UNITED NATIONS CONFERENCE ON TRADE AND DEVELOPMENT

REVIEW
OF MARITIME
TRANSPORT

2012

**REPORT BY
THE UNCTAD SECRETARIAT**

UNITED NATIONS
New York and Geneva, 2012

NOTE

The Review of Maritime Transport is a recurrent publication prepared by the UNCTAD secretariat since 1968 with the aim of fostering the transparency of maritime markets and analysing relevant developments. Any factual or editorial corrections that may prove necessary, based on comments made by Governments, will be reflected in a corrigendum to be issued subsequently.

*

* *

Symbols of United Nations documents are composed of capital letters combined with figures. Use of such a symbol indicates a reference to a United Nations document.

*

* *

The designations employed and the presentation of the material in this publication do not imply the expression of any opinion whatsoever on the part of the Secretariat of the United Nations concerning the legal status of any country, territory, city or area, or of its authorities, or concerning the delimitation of its frontiers or boundaries.

*

* *

Material in this publication may be freely quoted or reprinted, but acknowledgement is requested, with reference to the document number (see below). A copy of the publication containing the quotation or reprint should be sent to the UNCTAD secretariat at the following address: Palais des Nations, CH-1211 Geneva 10, Switzerland.

UNCTAD/RMT/2012

UNITED NATIONS PUBLICATION

Sales no. E.12.II.D.17

ISBN 978-92-1-112860-4

e-ISBN 978-92-1-055950-8

ISSN 0566-7682

ACKNOWLEDGEMENTS

The Review of Maritime Transport 2012 was prepared by the Trade Logistics Branch of the Division on Technology and Logistics, UNCTAD, under the coordination of Jan Hoffmann with administrative support by Florence Hudry, the supervision of José María Rubiato, and the overall guidance of Anne Miroux. The authors were Regina Asariotis, Hassiba Benamara, Hannes Finkenbrink, Jan Hoffmann, Anila Premti, Vincent Valentine and Frida Youssef.

The desktop publishing was undertaken by Nathalie Loriot. Additional desktop publishing and administrative support was carried out by Wendy Juan and the publication was edited by John Rogers.

This publication was externally reviewed by the following persons:

Chapter 1:   Clarkson Research Services (CRS), Wally Mandryk, Andrea Goldstein, Melissa Dawn Newhook.

Chapter 2:   Yann Alix, Peter Faust, Ricardo Sanchez.

Chapter 3:   Sam Bateman, Adolf K.Y. Ng, Harilaos N. Psaraftis.

Chapter 4:   Ki-Soon Hwang, Michael Manuel, Dong-Wook Song.

Chapter 5:   Mahin Faghfouri, André Stochniol.

Chapter 6:   Sudhir Gota, Sophie Punte, Ko Sakamoto.

In addition, the publication was internally reviewed in full by Vladislav Chouvalov.

TABLE OF CONTENTS

Annexes

LIST OF TABLES, FIGURES AND BOXES

Tables

Figures

Boxes

ABBREVIATIONS AND EXPLANATORY NOTES

ADB	Asian Development Bank
AEO	Authorized Economic Operator
AGF	United Nations Secretary-General's High-level Advisory Group on Climate Change Financing
APEC	Asia–Pacific Economic Cooperation
APMT	APM Terminals (A. P. Moller-Maersk Group)
APU	auxiliary power unit
BIMCO	Baltic and International Maritime Council
BP	British Petroleum
BRIC	Brazil, Russian Federation, India and China
BRICS	Brazil, Russian Federation, India, China and South Africa
BWM	International Convention for the Control and Management of Ships' Ballast Water and Sediments
CAI-Asia	Clean Air Initiative for Asian Cities
CBDR	common but differentiated responsibilities and respective capabilities
CBP	United States Customs and Border Protection
CDM	clean development mechanism
CEFIC	European Chemical Industry Council
CLC–IOPC Fund	Civil Liability Convention–International Oil Pollution Compensation Fund
CNTIC	China National Technical Import and Export Corporation
CO_2	carbon dioxide
CSI	United States Container Security Initiative
cSt	centistokes
C–TPAT	United States Customs–Trade Partnership Against Terrorism
DHS	United States Department of Homeland Security
DIS	Danish International Ship Register
DNV	Det Norske Veritas
dwt	deadweight ton
ECA	Emission Control Areas
ECSA	European Community Shipowners' Associations
EEDI	Energy Efficiency Design Index
EEOI	Energy Efficiency Operational Indicator
EPC	Electronic Port Clearance
ESC	European Shippers' Council
EU	European Union
EURIST	European Institute for Sustainable Transport
FAL	IMO Facilitation Committee
FDI	foreign direct investment
FEU	40-foot equivalent unit
FMC	United States Federal Maritime Commission
G12	MEPC 2012 Guidelines on Design and Construction to Facilitate Sediment Control on Ships
GAO	United States Government Accountability Office
GCF	United Nations Green Climate Fund
GDP	gross domestic product
GeSI	Global eSustainability Initiative
GHG	reenhouse gas
GHG-WG3	third intersessional meeting of the Working Group on GHG Emissions from Ships
GISIS	Global Integrated Shipping Information System

GT	gross tonnage
HAROPA	French port entity of the ports of Le Havre, Rouen and Paris
HNS	hazardous and noxious substances
IAPH	International Association of Ports and Harbours
ICC	International Chamber of Commerce
ICS	International Chamber of Shipping
ICT	information and communications technology
IDB	Inter-American Development Bank
IEA	International Energy Agency
IFC	International Finance Corporation
IMDG	International Maritime Dangerous Goods
IMF	International Monetary Fund
IMO	International Maritime Organization
IMSBC	International Maritime Solid Bulk Cargoes
IPCC	Intergovernmental Panel on Climate Change
ISF	International Shipping Federation
ISL	Institute of Shipping Economics and Logistics
ISO	International Organization for Standardization
ISO/PAS	ISO Publicly Available Specification
ISPS	International Ship and Port Facilities Security Code
ISO/TS	ISO Technical Specification
ITF	International Transport Forum
ITS	intelligent transport systems
LDC	least developed country
LEZ	low emission zone
LLMC	Convention on Limitation of Liability for Maritime Claims
LNG	liquefied natural gas
LPG	liquefied petroleum gas
LSCI	UNCTAD Liner Shipping Connectivity Index
MARPOL	International Convention for the Prevention of Pollution from Ships
MBM	market-based measure
MBM-EG	Expert Group on Feasibility Study and Impact Assessment of Possible Market-based Measures
MEB	Terminal Maritimo Muelles el Bosque
MEPC	Marine Environment Protection Committee
MRA	Mutual Recognition Agreement/Arrangement
MSC	IMO Maritime Safety Committee
NAFTA	North American Free Trade Agreement
NAMA	nationally appropriate mitigation action
NGTF	WTO Negotiating Group on Trade Facilitation
NII	Non- Intrusive Inspection
NIS	Norwegian International Ship Register
NOx	nitrogen oxide

NPA	Nigerian Ports Authority
ODA	official development assistance
OECD	Organization for Economic Cooperation and Development
OPEC	Organization of the Petroleum Exporting Countries
OPRC	Convention on Oil Pollution Preparedness, Response and Cooperation
OPRC HNS	Protocol to the OPRC relating to hazardous and noxious substances (OPRC-HNS Protocol)
pb	per barrel
PPP	public–private partnership
RAKIA	Ras Al Khaimah Investment Authority
SAFE	Framework of Standards to Secure and Facilitate Global Trade
SDR	Special Drawing Rights
SDT	special and differential treatment
SEEMP	Ship Energy Efficiency Management Plan
SFI	Secured Financial Initiative
SIDS	small island developing State
SME	small and medium-sized enterprise
SOLAS	International Convention for the Safety of Life at Sea
SOx	sulphur oxide
SRES	Special Report on Emissions Scenarios
SSCCAP	Sustainable Supply Chain Centre Asia Pacific
STCW	International Convention on Standards of Training, Certification and Watchkeeping for Seafarers
STCW-F	International Convention on Standards of Training, Certification and Watchkeeping for Fishing Vessel Personnel
TACB	technical assistance and capacity building
TEU	20-foot equivalent unit
TF	trade facilitation
TPT	transnet port terminals
ULCC	ultra-large crude carrier
ULCS	ultra-large container ship
UNCLOS	United Nations Convention on the Law of the Sea
UNCSD	United Nations Conference on Sustainable Development
UNECE	United Nations Economic Commission for Europe
UNFCCC	United Nations Framework Convention on Climate Change
UNLK	United Nations Layout Key
VLCC	very large crude carrier
VLOC	very large ore carrier
WBCSD	World Business Council for Sustainable Development
WCO	World Customs Organization
WTO	World Trade Organization
WWF	World Wide Fund for Nature

EXPLANATORY NOTES

- The *Review of Maritime Transport 2012* covers data and events from January 2011 until June 2012. Where possible, every effort has been made to reflect more recent developments.

- All references to dollars ($) are to United States dollars, unless otherwise stated.

- Unless otherwise stated, "ton" means metric ton (1,000 kg) and "mile" means nautical mile.

- Because of rounding, details and percentages presented in tables do not necessarily add up to the totals.

- n.a. Not available

- A hyphen (–) signifies that the amount is nil.

- In the tables and the text, the terms *countries* and *economies* refer to countries, territories or areas.

- Since 2007, the presentation of countries in the *Review of Maritime Transport* has been different from that in previous editions. Since 2007, the new classification is that used by the Statistics Division, United Nations Department of Economic and Social Affairs, and by UNCTAD in its *Handbook of Statistics*. For the purpose of statistical analysis, countries and territories are grouped by economic criteria into three categories, which are further divided into geographical regions. The main categories are developed economies, developing economies, and transition economies.

Vessel groupings used in the Review of Maritime Transport

As in the previous year's Review of Maritime Transport, five vessel groupings have been used in most of the shipping tables in this year's edition. The cut-off point for all tables, based on data from IHS Fairplay, is 100 gross tons (GT), except for the tables that deal with ownership, where the cut-off point is 1,000 GT. The groups aggregate 20 principal types of vessel category, as noted below.

Review group	Constituent ship types
Oil tankers	Oil tankers
Bulk carriers	Ore and bulk carriers, ore/bulk/oil carriers
General cargo ships	Refrigerated cargo, specialized cargo, roll-on roll-off (ro-ro) cargo, general cargo (single- and multi-deck), general cargo/passenger
Container ships	Fully cellular
Other ships	Oil/chemical tankers, chemical tankers, other tankers, liquefied gas carriers, passenger ro-ro, passenger, tank barges, general cargo barges, fishing, offshore supply, and (all other types)
Total all ships	Includes all the above-mentioned vessel types

Approximate vessel-size groups referred to in the *Review of Maritime Transport*, according to generally used shipping terminology

Crude oil tankers

ULCC, double hull	350,000 dwt plus
ULCC, single hull	320,000 dwt plus
VLCC, double hull	200,000–349,999 dwt
VLCC, single hull	200,000–319,999 dwt
Suezmax crude tanker	125,000–199,999 dwt
Aframax crude tanker	80,000–124,999 dwt; moulded breadth > 32.31m
Panamax crude tanker	50,000–79,999 dwt; moulded breadth < 32.31m

Dry bulk and ore carriers

Large capesize bulk carrier	150,000 dwt plus
Small capesize bulk carrier	80,000–149,999 dwt; moulded breadth > 32.31m
Panamax bulk carrier	55,000–84,999 dwt; moulded breadth < 32.31m
Handymax bulk carrier	35,000–54,999 dwt
Handysize bulk carrier	10,000–34,999 dwt

Ore/oil carriers

VLOO	200,000 dwt

Container ships

Post-Panamax container ship	moulded breadth > 32.31m
Panamax container ship	moulded breadth < 32.31m

Source: IHS Fairplay.

FOREWORD

Maritime transport is the backbone of international trade and a key engine driving globalization. Around 80 per cent of global trade by volume and over 70 per cent by value is carried by sea and is handled by ports worldwide; these shares are even higher in the case of most developing countries.

UNCTAD's *Review of Maritime Transport* has provided 44 years of uninterrupted coverage of the key developments affecting international seaborne trade, shipping, the world fleet, ports, freight markets, and transport-related regulatory and legal frameworks. The Review also covers inland transport and intermodal connections. Keeping track of both long-term trends and the latest developments, the Review has become a standard reference work in its field.

In common with previous issues, the 2012 Review contains critical analysis and a wealth of unique data, including long-term data series on seaborne trade, fleet capacity, shipping services and port handling activities. This year's Review notes that world seaborne trade grew by 4 per cent in 2011, whereas the tonnage of the world fleet grew at a greater rate, by almost 10 per cent, as shipowners took delivery of vessels that had been ordered before the economic crisis began. With supply outstripping demand, freight rates fell even further, to unprofitable levels for most shipping companies. For importers and exporters, however, the low freight rates helped to reduce transaction costs, which is important for helping to revive global trade.

As freight traffic continues to grow, the question of how to ensure the long-term sustainability of such growth is playing an increasingly important part in the policy debate on globalization, trade and development, environmental sustainability, energy security and climate change. Reflecting these new realities, this year's *Review of Maritime Transport* addresses a range of relevant issues in this context and includes a special chapter on sustainable freight transport. This chapter highlights the impacts of freight transport activity, for example on the environment, human health and the climate, and the consequent need to reduce the sector's energy consumption and emissions.

If left unchecked, such unsustainable patterns are likely to intensify, increasing the potential for global energy and environmental crises, and risk undermining progress being made on sustainable development and growth. Promoting a shift towards sustainable freight transport will help improve the sector's energy efficiency, reduce its heavy reliance on oil, and limit environmental and climate change impacts. In this context, developing effective policies and measures, including for the purpose of climate change mitigation and adaptation, and ensuring appropriate financing, are major challenges, especially for developing countries. Governments and the industry are becoming increasingly aware of the need to mainstream sustainability criteria into their transport planning and policies, and it is hoped that this year's *Review of Maritime Transport* will assist policymakers in their efforts to promote sustainable freight transport systems.

Supachai Panitchpakdi
Secretary-General of UNCTAD

EXECUTIVE SUMMARY

Seaborne trade reaches 8.7 billion tons

In tandem with developments in the world economy and global merchandise trade, international seaborne shipments continued to grow in 2011, albeit at a slower rate than in 2010. Fuelled by strong growth in container and dry bulk trades, world seaborne trade grew by 4 per cent in 2011, taking the total volume of goods loaded worldwide to 8.7 billion tons.

In addition to the sovereign debt crisis in Europe and other difficulties facing advanced economies, a number of factors have weighed down on global growth. These include heightened global financial risks, political and social unrest in North Africa and Western Asia, natural disasters in Japan and Thailand which have disrupted regional and global supply chains, rising oil prices and volatility, the impact of the austerity measures introduced in many countries and the fading of the stimulus effect of 2010, and growing geopolitical tensions. Many of these factors have remained relevant in 2012 and, depending on how they evolve, may impact dramatically on the global economic and trade outlook and international seaborne trade.

World fleet grew by 37 per cent in just four years

More than three years after the economic and financial crisis of 2008, the world fleet continued to expand during 2011, reaching more than 1.5 billion deadweight tons (dwt) in January 2012, an increase of over 37 per cent in just four years. At the same time, continued deliveries and a drastic downturn in new orders following the economic crisis has led to a reduction in the world order book by one third during the same period. Still largely responding to orders placed prior to the economic crisis, the major shipbuilders are reluctant to cancel or postpone deliveries. China, Japan and the Republic of Korea together built more than 93 per cent of the tonnage delivered in 2011, thus maintaining important employment in their shipyards. The resulting oversupply of ships represents a serious challenge for shipowners.

Developing countries continue to expand their market share in different maritime sectors, including shipbuilding, ownership, registration, operation, scrapping and manning. Shipowners of one third of the world fleet and 12 of the top 20 container operators are from developing countries. Almost 42 per cent of the world fleet are registered in Panama, Liberia and the Marshall Islands, and more than 92 per cent of scrapping in 2011 took place in India, China, Bangladesh and Pakistan.

Freight rates reported as unprofitable for carriers

Freight rates in 2011 and at the beginning of 2012 were often at unprofitable levels for ship owners. Substantial freight-rate reductions were reported within the dry bulk, liquid bulk and containerized cargo segments. Vessel oversupply continued to be a driving factor behind reductions in freight rates. Ship operators attempted to make savings through greater economies of scale by investing in large capacity ships in the tanker and dry bulk market segments.

Daily earnings of large Capesize vessels dropped below those of the significantly smaller Handysize class for several months. While smaller vessels offer greater flexibility by serving many kinds of ports, large vessels are constrained to navigate between the world's busiest trading centres that have seen both a downturn in business and increased oversupply in available tonnage.

The cost of transport expressed as a percentage of the value of the goods imported continues to decrease for developing countries in Asia and the Americas, converging to that of developed nations.

Container port throughput increased by 5.9 per cent

World container port throughput increased by an estimated 5.9 per cent to 572.8 million 20-foot equivalent units (TEUs) in 2011, its highest level ever. This increase was less than the 14.5 per cent increase of 2010 that sharply rebounded from the slump of 2009. Chinese mainland ports, utilized by many manufacturers and a partial indicator of the global demand for semi-manufactured and manufactured goods, maintained their share of total world container port throughput at 24.2 per cent.

The UNCTAD Liner Shipping Connectivity Index (LSCI) and its components showed a continuation in 2012 of the trend towards larger ships deployed by a smaller number of companies. Between 2011 and 2012, the number of companies providing services per country went down by 4.5 per cent, while the average size of the largest container ships increased by 11.5 per cent. Only 17.7 per cent of country pairs were served by direct liner shipping connections; for the remaining country pairs at least one trans-shipment port was required.

Legal issues and regulatory developments

Important issues include the recent adoption of amendments to the 1996 Convention on Limitation of Liability for Maritime Claims (1996 LLMC), as well as a range of regulatory developments relating to maritime and supply-chain security, maritime safety and environmental issues. Among the regulatory measures worth noting is a set of technical and operational measures to increase energy efficiency and reduce greenhouse gas (GHG) emissions from international shipping that was adopted under the auspices of the International Maritime Organization (IMO) in July 2011 and is expected to enter into force on 1 January 2013. To assist in the implementation of these new mandatory measures, four sets of guidelines were also adopted at IMO in March 2012. Discussions on possible market-based measures for the reduction of GHG emissions from international shipping continued and remained controversial. In respect of liability and compensation for ship-source oil pollution, a new UNCTAD report provides an overview of the international legal framework as well as some guidance for national policymaking.

At the World Trade Organization (WTO), negotiations continued on a future Trade Facilitation Agreement. While negotiators advanced on the draft negotiating text, it has been suggested that an agreement in trade facilitation might be reached earlier than in other areas of the Doha Development Round of negotiations.

Special focus: growing concerns regarding sustainable freight transport

The importance of freight transport as a trade enabler, an engine of growth and a driver of social development is widely recognized. However, the associated adverse impacts of freight transport activity on the environment, human health and the climate are also cause for concern.

Overall, transport consumes over 50 per cent of global liquid fossil fuels and is projected to grow by 1.4 per cent per year from 2008 to 2035 and to account for 82 per cent of the total projected increment in liquid fuel use. Energy demand of commercial transportation — trucks, aeroplanes, ships and trains — will rise by more than 70 per cent from 2010 to 2040, driven by economic growth, particularly in developing countries. At the same time, the transport sector accounts for 13 per cent of all world GHGs, of which 5.5 per cent are related to freight transport. Nearly 25 per cent of global energy-related carbon dioxide (CO_2) emissions are transport related and these are expected to increase by 57 per cent worldwide (1.7 per cent a year) between 2005 and 2030.

If left unchecked, these unsustainable patterns are likely to intensify and potentially result in global energy and environmental crises, and undermine any progress being made in world sustainable development and growth. Sustainability imperatives in the freight transport sector lead to the need to reduce the sector's energy consumption and emissions, including GHGs and air pollutants. Governments and industry have started to mainstream sustainability criteria into their planning processes, policies, and programmes; however, meeting effectively and in full the sector's sustainability objectives has yet to be achieved.

1

DEVELOPMENTS IN INTERNTIONAL SEABORNE TRADE

In tandem with the world economy and global merchandise trade, international seaborne shipments continued to grow in 2011, albeit at a slower rate than in 2010. Fuelled by strong growth in container and dry bulk trades, world seaborne trade grew by 4 per cent in 2011, taking the total volume of goods loaded worldwide to 8.7 billion tons. In addition to the sovereign debt crisis in Europe and other difficulties facing advanced economies, a number of factors have weighed down on global growth. These include, in particular, heightened global financial risks, political and social unrest in North Africa and Western Asia, natural disasters in Japan and Thailand which have disrupted regional and global supply chains, rising oil prices and volatility, austerity measures, the fading of the stimulus effect of 2010, and geopolitical tensions in the Strait of Hormuz. Many of these factors remained relevant in 2012 and, depending on how they evolve, they could impact dramatically on the global economic and trade outlook.

This chapter covers developments from January 2011 to June 2012, and where possible up to October 2012. Section A reviews the overall performance of the global economy and world merchandise trade. Section B considers developments in world seaborne trade volumes and examines trends unfolding in the economic sectors and activities that generate demand for shipping services, including oil and gas, mining, agriculture and steel production. Section C highlights selected trends that are currently transforming the landscape of international shipping and seaborne trade, focusing mainly on climate change, the current shift in global economic influence and changing trade patterns, and the rising bunker fuel prices and operating costs.

A. WORLD ECONOMIC SITUATION AND PROSPECTS[1]

1. World economic growth[2]

The global economy lost steam in 2011, with gross domestic product (GDP) growing by 2.7 per cent compared with 4.1 per cent in 2010. In addition to the sovereign debt crisis in Europe, the slow recovery in the United States of America, and other difficulties facing advanced economies, a number of factors have weighed down on global growth. These include, in particular, heightened global financial risks, political and social unrest in North Africa and Western Asia, natural disasters in Japan and Thailand which have disrupted regional and global supply chains, rising oil prices and volatility, austerity measures, the fading of the stimulus effect of 2010, and geopolitical tensions in the Strait of Hormuz. Many of these factors remained relevant in 2012, and, depending on how they evolve, they could impact dramatically on the global economic outlook.

In 2011, world GDP, industrial production, merchandise trade and seaborne shipments continued to move in tandem as shown in figure 1.1. During the year, industrial production decelerated in the countries of the Organization for Economic Cooperation and Development (OECD) and grew by a modest 2.1 per cent, down from 8.5 per cent in 2010. The industrial output of Japan was cut by over 2 per cent, reflecting the effects of the combined earthquake, tsunami and nuclear accident that hit the country in March 2011, as well as the interruptions to the supply chains caused by the November 2011 floods in Thailand.

Tighter monetary policies in many developing regions contributed to moderate growth in industrial activity. In China for example, industrial production grew by nearly 14 per cent, down from 16 per cent in 2010. Brazil, India and the Russian Federation also expanded their industrial output, albeit at a slower rate than in 2010. Flooding in Thailand strongly reduced the country's industrial output by 48 per cent in October and November, and drove down outputs in Singapore, Hong Kong (China), Malaysia

---

Figure 1.1. The OECD Industrial Production Index and indices for world GDP, world merchandise trade and world seaborne trade (1975–2012) (1990 = 100)

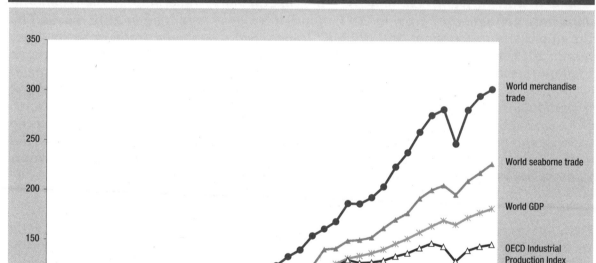

Source: UNCTAD secretariat, on the basis of OECD Main Economic Indicators, May 2012; UCTAD, *The Trade and Development Report 2012*; UNCTAD *Review of Maritime Transport*, various issues; World Trade Organization (WTO) (table A1a); the WTO press release 658, April 2012, *World Trade 2011*, Prospects for 2012. The 2012 index for seaborne trade is calculated on the basis of the growth rate forecast by Clarkson Research Services in *Shipping Review & Outlook*, spring 2012.

and Taiwan Province of China, due to the interrupted supply chains.

Table 1.1 provides an overview of annual GDP growth over the 2008-2011 period and a forecast for 2012. While growth in developed economies weakened in 2011, developing countries continued to drive world economic expansion and to account increasingly for a larger share of world GDP. This share is estimated by UNCTAD to have increased from 21.6 per cent in 1980 to 32.6 per cent of world GDP (at constant prices 2005) in 2010.[3] In 2011, growth in China remained robust, although it decelerated to 9.2 per cent. The country continues to be, however, the engine of

regional growth: on the one hand, the country's middle class is expanding and the government is adopting policies to encourage growth in private consumption; on the other hand, as China moves up the value chain, lower-value manufacturing companies are relocating to other low-wage countries such as Bangladesh and Viet Nam.[4]

Growth in Latin America slowed in 2011, reflecting the end of the stimulus effect, the sluggish growth in Europe and the hesitant recovery in the United States. Growth in Africa was held back by the unrest in North Africa and remains vulnerable to political instability, volatile commodity prices and potential

Table 1.1. World economic growth, 1991–2012[a] (Annual percentage change)

Region/country	1991–2004 Average[a]	2008	2009	2010	2011[b]	2012[b]
WORLD	2.9	1.5	-2.3	4.1	2.7	2.3
Developed economies	2.6	0.0	-3.9	2.8	1.4	1.1
of which:						
United States	3.4	-0.4	-3.5	3.0	1.7	2.0
Japan	1.0	-1.0	-5.5	4.4	-0.7	2.2
European Union (27)	2.3	0.3	-4.4	2.1	1.5	-0.3
of which:						
Germany	1.5	1.1	-5.1	3.7	3.0	0.9
France	2.0	-0.1	-3.1	1.7	1.7	0.3
Italy	1.6	-1.2	-5.5	1.8	0.4	-1.9
United Kingdom	3.1	-1.1	-4.4	2.1	0.7	-0.6
Developing economies	4.7	5.3	2.4	7.5	5.9	4.9
of which:						
Africa	3.2	4.8	0.9	4.5	2.5	4.1
South Africa	2.5	3.6	-1.7	2.8	3.1	2.7
Asia	5.9	5.9	4.1	8.4	6.8	5.5
Association of Southeast Asian Nations	4.9	4.0	1.3	8.0	4.5	4.9
China	9.9	9.6	9.2	10.4	9.2	7.9
India	5.9	7.5	7.0	9.0	7.0	6.0
Republic of Korea	5.0	2.3	0.3	6.2	3.6	3.3
Latin America and the Caribbean	2.7	4.0	-2.0	6.0	4.3	3.4
Brazil	2.6	5.2	-0.3	7.5	2.7	2.0
Least Developed Countries (LDCs)	5.2	7.7	5.0	5.8	4.0	4.1
Transition economies	..	5.2	-6.5	4.2	4.5	4.3
of which:						
Russian Federation	..	5.2	-7.8	4.0	4.3	4.7

Sources: UNCTAD Trade and Development Report, 2012, table 1.1. World Output Growth, 2004-2012.

[a]   Average percentage change.

[b]   Forecast.

droughts. Prospects for the region could, however, improve given large new gas discoveries in Tanzania and Mozambique and promising oil finds in Kenya and West Africa.[5] As to the least developed countries (LDCs), their economies expanded by 4 per cent in 2011, down from 5.8 per cent in 2010, reflecting in part a weaker global demand and a slowing Chinese economy. Economies in transition grew by 4.5 per cent in 2011, with growth being sustained by higher commodity prices, increased public infrastructure spending and strong agricultural output.

World economic developments in 2011 highlighted the continued strong interdependence among economies and to some extent weakened the case for a potential decoupling of growth between developed and developing countries. From the second quarter of 2011, economic growth in most developing countries and economies in transition started to decelerate, suggesting that these countries are not immune to the problems facing advanced economies and that they remain vulnerable to contagion through various channels, including trade, supply chains and the global financial system.

Looking to the future, global economic growth is projected to further decelerate in 2012. This outlook is subject to a high degree of uncertainty, and the risk cannot be excluded that it will be skewed to the downside. A potential escalation of the debt situation in Europe remains a major source of concern, despite ongoing efforts to contain the crisis and avoid contagion, such as, for example, increasing pledges to the International Monetary Fund (IMF) to raise its resources to above $1 trillion.[6] To put this into context, the IMF provided Greece with €30 billion and €28 billion in May 2010 and April 2012, respectively.[7]

Oil price developments constitute another concern as persistent high and volatile oil prices could become a drag on global demand. In 2011, oil prices increased by over 40 per cent and averaged $112 per barrel (pb) despite the release of strategic stocks from the International Energy Agency (IEA) member countries. The $32 increase in the average oil price during 2011 translated into a net transfer of $450 billion from oil-importing to oil-exporting countries.[8] It is estimated by IMF that a cut in oil supply from the Islamic Republic of Iran, due to sanctions, could lead to an initial world price increase of 20 to 30 per cent if other producers do not make up for the shortage.[9] Under relatively weak global economic conditions, an increase of 50 per cent in oil prices sustained over the coming two years could, according to IMF, lower growth by 0.5 to 1 per cent.[10]

2. World merchandise trade

In tandem with the world economy, growth in world merchandise trade by volume (that is, trade in real terms adjusted to account for inflation and exchange-rate fluctuations) progressively lost momentum in 2011 and expanded at an annual rate of 5.9 per cent, a sharp drop from the 13.9 per cent recorded in 2010. In addition to a weaker world economy, trade in 2011 was particularly hampered by natural shocks disrupting supply chains and production processes in Japan and Thailand, civil unrest in North Africa and oil supply disruption in Libya. Meanwhile, supported by high commodity prices, the value of world merchandise exports increased by 19 per cent to reach $18.2 trillion, a relative slowdown from the 22 per cent recorded in 2010.[11]

Developed economies performed better than expected with exports rising by 5.1 per cent due to strong, rapid export growth in the United States (7.2 per cent) and the European Union (6 per cent). Meanwhile, exports from Japan contracted by 0.4 per cent.

Exports of developing countries grew by 7 per cent, driven by Asia (4.5 per cent) and in particular India (13.7 per cent), China (12.8 per cent) and the Republic of Korea (11.2 per cent). Exports in Thailand contracted as a consequence of the floods in November 2011, while exports from Africa slumped by 5.1 per cent, due in particular to the 75 per cent drop of Libyan oil shipments.[12]

The slowdown in demand and the overall weak growth in advanced economies translated into weaker imports in developed regions. In 2011, imports grew at a modest 3.5 per cent, a sharp fall from the 11 per cent recorded in 2010. Japan recorded the slowest growth (1.9 per cent) followed, in ascending order, by the European Union (3.2 per cent) and the United States (3.7).

Imports into developing countries expanded at the much faster rate of 6.2 per cent, with resource-exporting regions benefiting from favourable commodity prices. Imports into Latin America and Africa grew by 7.1 per cent and 3.9 per cent, respectively. In a separate development, a recent decline in the normally large trade surpluses of Japan and China is changing the trade landscape and constitutes a welcome development, as it could imply a rebalancing of the world economy (see table 1.2).[13]

Looking to the future, WTO projects a further deceleration in trade growth with global merchandise trade volumes expected to grow by just 2.5 per cent in 2012, a rate below the 6 per cent average recorded over the period 1990–2008.

Apart from current global economic uncertainties, the outlook for merchandise trade is also clouded by the risk of a lack of trade finance.[14] A report by the International Chamber of Commerce (ICC) and IMF revealed a pessimistic outlook for trade finance in 2012.[15] More than 50 per cent of respondents to a relevant survey expected trade finance in Asia to improve and only 16 per cent were optimistic about trade finance in Europe.[16]

A surge in protectionist measures is another driver of uncertainty in view of the current difficult economic climate and the lack of progress on the adoption of a multilateral trading system under the WTO Doha Round negotiations. At the November 2011 meeting of the G20, participants underscored their commitment to free trade and to the multilateral trade system.[17] However, since mid-October 2011, 124 new restrictive measures have been recorded, affecting around 1.1 per cent of G20 merchandise imports, or 0.9 per cent of world imports.[18] Relevant measures include trade remedy actions, tariff increases, import licenses and customs controls.[19]

B. WORLD SEABORNE TRADE[20]

1. General trends in seaborne trade

Preliminary data indicate that world seaborne trade held steady in 2011 and grew by 4 per cent, with total volumes reaching a record 8.7 billion tons (tables 1.3 and 1.4, and figure 1.2). This expansion was driven by rapid growth in dry cargo volumes (5.6 per cent) propelled by upbeat container and major bulk trades, which grew by 8.6 per cent (expressed in tons) and 5.4 per cent, respectively.

Table 1.2	**Growth in the volume of merchandise[a] trade, by country groups and geographical region, 2008–2011 (Annual percentage change)**								
Exports				**Countries/regions**	**Imports**			
2008	**2009**	**2010**	**2011**		**2008**	**2009**	**2010**	**2011**
2.4	-13.1	13.9	5.9	**WORLD**	2.5	-13.4	14.1	5.0
2.5	-15.2	13.2	5.1	**Developed economies**	-0.2	-14.5	11.0	3.5
				of which:				
2.3	-24.9	27.5	-0.4	Japan	-0.6	-12.4	10.1	1.9
5.5	-14.9	15.3	7.2	United States	-3.7	-16.4	14.8	3.7
2.4	-14.3	12.0	6.0	European Union (27)	0.8	-14.2	10.0	3.2
3.2	-9.7	15.4	7.0	**Developing economies**	6.6	-9.9	19.2	6.2
				of which:				
-3.1	-9.7	8.7	-5.1	Africa	10.6	-3.9	7.1	3.9
-0.3	-11.0	10.3	3.4	Latin America and the Caribbean	8.5	-17.9	23.3	7.1
1.6	-10.9	18.8	4.5	**Asia**	8.0	-16.3	21.9	6.1
				of which:				
1.8	-10.9	18.8	4.5	ASEAN	8	-16.3	21.9	6.1
10.6	-13.9	29.0	12.8	China	2.3	-1.8	30.8	10.6
16.8	-6.6	5.9	13.7	India	29.7	-0.8	13.8	5.3
8.8	2.6	15.3	11.2	Republic of Korea	0.7	-2.7	17.4	6.7
-0.2	-14.4	11.5	6.0	**Transition economies**	15.5	-28.6	15.5	17.0

Sources: UNCTAD secretariat calculations, based on UNCTAD *Handbook of Statistics and Trade and Development Report*, 2012.
a   Data on trade volumes are derived from international merchandise trade values deflated by UNCTAD unit value indices.

Table 1.3.	Development in international seaborne trade, selected years (Millions of tons loaded)			
Year	Oil and gas	Main bulks[a]	Other dry cargo	Total (all cargoes)
1970	1 440	448	717	2 605
1980	1 871	608	1 225	3 704
1990	1 755	988	1 265	4 008
2000	2 163	1 295	2 526	5 984
2005	2 422	1 709	2 978	7 109
2006	2 698	1 814	3 188	7 700
2007	2 747	1 953	3 334	8 034
2008	2 742	2 065	3 422	8 229
2009	2 642	2 085	3 131	7 858
2010	2 772	2 335	3 302	8 409
2011	2 796	2 477	3 475	8 748

Sources: Compiled by the UNCTAD secretariat on the basis of data supplied by reporting countries and as published on the relevant government and port industry website, and by specialist sources. The data for 2006 onwards have been revised and upated to reflect improved reporting, including more recent figures and better information regarding the breakdown by cargo type. Figures for 2011 are estimated based on preliminary data or on the last year for which data were available.

[a]   Iron ore, grain, coal, bauxite/alumina and phosphate. The data for 2006 onwards are based on various issues of the *Dry Bulk Trade Outlook*, produced by Clarkson Research Services.

In 2011, container trade flows were sustained by non-mainlane trade as the United States and Europe continued to struggle with sluggish growth and uncertainty, while dry bulk volumes held strong with continued import demand for raw materials in large developing economies, notably China and India. Five major dry bulk flows were sustained by growth in iron ore trade (6 per cent), which caters to a strong import demand in China, a country accounting for about two thirds of global iron ore trade volumes in 2011. Tanker trade volumes (crude oil, refined petroleum products, and liquefied petroleum and gas) remained almost flat, growing by less than 1 per cent due to falling crude oil volumes. Together, trade in refined petroleum products and gas grew by 5.1 per cent, due mainly to the recent boom in liquefied natural gas (LNG) trade.

As shown in tables 1.3 and 1.4, and in figure 1.2, which feature global seaborne trade in volume terms (tons), oil trade continued to account for approximately one third of the total in 2011. During the same year, dry cargo, including major and minor dry bulks, containerized trade and general cargo held the remaining two thirds of the market. As a proportion of total dry cargo, major bulks accounted for 41.6 per cent, containerized trade for 23.3 per cent and minor bulks for 20.8 per cent. The remaining share of 14.3 per cent was accounted for by other dry goods including general cargo.

A different picture emerges, however, when one considers the contribution of these market segments

to the value of world seaborne trade. While recent data, including for 2011, are not readily available, existing estimates for 2007 may provide some insight into the distribution of world seaborne trade by value and allow for some comparisons to be made. In 2007, it was not tanker cargo (oil and gas) that accounted for the largest share of global trade, but containerized cargo, with more than 50 per cent of the total, this reflecting the higher value of goods carried in containers. Tanker trade accounted for less than 25 per cent, while general and dry cargo accounted for 20 per cent and 6 per cent of the value, respectively.[21] More recent analysis of the 2008 and 2009 United Nations trade data shows an increase in the value of dry bulk cargo reflecting to a large extent the strong import demand for these commodities from emerging developing countries, in particular China.[22]

As developing countries contribute increasingly larger shares and growth to both world GDP and merchandise trade, their contribution to world seaborne trade has also been increasing. In 2011, a total of 60 per cent of the volume of world seaborne trade originated in developing countries and 57 per cent of this trade was delivered on their territories (figure 1.3 (a)). Developing countries are now major world players both as exporters and importers, a remarkable shift away from earlier patterns when they served mainly as loading areas of high volume goods (mainly of high volume raw materials and resources)

| Table 1.4. | World seaborne trade in 2006–2011, by type of cargo, country group and region |||||||| |

Country group	Year	Goods loaded				Goods unloaded		
		Total	Crude	Petroleum products and gas	Dry cargo	Total	Crude	Petroleum products and gas	Dry cargo
		Millions of tons								
World	2006	7 700.3	1 783.4	914.8	5 002.1	7 878.3	1 931.2	893.7	5 053.4
	2007	8 034.1	1 813.4	933.5	5 287.1	8 140.2	1 995.7	903.8	5 240.8
	2008	8 229.5	1 785.2	957.0	5 487.2	8 286.3	1 942.3	934.9	5 409.2
	2009	7 858.0	1 710.5	931.1	5 216.4	7 832.0	1 874.1	921.3	5 036.6
	2010	8 408.9	1 787.7	983.8	5 637.5	8 443.8	1 933.2	979.2	5 531.4
	2011	8 747.7	1 762.4	1 033.5	5 951.9	8 769.3	1 907.0	1 038.6	5 823.7
Developed economies	2006	2 460.5	132.9	336.4	1 991.3	4 164.7	1 282.0	535.5	2 347.2
	2007	2 608.9	135.1	363.0	2 110.8	3 990.5	1 246.0	524.0	2 220.5
	2008	2 715.4	129.0	405.3	2 181.1	4 007.9	1 251.1	523.8	2 233.0
	2009	2 554.3	115.0	383.8	2 055.5	3 374.4	1 125.3	529.9	1 719.2
	2010	2 865.4	135.9	422.3	2 307.3	3 604.5	1 165.4	522.6	1 916.5
	2011	2 966.2	123.3	423.3	2 419.5	3 615.3	1 109.6	569.9	1 935.7
Transition economies	2006	410.3	123.1	41.3	245.9	70.6	5.6	3.1	61.9
	2007	407.9	124.4	39.9	243.7	76.8	7.3	3.5	66.0
	2008	431.5	138.2	36.7	256.6	89.3	6.3	3.8	79.2
	2009	505.3	142.1	44.4	318.8	93.3	3.5	4.6	85.3
	2010	515.7	150.2	45.9	319.7	122.1	3.5	4.6	114.0
	2011	510.4	138.7	49.7	322.0	154.7	4.2	4.4	146.1
Developing economies	2006	4 829.5	1 527.5	537.1	2 765.0	3 642.9	643.6	355.1	2 644.3
	2007	5 020.8	1 553.9	530.7	2 932.6	4 073.0	742.4	376.3	2 954.3
	2008	5 082.6	1 518.0	515.1	3 049.6	4 189.1	684.9	407.2	3 097.0
	2009	4 798.4	1 453.5	502.9	2 842.0	4 364.2	745.3	386.9	3 232.1
	2010	5 027.8	1 501.6	515.6	3 010.5	4 717.3	764.4	452.0	3 500.9
	2011	5 271.2	1 500.3	560.5	3 210.3	4 999.3	793.2	464.3	3 741.8
Africa	2006	721.9	353.8	86.0	282.2	349.8	41.3	39.4	269.1
	2007	732.0	362.5	81.8	287.6	380.0	45.7	44.5	289.8
	2008	766.7	379.2	83.3	304.2	376.6	45.0	43.5	288.1
	2009	708.0	354.0	83.0	271.0	386.8	44.6	39.7	302.5
	2010	754.0	351.1	92.0	310.9	416.9	42.7	40.5	333.7
	2011	787.7	344.5	108.9	334.2	371.3	40.1	43.4	287.8
America	2006	1 030.7	251.3	93.9	685.5	373.4	49.6	60.1	263.7
	2007	1 067.1	252.3	90.7	724.2	415.9	76.0	64.0	275.9
	2008	1 108.2	234.6	93.0	780.6	436.8	74.2	69.9	292.7
	2009	1 029.8	225.7	74.0	730.1	371.9	64.4	73.6	234.0
	2010	1 172.6	241.6	85.1	846.0	448.7	69.9	74.7	304.2
	2011	1 260.0	254.0	93.5	912.4	491.5	74.1	79.3	338.1
Asia	2006	3 073.1	921.2	357.0	1 794.8	2 906.8	552.7	248.8	2 105.3
	2007	3 214.6	938.2	358.1	1 918.3	3 263.6	620.7	260.8	2 382.1
	2008	3 203.6	902.7	338.6	1 962.2	3 361.9	565.6	286.8	2 509.5
	2009	3 054.3	872.3	345.8	1 836.3	3 592.4	636.3	269.9	2 686.2
	2010	3 094.6	907.5	338.3	1 848.8	3 838.2	651.8	333.1	2 853.4
	2011	3 216.4	900.1	357.9	1 958.4	4 122.0	679.0	337.7	3 105.3
Oceania	2006	3.8	1.2	0.1	2.5	12.9	0.0	6.7	6.2
	2007	7.1	0.9	0.1	2.5	13.5	0.0	7.0	6.5
	2008	4.2	1.5	0.1	2.6	13.8	0.0	7.1	6.7
	2009	6.3	1.5	0.2	4.6	13.1	0.0	3.6	9.5
	2010	6.5	1.5	0.2	4.8	13.4	0.0	3.7	9.7
	2011	7.1	1.6	0.2	5.3	14.5	0.0	3.9	10.6

Table 1.4. World seaborne trade in 2006–2011, by type of cargo, country group and region *(continued)*

Country group	Year	Goods loaded				Goods unloaded			
		Total	Crude	Petroleum products and gas	Dry cargo	Total	Crude	Petroleum products and gas	Dry cargo
		Percentage share							
World	2006	100.0	23	12	65	100	25	11	64
	2007	100.0	23	12	66	100	25	11	64
	2008	100.0	22	12	67	100	23	11	65
	2009	100.0	22	12	66	100	24	12	64
	2010	100.0	21	12	67	100	23	12	66
	2011	100.0	20	12	68	100	22	12	66
Developed economies	2006	32.0	7	37	40	53	66	60	46
	2007	32.5	7	39	40	49	62	58	42
	2008	33.0	7	42	40	48	64	56	41
	2009	32.5	7	41	39	43	60	58	34
	2010	34.1	8	43	41	43	60	53	35
	2011	33.9	7	41	41	41	58	55	33
Transition economies	2006	5.3	7	5	5	1	0	0	1
	2007	5.1	7	4	5	1	0	0	1
	2008	5.2	8	4	5	1	0	0	1
	2009	6.4	8	5	6	1	0	0	2
	2010	6.1	8	5	6	1	0	0	2
	2011	5.8	8	5	5	2	0	0	3
Developing economies	2006	62.7	86	59	55	46	33	40	52
	2007	62.5	86	57	55	50	37	42	56
	2008	61.8	85	54	56	51	35	44	57
	2009	61.1	85	54	54	56	40	42	64
	2010	59.8	84	52	53	56	40	46	63
	2011	60.3	85	54	54	57	42	45	64
Africa	2006	9.4	20	9	6	4	2	4	5
	2007	9.1	20	9	5	5	2	5	6
	2008	9.3	21	9	6	5	2	5	5
	2009	9.0	21	9	5	5	2	4	6
	2010	9.0	20	9	6	5	2	4	6
	2011	9.0	20	11	6	4	2	4	5
America	2006	13.4	14.1	10.3	13.7	4.7	2.6	6.7	5.2
	2007	13.3	13.9	9.7	13.7	5.1	3.8	7.1	5.3
	2008	13.5	13.1	9.7	14.2	5.3	3.8	7.5	5.4
	2009	13.1	13.2	7.9	14.0	4.7	3.4	8.0	4.6
	2010	13.9	13.5	8.7	15.0	5.3	3.6	7.6	5.5
	2011	14.4	14.4	9.0	15.3	5.6	3.9	7.6	5.8
Asia	2006	39.9	51.7	39.0	35.9	36.9	28.6	27.8	41.7
	2007	40.0	51.7	38.4	36.3	40.1	31.1	28.9	45.5
	2008	38.9	50.6	35.4	35.8	40.6	29.1	30.7	46.4
	2009	38.9	51.0	37.1	35.2	45.9	34.0	29.3	53.3
	2010	36.8	50.8	34.4	32.8	45.5	33.7	34.0	51.6
	2011	36.8	51.1	34.6	32.9	47.0	35.6	32.5	53.3
Oceania	2006	0.0	0.1	0.01	0.0	0.2	–	0.7	0.1
	2007	0.1	0.1	0.01	0.0	0.2	–	0.8	0.1
	2008	0.1	0.1	0.01	0.0	0.2	–	0.8	0.1
	2009	0.1	0.1	0.02	0.1	0.2	–	0.4	0.2
	2010	0.1	0.1	0.02	0.1	0.2	–	0.4	0.2
	2011	0.1	0.1	0.02	0.1	0.2	–	0.4	0.2

Source: Compiled by the UNCTAD secretariat on the basis of data supplied by reporting countries, and data obtained from the relevant government, port industry and other specialist websites and sources. The data for 2006 onwards have been revised and updated to reflect improved reporting, including more recent figures and better information regarding the breakdown by cargo type. Figures for 2011 are estimated based on preliminary data or on the last year for which data were avaialble.

Figure 1.2.	**International seaborne trade, by cargo type, selected years (Millions of tons loaded)**

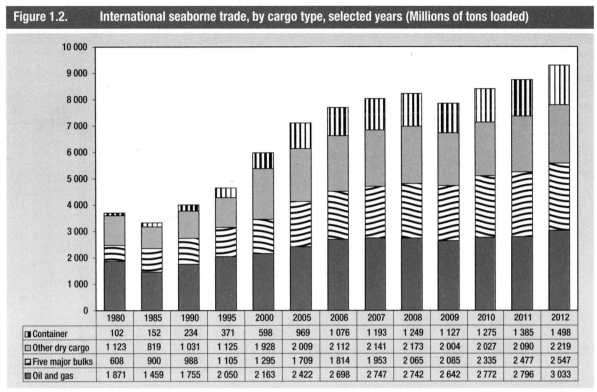

	1980	1985	1990	1995	2000	2005	2006	2007	2008	2009	2010	2011	2012
Container	102	152	234	371	598	969	1 076	1 193	1 249	1 127	1 275	1 385	1 498
Other dry cargo	1 123	819	1 031	1 125	1 928	2 009	2 112	2 141	2 173	2 004	2 027	2 090	2 219
Five major bulks	608	900	988	1 105	1 295	1 709	1 814	1 953	2 065	2 085	2 335	2 477	2 547
Oil and gas	1 871	1 459	1 755	2 050	2 163	2 422	2 698	2 747	2 742	2 642	2 772	2 796	3 033

Source: UNCTAD *Review of Maritime Transport*, various issues. For 2006–2012, the breakdown by type of dry cargo is based on Clarkson Research Services' *Shipping Review & Outlook*, various issues. Data for 2012 are based on a forecast by Clarkson Research Services in *Shipping Review & Outlook*, spring 2012.

Figure 1.3 (a).	**World seaborne trade, by country group, 2011 (Percentage share in world tonnage)**

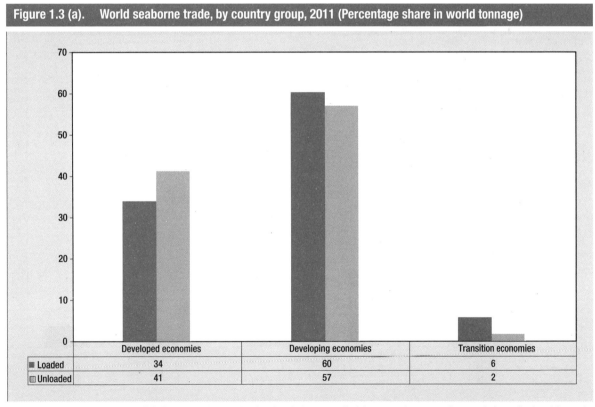

	Developed economies	Developing economies	Transition economies
Loaded	34	60	6
Unloaded	41	57	2

Source: Compiled by the UNCTAD secretariat on the basis of data supplied by reporting countries, and data obtained from the relevant government, port industry and other specialist websites and sources. Figures are estimated based on preliminary data or on the last year for which data were available.

Figure 1.3 (b).   Participation of developing economies in world seaborne trade, selected years (Percentage share in world tonnage)

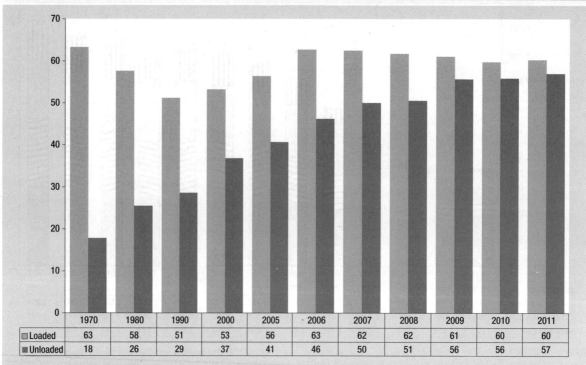

	1970	1980	1990	2000	2005	2006	2007	2008	2009	2010	2011
Loaded	63	58	51	53	56	63	62	62	61	60	60
Unloaded	18	26	29	37	41	46	50	51	56	56	57

Source: UNCTAD *Review of Maritime Transport*, various issues.

Figure 1.3 (c).   World seaborne trade, by region, 2011 (Percentage share in world tonnage)

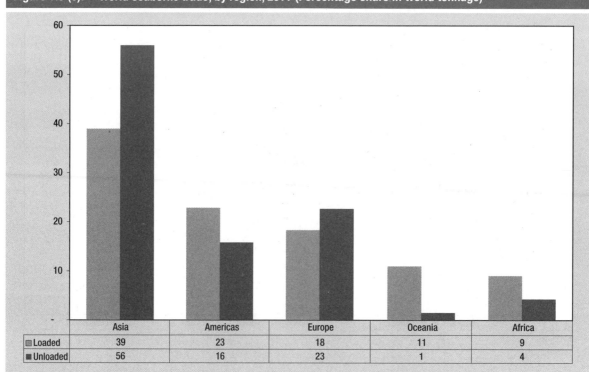

	Asia	Americas	Europe	Oceania	Africa
Loaded	39	23	18	11	9
Unloaded	56	16	23	1	4

Source: Compiled by the UNCTAD secretariat on the basis of data supplied by reporting countries, and data obtained from the relevant government, port industry and other specialist websites and sources. Figures are estimated based on preliminary data or on the last year for which data were available.

as shown in figure 1.3 (b). With regards to developed countries, their share of imports outweighed exports, totalling 41 per cent and 34 per cent, respectively. Transition economies continued to account for the remaining trade, their contribution to world seaborne exports and imports totalling 6.2 per cent and 2 per cent, respectively. Geographically, Asia maintained its lead position and continued to fuel world seaborne trade with its share of goods loaded amounting to 39 per cent, while that of goods unloaded reaching 56 per cent (figure 1.3 (c)).

For 2012, Clarkson Research Services are forecasting a 4.3 per cent annual growth rate in the volume of world seaborne trade. However, several downside risks continue to stand in the way of a robust and sustainable recovery in shipping, including the current global economic uncertainty, security concerns and maritime piracy, limited trade finance and geopolitical tensions, as well as a potential rise in trade restrictions.

2. Seaborne trade in ton-miles[23]

The unit of ton-miles offers a measure of true demand for shipping services and tonnage as it takes into account distance, which determines ships' availability. Between 1999 and 2011, ton-miles have increased for all cargoes, and are projected to rise further in 2012 (table 1.5 (a), figures 1.4 (a) and 1.4 (b)). The most impressive growth over this period has been in LNG (258 per cent), followed by iron ore (183 per cent), grain (71 per cent), coal (67 per cent), petroleum products (58 per cent) and crude oil (13 per cent). Since 2000, a surge in China of import demand for industrial commodities necessary for steel production has fuelled rapid growth in the iron ore and coal trades. The growing appetite of China for these commodities has heightened the need to diversify sources of supply, and include more distant locations such as Brazil, the United States and South Africa. While the estimated average distance of global iron ore trade increased from 5,451 miles in 1998 to 6,260 miles in 2011, iron ore ton-miles are expected to increase further as new mines in the Arctic and West Africa start up.[24]

Steam and coking coal ton-miles varied both over time and between the Atlantic and the Pacific regions.[25] In 2011, coal trade patterns shifted, with growth in ton-mile exports falling by 2 per cent in the Pacific and rising for the first time since 2006 in the Atlantic at an annualized rate of 12 per cent. The ton-mile decrease in the Pacific resulted in part from the Australian floods, which reduced supply and

drove coal prices up.[26] Meanwhile, higher demand for thermal coal in Europe and a rise in coal exports from the United States have boosted the Atlantic trade. The predominance of the Pacific coal trade continues, however, with China in particular emerging as a net importer, and with Indonesian exports predominantly catering for this demand. In view of the relatively short distances between China and Indonesia, compared with the United States or South Africa, estimated average distances fell from 4,998 miles in 1998 to 3,910 miles in 2011.[27]

Refined petroleum products (for example, gasoline and kerosene) and crude oil recorded the smallest ton-mile growth, reflecting the slow pace at which crude oil trade has been evolving over the past decade. Tanker trade patterns, including associated ton-mile demand, are changing as a result of the strategies seeking to diversify crude oil supply sources. In China, where crude imports increased nearly five times between 2001 and 2011, the share of the country's ton-mile trade sourced from Western Asia has been decreasing, while the proportion of its ton-miles sourced from the Caribbean has increased.[28] The share of crude ton-miles from Western Asia fell from 64 per cent of the country's total in 2001 to 52 per cent in 2011, while the Caribbean share increased from 1 per cent to 18 per cent.[29] The Western Asia share of crude ton-miles to North America fell from 62 per cent in 2001 to 53 per cent in 2011, while the shares of the Caribbean and West Africa helped offset this decline.[30] In 2014, the crude ton-mile demand of China is expected to surpass that of North America.[31]

In 2011, although crude oil flows declined, trade distances rose in certain regions. Europe, for example, replaced crude oil from Libya with longer-haul substitutes from Western Asia, the Black Sea, and Western Africa.[32] Furthermore, tankers trading between Western Asia and the Atlantic coast of the United States are increasingly travelling greater distances to avoid piracy off the coast of Somalia in the Indian Ocean.[33]

Oil products have also shown slower ton-mile growth over the past decade as an increased refinery capacity in Asia implies a lesser need for long-haul petroleum products imports. However, with the closing of three refineries in the East Coast of the United States, the country's ton-mile demand for crude oil imports will likely be reduced. This means, in parallel, that its ton-mile demand for refined products can be expected to rise with higher import volumes from Europe, India

Table 1.5 (a).		World seaborne trade in cargo ton-miles and by cago type, 1999–2012 (Estimated billions of ton-miles)										
Year	*Crude*	*Products*	*Oil trade*	*LPG*	*LNG*	*Gas trade*	*Iron ore*	*Coal*	*Grain*[a]	*Five main dry bulks*[b]	*Other dry cargoes*	*All cargoes*
1999	7 761	1 488	**9 249**	188	267	**456**	2 338	2 196	1 122	**6 046**	**11 191**	**26 942**
2000	8 014	1 487	**9 500**	199	317	**516**	2 620	2 420	1 224	**6 649**	**12 058**	**28 723**
2001	7 778	1 598	**9 376**	182	341	**523**	2 698	2 564	1 293	**6 922**	**12 347**	**29 168**
2002	7 553	1 594	**9 146**	192	360	**552**	2 956	2 577	1 295	**7 212**	**12 587**	**29 497**
2003	8 025	1 697	**9 723**	187	399	**586**	3 148	2 771	1 382	**7 710**	**13 072**	**31 091**
2004	8 550	1 836	**10 386**	192	429	**621**	3 667	2 901	1 397	**8 424**	**13 975**	**33 407**
2005	8 643	2 057	**10 701**	187	444	**631**	3 900	2 984	1 459	**8 819**	**14 570**	**34 720**
2006	8 875	2 192	**11 067**	195	537	**732**	4 413	3 103	1 496	**9 508**	**15 759**	**37 065**
2007	8 836	2 223	**11 060**	198	614	**812**	4 773	3 177	1 610	**10 090**	**16 390**	**38 351**
2008	8 965	2 277	**11 241**	205	660	**865**	5 000	3 260	1 721	**10 523**	**16 646**	**39 276**
2009	8 138	2 233	**10 371**	193	668	**862**	5 569	3 060	1 693	**10 715**	**14 988**	**36 936**
2010	8 688	2 272	**10 960**	198	861	**1 059**	6 121	3 540	1 948	**12 042**	**16 829**	**40 891**
2011[c]	8 762	2 351	**11 112**	201	955	**1 155**	6 608	3 664	1 920	**12 666**	**17 861**	**42 794**
2012[d]	8 918	2 449	**11 367**	213	1 065	**1 278**	6 948	3 763	1 940	**13 141**	**18 754**	**44 540**

Sources: Based on data from Clarkson Research Services' *Shipping Review & Outlook*, spring 2012.
[a]   Includes soybean period.
[b]   Includes iron ore, coal, grain bauxite/alumina and rock phosphate.
[c]   Estimated period.
[d]   Forecast period.

Figure 1.4 (a).	World seaborne trade in cargo ton-miles, 1999–2012 (Billions of ton-miles)

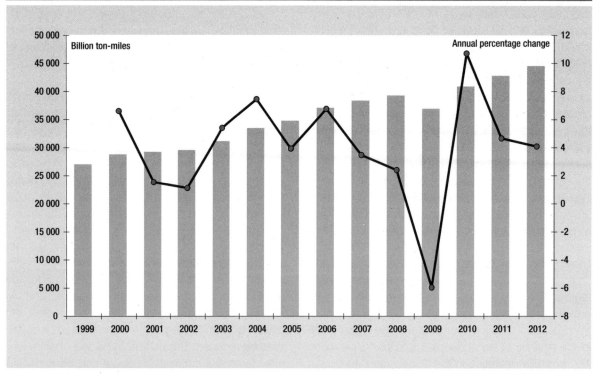

Source: UNCTAD secretariat based on data from Clarkson Research Services' *Shipping Review & Outlook*, spring 2012.

Figure 1.4 (b). World seaborne trade in cargo ton-miles and by cargo type, 1999–2012 (Billions of ton-miles)

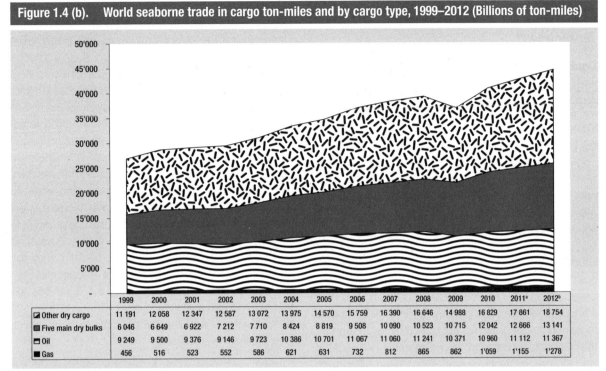

	1999	2000	2001	2002	2003	2004	2005	2006	2007	2008	2009	2010	2011[a]	2012[b]
Other dry cargo	11 191	12 058	12 347	12 587	13 072	13 975	14 570	15 759	16 390	16 646	14 988	16 829	17 861	18 754
Five main dry bulks	6 046	6 649	6 922	7 212	7 710	8 424	8 819	9 508	10 090	10 523	10 715	12 042	12 666	13 141
Oil	9 249	9 500	9 376	9 146	9 723	10 386	10 701	11 067	11 060	11 241	10 371	10 960	11 112	11 367
Gas	456	516	523	552	586	621	631	732	812	865	862	1'059	1'155	1'278

Source: UNCTAD secretariat based on data from Clarkson Research Services' *Shipping Review & Outlook*, spring 2012.
a   Estimated.
b   Forecast.

Table 1.5 (b). World seaborne trade in dwt-miles, 2008-2011 (Estimated billions of dwt-miles)

Year	Container	General Cargo	RoRo	Reefer	Dry Bulk	Oil	Gas	World Total
2008	18 400	2 800	1 812	496	25 606	29 310	2 538	80 962
2009	15 313	2 366	1 217	405	24 550	26 228	2 344	72 423
2010	16 508	2 457	1 468	333	26 784	27 787	3 322	78 659
2011	18 756	2 472	1 578	356	31 788	28 181	3 816	86 947

Source: Lloyd's List Intelligence, 2012. www.lloydslistintelligence.com

and Western Asia. Refinery developments in the oil-producing regions could help shift a larger share of the oil trade from crude oil to refined petroleum products (for example, gasoline, kerosene, and the like).

Table 1.5 (b) features estimated annual deadweight ton-miles (dwt-miles), which are calculated by multiplying the number of voyages between each port by the distance and individual vessel dwt. Therefore, unlike cargo ton-miles, dwt-miles measure total annual vessel activity not only when the ship is laden but also when in ballast. Thus, this measure is not equivalent to measuring the potential ton-mile capacity, as data in table 1.5 (b) reflect voyages actually made, and do not account for unused ship supply capacity (for example, ships that are laid up, waiting or out of service). Therefore, the dwt-mile data presented

in table 1.5 (b) do not measure supply or determine utilisation. The dwt-miles to cargo ton-miles ratio over the 2008–2011 period is around 2, reflecting, in part, the difference between the two measures.

Bearing in mind these differences, the evolution of dwt-miles as shown in table 1.5 (b) appears to be in line with the trends observed in cargo ton-miles as shown in table 1.5 (a). The performance of dwt-miles clearly highlights the impact of the 2009 downturn when global trade collapsed, as well as the strong rebound in trade volumes recorded since 2010. Rapid growth in gas trade and, more specifically, the recent surge in LNG trade have been key drivers of growth in dwt-miles over the 2010–2011 period. Table 1.5 (b) also shows the relative resilience of dry bulk trade owing to the booming Asian demand for commodities such as iron ore and coal.

3. Seaborne trade by cargo type

Tanker trade[34]

Crude oil production and consumption[35]

In 2011, world oil consumption grew marginally by 0.7 per cent to reach 88 million barrels per day (bpd). While consumption in the OECD countries declined by 1.3 per cent, it rose by 2.8 per cent in developing countries. Interestingly, after growing by an average of 12 per cent annually between 2006 and 2010, oil consumption growth in China slowed down in 2011, reflecting, in particular, the effect of the country's tighter monetary and fiscal policies.

Global production increased by 1.3 per cent to reach 83.6 million bpd in 2011, with members of the Organization of the Petroleum Exporting Countries (OPEC) leading the growth. Non-OPEC supply remained flat as growth in the United States, Canada, the Russian Federation and Colombia was offset by declines in Norway and the United Kingdom. An overview of major producers and consumers is presented in table 1.6.

Recent developments in drilling activity point to future oil supply increases. Drilling activity picked up in 2011 due in part to the allocation of new drilling permits in the Gulf of Mexico. This follows the end, in October 2010, of the moratorium established in this region after the Deepwater Horizon incident. Activity also revived with the emergence of new exploration of fields in Brazil and the Gulf of Guinea (Ghana, Angola, Equatorial Guinea and the Congo) and with new projects being launched in 2011.

Crude oil shipments

Over the past decade, crude oil volumes increased at a relatively slower pace than other market segments. Between 2000 and 2011, crude oil shipments grew annually at an average rate of less than 1 per cent while in 2011, they declined by 1.4 per cent. In 2011, the total volume of crude oil loaded globally amounted to about 1.8 billion tons. Western Asia remained the largest loading area, followed, Africa, developing America and the transition economies. Major importing areas were in ascending order, Japan, North America, Europe and developing Asia.

Tanker trade patterns are changing as crude oil source diversification continues. A new map of crude supplies is being drawn up as new oil discoveries are made in different regions and as new market suppliers emerge. Underpinning the diversification strategy is the active move by China to secure its energy supply through foreign investments.[36] In March 2009, China lent up to $40 billion to the Russian Federation, Kazakhstan, the Bolivarian Republic of Venezuela and Brazil,[37] in exchange for oil, while its investment in the mining sector in sub-Saharan Africa accounted for about one third of the country's foreign direct investment (FDI).[38] There are now 50 countries in which Chinese oil companies have more than 200 upstream investments.[39] The extent to which the international tanker market would benefit from the full opportunities arising from these projects remains unclear as the strategy being developed by China also aims to ensure that, by 2015, half the country's crude imports are shipped on domestic ship tonnage. Another trend reshaping the market is the falling demand in the United States – the world's largest oil consumer – and the consequent reorientation of cargo flows towards Asia.

Current sanctions applying to the oil trade of the Islamic Republic of Iran are also influencing the tanker market and raising uncertainties. The sanctions have a direct impact on this country's oil exports as well as on the oil trade that passes through the Strait of Hormuz. An escalation of these geopolitical tensions could lead to a shutdown of the Strait, which in turn would create oil shortages and raise oil prices to potentially extreme levels, including the range of $200–$400.[40] Although temporary waivers have been issued for a number of countries, concerns remain with respect to the likely severe impact of the sanctions, including those enacted by the European Union. These latter sanctions prohibit insurers in Europe – marine insurers are to a large extent based in Europe and the United States – from issuing or maintaining insurance to tankers involved in servicing the oil trade of the Islamic Republic of Iran. Pressure is particularly high for some key crude importers, which could be forced to provide sovereign guarantees to tankers.

In a separate development, tanker trade has also been affected by rising operating costs resulting from the higher oil and bunker fuel prices that prevailed in 2011. Tanker operators had to reduce speed to optimize fuel consumption and also absorb excess tonnage capacity. Slow steaming has been implemented in the tanker trade, with most voyages taking place at an average of 13 knots (compared to 14 knots), and at 10–11 knots when sailing in ballast (see also section C).

Table 1.6.	Major producers and consumers of oil and natural gas, 2011 (World market share in percentage)		
World oil production		**World oil consumption**	
Western Asia	33	Asia Pacific	32
Transition economies	16	North America	24
North America	14	Europe	16
Africa	11	Latin America	9
Latin America	12	Western Asia	10
Asia Pacific	10	Transition economies	5
Europe	5	Africa	4
World natural gas production		**World natural gas consumption**	
North America	25	North America	25
Transition economies	24	Europe	16
Western Asia	16	Asia	17
Asia Pacific	15	Transition economies	18
Europe	8	Western Asia	14
Latin America	7	Latin America	7
Africa	6	Africa	3

Source: UNCTAD secretariat on the basis of data published in the British Petroleum (BP) *Statistical Review of World Energy 2012* (June 2012).

Note: Oil includes crude oil, shale oil, oil sands and natural gas liquids NGLs – the liquid content of natural gas where this is recovered separately). The term excludes liquid fuels from other sources as biomass and coal derivatives.

Refinery developments, shipments of petroleum products and gas

In 2011, global refinery throughputs increased marginally by 0.5 per cent and averaged 75.7 million bpd. The drop in the OECD output was offset by increased production in developing countries, including India, China and those of Latin America. For the fifth time in six years, growth in throughput was outpaced by growth in the global refining capacities, which expanded by 1.5 per cent in 2011. The largest capacity growth continues to take place in the Asia–Pacific region and in Western Asia.

Refiners in Europe are confronted with a number of difficulties. These include a falling demand in Europe and the United States (the largest market for European gasoline), the shutdown of seven refineries, the need to seek alternative markets in Africa and Western Asia for European gasoline, and a supply and demand mismatch with refineries in Europe being geared towards gasoline production and global demand supporting diesel. The closing of refineries in Europe, however, could mean greater European imports of oil products in the future.

In 2011, world shipments of petroleum products and gas, including LNG and liquefied petroleum gas (LPG) increased by 5.1 per cent, taking the total to 1.03 billion tons. The growth rate reflects the booming LNG trade. If gas trade were to be excluded, and using estimates for LNG and LPG trade published by Clarkson Research Services (*Shipping Review & Outlook*, spring 2012), the growth rate would moderate and amount to 3.3 per cent. In 2011, the United States became a net exporter of refined petroleum products for the first time on record.

Natural gas supply and demand

Natural gas is the third largest source of energy consumed globally, after oil and coal. North America continues to account for the largest share of world gas consumption, although the largest growth rate was recorded in the Asian market.

In 2011, natural gas consumption increased by 2.2 per cent, with consumption in North America expanding by 3.2 per cent due to low gas prices. Elsewhere the largest growth was recorded in China, Qatar, Saudi Arabia and Japan. The combined effect of a weak economic situation, relatively high gas prices, warmer weather conditions and an incremental shift towards greater use of renewable power generation has led gas consumption in the European Union to drop by 10 per cent.

In 2011, global natural gas production grew by 3.1 per cent, with production in the United States growing by 7.7 per cent and this country ranking as the largest world producer. The United States has been gradually reducing its dependency on foreign energy supplies, in part through increased exploitation of its shale gas.

Output of natural gas grew rapidly in Qatar, the Russian Federation and Turkmenistan, which helped to offset the lost output from Libya and the United Kingdom. Production in the European Union also declined as demand in the region weakened and gas fields matured or were under maintenance.

Liquefied natural gas shipments

In 2011, global natural gas trade increased by 4 per cent, with 32 per cent of this trade being carried as LNG on board gas carriers and the remaining share being carried via pipelines. Shipments of LNG grew by 10.3 per cent in 2011, taking the total volume to 330.8 billion cubic meters. Growth was fuelled by increasing exports from Qatar and increasing imports into the United Kingdom (35.3 per cent), Japan (12.6 per cent) and the Republic of Korea (11 per cent). Asia accounted for 62.7 per cent of global LNG imports, with Japan remaining the world largest importer, followed by the Republic of Korea.

Over the past few years LNG has been one of the fastest-growing cargoes owing to the increasing interest in LNG as a greener alternative to other fossil fuels. Interest in LNG heightened in 2011 as the fallout from the disaster in Japan highlighted the risk of a great reliance on nuclear power over the long term. New and expanding LNG-receiving terminals (for example, in the United Kingdom, the United States, China, the United Arab Emirates, Chile, and Thailand) are being set up, and a total of five new liquefaction projects started operations between 2010 and 2011, including those in Qatar, Peru and Norway. Overall, the outlook for LNG is positive and is supported by growing demand from Asia, including a projected growth in demand from traditionally large LNG exporters such as Indonesia and Malaysia.

One study projects that by 2030 Norway and the Russian Federation will be driving global exports of LNG and that these two countries will lead the fourth wave of LNG exports.[41] The first wave is taking place at the present time and is led by Qatar, the second wave is projected to occur in 2014 with Australia and the Asia Pacific region being major players, and the third wave is expected to occur around 2020 and be driven by West Africa.[42]

Dry cargo trades: major and minor dry bulks and other dry cargo[43]

In 2011, the momentum was maintained for dry cargo trade, which increased by a firm 5.6 per cent, taking the total to nearly 6 billion tons. Dry bulk cargo, including the five major commodities (iron ore, coal, grain, bauxite/alumina and phosphate rock) and minor bulks (agribulks, fertilizers, metals, minerals, steel and forest products) increased by 5.6 per cent, down from the 12.3 per cent increase recorded in 2010. The total volume of dry bulk trade amounted to 3.7 billion tons in 2011.

Major dry bulks: iron ore, coal, grain, bauxite/alumina and phosphate rock

In 2011, the five major dry bulks accounted for approximately 42 per cent of total dry cargo, driven by iron ore volumes, which accounted for the largest share (42.5 per cent), followed by coal (38.1 per cent), grain (14 per cent), bauxite/alumina (4.4 per cent) and phosphate rock (1.1 per cent).

Growth in the five major bulks remained closely linked to steel production, growing infrastructure development needs of emerging developing countries, urbanization and the evolution of the global manufacturing base. World consumption and production of steel, a key product supplier to many industries, continued to expand in 2011 despite prevailing global economic uncertainties and volatilities. In 2011, world steel consumption grew by 6.5 per cent, down from 15.1 per cent in 2010. The deceleration reflects the overall weakness of the world economy and the slight slowdown in the economic expansion of China. With most of Chinese steel demand being driven by expenditure on investment and construction, the country's steel consumption grew by 8.9 per cent in 2011, a slower pace than in 2010.

World steel production is estimated to have grown by 6.8 per cent in 2011, reaching a record 1.6 billion tons. Steel production in China increased, albeit at a slower pace, and still accounted for almost half of the global output in 2011. Other emerging developing economies such as India, Brazil, the Republic of Korea and Turkey, which have featured among the top 10 steel producers for the past 40 years, also increased output. Major world steel producers and consumers are featured in table 1.7.

Coal production, consumption and shipments

With a share of 30.3 per cent of global energy consumption, coal is the second most important primary energy source and is used mainly in power generation. Global coal consumption grew by 5.4 per cent in 2011, with consumption outside the OECD countries, led by China (9.7 per cent), rising by 8.4 per cent. Despite growth in Europe, overall consumption in the OECD countries declined by 1.1 per cent due to falling demand in the United States and Japan.

Coal production grew by 6.1 per cent in 2011, with most of the growth occurring in developing countries and with China accounting for over two thirds of this expansion. Since China has emerged as a net importer of coal, coal prices have been rising, as have new investments in exporting countries, including Australia, Indonesia, the Russian Federation, Mongolia and more recently Mozambique, which has

Table 1.7.	Major dry bulks and steel: main producers, users, exporters and importers, 2011 (Market shares in percentages)		

Steel producers		Steel users	
China	46	China	45
Japan	7	European Union 27	11
United States	6	North America	9
Russian Federation	5	Confederation of Independent States	4
India	5	Middle East	4
Republic of Korea	4	Latin America	3
Germany	3	Africa	2
Ukraine	2	Other	22
Brazil	2		
Turkey	2		
Others	18		

Iron ore exporters		Iron ore importers	
Australia	42	China	63
Brazil	31	Japan	12
Others	10	European Union 15	10
India	7	Republic of Korea	6
South Africa	5	Middle East	2
Canada	3	Others	6
Sweden	2		

Coal exporters		Coal importers	
Indonesia	34	Japan	18
Australia	30	Europe	18
United States	10	China	13
Colombia	8	India	13
South Africa	7	Republic of Korea	13
Russian Federation	6	Taiwan Province of China	6
Canada	3	Malaysia	2
Others	2	Thailand	2
China	1	Israel	1
		Others	12

Grain exporters		Grain importers	
United States	36	Asia	33
European Union	12	Latin America	21
Argentina	11	Africa	22
Australia	10	Middle East	14
Canada	9	Europe	6
Others	23	Confederation of Independent States	3

Source: UNCTAD secretariat on the basis of data from the World Steel Association (2012), Clarkson Research Services, published in the June 2012 issue of *Dry bulk Trade Outlook*, and the World Grain Council, 2012.

been attracting investors, especially from Brazil and India. The year 2011 saw the first coal shipment from Mozambique.[44]

In 2011, the volume of coal shipments (thermal and coking) totalled 944 million tons, up by 5.1 per cent compared with 2010. In 2011, coking coal shipments declined by 5.5 per cent, reflecting developments on the demand side as well as supply side constraints resulting from tighter market conditions caused by output cuts from Australia. The floods in Australia interrupted coal mine operations, which reduced supply and raised coal prices. This in turn depressed demand, especially from China, where domestic supplies provide a better alternative to less competitive coal imports.

Growth in overall coal shipments held strong due to an increase of 8.7 per cent in thermal coal trade. Growing energy requirements in emerging developing countries in Asia, a stronger demand for steam coal in Europe, for a short while, high oil prices and the aftermath of the nuclear accident in Japan have all contributed to boost demand for thermal coal.

In 2011, Indonesia remained the leading exporter of thermal coal with a share of 44.9 per cent, followed by Australia (20.4 per cent). Strong demand in China and India as well as in Europe has boosted thermal coal imports. Import levels in Japan and the United States dropped due, in part, to the aftermath of the March 2011 disaster in Japan, stringent environmental regulation and comparatively low gas prices in the United States.

One study projects that Australia will overtake Indonesia as the biggest exporter of coal by 2016.[45] Australia is investing in the establishment of new mines and expanding existing ones. According to the Australian Bureau of Agricultural and Resource Economics and Sciences, by October 2011 there were 20 committed coal-mining projects in the country and 76 proposals.[46] Meanwhile, some observers are noting that the growing power generation needs in Indonesia may constrain the country's exports starting in 2014.[47] This would likely provide an opportunity for other suppliers, including those situated in locations distant from China, to step in and meet the growing demand. Potential new players that may develop a bigger role include the United States, the Russian Federation, South Africa and Mongolia. Main world coal importers and exporters are featured in table 1.7.

The outlook for coal trade remains promising, as developing nations continue to require more coal to meet their energy needs. It remains subject, however, to developments in coal production and consumption patterns in China, as the scale of the country's large domestic supply means that any small shift could turn the country into a net exporter again.[48] Additionally, the country's Five-Year Plan for the period 2011 to 2015, which aims to reduce the energy and carbon intensity of the economy, is likely to impact on coal trade.

Iron ore and steel production and consumption

In 2011, iron ore trade expanded by 6 per cent, taking the total volume past 1 billion tons. This growth remains highly concentrated with China being the main driver.

Major iron ore exporters in 2011 were Australia, Brazil, India, South Africa and Canada (table 1.7). With a joint market share of 73 per cent, Australia and Brazil increased their export volumes by 8.9 per cent and 6.4 per cent, respectively. Except for India, where iron ore exports were constrained by the introduction of mining and export bans, as well as higher export duties, all other exporters have recorded positive export growth.

Reflecting their weaker economic stance, European countries reduced their iron ore imports by 3.7 per cent, while Asian developing countries recorded an increase of 2 per cent. Although positive, this rate is dwarfed by the 32 per cent recorded in 2010. Import demand in China increased by a strong 10 per cent, anchoring the country's dominance in this particular trade. Most other Asian countries increased their imports, but Japan and Indonesia recorded a decline of 4.4 per cent and 21.7 per cent, respectively.

In 2011, concerns were raised regarding new port restrictions introduced by Chinese authorities. These would restrict access to the purpose-built very large ore carriers (VLOCs) of 400,000 dwt, owned or ordered by Vale to service booming iron ore demand from China (see also chapters 2 and 4 for more detailed information). For Brazil, in particular, the strategic importance of its bilateral trade with China cannot be overemphasized. Brazilian exports to China increased by 46.1 per cent in 2011 to reach $44.3 billion, up from $30.8 billion in 2010, while exports from China to Brazil grew by 34.6 per cent to $32.8 billion.[49] Iron ore accounts for 40 per cent of Brazilian exports to

China, soybeans for 27 per cent, crude oil for 10.5 per cent, pig iron for 4 per cent and sugar for 2.7 per cent. Brazil and China are increasingly investing in port infrastructure projects to address any potential bottlenecks that may hinder this trade.[50]

Although it remains subject to developments in the wider economy and the steel-making sector, and more importantly, to the effect of new macroeconomic policies being instigated by China, the outlook for iron trade remains positive, with shipments projected by Clarkson Research Services to grow by 6 per cent in 2012.

Grain shipments

Total grain production in the crop year 2010/2011 fell by 2.6 per cent to 1.75 billion tons, while production in the crop year 2011/2012 increased by 5.1 per cent, taking the total to 1.84 billion tons. World grain consumption increased by 1 per cent in 2010/2011 to reach 1.79 billion tons and further increased in 2011/2012 by 2.8 per cent, taking the total to 1.84 billion tons.

World wheat consumption is expected to increase from 657 million tons in 2010/2011 to 688 million tons in 2011/12, up by 4.7 per cent. Food use accounts for over two thirds of the total growth. However, with maize supplies being more limited and prices being higher, lower-grade wheat becomes a good alternative for use as feedstock. Industrial use remains small but is expected to grow as demand for wheat-based ethanol increases.

World grain shipments totalled 347 million tons in the full year 2011, up by 1.5 per cent over 2010. Wheat and coarse grain accounted for 73.8 per cent of the total grain shipments. For the crop year 2011/12, volumes of wheat exports increased by 15.6 per cent due to a strong demand, especially from developing economies, and improved harvests. These factors eased wheat prices. Wheat export increases were recorded in Argentina (50 per cent), Australia (24.9 per cent) and Canada (10.4 per cent). Exports by majors such as the United States and the European Union dropped by 21.9 per cent and 29.1 per cent, respectively, due in particular to better priced grain from other regions, including from the Black Sea. Meanwhile, shipments of coarse grains increased by 5.8 per cent, with large increases recorded in Australia (51.1 per cent) and Argentina (9.7 per cent).

Bauxite/alumina and phosphate rock

Bauxite ore is mined and then transferred to a refinery for the processing and extraction of alumina. The world's largest bauxite deposits are located in Guinea, Australia, Brazil and Jamaica. In 2011, world production of alumina increased by 8 per cent over 2010. Growth resulted mainly from the increased production of bauxite (6 per cent) from expanded, new and reopened mines in Brazil, China, Guinea, India, Jamaica, Suriname and the Bolivarian Republic of Venezuela. Bauxite production in Australia declined slightly because of the flooding that forced production cuts at some mines. World trade in bauxite/alumina increased by a strong 17.2 per cent, totalling 109 million tons in 2011.

World phosphate rock production capacity is projected to increase by nearly 20 per cent between 2011 and 2015, with most of the increases occurring in Africa, in particular Morocco. Other new mines are planned in Australia, Brazil, Namibia, and Saudi Arabia. World consumption of phosphate rock for fertilizers is projected to grow at a rate of 2.5 per cent per year during the next 5 years, with the largest increases being in Asia and South America. Phosphate rock volumes increased by 8.7 per cent, down from 15 per cent recorded in 2010. Total volumes reached 25 million tons, reflecting in part the continued improved economic situation in the first half of the year. With no substitutes for phosphorus in agriculture, increased demand for grain and improved production levels have also contributed to the continued growth. Growing demand for fertilizers and increased production by new or expanding plants in producing countries are expected to sustain growth in phosphate rock trade.

Dry cargo: minor bulks

In line with developments in the world economy and the deceleration of growth since the third quarter of 2011, growth in minor bulks trade decelerated to 6.1 per cent. Global volumes reached 1.2 billion tons, a level surpassing the pre-crisis peak of 1.1 billion tons achieved in 2007. Exports of metals and minerals recorded the second fastest growth (7.4 per cent) after agribulks (8.6 per cent), while manufactures expanded by 5.6 per cent and fertilizers (excluding phosphate rock) grew by 4.3 per cent. The only contraction recorded was in sugar volumes, which fell by 7.4 per cent, following a growth of 11.9 per cent in 2010. Looking to the future, trade in minor bulks is projected to expand further in 2012, albeit at a slower rate, reflecting in part the weakening in the world economy and the slowdown in steel production activity, an important source of demand for a number of minor bulks.

Containerized cargo

Accounting for about 62 per cent of the remaining 2.2 billion tons of dry cargoes, world container trade, expressed in 20-foot equivalent units (TEUs), grew by 7.1 per cent in 2011, down from 12.8 per cent in 2010. According to Clarkson Research Services, total container trade volumes amounted to 151 million TEUs in 2011, equivalent to about 1.4 billion tons. These headline figures conceal some differences at regional and route levels that have significantly impacted the container trade market during the year.

Global growth in 2011 was limited by the slowdown recorded on the mainlane East–West trade. As shown on table 1.8, trade on the trans-Pacific route declined by 0.5 per cent while volumes on the Asia–Europe and trans-Atlantic routes expanded by 6.3 per cent and 5.7 per cent, respectively (figures 1.5(a), 1.5 (b), 1.5 (c) and table 1.8).

Growth was mainly generated by increased demand for imports in developing regions, with container trade volumes expanding strongly on the non-mainlane East–West, North–South and intraregional lanes. Non-mainlane East–West trade grew by 8.9 per cent, while North–South and intraregional trades expanded by 8.9 per cent and 9.2 per cent respectively.[51] According to data from Clarkson Research Services, in 2011, the three mainlane trades totalled 47.3 million TEUs, while the non-mainlane trades reached 103.3 million TEUs.[52]

One current opinion maintains that greater containerization could help generate additional cargo for container shipping. It is argued that unconventional commodities can be carried increasingly in containers. These include, for example, larger volumes of scrap steel and recycled paper from North America and Europe to Asia, and general cargo and bulk commodities that can be transported in smaller batches and containerized (for example, segments of food commodities and raw materials). Other commodities include more refrigerated cargo, chemicals and even Handysize loads of bulk commodities, such as iron ore, which is reported to have already been shipped in small parcels from Africa to China. For these ideas to materialize, however, prevailing price and cost barriers need to be removed and cost-effectiveness and vessel specifications need to be assessed.[53]

Figure 1.5 (a).   Global container trade, 1996–2013 (Millions of TEUs and annual percentage change)

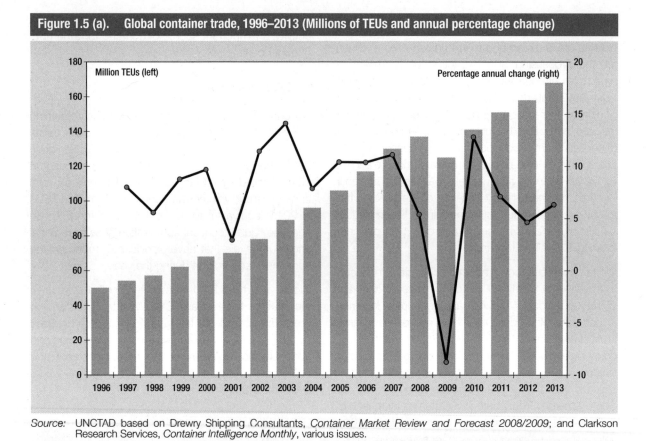

Source: UNCTAD based on Drewry Shipping Consultants, *Container Market Review and Forecast 2008/2009*; and Clarkson Research Services, *Container Intelligence Monthly*, various issues.

Figure 1.5 (b).   Global container trade, 1985–2012 (Millions of tons and annual percentage change)

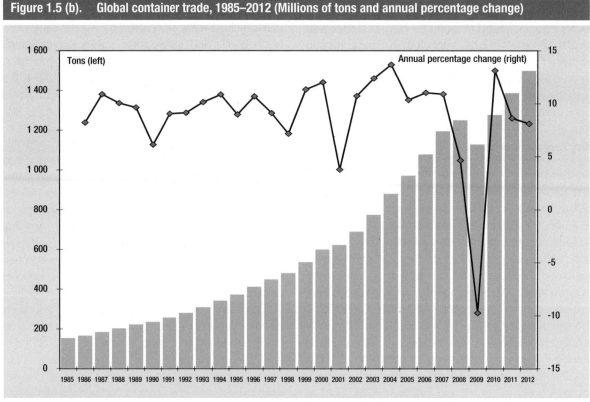

Source: UNCTAD based on Clarkson Research Services' *Shipping Review & Outlook*, spring 2012.

Table 1.8.	Estimated containerized cargo flows on major East–West container trade routes, 2009–2011 (Millions of TEUs and percentage change)					
Year	Transpacific		Europe Asia		Transatlantic	
	Asia–North America	North America–Asia	Asia–Europe	Europe–Asia	Europe–North America	North America–Europe
2009	10.6	6.1	11.5	5.5	2.8	2.5
2010	12.8	6.0	13.5	5.6	3.1	2.8
2011	12.7	6.0	14.1	6.2	3.4	2.8
Percentage change 2010–2011	1.2	0.9	4.6	10.6	8.3	2.8

Source: UNCTAD based on Container Trade Statistics, March 2012; *Containerisation International*, 1 September 2012; and the Global Insight Database as published in *Bulletin FAL*, issue number 288, number 8/2010 (*International maritime transport in Latin America and the Caribbean in 2009 and projections for 2010*), ECLAC.

The policy of China to move up the value chain in global manufacturing is causing manufacturing operations of low-value goods to relocate to other lower-cost production sites such as in Viet Nam, Bangladesh and Indonesia.[54] Chinese manufacturers have been moving up the value chain as exports in power equipment, auto parts and electronics are growing faster than average.[55] Research from the Boston Consulting Group

argues that with rapidly rising labour costs in China, manufacturing business could shift operations from China back to the United States.[56] Another research by Cost and Capital Partners suggests that relocation is taking place towards Mexico rather than the United States in view of Mexico's cost competitiveness and more reliable supply chains.[57] This is further illustrated by recent data from Piers indicating that exports from

Figure 1.5 (c).	Estimated containerized cargo flows on major East–West container trade routes, 1995–2011 (Millions of TEUs)

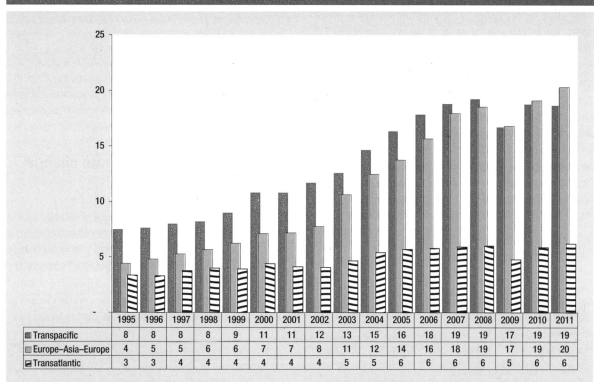

	1995	1996	1997	1998	1999	2000	2001	2002	2003	2004	2005	2006	2007	2008	2009	2010	2011
Transpacific	8	8	8	8	9	11	11	12	13	15	16	18	19	19	17	19	19
Europe–Asia–Europe	4	5	5	6	6	7	7	8	11	12	14	16	18	19	17	19	20
Transatlantic	3	3	4	4	4	4	4	4	5	5	6	6	6	6	5	6	6

Source: Based on the Global Insight Database as published in *Bulletin FAL*, issue number 288, number 8/2010 (*International maritime transport in Latin America and the Caribbean in 2009 and projections for 2010*). ECLAC. Data for 2010 and 2011 are based on table 1.8.

China to the United States have been growing at a much slower rate (2 per cent for the 12 month period up to January 2012) than exports from Mexico to the United States (68 per cent over the same period).[58] Overall, both the cost and the transit time of shipping are viewed as key considerations for moving from China to Mexico.

Import demand from China could also have a deep impact on future container trade patterns. Supported by the policy within China of promoting greater consumer spending, some rebalancing of container trade flows is emerging, breaking away from past trends as containerships are increasingly sailing full to China.[59] The shift not only reflects the robust Chinese demand for raw materials and commodities, including metals, waste paper and plastics, but also its growing demand for higher-value goods.[60] These include items such as machine tools and instruments, hi-tech products, luxury goods and cars.[61]

In a separate development and against a background of increasing costs and lower earnings, container shipping witnessed a structural change in 2011 with the emergence of alliances and oligopolistic competition (see chapter 2).[62] At the same time, decisions to maintain exemptions of liner shipping from the application of competition laws have been made by a number of administrations during the year. In February 2012, a study for the United States Federal Maritime Commission (FMC) did not confirm the merit of repealing the exemption, while in Singapore, the block exemption from competition rules for liner shipping agreements was extended until 2016. Japan also decided to maintain its antitrust immunity system till at least 2015, while an agreement by the Asia–Pacific Economic Cooperation (APEC) forum was adopted in 2011 setting up guidelines on maritime competition rules for consortia. In Europe, however, where such exemptions were repealed in 2008, compliance with the competition law continues to be enforced by the European Commission, which in March 2012 fined 14 international logistics companies, including UPS and Kuehne and Nagel, €169 million for operating four price-fixing cartels.[63]

Finally, another important concern for the container industry was dealt with in 2011 as the call by the shipping and port industries for mandatory controls on the weighing of freight containers received full attention at the International Maritime Organization

(IMO). An amendment to the International Convention for Safety of Life at Sea (SOLAS) to create a new legal obligation requiring containers' actual weight to be verified prior to loading aboard a ship is now being considered by IMO.[64]

C. SELECTED EMERGING TRENDS AFFECTING INTERNATIONAL SHIPPING

Against a background of economic uncertainty, faltering demand and the burden of ship tonnage overcapacity (see chapter 2), the shipping industry is also confronted by a rapidly changing operating environment, in which some trends are reshaping the industry's future and altering global seaborne trade patterns. Shipping and logistics will need to address these developments to adapt to the new realities and remain operational and competitive. Featuring high on the list of these trends are:

- Climate change;
- Shift in global economic influence and changing trade patterns;
- Rising bunker fuel prices and operating costs;
- Maritime piracy (see chapters 5 and 3);[65]
- Growing momentum of sustainability imperatives (see chapter 6).[66]

While all these issues warrant due consideration, the following section focuses on three developments that entail particularly long-term implications, namely climate change, shifting global economic mass and trade patterns, and rising fuel and operating costs.

1. Transport and the climate change challenge

Climate change is one of the greatest challenges facing our societies, economic structures and environmental systems. A significant risk multiplier, climate change undermines the objectives of sustainable development by exacerbating other interconnected global problems, including poverty, food shortages, water scarcity, energy insecurity and environmental degradation.

Transportation and the greenhouse gas (GHG) emissions that it generates are at the centre stage of the current climate change debate. While the entire sector needs to reduce its carbon footprint, international shipping, in particular, has attracted attention because the GHG emissions generated by this sector are not covered under the United Nations Framework Convention on Climate Change (UNFCCC). Another reason for this heightened interest is the renewed opportunity provided by the current climate negotiations under UNFCCC and IMO to adopt, for the first time, a binding international regime. Some regulatory measures focusing on technical and operational aspects of international shipping have recently been adopted by IMO while other measures, such as market-based instruments, are still being considered (see chapters 5 and 6). Mitigation action is also gathering momentum among the shipping and port industries with a number of measures being planned or having already been implemented (see chapter 6). However, although mitigation action in maritime transport is critical, it is not sufficient to effectively address climate change and its related impacts. Adaptation action based, as a prerequisite, on a good understanding of risks and vulnerabilities is fundamental to help minimize the effects of unmitigated climate change on transport and trade. While adaptation action in maritime transport is increasingly recognized as important, it should be noted that it is a newcomer to the climate change policy debate and has so far attracted much less interest than mitigation.

Within the transport sector, the special case of seaports calls for particular attention. With 80 per cent of world trade by volume being carried by sea, ports fulfil a critical function as links of global supply chains and constitute engines of economic growth. At the same time, these key infrastructural assets are vulnerable to climate change impacts and associated risks, given their location in coastal zones, low-lying areas and deltas.

Risks for maritime transport include accelerated coastal erosion, port and coastal road inundation or submersion, increased runoff and siltation requiring increased dredging, restrictions on access to docks, deterioration of conditions and problems with the structural integrity of pavements and railway tracks within port areas and related hinterland connections.[67] In addition to these impacts on physical infrastructure, climate change also affects shipping volumes and costs, cargo loading and capacity, sailing and/or loading schedules, storage and warehousing.[68] These impacts are likely to impose costs that will be correlated to the degree of exposure and vulnerability, as well as constraints on the adaptive capacity. Furthermore, greater global interconnectedness

and economic integration with supply chains acting as transmission channels entail additional costs. A localized impact on ports can have ripple effects that extend beyond borders to affect industries, stakeholders and economies in distant locations. Although not necessarily driven by climate change, supply chain disruptions resulting from damage to ports caused by natural disasters in Japan and Thailand in 2011 provide a poignant illustration.

The implications of any damage or disruption to transport networks, including ports, can be particularly challenging for the transport and trade of developing countries such as small island developing States (SIDS). The challenge for SIDS is of greater magnitude given their high economic, geographic and climatic vulnerabilities and their generally limited adaptive capacity.[69] In this context, building the capacities of developing countries, including SIDS, with a view to reducing their vulnerability and managing disaster risks is crucial and should be pursued as a matter of priority.[70]

Assessing with any certainty the costs for ports and their hinterland connections associated with the impacts of climate change is difficult. There is no doubt, however, that these impacts can reach extreme proportions in ports and port cities.[71] A study by OECD assessed the exposure of the world's largest port cities to coastal flooding in 2005 and has estimated the total value of assets exposed across all 136 port cities examined to be $3 trillion.[72] A more recent study examining the same 136 port megacities has found that, assuming a sea-level rise of 0.5 metres by 2050, the value of exposed assets may be as high as $28 trillion.[73] These costs are rising in tandem with ever increasing urbanization, population growth, investment in port and transport infrastructure, and wealth expansion around coastal areas.

Against this background, the case for designing and implementing appropriate adaptation strategies to address climate-change impacts on transport, and more specifically on ports is a strong one. Given the long lifetime of transport infrastructure, adaptation has to happen now to avoid high retrofitting costs.[74] However, a review of the available literature reveals that adaptation action in ports appears to be scarce.[75] Over recent years, various studies have addressed the impacts of climate change on transportation infrastructure generally, for example in the case of the United States,[76] Canada, Australia and the United Kingdom. Most of these studies, however, are not mode-specific and very few specifically focus on ports.[77] Within the existing literature available in the public domain, the United States report, *Impacts of Climate Change and Variability on Transportation Systems and Infrastructure: Gulf Coast Study, Phase I*, is of particular relevance for ports and their hinterland connections.[78] Other studies worth noting include the report commissioned by the International Finance Corporation (IFC), which focuses on the case of the Terminal Maritimo Muelles el Bosque (MEB), in Cartagena, Colombia. The aim of this study was to help develop knowledge, tools and methods for analysing climate-related risks and opportunities, and for evaluating adaptation responses. Equally relevant is the study commissioned by the International Association of Ports and Harbours (IAPH), *Seaports and Climate Change – An Analysis of Adaptation Measures*.[79]

While adaptation strategies in ports may vary (for example, retreat/relocate, protect, and/or accommodate), the ultimate objective is to enhance the resilience of facilities and systems. This may be achieved by, for example, changes in operations, management practices, planning activities, design specifications and standards. This may involve integrating climate change considerations into transport and port investment and planning decisions, as well as into broader transport and port design and development plans. A number of factors could, nevertheless, potentially delay or pose challenges to adaptation action. Firstly, as ports involve multiple players in the decision-making process, it may be difficult to proceed effectively with adaptation plans and strategies.[80] Secondly, factors such as a high perception of uncertainty, limited information about the cost-effectiveness of adaption options and about the cost of inaction, the need for realistic predictions of impacts and for science-based policy formulation that takes into consideration the specifics of the region, and resource intensiveness and costs could all, either individually or in combination, hamper adaptation action in ports.

More specifically, costs and the constraints of financial resources could pose a great challenge to adaptation action. Existing studies on adaptation costs provide only a wide range of estimates and have many information gaps. Much more knowledge is required regarding the impacts of climate change and how they interact, and regarding information on relevant adaptation options.[81] Although not specific to transport or ports, a study produced by the World Bank estimates that, for developing countries, the cost of adapting to an increase in temperature by approximately 2° C by 2050 would be, for the period 2010–2050, in the range of \$75 billion–\$100 billion annually.[82]

Estimates for Barbados that are more specific for transportation, based on the Intergovernmental Panel on Climate Change (IPCC) emission projection scenarios SRES B2[83] and SRES A2, indicate that by 2050 the total impact of climate change on international transport expenditures could range from \$12.7 billion (scenario SRES B2) to \$14.9 billion (scenario SRES A2).[84] The costs for maritime transportation alone range between \$2 billion (SRES B2) and \$2.6 billion (SRES A2).[85] Another study has estimated the total costs of climate change for international transportation in Montserrat to be between \$839 million and \$1.1 billion under scenarios SRES B2 and SRES A2, respectively,[86] while for maritime transport, estimates amounted to between \$209 million (SRES B2) and \$347 million (SRES A2).[87]

Nevertheless, the benefits of adaptation in terms of the effects on frictions to international trade and development are expected to outweigh the costs.[88] One study which compared the cost of adaptation with the cost of inaction at the European Union level finds that by 2020, the net benefit of adaption will range between €3.8 billion (low sea-level-rise scenario) and €4.2 billion (high sea-level-rise scenario). These benefits are expected to increase further by 2080.[89]

Some of these critical considerations have been considered as part of the activities of UNCTAD aimed at addressing the climate change challenge from the maritime transport perspective.[90] These include the 2009 first session of the Multiyear Expert Meeting on Transport and Trade Facilitation, which had as title Maritime Transport and the Climate Change Challenge, the 2010 Joint UNECE-UNCTAD Workshop on Climate Change Impacts on International Transport Networks, the 2011 UNCTAD Ad Hoc Expert Meeting entitled Climate Change Impacts and Adaptation: A Challenge for Global Ports, and the new book entitled *Maritime Transport and the Climate Change Challenge*, edited by UNCTAD and co-published by the United Nations and Earthscan/Routledge in May 2012.[91] Some of the key messages emerging from this work include the wide recognition that adaptation action in transport and more specifically in ports should be pursued without delay, and that adaptation planning for those impacts that are already known should be a priority. Furthermore, collaboration between scientists, engineers, policy makers, governments and industry is key and should be improved. Equally, compiling more data, in particular data on local impacts and vulnerabilities, and conducting cases studies and pilot projects is crucial. Awareness-raising activities need to continue and guidance as well as best practices should be compiled and widely disseminated.

To sum up, climate change impacts on ports and their hinterland connections and related adaptation requirements are development challenges with direct implications for trade and growth. While more work is needed to help advance understanding of the various issues at stake and better assess their full implications, adaptation action in transport generally and, especially, in ports, is an imperative and a sound investment with high returns in the long term.

2. Shift in global economic influence and changing trade patterns

Over the past few years developing countries have been leading a global transformation which entails major implications for the global economy, geopolitics and international trade. The 2008/2009 crisis has deepened the shift of influence and economic mass from advanced economies to emerging developing countries. This trend is creating a multipolar global economy[92] (see previous discussion on a global new design in the *Review of Maritime Transport 2011*, section C).

It is projected that, by 2025, fast-growing developing economies and transition economies, led by China, will grow on average by 4.7 per cent per year between 2011 and 2025, with Brazil, China, India, Indonesia, the Republic of Korea and the Russian Federation expected to account for more than 50 per cent of global growth.[93] By comparison, GDP growth in advanced economies is forecast to grow at less than half this rate (2.3 per cent) over the same period.[94] The share of merging developing economies in global real GDP is forecast to expand from 36.2 per cent in 2010 to 44.5 per cent in 2025.[95] In line with economic growth, the share of all developing countries in international trade flows has also increased over the past few decades, rising from 30 per cent in 1995 to an estimated 42 per cent in 2010. Much of this growth is being generated by South–South and intraregional trade.[96]

Some observers argue that the winner of globalization will be Asia, with rising intra-Asian trade becoming the focus of the global economy. South–South interregional trade is also expected to grow and gather momentum.[97] Supply chains, greater integration in the world economy, growing regional concentration and a shift of technology will all propel East Asian countries (led by China) to become the largest trading bloc in 2015, surpassing the areas of the North American Free Trade Agreement (NAFTA) and the Euro.[98] Such a development will have tangible implications for global transport and trade patterns. One recent analysis predicts that in 2015 China will be the top exporter and importer and that by 2030 the world's largest trade corridor will not involve the United States or Europe, but will instead extend from the advanced to the emerging Asia of Thailand and Viet Nam.[99] It is forecast that by 2050 60 per cent of exports from advanced Asia will go to emerging Asia, thus reinforcing the move eastwards and South–South trade.[100]

In parallel to projected economic and trade growth, freight transport is expected to expand. It has been projected by OECD that by 2050, world freight flows will be from two to four times above their 2010 levels, driven by growth outside OECD, where flows are expected to be between two and six times higher than in 2010.[101] This has implications for international shipping and seaborne trade and will require that appropriate policies and strategies be elaborated to effectively respond to the new realities. All shipping market segments are likely to be affected through changes and adjustments to infrastructure, services, equipment and operations, as well as to the underlying legal and regulatory frameworks. For its part, the transport and logistics industry is also making efforts to ensure that it remains relevant and maintains a competitive edge by being more responsive to the needs of its customers. This is illustrated by the increasing tendency within this industry to reach out to its customer base to solicit its input and help map out its needs and requirements.[102]

To better understand the full impact of the changing global transport and trade landscape, a number of key questions, however, remain and need to be addressed. Relevant considerations include how shipping energy consumption patterns and carbon emissions, production processes, decisions about production plant location and infrastructure investment will all be affected.

3. Rising bunker fuel prices and operating costs

Bunker fuel prices increased in tandem with global oil prices, as shown by the price of 380 centistokes (cSt) in Singapore, which increased by 40 per cent to reach $647 per ton in 2011. Higher fuel costs have a disproportionate effect on transportation companies, as fuel is a necessary cost input. Fuel costs are estimated to have made up 60 per cent of total freight earnings on the benchmark very large crude carrier (VLCC) Western Asia to Far East voyage – taking an average bunker price of $630 per ton for March 2011. This share was only 36 per cent in June 2010. To put this in perspective, in 2008 the annual capital cost for a new Panamax bulker was $6 million, and the annual bunker cost $3.3 million. In 2011, the costs were $2 million and $5.5 million, respectively (see also chapter 3).[103]

In addition to fuel expenses, other cost items are also increasing. Drewry estimates that ship-operating costs have risen between 4 and 6 per cent, depending on the market segment. This has been due to increases in commodity prices, which drove up lube, repair and maintenance costs, as well as to additional insurance cover against piracy.[104] These developments have significantly weighed down on the shipping industry and undermined its profitability – an industry which has been, in addition, struggling with excess tonnage capacity, slowing demand and falling freight rates. In the tanker market, for example, the Republic of Korean operator Samho Shipping filed for court protection against creditors following months of financial difficulties. Reasons cited included increasing bunker costs, low freight rates and the costs associated with piracy attacks against its vessels.[105] In the liner industry, the overall loss in 2011 was estimated at over $6 billion.[106]

In a context of increasingly higher costs and weak economic juncture, cost management and control is becoming important. Relevant cost-cutting measures include speed management through slow steaming, bunker adjustment, paper hedges and selection of the most economical routing options. Among these strategies, slow steaming has evolved into a key cost-cutting measure that reduces bunker fuel consumption and helps absorb capacity. Today, slow steaming is implemented across various market segments and in particular container trade, which

relied heavily on this strategy during the 2008/2009 crisis. The global containership fleet has been cutting sailing speeds by an average of 13 per cent in 2011 on a number of mainlane trades[107] and has continued to reduce sailing speed from 24–25 knots to 21 knots (slow steaming), 18 knots (extra-slow steaming) and 15 knots (super-slow steaming).[108] In the tanker trade, slow steaming has been implemented with most voyages occurring at an average of 13 knots (compared to 14 knots), and 10–11 knots when sailing in ballast (see also previous section on crude oil shipments and chapter 2).[109]

Some argue that slow steaming has its limitations and that it may not be advisable to implement it in all cases. First, slow steaming may be better limited to a few long-haul routes and not used for short-haul ones. Second, there is a need to assess the implications of employing additional ships and container equipment. Furthermore, increased transit time, especially for the dominant leg, may not be acceptable for supply chains, as shown by a study investigating the merits of slow steaming.[110] This study argued that other factors need to be accounted for, including the auxiliary bunker costs and the sensitivity of demand to transit time. Figures for January 2010 indicated a limited use of slow steaming on the Europe–South American trades (with around 30 per cent of services operating slow steaming) as compared with over 80 per cent of services operating slow steaming on those between Europe and the Far East. The study concludes that a differentiated strategy by shipping lines of sailing at a different speed depending on the leg, or of using hubs instead of direct services maybe recommended. Such differentiated strategy would also take into account the sensitivity of demand to transit time, such as, for example, by distinguishing between frozen and dry and fresh products.

While slow steaming is viewed by many as a short-term fix, others consider it to be a long-term trend. In view of current developments in the energy sector, growing demand, constrained and uncertain supply, as well as ongoing geopolitical risks affecting oil producing regions, oil prices and therefore bunker fuel costs will not doubt continue to trend upward.[111] Interestingly however, the historical correlation between bunker and crude prices seems to have changed slightly in 2011, as the rise in bunker prices exceeded that of crude oil. A potential reason for this could be that the large ship deliveries of recent years have increased demand for marine fuels against a slower supply.[112]

With bunker fuel being a residual of the refining process, it is possible that efforts by refineries to maximize the middle distillates output have reduced the quantity of residual marine fuels. Another reason that could have reduced the quantity of residual marine fuels is the combination of increased demand for petroleum products trom Japan that followed the disaster in March 2011 and the cuts in oil supply from Libya during the course of the year.[113]

World energy demand is projected to grow and add some 39 per cent to global consumption by 2030, with almost all the growth being generated in developing regions.[114] Whether adequate levels of energy at affordable prices will be available to match the increased global energy requirements remains uncertain (see *Review of Maritime Transport 2011*, for a detailed discussion of oil supply and demand fundamentals). It is worth noting in this respect that global replacement costs of existing fossil fuel and nuclear power infrastructure are estimated at $15 trillion to $20 trillion at least, equivalent to between 25 and 33 per cent of global GDP.[115] Geopolitical risks and tensions, including economic sanctions, civil unrest and conflicts also weigh down on the supply side. Some observers forecast that the price of crude oil will reach extreme levels if current geopolitical risks escalate and if strategic transit points for oil trade are closed. According to Drewry Supply Chain Advisors, Europe is reliant on Suez transits for about 15 per cent of its crude, and the bunker adjustment factor can be expected to increase by 7 to 9 per cent annually over the next three years on trade between South China and Northern Europe.[116]

Another major development with a bearing on the bunker market relates to the requirement under the IMO International Convention for the Prevention of Pollution from Ships (MARPOL) annex VI, governing air pollution and Emission Control Areas (ECAs) in the European Union and North America, for ships to use low-sulphur fuel (see chapter 5). Ships are required between now and 2020 to burn a more expensive but less polluting fuel, namely distillate grade fuel. The price differential with residual fuel is currently estimated at 50 per cent. While ships are allowed to use technology such as cleaning systems for exhaust gas (scrubbers), the effective widespread use of such scrubbers remains uncertain. These developments raise concerns about their potential economic impact

on shipping, especially at a time when fuel costs account for more than two thirds of operational ship expenditure. The price differential between low-sulphur fuel and residual bunker fuel is projected to increase further with growing demand not being matched by increased supply. Other concerns relate to the potential for inducing an undesirable modal shift. Recent studies supported by the European Community Shipowners' Associations (ECSA) have suggested that applying the 0.1 per cent limit on sulphur fuel could result in a modal shift from water to surface transport which could be detrimental for local shipping and the environment. This concern is shared with respect to trade in the Great Lakes of Canada and the United States.

To sum up, rising energy prices and fuel costs remain a great challenge for the shipping industry in view, in particular, of rising demand, supply pressures and increasing environmental regulation. Cost control and fuel consumption management is essential and may involve a range of strategies. These may include speed management through slow steaming, selection of the most economical routing options and technology-based solutions. These strategies will impact on the design of vessels and propulsion systems, as well as on other technology-related strategies and operational measures. While these may apply differently, depending on the vessel and type of operations, overall a combination of technology-based and operational measures have a significant potential to help address rising fuel and operational costs. As shipping has over recent years intensified efforts to optimize fuel consumption, in view in particular of the more stringent environmental regulatory framework and given the concerns over climate change, new options and solutions are being increasingly developed and tested.

The trends discussed above are all interconnected and entail both challenges and opportunities for the shipping industry. By altering costs, prices and comparative advantages, these developments and related impacts on shipping and seaborne trade can greatly determine countries' trade performance and competitiveness. Improved understanding of these issues and their impacts, both individually and in combination, is required, with active involvement by all stakeholders, including policy makers, investors, transport planners, operators and managers.

ENDNOTES

[1] This sections draws also from: World Bank (2011). *Global Development Horizons 2011. Multipolarity: The New Global Economy*; World Bank (2012). *Global Economic Prospects: Uncertainties and vulnerabilities*. Volume 4. January; Lanzeni ML (2012). *Emerging Markets, Fad or New Reality?* Deutsche Bank Research. April; United Nations Department of Economic and Social Affairs (2011). Monthly Briefing. *World Economic Situation and Prospects*. No 34. 11 August; United Nations Department of Economic and Social Affairs (2011). Monthly Briefing. *World Economic Situation and Prospects*. No 38. 20 December; United Nations Department of Economic and Social Affairs (2012). Monthly Briefing. *World Economic Situation and Prospects*. No 43. 29 May.

[2] For a more comprehensive overview of world economic developments, see UNCTAD *Trade and Development Report, 2012*. www.unctad.org.

[3] UNCTADstat, Nominal and real GDP, total and per capita, annual, 1970–2010. http://unctadstat.unctad.org/TableViewer/tableView.aspx?ReportId=96.

[4] Economist Intelligence Unit (EIU) (2012). *Country Forecast. Global Outlook*. June.

[5] Ibid.

[6] United Nations Department of Economic and Social Affairs (2012). Monthly Briefing. *World Economic Situation and Prospects*. No 43. 29 May.

[7] Ibid.

[8] United Nations Department of Economic and Social Affairs (2012). *World Economic Situation and Prospects, Update as of mid-2012*. United Nations. New York.

[9] Ibid.

[10] Ibid.

[11] World Trade Organization (WTO) (2012). *World trade 2011, prospects for 2012*. PRESS/658, 12 April.

[12] Ibid.

[13] Economist Intelligence Unit (EIU) (2012). *Country Forecast. Global Outlook*. June.

[14] International Monetary Fund (IMF) (2012). *World Economic Outlook. Growth Resuming, Dangers Remain*. World Economic and Financial Surveys (WEFS); Economist Intelligence Unit (EIU) (2012). *Country Forecast. Global Outlook*. June.

[15] Ibid.

[16] Ibid.

[17] World Trade Organization (WTO) (2012). *Report on G-20 Trade Measures (Mid-October 2011 to Mid-May 2012)*. Executive Summary.

[18] Ibid.

[19] Ibid.

[20] Data and information in on seaborne trade draw from relevant UNCTAD statistics and reports as well as on various specialized sources, including: (1) British Petroleum (BP) (2012). *Statistical Review of World Energy 2012*. June; (2) International Energy Agency (IEA) (2011). *World Energy Outlook 2011*; (3) British Petroleum (BP) (2012). *Energy Outlook 2030*. January; (4) International Energy Agency (IEA). *Oil Market Report*. Various issues; (5) Organization of the Petroleum Exporting Countries (OPEC) (2012). *Monthly Oil Market Report*. June; (6) Organization of the Petroleum Exporting Countries (OPEC) (2011). *World Oil Outlook*; (7) Economist Intelligence Unit (EIU) (2012). *World Commodity Forecasts: Industrial Raw Materials*. May; (8) Economist Intelligence Unit (EIU) (2012). *World Commodity Forecasts: Food, Feedstuffs and Beverages*. May; (9) World Steel Association (2012). *World Steel Short Range Outlook*. April; (10) International Grains Council (IGC) (2012). *Grain Market Report*. April; (11) Clarkson Research Services (2012). *Shipping Review & Outlook*. Spring; (12) Clarkson Research Services (2011). *Shipping Review & Outlook*. Fall; (13) Clarkson Research Services. *Container Intelligence Monthly*. Various issues; (14) Clarkson Research Services. *Dry Bulk Trade Outlook*. Various issues; (15) *Lloyd's Shipping Economist* (LSE). Various issues; (16) *Drewry Shipping Consultants* (2012). *Container Forecasters – Quarterly Forecast of the Container Market*. September; (17) Drewry Shipping Consultants. *Drewry Shipping Insight*. Monthly Analysis of the Shipping Markets. Various issues; (18) Institute of Shipping Economics and Logistics (ISL). *Shipping Statistics and Market Review*. Various issues; (19) Dynamar. *DynaLiners*. Various issues; (20) *IHS Fairplay*. Various press articles; (21) *BIMCO Bulletins*. Various issues; (22) *ICS/ISF Annual Review 2012*; (23) United States Geological Survey (2012). *Mineral Commodity Summaries*; (24) Organization for Economic Co-operation and Development (OECD)/International Transport Forum (ITF) (2012). *Transport Outlook Seamless Transport for Greener Growth*; (25) Deutsch Bank Research (2012). *On the Record. Prof. Burkhard Lemper on global shipping markets*, May 14; (26) Barry Rogliano Salles (BRS) (2012). *Shipping and shipbuilding markets, Annual Review 2012*; (27) Seatrade (2011). Issue 6. December; (28) Slater P (2012). No end in sight for the great shipping recession. *Lloyds' List*. 3 May; (29) Leander T (2012). Global shipping earnings to contract 5%–10% in 2012. *Lloyd's List*. 31 May; (30) Slater P (2012). CMA 2012: Bleak Outlook for Shipping. *Lloyd's List*. 19 March.

21   Lloyd's List Maritime Intelligence Unit (LLMIU) as published on the website of the World Shipping Council's (WSC) at www.worldshipping.org.

22   Estimated by Lloyds List Maritime Intelligence Unit (LLMIU), June 2012.

23   This sections draws mainly from Clarkson Research Services (2012). *Shipping Review & Outlook*. Spring; Clarkson Research Services (2011). *Shipping Review & Outlook*. Fall; Mantell C (2012). Variety is the Spice of Life: Regional Crude Sourcing. *Clarkson Shipping Intelligence Network*. 27 April.

24   Clarkson Research Services (2012). Is Trade Giving Enough Mileage? *World Fleet Monitor-Flag, Class, Ownership, Investment, Recycling, Markets, Trade*. Volume 3 No. 3. March.

25   Holden S(2012). Global Coal Flows: A Growing Imbalance? *Clarkson Shipping Intelligence Network*. 24 February.

26   Ibid.

27   Clarkson Research Services (2012). Is Trade Giving Enough Mileage? *World Fleet Monitor-Flag, Class, Ownership, Investment, Recycling, Markets, Trade*. Volume 3 No. 3. March.

28   Mantell C (2012). Variety is the Spice of Life: Regional Crude Sourcing. *Clarkson Shipping Intelligence Network*. 27 April.

29   Ibid.

30   Ibid.

31   Marsoft (2012). Marsoft *Tanker Market Report*. January.

32   Ibid.

33   Ibid.

34   This section draws mainly from: United Nations Department of Economic and Social Affairs (2012) *World Economic Situation and Prospects*. United Nations Publications. New York; Economist Intelligence Unit (EIU) (2012). *Country Forecast. Global Outlook*, June; Economist Intelligence Unit (EIU) (2012). *World Commodity Forecasts: Industrial Raw Materials*; *Shipping & Finance* (2012). Australia to become the world's largest gas exporter in 2030. March; *Shipping & Finance* (2012). How China will evolve until 2030. March; *Shipping & Finance* (2011). Asia to consume two-thirds of global LNG supplies by 2015. October; *Shipping & Finance* (2011). Is US going to cause another oil shock to the tanker market? November; *Shipping & Finance* (2012). LNG Shipping: From Bottom to the Top. March Clarkson Research Services (2012). *Tanker Outlook*. May; Clarkson Research Services (2012). *Oil & Tanker Trades Outlook*. Volume 17, No. 7. July; Clarkson Research Services (2011). *LNG Trade & Transport 2011. A comprehensive overview of the ships, the trades and the markets for LNG*; Organization of Petroleum Exporting Countries (OPEC) (2011). *World Oil Outlook 2011*; Barry Rogliano Salles (BRS) (2012). *Shipping and shipbuilding markets, Annual Review 2012*; Mantell C (2012). Anxious Times: Fear and Supply in the Crude Market. *Clarkson Shipping Intelligence Network*. 26 March; Mantell C (2012). Disaster and Recovery: Japanese Oil Trade in 2011. *Clarkson Shipping Intelligence Network*. 30 January; *BIMCO Bulletin* (2011). Volume 106 #6; Mühlberger M (2012). *Sub-Saharan Africa: the Continent of the 21st Century*. Deutsche Bank. April; Chan, C. (2011). VLs shouldn't rely on China for extra demand. *Fairplay*. 15 December; Brown H (2012). Norway and Russia to ride fourth wave of LNG exports. *Lloyd's List*. 22 March; Brown H (2012).Venezuela-China deal boosts VLCC demand. *Lloyd's List*. 24 May; Chan C (2011). Tanker operators assess changing trade patterns as new oil sources come on stream. *Fairplay*. 15 December; Brown H (2011). Exporters turned importers drive new LNG demand. *Lloyd's List*. 16 September; Osle D (2012). Venezuela's ties to China boost VLCC demand. *Lloyd's List*. 26 March.

35   This section draws mainly from British Petroleum (BP) (2012). *Statistical Review of World Energy 2012*.

36   See for example, Brown H (2012).Venezuela-China deal boosts VLCC demand. *Lloyd's List*. 24 May; Chan C (2011). Tanker operators assess changing trade patterns as new oil sources come on stream. *Fairplay*. 15 December; Osle D (2012). Venezuela's ties to China boost VLCC demand. *Lloyd's List*. 26 March.

37   Chan C (2011). VLs shouldn't rely on China for extra demand. *Fairplay*. 15 December.

38   Mühlberger M (2012). Sub-Saharan Africa: the Continent of the 21st Century. Deutsche Bank. April.

39   Chan C (2011). VLs shouldn't rely on China for extra demand. *Fairplay*. 15 December.

40   *Shipping & Finance* (2011). Is US going to cause another oil shock to the tanker market? November; *Shipping & Finance* (2012). LNG Shipping: From Bottom to the Top. March.

41   Brown H (2012). Norway and Russia to ride fourth wave of LNG exports. *Lloyd's List*. 22 March;

42   Ibid.

43   U.S. Geological Survey (2012). Bauxite and Alumina Statistics and Information. *Mineral Commodity Summaries*; U.S. Geological Survey (2012). Phosphate Rock Statistics and Information. *Mineral Commodity Summaries*; *Shipping & Finance* (2011). Brazil's trade with China 45% up causing port problems; *Shipping & Finance* (2012). China's reliance on imported ores to ease. April; Clarkson Research Services (2012). *Shipping Review & Outlook*, Spring. Clarkson Research Services (2011). *Shipping Review & Outlook*, Fall; World Steel Association (2012). *Global economic outlook and steel demand trends*. April; Economist Intelligence Unit (EIU) (2012). *Global World Commodity Forecasts: Food, Feedstuffs and Beverages*. June; Economist Intelligence Unit (EIU) (2012). *World Commodity Forecasts: Industrial Raw Materials*. June; International Energy Agency (IEA) (2011). *World Energy*

Outlook 2011. November. British Petroleum (BP) (2012). Statistical Review of World Energy 2012.June; Fairplay (2011). Mozambique vital to Essar's African Plan. 1 December. Holden, S. (2012*). Metal Smelting: A Major Driver Under Pressure. Clarkson Shipping Intelligence Network*. 10 February; de Groot, B. (2012). Bolting the door on Valemaxes. *Fairplay*. April; Van den Berg, E. (2012). Seaborne coal trade will top 1 trillion tonnes by 2016. *Lloyd's List*. 30 March.

44   Hutson T (2011). Coal boom seeks new port. *Fairplay*. 27 October.

45   Van den Berg E (2012). Seaborne coal trade will top 1trn tonnes by 2016. *Lloyd's List*. 30 March.

46   Economist Intelligence Unit (EIU) (2012). *World Commodity Forecasts: Industrial Raw Materials*. June.

47   *Fairplay* (2011). Indonesia's coal export dilemma. 17 November.

48   See for example, *Fairplay* (2012). China is key to world coal balance. 5 January.

49   *Shipping & Finance* (2012). China-Brazil bilateral trade soars. April.

50   Ibid.

51   Clarkson Research Services. *Container Intelligence Monthly.* October 2012.

52   Ibid.

53   *Fairplay* (2012). Containers may aid recovery. 23 Feb.

54   Van Marle G (2012). Box lines' China trade could be swamped by a Mexican wave. *Lloyd's List*. March.

55   Leander T (2012). China feels the pinch. *Lloyd's List*. 22 May.

56   Van Marle G. Box lines' China trade could be swamped by a Mexican wave. *Lloyd's List*. March.

57   Ibid.

58   Ibid.

59   Porter J (2012). China's hunger for imports reshapes east-west trade patterns. *Lloyd's List*. 20 June.

60   Ibid.

61   Ibid.

62   Clayton R (2011). Outside the box. *Fairplay*. 22 December.

63   European Commission Press Release (2012). *Antitrust: Commission imposes € 169 million fine on freight forwarders for operating four price fixing cartels*. IP/12/314. 23 March. http://europa.eu/rapid/pressReleasesAction.do?reference=IP/12/314.

64   *Ports & Harbors*. Looking back at 2011 it seems we have seen more negatives than positives. January/February 2012.

65   See also UNCTAD Review of Maritime Transport 2011, Chapter 1, Section C.

66   Ibid.

67   UNCTAD (2011). Ad Hoc Expert Meeting on Climate Change Impacts and Adaptation: A Challenge for Global Ports. *Information Note*. 29 September. UNCTAD/DTL/TLB/2011/2.

68   Ibid.

69   For further information on the challenge of climate change for maritime transport see relevant work in the field from UNCTAD available at www.unctad.org/ttl/legal. See in particular relevant documents and information relating to the Multi-year Expert Meeting on Transport and Trade Facilitation: Maritime Transport and the Climate Change Challenge, 2009; Joint UNECE–UNCTAD Workshop on Climate Change Impacts on International Transport Networks, 2010; Ad Hoc Expert Meeting on Climate Change Impacts and Adaptation: A Challenge for Global Ports, 2011; and, *Maritime Transport and the Climate Change Challenge*, a new book edited by UNCTAD and co-published by the United Nations and Earthscan/Routeledge in May 2012. The book offers information and analysis on the climate change challenge from the perspective of maritime transport and trade.

70   Vulnerability reduction is a core common element of adaptation and disaster risk management. See for example, the special report of the Intergovernmental Panel on Climate Change (2012) entitled *Managing the Risks of Extreme Events and Disasters to Advance Climate Change Adaptation*, Cambridge University Press, New York.

71   Hanson S and Nicholls R (2012). Extreme floods and port cities through the twenty-first century: Implications of climate change and other drivers. *Maritime Transport and the Climate Change Challenge*. Earthscan/United Nations, London.

72   Nicholls R J et al (2008). *Ranking Port Cities with High Exposure and Vulnerability to Climate Extremes: Exposure Estimates*. OECD Environment Working Papers, No. 1. OECD Publishing.

73   Lenton T, Footitt A and Dlugolecki A (2009). *Major Tipping Points in the Earth's Climate System and Consequences for the Insurance Sector*.

74   Kopp A (2012). Transport costs, trade and climate change. *Maritime Transport and the Climate Change Challenge*. Earthscan/United Nations, London, 2012. See also, UNCTAD (2011). Ad Hoc Expert Meeting on Climate Change Impacts and Adaptation: A Challenge for Global Ports. *Information Note*. 29 September. UNCTAD/DTL/TLB/2011/2.

75 Velegrakis AF (2011). *Climate Change: an overview of the scientific background and potential impacts affecting transport infrastructure and networks*. DRAFT Report for consideration and discussion by the Expert Group on Climate Change Impacts and Adaptation for International Transport Networks at its second session (8 November 2011). Informal document No. 2. 4 November.

76 See for example, the 2008 Special Report 290 of the Transportation Research Board, National Academy of Sciences, Washington, DC, entitled "*The Potential Impacts of Climate Change on U.S. Transportation*". See in particular, Appendix C containing a commissioned paper on *Climate Vulnerability and Change with Implications for U.S. Transportation*, December 2006.

77 Ibid.

78 U.S. Climate Change Science Program and Subcommittee on global Change Research (2008). *Impacts of Climate Change and Variability on Transportation Systems and Infrastructure: Gulf Coast Study, Phase I*. [Savonis MJ, Burkett VR and Potter JR (eds.)]Department of Transportation, Washington, DC.

79 Seaports and Climate Change - An Analysis of Adaptation Measures. (2010). Study commissioned by the International Association of Ports and Harbors (IAPH)-Port Planning and Development Committee. Unpublished Draft, November 2010.

80 Asam S (2010). *Climate change Adaptation for Transportation Infrastructure*. ICF International. March 2. North Carolina Workshop on Climate Change Adaptation.

81 Fankhauser S (2009). *The Cost of Adaptation*. Grantham Research Institute. London School of Economics. 1 November.

82 World Bank (2010). *The Economics of Adaptation to Climate Change (EACC) Synthesis Report*.

83 The IPCC published a new set of scenarios in 2000 for use in the Third Assessment Report (Special Report on Emissions Scenarios - SRES). A2 storyline and scenario family: a very heterogeneous world with continuously increasing global population and regionally oriented economic growth that is more fragmented and slower than in other storylines. B2 storyline and scenario family: a world in which the emphasis is on local solutions to economic, social, and environmental sustainability, with continuously increasing population (lower than A2) and intermediate economic development.

84 United Nations Economic Commission for Latin America and the Caribbean (2011). *An Assessment of the Economic Impact of Climate Change on the Transportation Sector in Barbados*. LC/CAR/L.309. 22 October.

85 Ibid.

86 United Nations Economic Commission for Latin America and the Caribbean (2011). *An Assessment of the Economic Impact of Climate Change on the Transportation Sector in Montserrat*.

87 Ibid.

88 Kopp A (2012). Transport costs, trade and climate change. *Maritime Transport and the Climate Change Challenge*. Earthscan/United Nations. London.

89 Richards JA and Nicholls RJ (2009). *Impacts of climate change in coastal systems in Europe*. PESETA-Coastal Systems study. European Commission Joint Research Centre Institute for Prospective Technological Studies.

90 For additional information about UNCTAD work in the field and direct links to the relevant meetings website, see www.unctad.org/ttl/legal. See also relevant documents and outcome of the International Conference on Adaptation of Transport Networks to Climate Change organized by the UNECE and held on 25-26 June 2012 in Greece (http://www.unece.org/trans/main/wp5/wp5_conf_2012_june.html).

91 The book is the first of its kind, adopting a multidisciplinary approach and providing detailed insight on a range of the potential implications of climate change for this key sector of global trade. It includes contributions from experts from academia, international organizations - such as the IMO, the UNFCCC secretariat, OECD, IEA and the World Bank - as well as the shipping and port industries. For further information see www.unctad.org/ttl/legal.

92 World Bank (2011). *Global Development Horizons 2011-Multipolarity: The New Global Economy*.

93 Ibid.

94 Ibid.

95 Ibid.

96 Ibid.

97 *Shipping & Finance* (2012). International trade to accelerate from 2014. March.

98 *Shipping & Finance* (2011) Analysis on the changing patterns of global trade. August 2011.

99 McMahon, L. (2012). Shipping may seem downbeat and dreadful but better times lie ahead. Lloyd's List.31 May.

100 Ibid.

101 Organization for Co-operation and Economic Development (OECD)/International Transport Forum (ITF) (2012). *Transport Outlook Seamless Transport for Greener Growth*. .

102 See for example, Deutsche Post AG. *Delivering Tomorrow, Customer Needs in 2020 and Beyond A Global Delphi Study*. June 2009.

103   *Shipping & Finance* (2011). Bunker costs up 5 times in a decade. August.

104   Beddow M (2011). Drewry projects more misery for ocean carriers. *Containerisation International*. October.

105   Taib A (2011). *Rising Bunkers Put Shipping Companies on Edge.* Bunker World.

106   Porter J (2012). Box lines' 2011 losses balloon to $6bn. *Lloyd's List*. April.

107   McCarthy L (2012). Containerhsip fleet slows speeds 13% over a year to an average 14.9 knots. *Lloyd's List*. March.

108   McCarthy L (2012). Maersk to super-slow steam on five Europe-Asia containership loops. *Lloyd's List*. April.

109   Barry Rogliano Salles (BRS) (2012). *Shipping and shipbuilding markets. Annual Review 2012.*

110   Cheaitou A and Cariou P (2011). *Containership speed and fleet size optimization with semi-elastic demand: an application to Northern Europe-South America Trade*. IAME Conference 2011, 25–28 October.

111   Deutsche Post AG (2009). *Delivering Tomorrow Customer Needs in 2010 and Beyond. A Global Delphi Study*. June.

112   Clarkson Research Services (2011). *Shipping Review & Outlook*. Spring.

113   BIMCO Bulletin 2011. Volume 106 # 6.

114   British Petroleum (2012). *Energy Outlook 2030*. January.

115   United Nations Department of Economic and Social Affairs (2011). The Great Green Technological Transformation Overview. *World Economic and Social Survey 2011*.

116   IFW News (2011). Asia-Europe bunker rates still on the rise. 24 March.

2

STRUCTURE, OWNERSHIP AND REGISTRATION OF THE WORLD FLEET

This chapter presents the supply-side of the shipping industry. It covers the vessel types, age profile, ownership and registration of the world fleet. The chapter also reviews deliveries, demolitions and tonnage on order.

More than three years after the economic and financial crisis of 2008, the world fleet continued to expand during 2011, reaching more than 1.5 billion deadweight tons (dwt) in January 2012, an increase of over 37 per cent in just four years. At the same time, continued deliveries and a drastic downturn in new orders following the economic crisis has led to a reduction in the world order book by one third during the same period. The order book in early 2012 amounts to approximately 21 per cent of the existing fleet tonnage, down from about 44 per cent four years earlier.

Still largely responding to orders placed prior to the economic crisis, the major shipbuilders are reluctant to cancel or postpone deliveries. China, Japan and the Republic of Korea together built more than 93 per cent of the tonnage delivered in 2011, thus maintaining important employment in their shipyards. The resulting oversupply of ships represents a serious challenge for shipowners. Importers and exporters, on the other hand, potentially benefit from ample supply of shipping capacity to transport international seaborne trade.

Developing countries continue to expand their market share in different maritime sectors, including shipbuilding, ownership, registration, operation, scrapping and manning. One third of the world fleet is owned by shipowners in developing countries, and 12 of the top 20 container operators are from developing countries. Almost 42 per cent of the world fleet are registered in Panama, Liberia and the Marshall Islands, and more than 92 per cent of scrapping in 2011 took place in India, China, Bangladesh and Pakistan.

A. STRUCTURE OF THE WORLD FLEET

1. World fleet growth and principal vessel types

Following an annual growth of almost 10 per cent, in January 2012 the world fleet reached a total tonnage of 1,534 million dwt. At the beginning of the year, there were 104,305 seagoing commercial ships in service (see annex II). The largest growth of tonnage was in dry bulk carriers, plus 17 per cent, bringing this category to 40.6 per cent of the world total capacity; the world dry bulk fleet has surged by 60 per cent in just four years. Oil tanker capacity, which grew by 6.9 per cent, now accounts for 33.1 per cent of the world fleet. Containerships, after an increase of 7.7 per cent, make up 12.9 per cent of the world tonnage. The conventional general cargo fleet continued its relative decline, being the only major vessel type with a smaller tonnage in January 2012 than one year earlier. Since 1980, the general cargo fleet has declined by 7 per cent, while the remainder of the world fleet grew by more than 150 per cent (table 2.1, figure 2.1).

Dry bulk ships

Freight costs are an important component of the landed price of most dry bulk commodities. In order to remain competitive and maintain reasonable profit margins, distant suppliers such as Brazilian iron ore producers see the use of large ships as a prerequisite to achieve economies of scale. It may be useful to recall that transporting dry bulk in a small Handymax ship was, in March 2012, three times as expensive per ton-mile than shipping the cargo in a large Capesize bulk carrier.[1]

The year 2011 saw a particularly interesting development in the dry bulk market, as a major supplier of iron ore aimed at gaining more control over the supply chain by ordering historically large vessels. To benefit from the above-mentioned economies of scale in the iron ore trade, in 2011 and early 2012 the Brazilian mining conglomerate Vale took delivery of the largest existing cargo carrying ships, the so-called Valemax ships of up to 400,000 dwt capacity.[2] The ships created a difficult situation for Vale, however, as permission for them to enter Chinese ports was still under discussion with Chinese authorities. Reportedly,

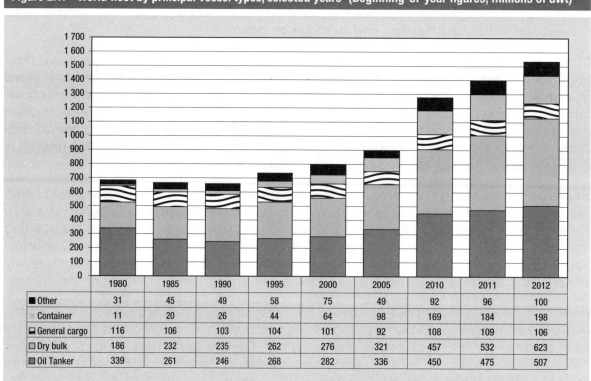

Figure 2.1. World fleet by principal vessel types, selected years[a] (Beginning-of-year figures, millions of dwt)

	1980	1985	1990	1995	2000	2005	2010	2011	2012
■ Other	31	45	49	58	75	49	92	96	100
Container	11	20	26	44	64	98	169	184	198
▣ General cargo	116	106	103	104	101	92	108	109	106
▢ Dry bulk	186	232	235	262	276	321	457	532	623
▣ Oil Tanker	339	261	246	268	282	336	450	475	507

Source: Compiled by the UNCTAD secretariat, on the basis of data supplied by *IHS Fairplay*.
[a] Seagoing propelled merchant ships of 100 gross tonnage (GT) and above.

Table 2.1.	World fleet by principal vessel types, 2011–2012[a] (Beginning-of-year figures, thousands of dwt; percentage share in italics)		
Principal types	**2011**	**2012**	**Percentage change 2012/2011**
Oil tankers	474 846	507 454	6.9
	34.0	*33.1*	*-0.9*
Bulk carriers	532 039	622 536	17.0
	38.1	*40.6*	*2.5*
General cargo ships	108 971	106 385	-2.4
	7.8	*6.9*	*-0.9*
Container ships	183 859	198 002	7.7
	13.2	*12.9*	*-0.3*
Other types of ships	96 028	99 642	3.8
	6.9	*6.5*	*-0.4*
Liquefied gas carriers	43 339	44 622	3.0
	3.1	*2.9*	*-0.2*
Offshore supply	33 227	37 468	12.8
	2.4	*2.4*	*0.1*
Ferries and passenger ships	6 164	6 224	1.0
	0.4	*0.4*	*0.0*
Other/ n.a.	13 299	11 328	-14.8
	1.0	*0.7*	*-0.2*
World total	1 395 743	1 534 019	9.9
	100.0	*100.0*	

Source: Compiled by the UNCTAD secretariat, on the basis of data supplied by *IHS Fairplay*.

[a] Seagoing propelled merchant ships of 100 GT and above. Percentage shares are shown in italics.

Chinese shipowners and iron ore producers opposed the entry of the Brazilian Valemax ships into Chinese ports, arguing that the operation of such large ships might not be safe, and fearing that Vale could gain monopolistic control of the supply chain for iron ore. Ports would also need to expand stockpiling capacity to store the imported ore.[3]

Vale is planning to take delivery of 35 such ships by the end of 2013, with a total investment of $4.2 billion. The Valemax ships are built in shipyards in the Republic of Korea and in China. Keeping in mind the benefits of lower transport costs, energy efficiency and further

South-South trade and collaboration between Brazil and China, several industry observers expressed hope that the ban for Valemax ships to enter Chinese ports would soon be lifted.[4] History has shown, however, that attempts by exporters to control the maritime supply chain have often been short-lived, and in the longer term the traditional shipowners may resume their role as providers of maritime transport services.

Oil tankers

The oil tanker tonnage reached more than half a billion dwt in January 2012. A part of this tonnage is used for storage, rather than for transporting oil. For example, in March 2012, the world's second-largest oil tanker was booked by Petroleo Brasileiro to be deployed as a storage facility. Increasing production in Latin America has spurred demand for more ships to store crude oil.[5] The increase in oil stocks also reflects fears of a possible future shortage of oil – for example, due to political conflict in the Persian Gulf. In the short term, the increase in the use of ships to store oil helps to reduce the oversupply of tonnage. In the medium-term future, the release of the stored oil will reduce the demand for oil transport and at the same time will increase available tanker capacity, again resulting in an oversupply of tonnage.

Container ships

In terms of deadweight tonnage, container ships have a share of just 12.9 per cent of the world fleet. The role of container ships for global trade is, however, more important than this tonnage share would suggest, as 52 per cent of seaborne trade in dollar terms are containerized.[6] If the deadweight tonnage share of different vessel types is compared with the share of the value of the cargo carried, on average each dwt of container ships carries 27 times more seaborne trade (in monetary terms) than a dwt of dry bulk carriers (see also table 2.5 below).

In terms of actual transport capacity, the average box-carrying capacity of container ships reached 3,074 20-foot equivalent units (TEU) in early 2012, a further increase of 6 per cent over the previous year (table 2.2). New container ships delivered in 2011 were 34 per cent larger than those delivered throughout 2010.

More than 93 per cent of the newly delivered container ships were gearless, that is, consisting of ships dependent on specialized container cranes in the ports (figure 2.2). Geared ships, which cater more for secondary ports, often in developing countries, tend to be smaller than gearless ones, which serve on the

Table 2.2.	Long-term trends in the cellular container ship fleet[a]		
Beginning of year	Number of vessels	TEU capacity	Average vessel size (TEU)
1987	1 052	1 215 215	1 155
1997	1 954	3 089 682	1 581
2007	3 904	9 436 377	2 417
2008	4 276	10 760 173	2 516
2009	4 638	12 142 444	2 618
2010	4 677	12 824 648	2 742
2011	4 868	14 081 957	2 893
2012	5 012	15 406 610	3 074
Growth 2012/2011 (per cent)	2.96	9.41	6.26

Source: Compiled by the UNCTAD secretariat, on the basis of data supplied by *IHS Fairplay*.

[a]   Fully cellular container ships of 100 GT and above. Beginning-of-year figures, except those from 1987, which are mid-year figures.

major routes for the larger volumes of containerized trade. In 2011, new geared ships were on average two fifths of the size (in TEU) of gearless ships.

In parallel with this long-term development, seaports increasingly deploy ship-to-shore gantry cranes to cater for gearless vessels. Between 2000 and

2010, the number of gantries deployed increased by 88 per cent to reach 4,900 units worldwide.[7] For some developing countries, however, this trend poses a challenge, as their ports may not always be able to catch up with market requirements. During the same period, gantries deployed in Africa, for example, increased by just 66 per cent, reaching only 200 units in 2010. Many African ports are not yet ready to accommodate the latest gearless container ships.

Specialized ships

Owners of specialized reefer tonnage have suffered from the competition of container ships that also cater for refrigerated containers. Containers today account for about 60 per cent of reefer cargo, and new container ships increasingly include large reefer capacities.[8] While the trend of containerization of refrigerated cargo will continue, the replacement of older dedicated reefer ships by more modern tonnage in coming years will allow a minimum fleet of these specialized vessels to be maintained. This should be able to cater for surges in demand during harvest time in many developing countries, which the regular container lines would not cover on their own.

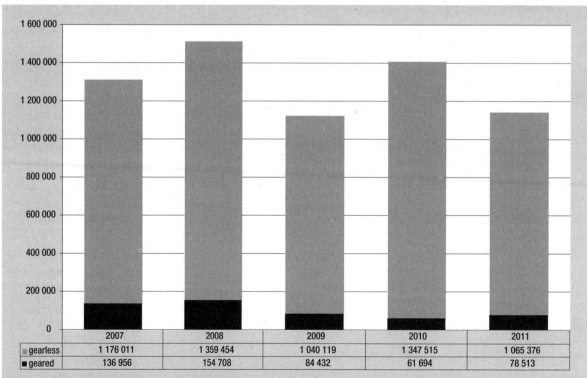

Figure 2.2.   Trends in deliveries of container ships (New container ships, in TEU, 2007–2011)

	2007	2008	2009	2010	2011
gearless	1 176 011	1 359 454	1 040 119	1 347 515	1 065 376
geared	136 956	154 708	84 432	61 694	78 513

Source: Compiled by the UNCTAD secretariat, based on data provided by *Lloyd's List Intelligence*: www.lloydslistintelligence.com.

Table 2.3.	Age distribution of the world merchant fleet, by vessel type, as of 1 January 2012 (Percentage of total ships and dwt)							

Country grouping and types of vessels	0–4 years	5–9 years	10–14 years	15–19 years	20 years and +	Average age (years) 2012	Average age (years) 2011	Percentage change 2012/2011
WORLD								
Bulk carriers	33.7	14.3	11.3	12.4	28.2	13.18	15.29	-2.11
Dwt	41.5	16.6	11.3	13.1	17.6	10.52	12.49	-1.97
Average vessel size (dwt)	78 098	73 344	63 300	66 520	39 569			
Container ships	23.8	27.9	18.3	17.4	12.6	10.90	10.70	0.20
Dwt	32.8	31.0	16.6	12.0	7.5	8.93	8.84	0.09
Average vessel size (dwt)	54 465	43 915	35 837	27 267	23 718			
General cargo	11.5	10.7	8.2	11.2	58.4	23.26	24.15	-0.89
Dwt	21.4	13.7	11.8	10.2	42.8	18.80	20.27	-1.47
Average vessel size (dwt)	9 698	6 670	7 451	4 723	3 795			
Oil tankers	24.7	21.2	11.0	10.5	32.6	15.70	16.37	-0.66
Dwt	34.7	29.0	18.4	9.4	8.5	9.44	9.74	-0.30
Average vessel size (dwt)	63 483	61 884	75 896	40 588	11 756			
Other types	10.6	9.7	9.2	8.4	62.0	25.06	25.19	-0.13
Dwt	27.2	18.3	10.7	7.7	36.1	17.12	17.11	0.01
Average vessel size (dwt)	4 417	3 240	1 992	1 580	1 006			
All ships	15.1	12.5	9.9	10.0	52.6	21.90	22.49	-0.58
Dwt	35.8	22.5	14.3	11.2	16.2	11.51	12.59	-1.07
Average vessel size (dwt)	34 827	26 518	21 378	16 431	4 543			
DEVELOPING ECONOMIES								
Bulk carriers	34.9	14.3	9.9	12.1	28.8	12.96	14.99	-2.03
Dwt	41.4	16.0	9.5	13.2	19.8	10.81	12.77	-1.97
Average vessel size (dwt)	77 386	72 977	62 730	71 136	44 843			
Container ships	25.1	26.7	16.8	18.0	13.3	11.00	10.83	0.17
Dwt	34.7	30.7	14.6	12.3	7.7	8.80	8.71	0.10
Average vessel size (dwt)	51 780	43 083	32 702	25 532	21 563			
General cargo	11.5	11.3	7.5	9.1	60.5	23.31	24.07	-0.76
Dwt	22.1	13.4	9.8	9.8	44.8	19.00	20.39	-1.39
Average vessel size (dwt)	10 547	6 487	7 160	5 932	4 074			
Oil tankers	24.0	18.6	9.8	9.9	37.7	16.69	17.15	-0.45
Dwt	35.4	27.7	15.8	9.9	11.2	9.94	10.33	-0.38
Average vessel size (dwt)	65 045	65 891	71 308	44 408	13 102			
Other types	14.2	11.0	7.7	8.3	58.9	23.67	24.33	-0.65
Dwt	24.2	15.5	9.4	7.7	43.2	18.94	19.06	-0.11
Average vessel size (dwt)	3 384	2 802	2 442	1 839	1 454			
All ships	17.8	13.3	8.7	9.7	50.4	20.74	21.61	-0.87
Dwt	36.4	21.2	12.1	11.6	18.7	11.92	13.11	-1.19
Average vessel size (dwt)	35 395	27 677	24 061	20 607	6 435			
DEVELOPED ECONOMIES								
Bulk carriers	23.2	11.4	15.1	16.7	33.6	16.51	18.13	-1.62
Dwt	37.3	17.2	17.8	13.8	13.8	10.78	12.06	-1.28
Average vessel size (dwt)	94 354	88 638	69 250	48 620	24 230			
Container ships	16.3	33.5	24.7	17.0	8.4	10.84	10.28	0.56
Dwt	23.1	35.5	23.8	12.0	5.5	9.44	9.12	0.32
Average vessel size (dwt)	74 141	55 339	50 293	36 726	34 295			
General cargo	16.8	13.3	14.1	20.8	35.0	19.00	19.66	-0.66
Dwt	27.4	18.2	20.4	12.3	21.7	14.14	15.19	-1.04
Average vessel size (dwt)	7 234	6 040	6 395	2 613	2 741			

| Table 2.3. | Age distribution of the world merchant fleet, by vessel type, as of 1 January 2012 (Percentage of total ships and dwt) (continued) |

Country grouping and types of vessels	0–4 years	5–9 years	10–14 years	15–19 years	20 years and +	Average age (years) 2012	Average age (years) 2011	Percentage change 2012/2011
Oil tankers	21.5	29.1	15.1	16.7	17.6	13.47	13.67	-0.20
Dwt	27.9	37.5	23.8	8.5	2.3	8.45	8.18	0.27
Average vessel size (dwt)	57 139	56 766	69 511	22 286	5 730			
Other types	8.1	10.2	13.3	9.6	58.7	24.96	24.91	0.04
Dwt	21.8	24.1	18.8	10.9	24.4	15.02	15.49	-0.47
Average vessel size (dwt)	2 789	2 454	1 467	1 185	434			
All ships	10.8	12.6	13.6	11.9	51.1	22.54	22.66	-0.12
Dwt	28.3	29.9	20.7	10.3	10.7	10.49	10.78	-0.29
Average vessel size (dwt)	20 949	18 961	12 106	6 846	1 675			
COUNTRIES WITH ECONOMIES IN TRANSITION								
Bulk carriers	35.0	5.9	4.2	13.7	41.2	15.73	17.99	-2.26
Dwt	34.1	6.9	5.9	17.3	35.8	15.06	17.33	-2.27
Average vessel size (dwt)	37 094	44 555	55 500	48 770	37 922			
Container ships	14.5	20.3	6.3	23.8	35.2	16.16	15.95	0.22
Dwt	21.0	33.1	2.5	16.0	27.4	13.30	12.35	0.94
Average vessel size (dwt)	40 165	42 901	10 454	17 638	21 347			
General cargo	7.5	10.9	6.3	8.9	66.4	24.19	24.68	-0.49
Dwt	10.1	9.7	5.5	5.8	68.9	24.34	25.68	-1.34
Average vessel size (dwt)	4 713	2 980	2 987	1 932	4 098			
Oil tankers	18.1	14.8	5.5	8.2	53.3	20.76	22.19	-1.43
Dwt	38.4	30.0	6.8	10.9	13.8	10.04	10.97	-0.93
Average vessel size (dwt)	41 006	38 211	25 681	22 196	5 051			
Other types	7.1	6.7	3.9	7.4	74.9	25.69	25.71	-0.02
Dwt	37.6	29.1	7.2	9.2	17.0	10.57	11.55	-0.98
Average vessel size (dwt)	41 006	38 211	25 681	22 196	5 051			
All ships	11.7	9.6	5.1	9.2	64.4	23.21	23.90	-0.69
Dwt	31.3	17.9	6.0	12.9	31.9	14.84	16.24	-1.41
Average vessel size (dwt)	29 687	21 209	14 351	19 149	10 267			
TEN MAJOR OPEN AND INTERNATIONAL REGISTRIES								
Bulk carriers	38.0	16.9	11.6	11.8	21.6	11.20	13.08	-1.89
Dwt	43.2	18.0	10.5	12.4	15.9	9.75	11.49	-1.73
Average vessel size (dwt)	82 215	76 751	65 422	75 977	53 264			
Container ships	26.2	30.0	17.5	16.9	9.4	9.86	9.61	0.25
Dwt	35.8	30.6	14.9	11.6	7.0	8.40	8.28	0.12
Average vessel size (dwt)	54 691	40 978	34 341	27 591	29 737			
General cargo	18.6	13.9	12.2	12.0	43.3	17.90	18.58	-0.68
Dwt	27.0	15.7	13.4	10.0	33.8	15.20	16.21	-1.01
Average vessel size (dwt)	14 264	11 140	10 834	8 236	7 680			
Oil tankers	35.9	29.7	14.9	7.1	12.4	9.53	9.81	-0.29
Dwt	35.4	28.1	20.7	9.1	6.8	8.80	9.14	-0.33
Average vessel size (dwt)	77 377	74 168	109 146	99 893	42 802			
Other types	23.6	12.6	10.6	7.0	46.2	19.72	20.49	-0.77
Dwt	32.2	17.9	9.1	5.6	35.2	16.09	15.84	0.25
Average vessel size (dwt)	17 049	17 780	10 687	10 034	9 507			
All ships	28.9	19.5	12.9	10.8	27.9	13.88	14.79	-0.92
Dwt	38.3	22.8	14.5	10.7	13.8	10.16	11.10	-0.93
Average vessel size (dwt)	57 487	50 618	48 467	43 152	21 396			

Source: Compiled by the UNCTAD secretariat, on the basis of data supplied by *IHS Fairplay*.
a   Seagoing propelled merchant ships of 100 GT and above.

The supply–demand balance is more favourable for shipowners of product tankers, for which fewer orders have been placed in recent years, but demand has increased due to longer distances between regions of supply and demand.

Regarding other types of specialized ships, offshore supply vessels continued to grow in 2011 at an above-average rate (plus 12.8 per cent), reaching a share of 2.4 per cent of the world fleet in January 2012. Offshore specialized ships have been in growing demand, notably in Nigeria, Ghana and other Western African countries, where oil exploration has recently expanded.

2. Age distribution of the world merchant fleet

The average age of the world fleet decreased slightly during 2011 as a result of continued newbuilding deliveries and increased demolitions. In January 2012, the average age of the fleet per dwt was 11.5 years, while the average age per vessel was almost twice as high at 21.9 years, indicating that older ships tend to be much smaller (table 2.3). An impressive 41.5 per cent of dry bulk tonnage is less than five years old,

following the historical spree of new construction of the last few years. Container ships continue to be the youngest market segment, with an average age per dwt of below nine years, and almost 64 per cent of the fleet younger than 10 years. The oldest ships continue to be general cargo and other types of vessels, with about three out of five ships being older than 20 years.

Among country groupings, the major open registries continued to have the youngest fleet, after recording a further reduction in the average age, from 11.1 to 10.2 years per dwt. The modernization of the open registry fleet is also reflected in the particularly high share of foreign-flagged ships among the 2011 deliveries (figures 2.3 and 2.4).

The recent growth of the world fleet is illustrated in figure 2.3. In spite of the economic crisis of 2008–2009, more tonnage was added to the world fleet in 2010 and 2011 than in any previous year, this fact resulting from orders placed prior to the economic crisis (see also figure 2.9). The high volume of one-year-old tonnage also explains the reduction in the average age of the fleet (table 2.3). Most of the additions to the world fleet during 2011 were registered under foreign flags.

Figure 2.3. Age structure of world fleet, national and foreign flags (Thousands of dwt)

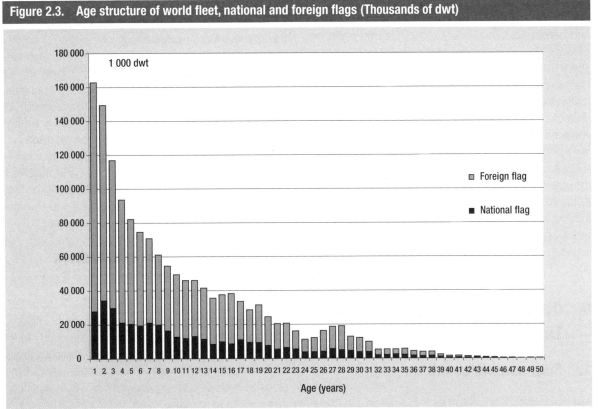

Source: Compiled by the UNCTAD secretariat, on the basis of data from *IHS Fairplay*, for vessels of 1000 GT and above.

3. Domestic shipping

Apart from international seaborne trade, domestic shipping is an important additional source of employment for ships, and policy makers frequently aim at supporting coastal maritime transport because of the environmental benefits of reducing the cargo moved by road. Demand for intra-country (cabotage) shipping has helped to absorb some of the new tonnage that entered into service in 2011. For example, about 10 per cent of smaller dry bulk carriers built in China are deployed exclusively in Chinese cabotage.[9]

Cabotage shipping is not governed by most of the international maritime regulations, such as the phasing out of single-hull tankers. Nigerian shipowners, for example, mostly deploy single-hull tankers for the coastal transport of oil.[10] Vessels deployed in cabotage services are also often older than the internationally deployed fleet; in the United States, for example, more than half of the cabotage fleet is older than 25 years.[11] The dry bulk fleet owned by Chinese interests includes about 50 per cent more ships of 25 years and older than the world average, which is mostly due to its deployment in coastal shipping.[12]

In many countries, cabotage is reserved for nationally flagged ships, which reduces competition from foreign providers. In order to further promote coastal shipping and benefit from more competitive maritime transport services, some countries are considering opening certain cabotage services to non-national operators. For the case of India, for example, it has been argued that a relaxation of the cabotage restrictions would help promote trans-shipment in Indian ports.[13] In Nigeria, the issuance of waivers for foreign providers of cabotage services has in practice become the rule rather than an exception.[14] Other countries have chosen to maintain a more restrictive policy, with a view to promoting national shipbuilding and the employment of national seafarers. Indonesia, for example, is reportedly considering prohibiting the import of older ships for cabotage services, hoping that this will increase the demand for shipbuilding in Indonesian yards.[15]

B. OWNERSHIP AND OPERATION OF THE WORLD FLEET

1. Ship-owning countries

Among the top 35 ship-owning economies, there are 17 in Asia, 14 in Europe and 4 in the Americas

(table 2.4). Practically half of the world tonnage (49.7 per cent) is owned by shipping companies from just four countries – Greece, Japan, Germany and China. Owners from Bermuda, Brazil and the Isle of Man specialize mostly in large ships, notably tankers and dry bulk carriers. Owners from Indonesia, the Russian Federation and Viet Nam have a large number of smaller ships, including vessels deployed in coastal and inter-island services.

Table 2.5 depicts the major ship-owning countries and their share in different market segments (in dwt percentage share), as well as an estimation of their share in the transport of global seaborne trade (in $ percentage share). Containerized cargo accounts for an estimated 52 per cent of the value of global seaborne trade and countries with a high share of containerized tonnage will thus also have a high share in global seaborne trade that is transported by their nationally owned ships.

As the largest owner of ship containerized tonnage, Germany (37 per cent of the container ship fleet) becomes the country whose ships also account for the largest share (more than 23 per cent) of global seaborne trade carried. The second largest shipowner is Japan with a share of 11.2 per cent of global seaborne trade carried, followed by Greece (9.8 per cent), China (7.5 per cent) and Denmark (5.6 per cent).

Ownership of the fleet does not necessarily imply that the ship-owning countries effectively operate or control the shipping operations. In particular, the German-owned container ships are frequently chartered out to liner shipping operators based in other countries, such as Maersk (Denmark), MSC (Switzerland) or CSAV (Chile). Neither would there necessarily exist a relationship between a country's own foreign trade and its fleet ownership. Previous analysis indicates that oil-exporting countries are more likely to own the oil tankers used for their own national exports, while the exporters of containerized cargo are much less likely to own the container ships used for their own foreign trade.[16]

2. Container shipping operators

The top 20 carriers

The largest container ship operators in January 2012 continue to be Maersk Line (Denmark), MSC (Switzerland) and CMA CGM (France). Together, these three companies operate almost 30 per cent of the global container carrying capacity (in TEU), reflecting the continued process of industry concentration of the last few years. Compared with January 2011,

Table 2.4.	The 35 countries and territories with the largest owned fleets, as of 1 January 2012[a] (Dwt)							
	Number of vessels			Deadweight tonnage				
Country or territory of ownership [b]	National flag[c]	Foreign flag	Total	National flag[c]	Foreign flag	Total	Foreign flag as a percentage of total	Estimated market share 1 January 2012
Greece	738	2 583	3 321	64 921 486	159 130 395	224 051 881	71.02	16.10
Japan	717	3 243	3 960	20 452 832	197 210 070	217 662 902	90.60	15.64
Germany	422	3 567	3 989	17 296 198	108 330 510	125 626 708	86.23	9.03
China	2 060	1 569	3 629	51 716 318	72 285 422	124 001 740	58.29	8.91
Korea, Republic of	740	496	1 236	17 102 300	39 083 270	56 185 570	69.56	4.04
United States	741	1 314	2 055	7 162 685	47 460 048	54 622 733	86.89	3.92
China, Taiwan Province of	470	383	853	28 884 470	16 601 518	45 485 988	36.50	3.27
Norway	851	1 141	1 992	15 772 288	27 327 579	43 099 867	63.41	3.10
Denmark	394	649	1 043	13 463 727	26 527 607	39 991 334	66.33	2.87
Chinese Taipei	102	601	703	4 076 815	34 968 474	39 045 289	89.56	2.81
Singapore	712	398	1 110	22 082 648	16 480 079	38 562 727	42.74	2.77
Bermuda	17	251	268	2 297 441	27 698 605	29 996 046	92.34	2.16
Italy	608	226	834	18 113 984	6 874 748	24 988 732	27.51	1.80
Turkey	527	647	1 174	8 554 745	14 925 883	23 480 628	63.57	1.69
Canada	205	251	456	2 489 989	19 360 007	21 849 996	88.60	1.57
India	455	105	560	15 276 544	6 086 410	21 362 954	28.49	1.53
Russian Federation	1 336	451	1 787	5 410 608	14 957 599	20 368 207	73.44	1.46
United Kingdom	230	480	710	2 034 570	16 395 185	18 429 755	88.96	1.32
Belgium	97	180	277	6 319 103	8 202 208	14 521 311	56.48	1.04
Malaysia	432	107	539	9 710 922	4 734 174	14 445 096	32.77	1.04
Brazil	113	59	172	2 279 733	11 481 795	13 761 528	83.43	0.99
Saudi Arabia	75	117	192	1 852 378	10 887 737	12 740 115	85.46	0.92
Netherlands	576	386	962	4 901 301	6 799 943	11 701 244	58.11	0.84
Indonesia	951	91	1 042	9 300 711	2 292 255	11 592 966	19.77	0.83
Iran	67	71	138	829 704	10 634 685	11 464 389	92.76	0.82
France	188	297	485	3 430 417	7 740 496	11 170 913	69.29	0.80
United Arab Emirates	65	365	430	609 032	8 187 103	8 796 135	93.08	0.63
Cyprus	62	152	214	2 044 256	5 092 849	7 137 105	71.36	0.51
Viet Nam	477	79	556	4 706 563	1 988 446	6 695 009	29.70	0.48
Kuwait	44	42	86	3 956 910	2 735 309	6 692 219	40.87	0.48
Sweden	99	208	307	1 070 563	5 325 853	6 396 416	83.26	0.46
Isle of Man	6	38	44	226 810	6 131 401	6 358 211	96.43	0.46
Thailand	277	67	344	3 610 570	1 542 980	5 153 550	29.94	0.37
Switzerland	39	142	181	1 189 376	3 700 886	4 890 262	75.68	0.35
Qatar	48	37	85	881 688	3 745 663	4 627 351	80.95	0.33
Total top 35 economies	14 941	20 793	35 734	374 029 685	952 927 192	1 326 956 877	71.81	95.34
Other owners	2 172	1 816	3 988	22 491 261	42 344 181	64 835 442	65.31	4.66
Total of known economy of ownership	17 113	22 609	39 722	396 520 946	995 271 373	1 391 792 319	71.51	100.00
Others, unknown economy of ownership		7 179			126 317 184			
World Total		46 901			1 518 109 503			

Source: Compiled by the UNCTAD secretariat, on the basis of data supplied by *IHS Fairplay*.

[a]   Vessels of 1000 GT and above, ranked by deadweight tonnage – excluding the United States Reserve Fleet and the United States and Canadian Great Lakes fleets (which have a combined tonnage of 5.3 million dwt).

[b]   The country of ownership indicates where the true controlling interest (that is, the parent company) of the fleet is located. In several cases, determining this has required making certain judgements. Thus, for example, Greece is shown as the country of ownership for vessels owned by a Greek national with representative offices in New York, London and Piraeus, although the owner may be domiciled in the United States.

[c]   Includes vessels flying the national flag but registered in second registries such as the Danish International Ship Register (DIS), the Norwegian International Ship Register (NIS) or the French International Ship Register (FIS).

Table 2.5.   **Countries/territories of ownership, by main vessel types (Dwt and dollars as percentages, January 2012 estimates)**

	Total	Germany	Japan	Greece	China	Denmark	China Taiwan, Province of	Norway	Korea, Republic of	Singapore	China, Hong Kong SAR	United States	Canada	Russian Federation	Turkey	Netherlands	Italy	United Kingdom	All other economies
Estimated share of world fleet (dwt), by main vessel type																			
Container	100	37.0	8.8	6.8	6.3	8.8	4.8	0.3	3.2	3.3	2.2	1.5	2.3	0.2	0.6	0.4	0.1	0.4	13.1
Dry bulk	100	4.8	22.7	19.9	14.0	1.1	3.4	1.4	6.3	2.0	4.5	3.1	0.4	0.3	2.1	0.2	1.5	0.9	11.3
Tankers	100	4.6	12.5	20.8	5.2	3.4	1.7	3.4	2.8	3.9	3.0	5.0	1.8	2.8	1.6	0.8	2.7	2.2	21.7
General cargo	100	13.3	12.4	2.4	11.0	1.1	1.6	12.0	2.3	1.4	1.8	1.0	0.2	3.7	3.4	4.5	2.2	2.0	23.7
Estimated share of global seaborne trade ($), carried by nationally owned ships, by main vessel type																			
Container	52	19.2	4.6	3.5	3.3	4.6	2.5	0.2	1.7	1.7	1.1	0.8	1.2	0.1	0.3	0.2	0.0	0.2	6.8
Dry bulk	6	0.3	1.4	1.2	0.8	0.1	0.2	0.1	0.4	0.1	0.3	0.2	0.0	0.0	0.1	0.0	0.1	0.1	0.7
Tankers	22	1.0	2.7	4.6	1.1	0.7	0.4	0.7	0.6	0.9	0.7	1.1	0.4	0.6	0.4	0.2	0.6	0.5	4.8
General cargo	20	2.7	2.5	0.5	2.2	0.2	0.3	2.4	0.5	0.3	0.4	0.2	0.0	0.7	0.7	0.9	0.4	0.4	4.7
TOTAL	100	23.2	11.2	9.8	7.5	5.6	3.4	3.4	3.1	3.0	2.4	2.3	1.6	1.5	1.4	1.3	1.2	1.2	17.0

Source: Estimations by the UNCTAD secretariat, on the basis of data supplied by *IHS Fairplay* (world fleet) and the World Shipping Council (share of seaborne trade by vessel type).

the largest growth was recorded by MOL (Japan), with an increase in TEU of 23.6 per cent, followed by CSCL (China, 20.9 per cent increase) and Hapag-Lloyd (Germany, 15.8 per cent increase). The largest decline in capacity was recorded by CSAV (Chile), which saw its operated TEU decrease by 9.1 per cent (table 2.6).

Financial performance

As a consequence of the continued oversupply of tonnage, which effectively continued to worsen throughout 2011, most carriers incurred important financial losses. The container shipping companies' combined loss was estimated at over $5 billion in 2011, following a profit of $17 billion in 2010, and a loss of $19 billion in 2009.[17] A loss of $1.7 billion in 2011 was reported by COSCO (including non-container shipping businesses), CSAV reported a loss of $1.2 billion, CMA CGM $30 million, Hanjin $730 million, and NOL $478 million. The year 2012 does not appear to be more positive. During the first quarter of 2012, CSAV reported a loss of $205 million, Hanjin of $208 million, Hapag-Lloyd of $172 million, Maersk Line of $599 million and NOL of $254 million.[18] Confronted with such a bleak picture, many industry observers expect a surge in bankruptcies in coming years, as banks "are seeking to recover what they can from a debacle they helped to create".[19]

Investing in circles

Carriers have invested in ever larger ships to benefit from economies of scale. The pressure to reduce costs is increased by historically low freight rates. However, building more and larger ships also adds to the general oversupply of capacity, thus putting further downward pressure on the freight rates. While an investment in larger ships may make sense for an individual company, for the industry as a whole this actually leads to a vicious cycle of more oversupply of tonnage and a further worsened financial performance. From the clients' perspective this pattern could also be considered as a virtuous cycle, where technological progress and energy efficiency help to reduce transport costs, which in turn help to promote trade and investment in larger and more energy-efficient ships.

Not all carriers have shown procyclical investment patterns. Evergreen, which in recent years had been the only major carrier that had not expanded and invested in ultralarge container ships, has in early 2012 placed an order for 10 vessels of 13,800 TEU each, this being the highest capacity range of container ships. The new container ships are reportedly to be among the most energy efficient ever built. Combined with other orders for new tonnage, Evergreen's order book in May 2012 amounted to 62 per cent of its existing fleet, pointing to an ambitious anticyclical expansion plan.[20]

Table 2.6.	The 20 leading service operators of container ships, 1 January 2012 (Number of ships and total shipboard capacity deployed, in TEUs)							
Ranking (TEU)	Operator	Country/ territory	Number of vessels	Average vessel size	TEU	Share of world total, TEU (percentage)	Cumulated share, TEU (percentage)	Growth in TEU over 2011 (percentage)
1	Maersk Line	Denmark	453	4 646	2 104 825	11.8	11.8	15.6
2	MSC	Switzerland	432	4 688	2 025 179	11.3	23.1	14.9
3	CMA CGM Group	France	290	4 004	1 161 141	6.5	29.5	8.5
4	APL	Singapore	144	4 168	600 168	3.4	32.9	1.4
5	COSCO	China	145	4 304	624 055	3.5	36.4	10.3
6	Evergreen Line	China, Taiwan Province of	159	3 590	570 843	3.2	39.6	-3.9
7	Hapag-Lloyd Group	Germany	145	4 476	648 976	3.6	43.2	15.8
8	CSCL	China	124	4 493	557 168	3.1	46.3	20.9
9	Hanjin	Korea, Republic of	101	4 927	497 641	2.8	49.1	11.2
10	MOL	Japan	107	4 194	448 727	2.5	51.6	23.6
11	OOCL	China, Hong Kong SAR	88	4 516	397 433	2.2	53.8	6.1
12	Zim	Israel	82	3 708	304 074	1.7	55.5	8.0
13	HMM	Korea, Republic of	70	4 497	314 770	1.8	57.3	10.4
14	NYK	Japan	93	4 129	383 964	2.1	59.4	8.8
15	Yang Ming	China, Taiwan Province of	84	4 089	343 476	1.9	61.3	6.4
16	Hamburg Sud	Germany	99	3 728	369 057	2.1	63.4	10.0
17	K Line	Japan	79	4 336	342 572	1.9	65.3	-1.6
18	CSAV	Chile	85	4 095	348 035	1.9	67.2	-9.1
19	PIL	Singapore	104	2 279	236 978	1.3	68.6	-0.5
20	Wan Hai Lines Limited	China, Taiwan Province of	89	2 080	185 146	1.0	69.6	8.8
Total top 20 carriers			2 973	3 979	12 464 228	69.6	69.6	10.0
Others			7 093	768	5 445 054	30.3	30.4	10.7
World container ship fleet			10 066	1 678	17 909 282	100.0	100.0	10.2

Source: UNCTAD secretariat, based on data provided by *Lloyd's List Intelligence*: www.lloydslistintelligence.com.
Note: Includes all container carrying ships. Not fully comparable to table 2.2, which covers only the specialized fully cellular container ships.

Consolidation and restructuring

Lines are taking different approaches to confront losses. The Malaysian shipping company MISC has effectively discontinued its container activities and now focuses solely on dry and liquid bulk. The Chilean carrier CSAV has in 2012 drastically modified its strategy, increasing the share of jointly operated services from 30 to more than 90 per cent and increasing the share of owned versus chartered-in tonnage.[21] Zim (Israel) is in negotiations with creditors to obtain additional funding and with shipyards to delay the delivery of previously ordered ships. Reports suggest that both CMA CGM and MSC are considering selling stakes in port operation businesses.

Several industry representatives suggest that further mergers among shipping lines can be expected and

would be positive for carrier profitability; proposed candidates for mergers were, for example, the three largest Japanese lines.[22] Some analysts predict that the major East–West companies "will shrink to 7 to 10 carriers by the mid-2020s".[23] All major shipping lines have in recent years increased vessel-sharing arrangements with other carriers, and two major alliances – the Grand Alliance and the New World Alliance – have joined forces to form the new G6 Alliance.[24] Feeder operators have also created alliances among themselves to better defend themselves against competition from the larger shipping lines.[25]

Several lines sought support from the public sector. The French CMA CGM has reportedly "approached a French sovereign wealth fund".[26] The China Shipowners' Association reportedly demanded carriers to seek government support and set freight

Table 2.7. The 35 flags of registration with the largest registered deadweight tonnage (ranked by deadweight tonnage), as of 1 January 2012[a]

Flag of registrations	Number of vessels	Deadweight tonnage, in thousands dwt	Average vessel size, dwt	Share of world total, dwt (per cent)	Cumulated share, dwt (per cent)	Tonnage registered for foreign owners in thousands dwt	Per cent of tonnage owned by foreigners	Dwt growth 2012/2011, (per cent)
Panama	8 127	328 210	40 385	21.39	21.39	328 112	99.97	7.25
Liberia	3 030	189 911	62 677	12.38	33.77	189 911	100.00	14.24
Marshall Islands	1 876	122 857	65 489	8.01	41.78	122 857	100.00	24.40
China, Hong Kong SAR	1 935	116 806	60 365	7.61	49.40	87 907	75.26	27.33
Singapore	2 877	82 084	28 531	5.35	54.75	59 910	72.99	21.99
Greece	1 386	72 558	52 351	4.73	59.48	7 520	10.36	1.59
Malta	1 815	71 287	39 277	4.65	64.12	71 241	99.94	16.30
Bahamas	1 409	69 105	49 046	4.50	68.63	68 620	99.30	2.43
China	4 148	58 195	14 030	3.79	72.42	5 983	10.28	10.34
Cyprus	1 022	32 986	32 276	2.15	74.57	30 940	93.80	2.06
Japan	5 619	23 572	4 195	1.54	76.11	398	1.69	6.18
Isle Of Man	410	22 542	54 980	1.47	77.58	22 315	98.99	16.06
Italy	1 667	21 763	13 055	1.42	79.00	3 523	16.19	11.95
Republic Of Korea	2 916	19 157	6 570	1.25	80.25	1 460	7.62	-4.95
United Kingdom	1 662	18 664	11 230	1.22	81.46	16 615	89.02	9.80
Norway (NIS)	535	17 896	33 450	1.17	82.63	3 248	18.15	-0.94
Germany	868	17 482	20 141	1.14	83.77	123	0.70	-0.48
India	1 443	16 141	11 186	1.05	84.82	668	4.14	5.65
Antigua and Barbuda	1 322	14 402	10 894	0.94	85.76	14 402	100.00	3.67
Denmark (DIS)	534	13 846	25 929	0.90	86.66	372	2.69	-3.20
Indonesia	6 332	13 512	2 134	0.88	87.54	3 483	25.78	11.63
United States	6 461	11 997	1 857	0.78	88.32	4 585	38.22	-5.25
Bermuda	164	11 598	70 722	0.76	89.08	9 301	80.19	6.80
Malaysia	1 449	10 895	7 519	0.71	89.79	990	9.09	1.58
Turkey	1 360	9 535	7 011	0.62	90.41	710	7.45	9.03
Netherlands	1 382	8 279	5 991	0.54	90.95	3 338	40.31	17.67
France (FIS)	161	7 973	49 521	0.52	91.47	4 980	62.47	1.17
Russian Federation	3 362	7 413	2 205	0.48	91.95	1 632	22.01	0.18
Philippines	1 995	6 694	3 355	0.44	92.39	5 834	87.16	-3.63
Belgium	235	6 663	28 352	0.43	92.83	326	4.90	-2.02
Viet Nam	1 525	6 072	3 982	0.40	93.22	845	13.92	2.94
Saint Vincent and the Grenadines	857	5 636	6 577	0.37	93.59	5 636	100.00	-15.89
China, Taiwan Province of	906	4 328	4 777	0.28	93.87	147	3.40	0.43
Thailand	850	4 249	4 999	0.28	94.15	398	9.36	-6.90
Kuwait	206	3 976	19 301	0.26	94.41	1	0.02	32.27
Total top 35 flags of registration	71 846	1 448 285	20 158	94.41	94.41	1 082 977		10.65
World total	104 305	1 534 019	14 707	100.00	100.00	1 133 417		9.91

Source: Compiled by the UNCTAD secretariat, on the basis of data supplied by *IHS Fairplay.*
[a] Seagoing propelled merchant ships of 100 GT and above; ranked by deadweight tonnage.

rates jointly.[27] The German Federal State of Hamburg has increased its share in Hapag-Lloyd, to avoid that the company would "fall victim to a global monopoly".[28]

Container ships are often owned by charterers, that is, companies that do not themselves provide the liner shipping service, but rather charter their vessels out to the operators. Many of these charterer owners have been under financial pressure and some were forced to auction their ships.[29] Such sales, however, will not withdraw the capacity from the market.

C. REGISTRATION OF SHIPS

1. Flags of registration

The year 2011 saw a further increase in the use of open registries. Among the tonnage delivered in 2011, an estimated 83 per cent was registered abroad (figure 2.3), and an estimated 71.5 per cent of the world tonnage is now registered under a foreign flag, that is, vessels operate under a different flag to that of the nationality of the owner (figure 2.4). Accordingly, the growth of most of the major flags of registration was higher than the growth of the total fleet. The registries of Hong Kong, China (plus 27.3 per cent), the Marshall

Islands (plus 24.4 per cent) and Singapore (plus 22 per cent) saw particularly impressive increases in their fleets (table 2.7).

A process of concentration is also observed in this maritime sector. Among the different country groupings, the 10 major open registries continued to expand their market share, amounting to 56.6 per cent in January 2012. The open-registry fleet has its highest share in bulk carriers (61.3 per cent). The share of the fleet registered in the developing countries of Asia also experienced a positive growth, while all other country groupings saw their market share decline between 2011 and 2012 (table 2.8).

2. Nationality of controlling interests

As vessel registries compete for business, the traditional distinction between open flags of registration as compared with flags that cater only for national owners becomes increasingly blurred. As illustrated in figure 2.5, today, almost all registries cater for national and foreign owners.

Among the top 30 flags of registration, three cater exclusively for foreign-owned tonnage, notably Liberia, the Marshall Islands, and Antigua and

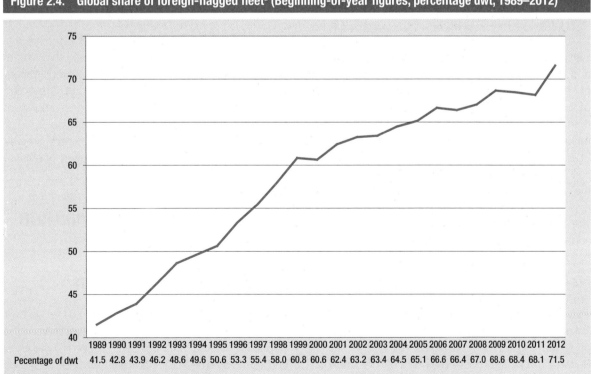

Figure 2.4. Global share of foreign-flagged fleet[a] (Beginning-of-year figures, percentage dwt, 1989–2012)

	1989	1990	1991	1992	1993	1994	1995	1996	1997	1998	1999	2000	2001	2002	2003	2004	2005	2006	2007	2008	2009	2010	2011	2012
Pecentage of dwt	41.5	42.8	43.9	46.2	48.6	49.6	50.6	53.3	55.4	58.0	60.8	60.6	62.4	63.2	63.4	64.5	65.1	66.6	66.4	67.0	68.6	68.4	68.1	71.5

Source: Compiled by the UNCTAD secretariat, on the basis of data supplied by *IHS Fairplay*.
[a]   Estimate based on available information of commercial seagoing vessels of 1000 GT and above.

Table 2.8. Distribution of dwt capacity of vessel types, by country group of registration, 2012[a] (Percentage change 2012/2011 in italics)

	Total fleet	Oil tankers	Bulk carriers	General cargo	Container ships	Other types
World total	100.00	100.00	100.00	100.00	100.00	100.00
Developed countries	15.85	18.32	10.15	18.02	22.75	22.85
	-1.11	*-1.10*	*-0.80*	*0.34*	*-1.23*	*-0.96*
Countries with economies in transition	0.82	0.79	0.33	4.23	0.08	1.85
	-0.11	*-0.02*	*-0.08*	*-0.30*	*-0.01*	*-0.11*
Developing countries	26.41	24.86	28.14	35.17	21.17	24.58
	0.00	*0.00*	*0.00*	*0.00*	*0.00*	*0.00*
Of which:						
Africa	0.65	0.75	0.29	2.25	0.11	1.77
	-0.03	*0.03*	*-0.06*	*0.15*	*0.00*	*-0.01*
America	1.52	1.82	0.90	4.17	0.42	3.26
	-0.12	*-0.01*	*-0.16*	*0.00*	*0.05*	*-0.23*
Asia	23.87	22.00	26.60	28.05	20.60	18.39
	1.07	*1.21*	*1.30*	*0.08*	*0.49*	*0.13*
Oceania	0.37	0.30	0.35	0.69	0.03	1.16
	-0.01	*0.12*	*-0.11*	*-0.11*	*0.01*	*0.02*
Other, unallocated	0.30	0.18	0.12	1.55	0.06	1.24
	-0.21	*-0.06*	*-0.19*	*-1.06*	*-0.07*	*-0.09*
Ten major open registries[b]	56.62	55.85	61.27	41.04	55.93	49.48
	0.52	*-0.17*	*0.10*	*0.89*	*0.75*	*1.24*

Source: Compiled by the UNCTAD secretariat, on the basis of data supplied by *IHS Fairplay*.
[a] Seagoing propelled merchant ships of 100 GT and above.
[b] There exists no clear definition of the term major open registries. The 10 major open and international registries have been grouped by UNCTAD to include the 10 largest fleets with more than 90 per cent foreign-controlled tonnage in 2007 (see annex II for the list of registries). The composition of this list has been kept constant to allow for year-to-year comparisons. Note, however, that the market shares and the percentage of foreign controlled tonnage changes from year to year (see also figure 2.5 for an estimated share of foreign-controlled tonnage for the top 30 flags of registration).

Barbuda. The flags of Panama, Malta, the Bahamas and the Isle of Man are also used by a small number of national shipowners, although the majority of users of these flags are foreign. Other flags for which more than 50 per cent of the tonnage is owned by foreign nationals are those of Cyprus, the United Kingdom, the Philippines, Bermuda, Hong Kong (China), Singapore and France (including the international registry FIS). In the case of the Netherlands and the United States, approximately two out of every five owners are foreign. The flags of Belgium, India, Denmark (including DIS), Japan and Germany are almost exclusively used by national owners.

Figures 2.6 and 2.7 and annex III combine data on the top 35 ship-owning countries (table 2.4) with information on the top 35 flags of registration (table 2.7). Most owners from Japan and the Republic of Korea register their tonnage under the flag of Panama, while the most common flag of choice for German owners is Liberia. Owners from the United States are most likely to register their tonnage under

the flag of the Marshall Islands. Greek shipowners have the most diverse portfolio of flags of registration, including a large share under the national Greek flag (figure 2.6). A mirror image of the most important owner–flag combination is obtained in figure 2.7. For the Panamanian registry, Japanese owners are the most important clients, while for the registry of Liberia, owners from Germany are most important.

D. SHIPBUILDING, DEMOLITION AND NEW ORDERS

1. Deliveries of newbuildings

Almost 39 per cent of GT delivered in 2011 was built by Chinese shipyards, followed by shipyards from the Republic of Korea (35.2 per cent), Japan (19 per cent) and the Philippines (1.6 per cent). All other countries of the world together accounted for only 5.3 per cent of GT built in 2011, mostly in shipyards in Viet Nam,

Figure 2.5. Foreign and national ownership of the top 30 fleets by flag of registration, 2012 (Percentage share of fleet dwt)

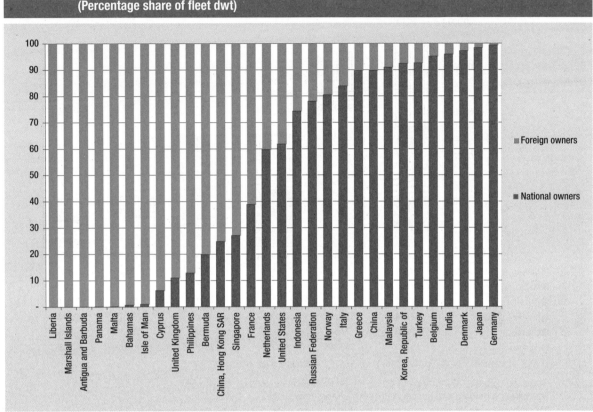

Source: Compiled by the UNCTAD secretariat, based on data provided by *IHS Fairplay*.
Note: The term national owners in the nationally flagged fleet includes nationals making use of the country's international registry, such as DIS (Denmark), FIS (France) and NIS (Norway). The term foreign owners includes tonnage where the nationality of the owner is not known.

Brazil and India (table 2.9). More than half of dry bulk carriers (in GT) were built by China, while the Republic of Korea had a 55 per cent share of container and other dry cargo ships. The Republic of Korea's lead in container ship building was further evidenced by the beginning of the construction of the world's largest container ship, the first of Maersk's Tripple-E class, in a Daewoo shipyard in the Republic of Korea in May 2012.

Deliveries during the three years following the economic and financial crisis are almost 80 per cent higher than the tonnage built and delivered during the three years prior to the crisis. For new orders, the picture is just the opposite: during the three years prior to 2009, shipowners ordered on average 200 million dwt per year, which is 2.5 times as much as the annual new orders placed between 2009 and 2011.[30]

It is, largely, the orders placed prior to 2009 that are the cause of the present boom in deliveries. Based on the current order book, deliveries in 2012 are expected to be even higher than last year's historical record; 73 per cent of containerships that are to be delivered

during 2012 were ordered in 2008 or earlier.[31] Only in 2013 will the decline of new orders since 2009 finally also lead to a decline in shipbuilding.

Chinese shipyards and Chinese traders have a common interest in continuing deliveries of new ships by Chinese shipyards. The building activities maintain employment in shipbuilding, and the delivered tonnage ensures a high supply of maritime transport capacity, which is to the benefit of importers and exporters. Shipowners, on the other hand, have reportedly expressed concerns that a continued oversupply of ships could prove devastating for them.[32]

In the longer term, in view of the reduced numbers of new orders, shipyards in most countries have been forced to reduce their capacity.[33] An exception is the Philippines, which is expanding its shipbuilding capacity; factors contributing to this expansion include investment by Hanjin (Republic of Korea), which is reportedly planning to hire 10,000 additional workers for its facility in Subic Bay.[34] India, too, is expected to expand its shipbuilding and repair capacity by 2015.[35]

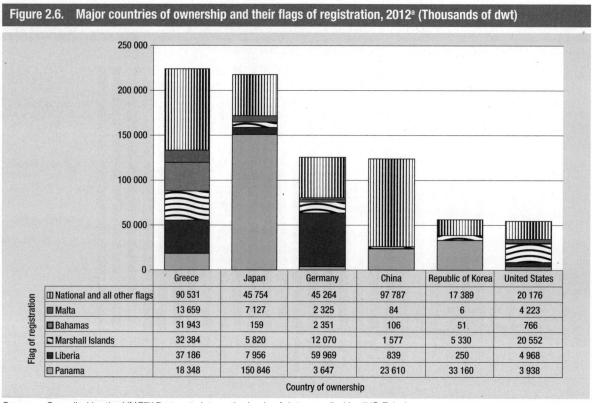

Figure 2.6. Major countries of ownership and their flags of registration, 2012ᵃ (Thousands of dwt)

Flag of registration	Greece	Japan	Germany	China	Republic of Korea	United States
National and all other flags	90 531	45 754	45 264	97 787	17 389	20 176
Malta	13 659	7 127	2 325	84	6	4 223
Bahamas	31 943	159	2 351	106	51	766
Marshall Islands	32 384	5 820	12 070	1 577	5 330	20 552
Liberia	37 186	7 956	59 969	839	250	4 968
Panama	18 348	150 846	3 647	23 610	33 160	3 938

Country of ownership

Source: Compiled by the UNCTAD secretariat, on the basis of data supplied by *IHS Fairplay*.
ᵃ   Seagoing propelled merchant ships of 1000 GT and above.

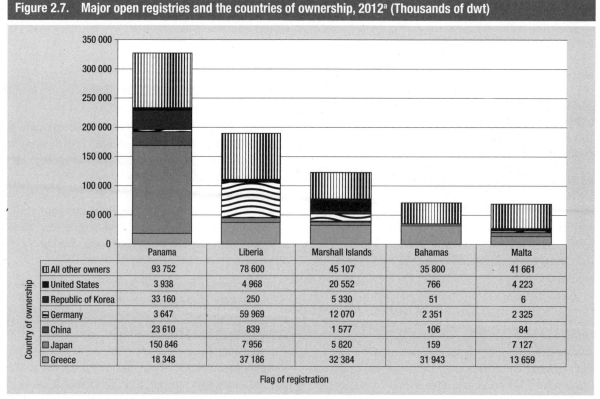

Figure 2.7. Major open registries and the countries of ownership, 2012ᵃ (Thousands of dwt)

Country of ownership	Panama	Liberia	Marshall Islands	Bahamas	Malta
All other owners	93 752	78 600	45 107	35 800	41 661
United States	3 938	4 968	20 552	766	4 223
Republic of Korea	33 160	250	5 330	51	6
Germany	3 647	59 969	12 070	2 351	2 325
China	23 610	839	1 577	106	84
Japan	150 846	7 956	5 820	159	7 127
Greece	18 348	37 186	32 384	31 943	13 659

Flag of registration

Source: Compiled by the UNCTAD secretariat, on the basis of data supplied by *IHS Fairplay*.
ᵃ   Cargo-carrying vessels of 1000 GT and above.

Table 2.9.   Deliveries of newbuildings, major vessel types and countries where built (2011, thousands of GT)

	China	Korea, Republic of	Japan	Philippines	Rest of world	World total
Tankers	7 613	11 370	4 764	-	617	24 365
Bulk carriers	26 719	11 678	11 656	1 658	1 290	53 001
Container and other passenger	4 291	11 794	2 921	3	2 418	21 427
Offshore and other work vessels	986	1 008	26	0	1 032	3 052
Total	39 609	35 850	19 367	1 661	5 357	101 845

Source: Compiled by the UNCTAD secretariat, on the basis of data supplied by *IHS Fairplay*.

Table 2.10.   Tonnage reported sold for demolition, major vessel types and country of demolition (2011, thousands of GT)

	India	China	Bangladesh	Pakistan	Turkey	Rest of world	Total
Tankers	1 811	610	830	1 485	98	157	4 992
Bulk carriers	3 215	4 367	4 527	1 240	205	114	13 668
Container and other passenger	3 370	1 318	464	176	830	353	6 511
Offshore and other work vessels	366	59	136	548	18	260	1 388
Total	8 762	6 354	5 957	3 449	1 152	884	26 558

Source: Compiled by the UNCTAD secretariat, on the basis of data supplied by *IHS Fairplay*.

2.   Demolition of ships

Most of the world's ship recycling takes place in developing countries in Asia. India accounted for 33 per cent of GT demolished in 2011, followed by China (23.9 per cent), Bangladesh (22.4 per cent) and Pakistan (13 per cent). There is also a pattern of specialization in India, which had its highest market share in the scrapping of container and other dry cargo ships. Scrapyards of Bangladesh and China purchased more tonnage of bulk carriers, while those of Pakistan mostly demolished tankers (table 2.10).

The large majority of ships demolished in 2011 were between 20 and 40 years of age, with a peak at the age of 30 (figure 2.8). Tankers tended to be demolished at a younger age, while general cargo and container ships were more likely to be kept in business beyond the age of 30. The shorter life cycle of oil tankers is in part the result of increasingly stringent environmental regulations.

In early 2012, MOL (Japan) reportedly sold five oil tankers for scrapping, including modern double-hull ships, "to help alleviate overcapacity in the charter market".[36] Rather than sell the ships to other owners, who would then compete for the same cargo, it was considered preferable to demolish the ships – even if the immediate earnings from such a sale would be lower than from a sale on the second-hand market.

In total, the quantity of tonnage sold for demolition increased by 31 per cent in 2011 compared with 2010. The increase was due to the surge in the scrapping of dry bulk ships (plus 356 per cent), while some other vessel types actually saw a slight decline in demolitions. Many of the dry bulk ships demolished were effectively still seaworthy, built in the eighties and with valid certificates for several more years of trading. However, as new tonnage is more energy efficient, given the extremely low charter rates, many owners still found it more profitable to sell for scrap instead of continuing trading at a financial loss. This economic context, combined with renewed demand from scrapyards in Bangladesh, has led to a further surge in ship recycling in early 2012. In May 2012, a 13-year-old container ship was sold for demolition, making it the youngest merchant vessel to be demolished since the economic crisis in 2008.[37]

3.   Tonnage on order

Since the economic and financial crisis of 2008 and 2009, far fewer new orders have been placed than tonnage delivered by the world's shipyards. This has helped to reduce significantly the existing order book (figure 2.9 and table 2.11). Since its peak in autumn 2008, the total order book has decreased by 43 per cent. The reduction in the order book for tankers has

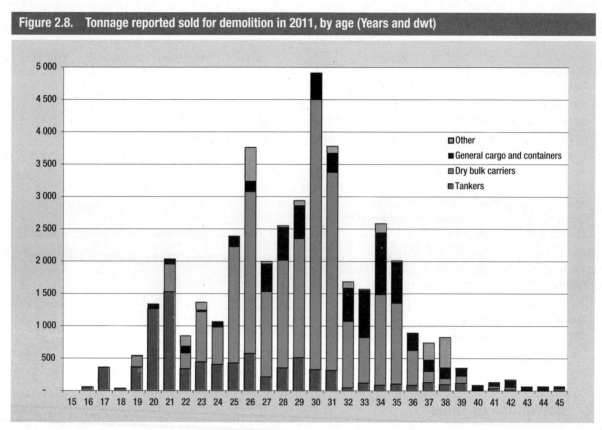

Figure 2.8.   Tonnage reported sold for demolition in 2011, by age (Years and dwt)

Source: Compiled by the UNCTAD secretariat, on the basis of data supplied by *IHS Fairplay*.

been even more impressive – at the end of 2011 tanker tonnage on order had declined by 57 per cent compared with three years earlier. In terms of dwt, more than half of the existing order book is for dry bulk carriers.

Compared with the existing fleet (table 2.1), the order book for dry bulk carriers also continues to be the largest, amounting to almost 30 per cent of the tonnage existing in January 2012. Container ships on order are almost 25 per cent of the current fleet, and oil tankers under 13 per cent. As an exception among the major vessel types, for the first time since 2006, the order book for container ships actually increased between the end of 2010 and the end of 2011.

Among specialized vessels, the most important increase was recorded for liquefied natural gas (LNG) tankers, for which the current order book now stands at more than 20 per cent of the existing fleet. As a response to the expected further surge in demand for LNG transport following opposition to the use of nuclear energy in Japan and other countries (this opposition being expected to increase the use of LNG), a historically high number of new orders for LNG carriers was placed in 2011. Several new orders are

of the tri-fuel design, enabling the ship to run on either fuel oil, diesel, or natural gas.[38] Another important increase was recorded for offshore vessels, including orders placed for drilling and support ships to serve new explorations in Brazil and West Africa.

New orders for dry cargo ships (bulk and containers) in 2011 were about as high as in 2006, that is, during the boom years before the financial and economic crisis, while new orders for tankers were among the lowest in recent history.[39] Among container ships, the majority of new orders are for ships above 10,000 TEU; these so-called mega-ships will account for more than half of the container fleet (in TEU) by 2015.[40]

Most of the world's shipbuilding takes place in Asia. China is estimated to hold about 44 per cent of the current order book, followed by the Republic of Korea (30 per cent) and Japan (17 per cent).[41] However, considering new orders placed in 2011, builders in the Republic of Korea generated more new business during the year than Chinese shipyards. Orders at Chinese shipyards tended to be largely for dry bulk ships, while the Republic of Korea has a larger share in higher value container and specialized ships.

Figure 2.9. World tonnage on order, 2000–2011ᵃ (Thousands of dwt)

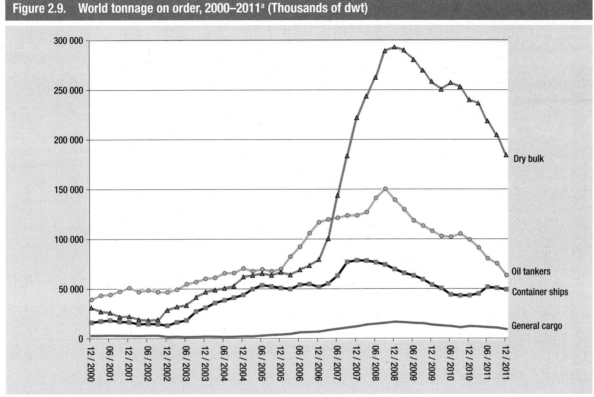

Source: Compiled by the UNCTAD secretariat, on the basis of data supplied by *IHS Fairplay*.
ᵃ Seagoing propelled merchant ships of 100 GT and above.

4. Tonnage utilization

Tonnage reported as idle

By the end of 2011, less than 1 per cent of the world merchant fleet of tankers, dry bulk and general cargo carriers was reported as idle, which is less than half of the idle share at the end of 2008 (table 2.12). Among the different vessel types, the highest idle shares were reported for LNG tankers (1.9 per cent) and for the ro-ro fleet (1.7 per cent) (table 2.13).

While there is no agreed definition of the term idle, for the purposes of this report the idle fleet includes ships that are reported as laid up. However, not being reported as laid up does not necessarily imply that the ship is at present transporting cargo. For example, the available tanker capacity waiting and ready to take cargo in the oil-exporting Persian Gulf region was reportedly 10 per cent higher than the available cargo in early 2012.[42]

The share of idle tonnage in container shipping is not quite comparable with the idle bulk and general cargo fleet. While tankers, bulk carriers and general cargo ships in the tramp business may be waiting for new cargo without immediately being considered "idle",

a containership that is not participating in a regular liner service is reported as idle. In early 2012, about 5 per cent of the container ship fleet was thus inactive, including six ships larger than 10,000 TEU.

Slow steaming in container shipping

Since 2008, container shipping companies have systematically reduced the speed of their services by introducing slow steaming. This has allowed them to absorb additional vessel capacity, thus reducing the oversupply of tonnage. It has also helped to significantly reduce fuel consumption. When initially introduced, slow steaming did not meet much opposition from shippers, because during the economic downturn many importers were not particularly concerned about replenishing their inventories. At present, an estimated 5 per cent of the total container fleet capacity is absorbed by slow steaming.[43]

Estimates for the average speed of shipping lines point to 15 to 20 knots for different levels of slow steaming. This is still faster than the usual sailing speeds for dry and liquid bulk ships, which tend to be around 10 to 15 knots. Depending on distance and speed, cost savings can amount to between 3 and 5 per cent of vessel operating costs.[44]

Table 2.11. World tonnage on order, 2000–2011[a]

Beginning of month	Tankers			Bulk carriers			General cargo ships			Container vessels			Other ships			Total		
	Thousands of dwt	Ships	Average vessel size (dwt)	Thousands of dwt	Ships	Average vessel size (dwt)	Thousands of dwt	Ships	Average vessel size (dwt)	Thousands of dwt	Ships	Average vessel size (dwt)	Thousands of dwt	Ships	Average vessel size (dwt)	Thousands of dwt	Ships	Average vessel size (dwt)
December 2000	40 328	284	142 001	31 208	486	64 214	3 966	446	8 892	16 140	394	40 964	8 870	1 087	8 160	100 513	2 697	37 268
December 2001	51 894	399	130 060	22 184	353	62 845	3 826	372	10 286	16 550	393	42 111	13 501	1 201	11 242	107 955	2 718	39 719
December 2002	47 591	488	97 523	28 641	391	73 251	2 832	257	11 018	13 000	296	43 919	16 174	1 386	11 669	108 238	2 818	38 409
December 2003	61 123	631	96 867	46 732	640	73 019	3 068	295	10 400	30 974	580	53 403	19 277	1 492	12 920	161 174	3 638	44 303
December 2004	71 563	701	102 087	62 051	796	77 953	3 306	370	8 935	43 904	880	49 891	27 361	1 898	14 416	208 185	4 645	44 819
December 2005	70 847	724	97 855	66 614	805	82 750	5 088	584	8 712	50 856	1 124	45 245	33 147	2 285	14 506	226 551	5 522	41 027
December 2006	118 008	1 078	109 470	79 364	988	80 328	8 004	737	10 860	51 717	1 143	45 247	45 612	2 962	15 399	302 706	6 908	43 820
December 2007	124 845	1 134	110 093	221 808	2 573	86 206	13 360	1 035	12 908	78 348	1 435	54 598	56 947	3 876	14 692	495 309	10 053	49 270
March 2008	128 128	1 139	112 492	243 600	2 804	86 876	15 097	1 195	12 633	73 042	1 419	54 998	58 304	4 174	13 968	523 171	10 731	48 753
June 2008	142 333	1 202	118 413	262 452	3 009	87 222	15 911	1 255	12 678	76 388	1 352	56 500	57 574	4 302	13 383	554 657	11 120	49 879
September 2008	151 423	1 245	121 625	288 959	3 316	87 141	16 787	1 332	12 603	74 090	1 322	56 044	56 563	4 442	12 734	587 823	11 657	50 427

Table 2.11. World tonnage on order, 2000–2011ª (continued)

December 2008	140 504	1 154	121 754	292 837	3 347	87 492	1 374	17 849	12 991	69 593	1 209	57 563	52 088	4 256	12 239	572 871	11 340	50 518
March 2009	130 777	1 088	120 200	289 763	3 303	87 727	1 363	17 439	12 795	65 610	1 121	58 528	48 131	4 117	11 691	551 720	10 992	50 193
June 2009	119 709	986	121 409	280 102	3 194	87 696	1 296	16 684	12 874	63 064	1 028	61 346	43 989	3 796	11 588	523 548	10 300	50 830
September 2009	114 460	934	122 548	269 558	3 050	88 380	1 264	16 354	12 939	59 314	948	62 567	40 947	3 591	11 403	500 632	9 787	51 153
December 2009	109 310	884	123 654	258 343	2 918	88 534	1 179	15 018	12 738	53 903	813	66 301	37 434	3 428	10 920	474 008	9 222	51 400
March 2010	104 062	849	122 570	250 383	2 890	86 638	1 139	14 199	12 466	50 416	732	68 874	34 804	3 396	10 248	453 864	9 006	50 396
June 2010	103 245	824	125 297	257 229	2 951	87 167	1 095	13 480	12 311	44 071	628	70 176	30 135	3 137	9 606	448 160	8 635	51 900
September 2010	106 599	791	134 765	252 924	2 887	87 608	1 023	12 361	12 083	43 060	600	71 766	26 003	2 849	9 127	440 946	8 150	54 104
December 2010	100 442	741	135 549	239 898	2 823	84 980	989	13 487	13 637	43 180	566	76 289	24 888	2 702	9 211	421 895	7 821	53 944
March 2011	92 367	710	130 094	236 431	2 786	84 864	967	13 172	13 621	45 011	577	78 009	24 106	2 703	8 918	411 087	7 743	53 091
June 2011	81 566	657	124 149	218 453	2 601	83 988	930	12 485	13 425	51 642	652	79 205	24 404	2 687	9 082	388 549	7 527	51 621
September 2011	76 536	635	120 530	204 580	2 470	82 826	880	11 994	13 630	50 661	633	80 034	25 445	2 687	9 470	369 218	7 305	50 543
December 2011	64 618	588	109 895	184 353	2 268	81 284	785	10 464	13 330	49 088	602	81 542	24 527	2 613	9 387	333 051	6 856	48 578
Percentage of total, December 2011	19.4	8.6		55.4	33.1		11.4	3.1		14.7	8.8		7.4	38.1		100.0	100.0	

Source: Compiled by the UNCTAD secretariat, on the basis of data supplied by *IHS Fairplay*.
ª   Seagoing propelled merchant ships of 100 GT and above.

Table 2.12.	Tonnage reported as idle, 2005–2011 (End-of-year figures)						
	2005	*2006*	*2007*	*2008*	*2009*	*2010*	*2011*
	Millions of dwt						
Merchant fleet, three main vessel types[a]	697.9	773.9	830.7	876.2	930.3	1,023.3	1,135.4
Idle fleet[b]	7.2	10.1	12.1	19.0	12.0	14.1	10.7
Active fleet	690.7	763.7	818.6	857.2	918.3	1,009.1	1,124.7
Idle fleet as percentage of merchant fleet	1.0	1.3	1.5	2.2	1.3	1.4	0.9

Source: Compiled by the UNCTAD secretariat, on the basis of data supplied by *Lloyd's Shipping Economist*, various issues.
[a] Tankers and dry bulk carriers of 10 000 dwt and above, and conventional general cargo vessels of 5,000 dwt and above.
[b] The idle fleet is defined as tonnage that is reported as laid up.

Table 2.13.	Analysis of idle tonnage by main type of vessel, 2005–2011[a] (Millions of dwt or m³)						
	2005	*2006*	*2007*	*2008*	*2009*	*2010*	*2011*
World tanker fleet (dwt)	**312.9**	**367.4**	**393.5**	**414.04**	**435.25**	**447.64**	**473.91**
Idle tanker fleet (dwt)	4.5	6.1	7.8	14.35	8.51	10.48	6.96
Share of idle fleet in tanker fleet (%)	1.4	1.7	2.0	3.47	1.96	2.34	1.47
World dry bulk fleet (dwt)	**340.0**	**361.8**	**393.5**	**417.62**	**452.52**	**522.52**	**608.60**
Idle dry bulk fleet (dwt)	2.0	3.4	3.6	3.68	2.64	2.86	2.87
Share of idle fleet in dry bulk fleet (%)	0.6	0.9	0.9	0.88	0.58	0.55	0.47
World conventional general cargo fleet (dwt)	**45.0**	**44.7**	**43.8**	**44.54**	**42.53**	**53.10**	**52.90**
Idle conventional general cargo fleet (dwt)	0.7	0.6	0.7	0.97	0.83	0.78	0.85
Share of idle fleet in general cargo fleet (%)	1.6	1.4	1.6	2.18	1.95	1.47	1.61
World ro-ro fleet (dwt)	**n.a.**	**n.a.**	**n.a.**	**11.37**	**10.93**	**10.28**	**9.99**
Idle ro-ro fleet (dwt)	n.a.	n.a.	n.a.	0.89	0.73	0.33	0.17
Share of idle fleet in ro-ro fleet (%)	n.a.	n.a.	n.a.	7.83	6.68	3.21	1.70
World vehicle carrier fleet (dwt)	**n.a.**	**n.a.**	**n.a.**	**11.27**	**11.20**	**11.48**	**12.42**
Idle Vehicle carrier fleet (dwt)	n.a.	n.a.	n.a.	0.24	0.55	0.13	0.06
Share of idle fleet in vehicle carrier fleet (%)	n.a.	n.a.	n.a.	2.13	4.91	1.13	0.48
World LNG carrier fleet (m³)	**n.a.**	**n.a.**	**n.a.**	**44.43**	**46.90**	**51.15**	**51.32**
Idle LNG carrier fleet (m3)	n.a.	n.a.	n.a.	5.87	1.29	1.53	0.98
Share of idle fleet in LNG fleet (%)	n.a.	n.a.	n.a.	13.21	2.75	2.99	1.91
World Liquefied petoleum gas(LPG) fleet (m³)	**n.a.**	**n.a.**	**n.a.**	**11.56**	**18.50**	**19.42**	**19.44**
Idle LPG carrier fleet (m³)	n.a.	n.a.	n.a.	0.94	0.10	0.13	0.11
Share of idle fleet in LNG fleet (%)	n.a.	n.a.	n.a.	8.13	0.54	0.67	0.57

Source: Compiled by the UNCTAD secretariat, on the basis of data from *Lloyd's Shipping Economist*, various issues.
[a] This table excludes tankers and dry bulk carriers of less than 10 000 dwt and conventional general cargo vessels of less than 5,000 dwt.

The inventory cost (capital, depreciation) of the goods that spend more time en route may well be higher than the cost savings made by the carriers. Shippers, who have to bear the inventory costs, have accordingly complained about this situation. Nevertheless, shippers have also realized that slow steaming may improve service reliability, and in the end may not be too concerned about the speed of delivery.[45]

A further reduction of service speed would not make technological or economic sense – engines would suffer, and the savings made in fuel reduction would be outweighed by additional operating costs resulting from the need to deploy additional ships. Returning to the previous higher speeds appears unlikely, too, as businesses have now adapted to the inventory held on the ships, and in view of the continuing oversupply of tonnage, the carriers have no room to re-absorb additional capacity should it be released from slow steaming. It appears that the current speeds may become the norm, with high speeding being considered as a form of premium service.

ENDNOTES

1   Clarkson (2012). Dry Bulk Trade Outlook. London, May 2012.

2   www.vale.com.

3   *IHS Fairplay* (2012). Bolting the door on Valemaxes. London, 9 February.

4   *Lloyd's List* (2012). Vale in talks over access to China. London, 17 May.

5   Bloomberg (2012). Petrobras Books World's Second-Biggest Oil Tanker. www.bloomberg.com. 9 March.

6   World Shipping Council website (2012). www.worldshipping.org. Accessed on 28 May 2012.

7   Drewry Shipping Consultants (2011). Global Container Terminal Operators, Annual Review and Forecast 2011. London, August.

8   *Containerisation International* (2012). Reefers on the slide. London, April.

9   *Lloyd's List* (2012). China's coastal trades absorb newbuilding surplus. London, 15 May, and: *Lloyd's List* (2012). China hints at intervention for ailing industry. London, 21 March.

10   *IHS Fairplay* (2011). New dawn for African shipping. London, 15 September.

11   United States Department of Transportation Maritime Administration (2011). U.S. Water Transportation Statistical Snapshot. The share refers to the "Jones-Act" fleet. Washington, February.

12   Clarksons Shipping Intelligence Network (2011). Elderly Chinese Bulkers – Not A Clear Solution. www.clarksons.net. 19 December.

13   *The New Indian Express* (2012). Not enough feeders, say steamer agents. http://expressbuzz.com. 3 April.

14   *All Africa* (2012). Nigeria: NIMASA poised to implement cabotage. http://allafrica.com/stories/201203300693.html. 30 March.

15   *The Jakarta Post* (2012). Government mulls reducing age limit for imported ships. www.thejakartapost.com. 20 March.

16   1UNCTAD (2008). Review of Maritime Transport. Geneva.

17   Bloomberg (2012). No slower steaming as container lines run like clippers. www.bloomberg.com. 26 January.

18   Specialized press reporting, including Dynamar, *Journal of Commerce*, *IHS Fairplay* and *Lloyd's List*, various issues.

19   *Lloyd's List* (2012). No end in sight for the great shipping recession. London, 3 May.

20   *Lloyd's List* (2012). Timing is everything. Whether Evergreen will in the end own or charter the ships is not yet decided. London, 26 April.

21   *Lloyd's List* (2012). CSAV sees glimmers of improvement. London, 23 April.

22   *IHS Fairplay* (2011).Box lines poised to consolidate. London, 1 December.

23   *Journal of Commerce* (2012). Mega-ship trend comes with consequences. www.joc.com. 5 March.

24   *IHS Fairplay* (2011). Outside the box. London, 22 December.

25   *Lloyd's List* (2012). Shortsea and feeder trades will consolidate. London, 1 February.

26   *Lloyd's List* (2012). No more smoke and mirrors. London, 10 May.

27   *Lloyd's List* (2012). CSA urges China shipowners to seek government aid. London, 2 April.

28   *Lloyd's List* (2012). State of Hamburg defends decision to buy more Hapag-Lloyd shares. London, 23 February.

29   *Lloyd's List* (2012). Forced sales to flood small boxship market as banks lose patience. London, 30 April.

30   BRS (2012). *World Shipping and Shipbuilding Markets Annual Review, 2012*. Paris.

31   *Clarkson Container Intelligence Monthly* (2012). A little patience can go a long way. London, May.

32   *Lloyd's List* (2012). Shipyard survival is zero-sum game. London, 20 March.

33   Helenic Shipping News: "Shipyards looking to trim capacity as demand slows down", www.hellenicshippingnews.com, 7 May 2012; Reuters: "China's shipyards founder as building boom ends", www.reuters.com, 2 May 2012.

34   Ground Report: "SUBIC Freeport: Hanjin shipyard expanding to hire 10.000 workers", www.groundreport.com, 15 May 2012.

35   Associated Chambers of Commerce and Industry of India: "Shipbuilding & ship repair industry to reach Rs 9,200 crore by 2015", www.assocham.org, 16 April 2012.

36   *Lloyd's List*: "United action", London, 30 January 2012; see also Hellenic Shipping News: "Demolition activity maintains pace as owners seek to easy oversupply issues", www.hellenicshippingnews.com, 18 February 2012.

37   *Lloyd's List*: "Downturn claims youngest vessel sold for scrap", London, 22 May 2012.

38   *IHS Fairplay* Daily News: "Ten places LNG bet", London, 10 April 2012.

39   BRS: "Shipping and Shipbuilding Markets Annual Review 2012", Paris, 2012.

40   Shipping Finance: "Containership industry consolidation to start again by 2015", Athens, March 2012.

41   BRS: "Shipping and Shipbuilding Markets Annual Review 2012", Paris, 2012.

42   Bloomberg: "Crude oil-tanker glut stays at four-week high, survey shows", www.bloomberg.com, 14 February 2012. Concerning the definitions of "idle" or "laid-up", it can be argued that operators "are brining into use a number of interim ship states before they acknowledge that a ship is, in fact, laid up"; see *Lloyd's List*: "Are ships idle or simply resting", London, 21 March 2012.

43   *IHS Fairplay* Daily News: "More box ship idling seen", London, 1 February 2012.

44   DC Velocity: "Slow steam ahead", www.dcvelocity.com, 5 March 2012.

45   Bloomberg: "No slower steaming as container lines run like clippers", www.bloomberg.com, 26 January 2012; Clarkson Container Intelligence Monthly: "A little patience can go a long way", London, May 2012.

3

FREIGHT RATES AND MARITIME TRANSPORT COSTS

Freight rates in 2011 and the beginning of 2012 have often remained at unprofitable levels. Within the three segments – dry bulk, liquid bulk and containerized cargo – substantial freight rate drops have been reported. Vessel oversupply can be identified as a driving factor behind this development. The investment in large capacity ships within the tanker and the dry bulk segment accelerated competition as ship operators were willing to accept freight rates below or close to operating costs.

Daily earnings of Capesize vessels dropped below those of the significantly smaller Handysize class for several months. This fuels an ongoing debate at a time when ship size rallies are coming to an end. While smaller vessels offer greater flexibility and serve ports that are not equipped with state of the art handling equipment, large vessels are constraint to navigate between the world's busiest ports, and these routes have often experienced a pronounced capacity oversupply this year.

While freight rates have declined or remained at historically low levels, ship operating costs have grown moderately. In addition, bunkering prices continue to recover from their collapse during the economic crisis, offsetting temporary freight-rate increases.

For developing countries in Asia and the Americas, the cost of transport expressed as a percentage of the value of the goods imported continues to diminish, thus converging to that of developed nations. Africa also followed this trend until 2001, but currently, these transport cost shares are stagnating on the continent at relatively high levels.

This chapter also discusses three generic strategies for individual countries to influence transport costs within their seaborne trade network. These include the development of coastal shipping and efficiency programmes for ports. In addition, policies should be applied that aim at improving the port connections with hinterland markets.

This chapter covers the development of freight rates and maritime transport costs and is structured in the following order. Section A analyses developments in maritime freight rates in 2011 and the beginning of 2012 for three major cargo types: containers, liquid bulk and dry bulk. Building on this, section B discusses the factors behind freight rate volatilities, mainly focusing on transport costs and the demand and supply structure in the individual shipping segments. Finally, section C proposes three generic strategies to reduce maritime freight rates and evaluates the impact of these measures on the components of freight rate costs.

A. FREIGHT RATES

This section presents an analysis of maritime freight rate developments for containers, dry bulk and liquid bulk shipping. It highlights significant events leading to major price fluctuations, discusses recent industry trends and gives a selective outlook on future developments of freight markets.

1. Container freight rates

Having experienced one of the steepest freight rate cuts in history in 2008, the recovery remains sluggish in 2011. Current freight rates are still far from reaching pre-crisis levels, having experienced another downturn in the second half of 2011 after a temporary resurgence. Time charter rates for container ships have declined from May to December 2011 for most ship types, reaching a loss of 66 per cent within the 2,300–3,400 20-foot equivalent units (TEUs) class (table 3.1). This is reflected by the New ConTex index, a condensed container freight rate indicator covering a wide range of ship sizes, which experienced a dip of almost 60 per cent of its value from May to December 2011 (figure 3.1).[1]

An overstretched container cargo market on the supply side precipitated the low freight rate levels in 2011. While the demand is currently still recovering from the seaborne trade collapse during the financial crisis, the growth rates of the global container carrier capacity have remained relatively stable (figure 3.2), due in part to shipowners not being able to withdraw from their buying contracts. In addition, ship operators suffer from substantial bunkering price increases that are not reflected in developments in freight rates.

As a result, the industry has experienced aggressive pricing policies of boxship operators competing for market shares.[2] Many box carriers are still operating at a loss, inciting them to cull capacity on unprofitable trade routes and/or raise prices for shippers. An example is Hanjin, which announced freight price increases of between $200 and $400 on routes linking Asia to Northern Europe and Western Africa. Companies such as CMA CGM, CKYH and OOCL cut their capacity on the transatlantic lanes.[3] These measures did not, however, lead to a substantial freight rate increase in the overall container shipping market in 2011. It is estimated that the total loss to the industry will reach $5.2 billion this year.[4]

High-volume routes, in particular, are experiencing an increasing competition. Operators place their largest

ships in these networks and aim at offering more regular services. As a result, shipping lines build alliances to share costs, bundle capacity and streamline their operations. Examples of this industry trend include the partnership of MSC and CMA CGM, or the merging of Asia–Europe services between the Grand Alliance (Hapag-Lloyd, NYK and OOCL) and the New World Alliance (HMM, APL and MOL).[5] Individual shipping lines with smaller vessels will find it increasingly difficult to remain competitive on the world's busiest shipping lanes. Furthermore, with a growth rate predicted at 25 per cent for the above-8,000 TEUs fleet in 2012, large-scale capacity is continuing to enter this market segment.[6]

Container ship operators entering the reefer business

The decline in freight rates in the container shipping business increasingly puts competitive pressures on specialized reefers. Refrigerated cargo is used by container ship operators as an opportunity to fill some of the idle capacity in the business. This trend is also reflected in the ship buyers' orderbook, which contains an increasing share of vessels with large reefer capacity (see also chapter 2).[7]

Industry-leader reefers such as Star Reefers have described 2011, as for 2010, as one of the poorest years in the industry's history, companies being hit hard by the low freight rates and increased competition from container ship operators.[8] The spot market rates for larger reefer ships reached an average of 43 cents per cubic feet per 30 days in 2011, following 42 cents in 2010.[9] The near collapse of banana exports from Ecuador and Central America since April 2011 brought additional stress to reefer freight rates. Although a strong growth in demand for the transport of perishable goods is being predicted, the shipping industry will most likely also experience an ongoing cargo shift from specialized reefers to container ships. International container lines are constantly introducing new regular services for the transportation of perishable goods connecting the major production centres with the largest consumer markets, such as Europe and North America. According to Drewry, in 2014 about 74 per cent of perishable reefer goods will be transported by container ships, these providing some 95 per cent of the entire reefer market cargo capacity.[10]

This industry trend is also reflected in the structure of the reefer fleet and the orderbook for specialized reefer vessels. The reefer fleet is comparably old, with

Figure 3.1. New ConTex 2007–2012 (Index base October 2007, 1,000 points)

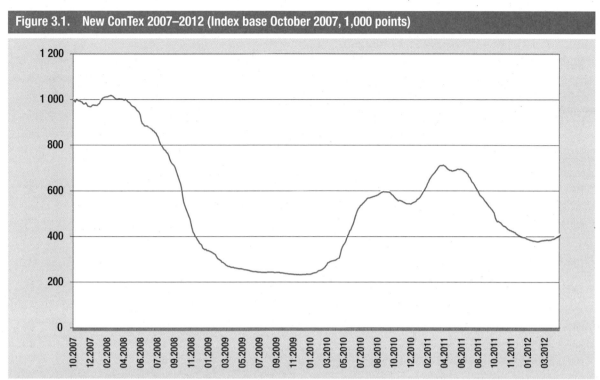

Source: Compiled by the UNCTAD secretariat, using the New ConTex index produced by the Hamburg Shipbrokers' Association. See http://www.vhss.de.

Note: New ConTex is a container ship time charter assessment index calculated as an equivalent weight of percentage change from six ConTex assessments, including the following ship sizes: 1,100, 1,700, 2,500, 2,700, 3,500 and 4,250 TEUs.

Figure 3.2. Growth of demand and supply in container shipping, 2000–2012 (Annual growth rates)

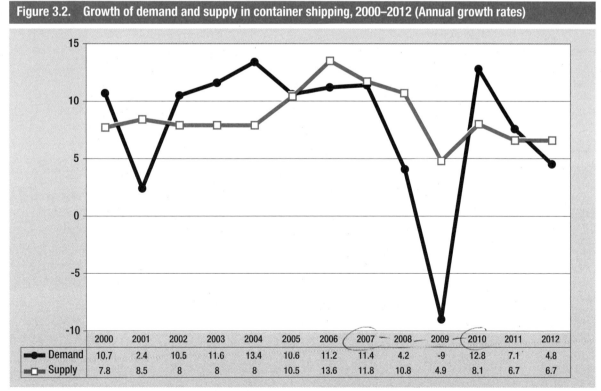

	2000	2001	2002	2003	2004	2005	2006	2007	2008	2009	2010	2011	2012
Demand	10.7	2.4	10.5	11.6	13.4	10.6	11.2	11.4	4.2	-9	12.8	7.1	4.8
Supply	7.8	8.5	8	8	8	10.5	13.6	11.8	10.8	4.9	8.1	6.7	6.7

Source: Compiled by UNCTAD secretariat on the basis of data from *Clarkson Container Intelligence Monthly*, various issues.

Note: Supply data refers to total container-carrying fleet capacity, including multi-purpose and other vessels with some container-carrying capacity. Demand growth based on million TEU lifts. The data for 2012 are forecast figures.

Table 3.1.   Container ship time charter rates (Dollars per 14-ton slot per day)

Ship type and sailing speed (TEUs)	Yearly averages									
	2002	2003	2004	2005	2006	2007	2008	2009	2010	2011
Gearless										
200–299 (min 14 kn)	16.9	19.6	25.0	31.7	26.7	27.2	26.0	12.5	12.4	12.4
300–500 (min 15 kn)	15.1	17.5	21.7	28.3	21.7	22.3	20.0	8.8	9.9	12.8
Geared/gearless										
2 000–2 299 (min 22 kn)	4.9	9.8	13.8	16.4	10.5	11.7	10.0	2.7	4.8	6.3
2 300–3 400 (min 22.5 kn)	6.0	9.3	13.2	13.0	10.2	10.7	10.7	4.9	4.7	6.2
Geared										
200–299 (min 14 kn)	17.0	18.9	27.0	35.4	28.0	29.8	32.1	16.7	18.3	22.1
300–500 (min 15 kn)	13.4	15.6	22.2	28.8	22.0	21.3	21.4	9.8	11.7	15.4
600–799 (min 17 - 17.9 kn)	9.3	12.3	19.6	23.7	16.6	16.1	15.6	6.6	8.4	11.2
700–999 (min 18 kn)	9.1	12.1	18.4	22.0	16.7	16.9	15.4	6.0	8.5	11.5
800–999 (min 18 kn)	n.a.	n.a.	n.a.	n.a.	n.a.	n.a.	n.a.	4.9	7.8	10.8
1 000–1 260 (min 18 kn)	6.9	11.6	19.1	22.6	14.3	13.7	12.2	4.0	5.9	8.7
1 261–1 350 (min 19 kn)	n.a.	n.a.	n.a.	n.a.	n.a.	n.a.	n.a.	3.7	4.9	8.1
1 600–1 999 (min 20 kn)	5.7	10.0	16.1	15.8	11.8	12.8	10.8	3.5	5.0	6.8

Ship type and sailing speed (TEUs)	Monthly averages for 2011												Monthly averages for 2012	
	Jan	Feb	Mar	Apr	May	Jun	Jul	Aug	Sep	Oct	Nov	Dec	Jan	Feb
Gearless														
200–299 (min 14 kn)	13.3	14.4	14.9	15.6	15.7	13.8	15.4	15.5	14.3	15.1	12.6	14.4	13.1	14.4
300–500 (min 15 kn)	11.3	12.3	13.4	14.4	14.4	14.1	13.6	13.1	12.6	12.4	11.9	10.3	9.8	12.3
Geared/gearless														
2 000–2 299 (min 22 kn)	6.6	7.3	7.4	8.2	7.5	7.8	6.6	6.3	5.1	4.8	4.3	3.6	3.4	7.3
2 300–3 400 (min 22.5 kn)	7.6	8.5	9.1	8.6	8.7	8.1	6.7	5.1	3.3	2.7	2.7	2.7	3.0	
Geared														
200–299 (min 14 kn)	22.1	22.9	22.5	22.5	27.2	24.7	23.0	22.1	20.5	19.5	19.1	19.1	13.5	22.9
300–500 (min 15 kn)	17.2	16.1	17.2	15.5	15.3	18.2	17.1	15.4	14.6	13.2	13.6	11.4	12.3	16.1
600–799 (min 17 - 17.9 kn)	10.4	12.9	12.6	12.4	13.4	12.7	11.7	11.3	10.6	9.8	8.9	7.9	7.4	12.9
700–999 (min 18 kn)	11.9	12.7	13.4	13.8	13.5	13.3	12.3	11.0	10.4	9.5	8.7	7.8	7.7	12.7
800–999 (min 18 kn)	10.3	12.7	12.2	12.3	12.4	12.1	11.8	10.8	9.8	9.0	8.7	7.1	7.3	12.7
1 000–1 260 (min 18 kn)	7.5	8.7	9.9	10.1	10.4	10.3	9.6	8.9	8.4	7.9	6.9	6.2	6.3	8.7
1 261–1 350 (min 19 kn)	7.6	8.0	8.9	9.4	9.5	9.6	8.9	8.2	7.8	7.3	6.1	5.4	5.2	
1 600–1 999 (min 20 kn)	6.7	7.5	7.9	7.8	8.0	8.0	7.3	6.9	6.2	5.7	4.8	4.4	4.1	7.5

Source: Compiled by the UNCTAD secretariat based on data from *Shipping Statistics and Market Review*, various issues from 2002–2012, produced by the Institute of Shipping Economics and Logistics, Bremen, Germany. See also www.isl.org.

50 per cent of the tonnage having operated for more then 20 years and only 2 per cent of the ships with an operating age below six years.[11] Despite this fact, most carriers were not willing to invest in modern vessels to upgrade their ageing fleets and the orderbook dropped to zero in September 2011 for the first time. In addition, an annual average of 36 reefer ships was sent for scrapping between 2008 and 2010.[12]

2. Tanker freight rates

The tanker market, which encompasses the transportation of crude oil and petroleum products, represents approximately one third of the world seaborne trade volume.

Freight rates for different ship sizes

Figure 3.3 visualizes tanker freight rates for different vessel sizes in dollars per 10,000 dwt capacity. The results confirm the significance of economies of scale in the tanker business, with substantial price gaps between the largest (310,000 dwt) and the smallest (47,000 dwt) ship category.

The comparison of oil prices and tanker market freight rates in the same figure demonstrates that freight rates and oil prices trend in similar patterns.[13] This is because vessel bunkering contributes a large share to the total ship operating costs (see also the vessel operating cost split in figure 3.7). In addition, the world demand for oil and maritime transport services are both strongly linked to overall economic growth. During times of economic growth, the demand for maritime transport services and oil increases substantially, possibly outweighing, in parallel, their demand and supply balance and thus leading to price increases. In the past, seaborne trade has grown approximately two times faster than the world's gross domestic product (GDP) (see also chapter 1). Oil demand increases during periods of economic prosperity not only because it is a major source of energy for the transport of goods, but also because it is used in some 70,000 manufactured products, such as synthetic fabrics, plastics and medicines.

From 2009 onwards, however, a divergence between the trends of oil price and freight rates can be observed. While the crude oil price has recovered to

Figure 3.3.   Daily tanker time charter rate in dollars per 10 000 dwt capacity for various vessel sizes, 2001–2012 (Dollars per day per 10 000 dwt)

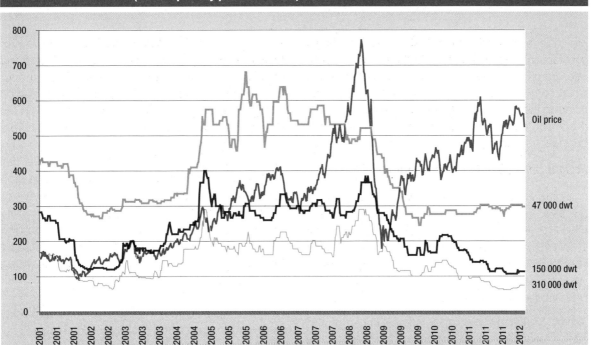

Source: Compiled by UNCTAD secretariat based on information from *Clarkson Shipping Intelligence Network*. Oil price data from United States of America Energy Information Administration, available at http://205.254.135.7/dnav/pet/pet_pri_spt_s1_w.htm.

Note: The x-axis represents weekly figures. The y-axis represents daily time charter rate in dollars per 10,000 dwt capacity for a modern tanker. Oil price is indexed with index base 150 in May 2001. Ship sizes are expressed in deadweight capacity (in thousands of dwt).

Table 3.2.   Daily time charter rates and tanker indices, 2011–2012 (monthly figures)

2011	Daily tanker time charter rate in $, monthly average					Exchange Baltic Tanker	
	310	150	110	74	48	Dirty Index	Clean Index
January	30 250	24 375	17 875	14 750	13 000	842	635
February	29 500	21 750	16 875	14 750	13 000	660	642
March	30 000	21 000	16 125	15 188	13 188	965	749
April	30 000	21 000	16 000	15 800	13 700	927	836
May	27 250	21 500	15 812	15 562	14 250	822	882
June	26 125	21 000	15 375	15 500	14 250	750	706
July	25 800	18 600	15 450	15 450	14 150	746	690
August	22 125	17 000	15 312	14 875	13 875	720	682
September	21 000	17 700	15 050	14 650	13 850	677	679
October	19 750	18 250	14 500	14 000	13 688	704	721
November	19 562	17 750	13 938	13 438	13 250	763	721
December	19 000	16 300	13 600	13 000	13 650	784	725
Average 2011	25 030	19 685	15 493	14 747	13 654	780	722
January	19 250	16 000	13 625	13 000	14 000	783	762
February	20 375	16 000	13 938	13 000	14 250	803	645
March	20 700	16 400	13 650	13 000	14 250	781	711
April	22 750	17 000	13 750	12 500	14 250	819	645

Source: Daily time charter rates expressed as monthly averages are based on information from *Clarkson Shipping Intelligence Network*. The indices are produced by the Baltic Exchange, the figures represent the value at the first working date of each month.

Note: The numbers in the second row, columns 2–6, refer to vessel size expressed in thousands of dwt.

pre-crisis levels, tanker freight rates have not shown substantial signs of recovery. On the contrary, freight rates on most routes can be seen to have decreased when comparing the figures from the beginning with those at the end of 2011 (table 3.2). Tanker capacity oversupply can be identified as one of the main factors behind these discrepancies.

Freight rates on different trade routes

Freight rates vary on different trade routes depending on their specific demand and supply structure. table 3.3 illustrates average freight rates quantified in Worldscale, a unified measure for establishing spot rates on major tanker routes for various vessel sizes. Developments on some of these routes will be presented in this section.

Almost 17 million barrels of oil, accounting for 35 per cent of seaborne petroleum trade, were transported through the Persian Gulf in 2011, making it the world's busiest shipping strait for this product.[14] In terms of voyages, 73 per cent of the world's 3,722 very large crude carrier (VLCC) trips have passed through the Persian Gulf.[15] Transport restrictions due to the

oil embargo on the Islamic Republic of Iran could, therefore, heavily affect the world tanker shipping market as a whole. The cut in transport demand for oil from the Islamic Republic of Iran was expected to trigger freight rate drops. However, prices on the Persian Gulf–Europe route, as an example, rose from 37 to 44 on the Worldscale from February to April 2012 (table 3.3). This is because Saudi Arabia has ramped up oil production to compensate for the drop in exports from the Islamic Republic of Iran. Other oil producers filling the supply gap are located in West Africa, the Caribbean and the North Sea region. The routes from these sources to Asia are much longer than those from the Persian Gulf, thus increasing tanker ton miles and capacity utilization rates.[16] With oil-consuming countries such as the United States and China building up their energy reservoirs, additional vessels have been taken out of the spot market.[17]

Freight rates on routes from West Africa were exposed to volatilities in 2011, with drops in the West Africa–North-West Europe route from 107 on the Worldscale in March to 69 in August. Increasing demand for cargo and resistance of Suezmax tanker owners to accept

Table 3.3. Tanker market summary: clean and dirty spot rates, 2011–2012 (Worldscale)

Routes	2010 Dec	2011 Jan	Feb	Mar	Apr	May	Jun	Jul	Aug	Sept	Oct	Nov	Dec	Percentage change Dec 2011/ Dec 2010	2012 Jan	Feb	Mar	Apr
VLCC/ULCC (200,000 dwt+)																		
Persian Gulf–Japan	61	48	74	63	50	51	53	50	48	45	50	57	59	3.3%	67	52	59	63
Persian Gulf–Republic of Korea	56	50	55	60	49	49	54	48	46	43	46	54	57	-1.8%	61	51	58	58
Persian Gulf–Europe	57	34	37	..	38	38	43	43	39	34	32	34	..	..	..	35	40	44
"Persian Gulf–Caribbean/East Coast of North America"	36	32	37	42	38	37	39	37	35	34	33	39	37	-2.8%	40	34	35	42
Suezmax (100,000–160,000 dwt)																		
West Africa–North-West Europe	118	63	75	107	83	84	..	74	69	70	89	79	86	27.1%	91	77	87	68
"West Africa–Caribbean/East Coast of North America"	103	60	72	101	79	81	66	69	66	69	84	75	83	19.4%	85	75	84	65
Mediterranean–Mediterranean	113	71	82	130	86	80	74	75	69	81	110	74	86	23.9%	98	86	84	73
Aframax (70,000–100,000 dwt)																		
North-West Europe–North-West Europe	162	88	97	121	107	110	98	102	98	96	117	104	122	24.7%	111	93	95	99
"North-West Europe–Caribbean/East Coast of North America"	120	131	90	109	95	102	80	..	92	..	98	92	..	..	119	99	..	..
"Caribbean–Caribbean/East Coast of North America"	146	125	98	125	123	104	98	110	113	90	104	104	112	23.3%	118	129	112	131
Mediterranean–Mediterranean	138	75	97	122	95	99	94	88	90	87	127	87	130	5.8%	105	82	104	94
Mediterranean–North-West Europe	133	69	103	135	85	90	84	86	88	84	138	84	118	11.3%	97	82	105	91
Indonesia–Far East	111	88	87	110	115	99	98	98	96	91	91	102	104	6.3%	100	90	60	85
Handy size (less than 50,000 dwt)																		
Mediterranean–Mediterranean	168	140	116	134	155	138	130	132	107	119	135	134	153	8.9%	147	157	147	140
"Mediterranean–Caribbean/East Coast of North America"	146	134	111	147	139	133	116	115	115	114	116	125	121	17.1%	124	121	118	127
"Caribbean–East Coast of North America/Gulf of Mexico"	200	155	105	174	155	139	128	118	122	124	121	141	133	33.5%	113	148	145	131
All clean tankers																		
70,000–80,000 dwt Persian Gulf–Japan	125	107	98	105	123	129	111	125	124	124	115	100	105	16.0%	100	86	84	91
50,000–60,000 dwt Persian Gulf–Japan	128	119	111	122	142	145	124	125	142	133	114	118	119	7.0%	107	101	100	117
35,000–50,000 dwt "Caribbean–East Coast of North America/Gulf of Mexico"	158	133	120	190	191	171	152	152	155	136	151	167	155	1.9%	150	165	152	155
25,000–35,000 dwt Singapore–East Asia	193	139	135	159	185	..	177	..	185	..	234	216	..	..	..	150	155	183

Source: UNCTAD secretariat, based on Drewry's *Shipping Insight*, various issues.

Note: The figures are indexed per ton voyage charter rates for a 75,000 dwt tanker. The basis is the Worldscale value 100, which represents the per ton break-even costs for this tanker size, estimated individually for each tanker route.

lower freight rates pushed price levels up again to 89 on the Worldscale in October.[18] While piracy along the Gulf of Guinea was almost non-existent about 10 years ago, it has become an issue of growing concern, leading to insurance premium increases for vessels operating in the region.[19] Expenses for rerouting to avoid high-risk piracy areas and investment in security equipment are additional cost drivers caused by piracy. Ships also navigate at higher speeds to avoid hijackings, which increases fuel costs. Up to 2011, no ship has been successfully hijacked that operated at 18 knots or higher.[20] The direct costs of piracy for the maritime industry were estimated to have reached a value of between $3.4 billion and $8.7 billion in 2010.[21] The International Maritime Organization (IMO) reported 46 piracy incidents in 7 countries in 2010 along the Gulf of Guinea. This number expanded to 64 incidents in 9 countries in 2011.[22]

Freight rates on export routes from the Mediterranean dropped in mid-2011 compared with the previous year. Price increases during 2011 were mostly caused by exceptional events and do not imply a long-term change in the market. The freight-level jumps in March 2011 were mostly caused by the unrest and military operations in Libya that pushed buyers to ship their cargo out of the country. Due to the war, oil-extraction volumes dropped in Libya from 1.57 million barrels to around 300 thousand barrels per day. This dragged the freight rates down again and reduced the likelihood of a quick recovery.[23] The rally in freight rates in October was triggered by congestions on the Bosporus Strait, which is one of the maritime choke points for oil shipments. These were caused by bad weather conditions, which increased tanker freight prices across the Mediterranean and on routes out of West Africa. Three million barrels of oil pass through this bottleneck on Suezmax tankers every day.[24]

The announcement of the closure of the oil refinery on Saint Croix, one of the United States Virgin Islands, in January 2012, one of the world's largest refineries, caused short-term freight rate drops on the route linking the Caribbean to the United States Atlantic Coast. The closure has been caused by the economic slowdown during the financial crisis and a growing competition from new-build oil-refining capacity in emerging markets.[25] The facility will now be used as a trans-shipment hub. Refined oil for the United States market will have to be imported from more distant sources to compensate for the capacity loss. This can positively affect product tanker freight rates on long-

haul voyages from refineries in the Middle East and Asia. The added ton-miles may also increase freight rates within the product tanker market as a whole.[26]

Tanker market outlook

Tankers connect oil producing countries with energy consumers. A change in the geographical structure of oil demand and supply will therefore cause modifications within the global tanker route network. British Petroleum (BP) predicts liquid-market developments until the year 2030 (figure 3.4) and it forecasts an ongoing oil-demand shift from the Organization for Economic Cooperation and Development (OECD) countries to Asia, with China contributing 50 per cent to the oil consumption growth until 2030. The BP analysis foresees that productions from the Middle East, and South and Central America together will add another 30 per cent to the demand expansion. On the production side, the Middle East will supply more than 60 per cent of the growth in oil production capacity, including large shares from Iraq and Saudi Arabia. Another 35 per cent of the projected growth will be delivered by countries from North and South America, with significant contributions from Brazil.

An ongoing volume expansion on the routes linking the traditional production centres around the Persian Gulf to major Asian markets will be the consequence if these predictions materialize. At the other end, we will observe a sluggish capacity development on tanker routes to most developed economies. British Petroleum have predicted a balanced growth of oil supply and demand in Africa – accordingly the continent's role as a world energy supplier will not significantly increase.

Developments in tanker freight rates will also depend heavily on the willingness of oil producing and buying countries to invest in their tanker fleets. China, for example, has announced that it aims to ship more of its seaborne oil imports with a domestically owned fleet. This strategic goal is also reflected in the growth of the country's VLCC fleet, which has increased from 11 vessels in 2006 to 38 in 2011. Competitive pressures have driven existing tanker operators out of the business. European shipowners have halved their market share to around 16 per cent on the Middle East–China lane from 2006 to 2011, losing capacity to their Chinese competitors.[27] If industry policies of emerging economies increasingly focus on expanding their market shares in oil transportation, this will add more capacity to the current oversupply and keep freight rates at low levels. McQuilling predicts that

Figure 3.4.   Growth in liquids demand and supply until 2030

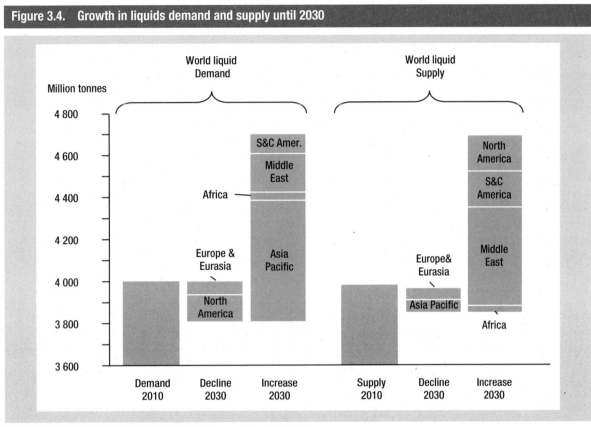

Source: UNCTAD secretariat based on *BP Energy Outlook 2030*.

tanker freight rates will continue to be under pressure, estimating a total delivery of 767 tankers over the next five years. Surplus increases are going to be more pronounced among larger ship sizes with a forecasted number of 62 VLCCs and 43 Suezmax entering the market in 2012.[28]

3.   Dry bulk freight rates

The dry bulk shipping market can be classified into the two categories major bulk and minor bulk. Major bulk includes iron ore, coal and grain, typically transported by large Capesize and Panamax vessels. They contribute about two thirds of the world dry bulk trade. Minor bulks include fertilizers, steel products, construction materials such as cement and aluminium, non-grain agricultural products, forest products and sundry minerals (for example, phosphate rock), these adding another third to the total dry bulk seaborne trade. These goods are most commonly shipped by the smaller Handymax and Handysize vessels.[29]

The increasing vessel utilization rate reinforced hopes of a market recovery in mid-2011. This indicator

reached 88 per cent in August 2011, making the difference between a sluggish and a firm market environment.[30] Freight-rate increases were reflected in the development of the Baltic Exchange Dry Index (figure 3.5). The index picked up in August 2011 from 1,256 points to 2,173 points in October. One of several factors behind the rally was the increasing Asian demand for iron ore and coal.[31] Japan, for example, increased its imports of these raw materials for reconstruction of areas affected by destruction as a result of the tsunami and earthquake.[32] However, this has been a short-lived trend. Since October a continuous decrease of the index can be observed, persisting until February 2012 where it reached its bottom value of 647 points.

Because of the unique characteristics of each individual ship class, large gaps in freight rates occur between the different dry bulk vessel segments. Small dry bulk carriers performed better than their larger counterparts (figure 3.6). Hence the need, in this section, to look at the individual developments within the four segments: Handysize, Supramax, Panamax and Capesize.

Figure 3.5.   Baltic Exchange Dry Index, 2010–2012   (Index base year 1985, 1000 points)

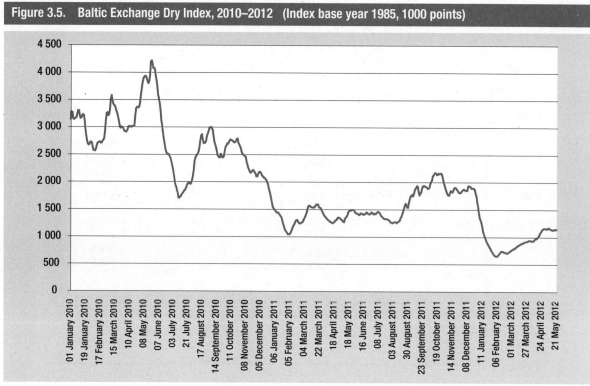

Source: UNCTAD, based on London Baltic Exchange data.

Note: The index is made up of 20 key dry bulk routes measured on a time charter basis. The index covers Handysize, Supramax, Panamax and Capesize dry bulk carriers, carrying commodities such as coal, iron ore and grain.

Figure 3.6. Daily earnings of bulker vessels, 2010–2012 (Dollars per day)

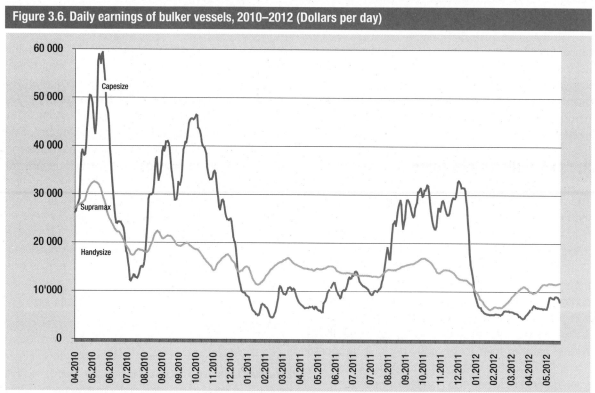

Source: UNCTAD, based on data from Clarkson Shipping Intelligence Network, figures published by the London Baltic Exchange.

Note: Handysize: average of the six time charter (T/C) routes; Supramax: average of the five T/C routes; Panamax: average of the four T/C routes; Capesize: average of the four T/C routes.

Capesize vessels

Figure 3.6 illustrates daily earnings of the four different vessel sizes described in this section. The results underline that Capesize vessels are facing the most difficult market environment when compared to smaller bulk ships. From January 2011, daily earnings of Capesize carriers dropped over a period of several months to levels below those of the smaller Handysize, Supramax and Panamax ships.[33] This can be described as a post-financial-crisis phenomenon. According to Baltic Exchange, between 2000 and 2008 Capesize vessels have constantly reached higher daily earnings than smaller ships. On 5 June 2008, Baltic Exchange reported record earnings for Capesize vessels of $244,000 per day. Four years later, in May 2012, the same ships could be chartered for around $8,000 dollars.

Pronounced fluctuations of freight rate in the Capesize segment are often the result of demand volatility in the coal and iron-ore market, these being goods typically transported by large bulk carriers. Low raw material prices most commonly indicate a sluggish world demand for these goods. However, in 2011, prices for iron ore were are at highs ($140.4 per ton in February 2012).[34] In addition, thermal coal prices had not fluctuated much since December 2010, reaching a historically firm level of $123.4 per ton in February 2012.[35] Therefore, the supply-side overcapacity in the largest dry bulk segment appears again as the decisive factor precipitating current declines in freight rate.[36] Bulk carriers accounted for two thirds of all newbuildings delivered in 2011. Recent investment figures do not suggest a cessation of competitive pressures in the Capesize segment. The orderbook for ships with a dwt of more than 200,000 amounts, in February 2012, to a 93 per cent share of the existing fleet.[37] Competitive pressures are also triggered by the specific characteristics of this market segment. Large Capesize vessels are restricted to navigate between a few ports mostly located in Australia, China and Brazil.[38] Demand fluctuations on one key route between these countries can therefore cause pronounced fluctuations of freight rate in the market as a whole.

Panamax vessels

Freight rates in the Panamax segment have been exposed to a long-term downward trend. Clarksons counted 1,632 Panamax bulkers at the beginning of 2010 and during the same period the Baltic Exchange

Panamax average time charter fluctuated between $24,000 and $34,000 (figure 3.6). In early 2011, the fleet grew to 1,818 vessels and freight rates slumped to a $11,000–$15,000 corridor.[39] In 2012, this trend has not yet reversed: the deployed fleet now counts 2,035 ships and the average daily time charter rate of below $9,000 reached its lowest level since July 2008.[40]

The turbulent economic environment and mild weather conditions in Europe reduced the coal demand from the continent, thus leading to weak prices on the Atlantic route in early 2012. Per-day charges fell to $4,000 on the Baltic Exchange United States–Europe/Europe–United States route. Pacific daily rates increased by more than a factor of two, this also provoked by the demand for coal shipments from Indonesia to Asia.[41] With the grain season ramping up in March in South America, freight rates on the spot market have risen, but this momentum has been lost again in May with the ebbing of the season.[42]

Supramax vessels

Supramax vessels increasingly compete with Panamax ships. This is due to their growing size. In 2008, Supramax vessels had an average capacity of 55,554 dwt, and this figure has, in 2011, increased to 57,037 dwt. Some of the modern carriers being handed over from shipyards reach a capacity of 61,000 dwt. In addition, they benefit from better fuel efficiency. These vessels are often geared with cranes on board for loading and unloading, which can be an advantage in small and medium-sized ports in developing countries that often do not provide sufficient handling facilities.[43] The competitiveness of Supramax vessels when compared to Panamax is also reflected in the freight rate developments.[44] The estimated three-year dry bulk time charter rates in 2011 were higher in 6 out of 12 months for Supramax than the larger Panamax vessels (table 3.4).[45] However, the segment also experienced a steep cut in freight rate, with daily rates falling from $12,296 at the end of 2011 to $6,348 in February 2012. Nevertheless, the subsequent recovery of Supramax chartering prices has been more sustainable, reaching earnings mostly above those of the larger Panamax class (table 3.6).

Handysize vessels

Handysize vessels have been more resilient in the bleak dry bulk market and benefit from several competitive advantages. They can load more than 30 cargo types, compared to only a handful of different goods carried

Table 3.4.	Estimated three-year dry bulk time charter rates 2011–2012 (Thousands of dollars per day)							
	Handysize 37 000 dwt		Supramax 55 000 dwt		Panamax 75 000 dwt		Capesize 170 000 dwt	
	2011	2012	2011	2012	2011	2012	2011	2012
January	13.0	10.5	15.2	11.0	16.5	11.0	12.0	12.0
February	13.0	9.5	15.2	10.0	16.7	10.0	20.5	11.0
March	13.1	10.5	15.5	10.8	17.0	10.9	20.5	10.0
April	13.5	10.7	16.3	11.0	15.5	11.2	16.0	11.5
May	13.1		16.0		16.5		13.5	
June	12.5		15.0		14.0		12.0	
July	12.0		14.0		13.0		12.5	
August	12.5		14.0		13.5		14.5	
September	13.0		14.5		14.0		16.5	
October	13.5		14.5		14.0		17.0	
November	12.0		13.0		13.0		16.0	
December	11.3		12.5		12.5		18.0	
Annual average	12.7	10.3	14.6	10.7	14.7	10.8	15.8	11.1

Source: UNCTAD secretariat, based on various issues of *Shipping Insight*, produced by Drewry Publishing.

by larger vessels. Secondly, smaller ships can enter almost any port, while larger carriers are restricted to the high volume routes connecting the world's busiest ports. Thirdly, ship oversupply ratios have been more pronounced among larger vessels: the yearly fleet growth rate beginning in December 2011 reached 19 per cent for Capesize and 13 per cent for Panamax vessels, while the Handysize fleet only grew by around 4 per cent during the same period.[46] Three-year time charter rates for Handysize and Panamax vessels were almost equal between January and April 2012 (table 3.4). Bearing in mind that Panamax vessels can carry about two times more than the Handysize class, this comparison underlines the weak demand for the larger vessel types.

B. FREIGHT MARKETS AND TRANSPORT COSTS

The uniqueness of freight rate patterns for bulkers, tankers and container ships can be quantified through a comparison of the maximum fluctuation of freight rate within each segment. The maximum freight rate fluctuation refers to the divisor between the highest and the lowest freight rate reported between March 2011 and April 2012. Freight rates have fluctuated most in the bulker segment, with rates being 2.17 times higher at the top level when compared with their lowest value. The two other segments appear to be much more stable, with a maximum fluctuation rate of 1.4 for tankers and 1.87 for container ships during the same period.[47]

Three major factors can trigger price fluctuations in a competitive market environment: first, the costs of running a maritime shipping business; second, to break even the freight rates must cover all incurred expenses; third, the minimum freight price range that a vessel operator is willing to accept. Two other major external factors determine the price in a fundamental way: the demand and the supply in the maritime transport market. The following sections discuss these pricing factors.

1. Maritime transport costs components

Maritime transport service providers that invest in the procurement and operation of a vessel aim at creating a profit on their capital employed. Fluctuations in the costs of buying and maintaining a vessel will impact on the freight rate a ship operator is willing to accept to ensure cost recovery and profit. A cost breakdown of the total vessel expenses allows an assessment of how each component affects freight rates and contributes to the total vessel costs. In addition, the volatility of each cost component is of importance when assessing freight rate fluctuations.

Figure 3.7 illustrates freight rate cost components for a 10,000 dwt tanker with an assumed operating life of 20 years. Fuel consumption, representing 35 per cent of total expenditures, is the largest cost factor. Crewing is the second largest, contributing 18.5 per cent, followed by port charges at 10 per cent. Most cost input factors do not appear to be subject to

Figure 3.7.   Freight rate cost components for a tanker of 10,000 dwt with 20 years of economical life

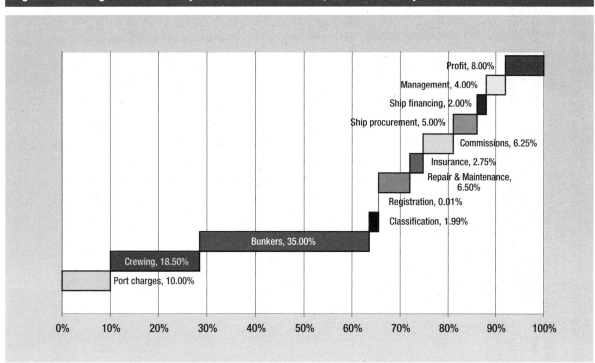

Source: Data received from a ship operator in February 2012.
Note: Figures refer to share of cost component as a percentage of total costs. Results are based on the assumption that the ship
            is staffed with a Turkish crew. Relative costs depend on many factors that may change over time.

major price fluctuations. The price of crude oil is an exception, as shown in figure 3.3, and is a major influencing factor on freight rate volatility.

2.   Maritime transport cost and revenue comparison

Based upon the information from the freight rate cost breakdown, a more comprehensive cost and revenue comparison is conducted below for the three shipping sectors and their different vessel sizes. Such an analysis allows the identification of characteristic cost structures for different vessel types and potential changes in the cost structure over time. table 3.5 illustrates the results of the calculations for 2006 and 2011.

The yearly time charter rate represents the revenue side of the analysis. The ship operating costs have been derived from a yearly survey that is based on indications from ship operators, owners and brokers for over 2,600 vessels.[48] As bunker costs and port handling charges are usually not included in the time charter rates, these expenses have also been excluded from the calculations. Assumptions have been made

for several variables influencing cost, such as ship utilization rates, interest rates or the commercial life expectancy of the ship, with the aim of obtaining a comparable dataset.[49]

Results for 2011

The results in table 3.5 illustrate the effect of economies of scale that can be reached with large scale vessels. Panamax tankers, for example, reported daily ship operating costs of $8,871 while the same expenses for the four-times-larger VLCC tanker were less than 30 per cent above this value. It can also be observed that the share of vessel procurement costs as a percentage of the total vessel costs increases with a larger vessel size. This indicator reaches 42.2 per cent for a Handysize bulker and 51.9 per cent for a Capesize carrier.

The ship profitability figures for 2011 illustrate that year's unfavourable economic environment for maritime transport service providers and show that most ship segments have had negative profitability rates. Only the bulker segment has estimated positive margins. The results also show that, in 2011, larger ship sizes mostly operated on a lower profitability rate

Table 3.5. Baltic Exchange Dry Index, 2010–2012 (Index base year 1985, 1000 points)

Ship type	Daily time charter rate in 2011, daily rate in $[a]	Costs for operations in 2011, daily in $[b]	Contribution margin I[c]	Newbuilding prices 2011, in $	Linear vessel depreciation costs, daily in $[d]	Costs for capital employed, daily in $[e]	Total vessel procurement costs, daily in $	Total costs (operations + vessel), daily in $	Percentage share, procurement costs of total vessel costs	Contribution margin II, daily in $[f]	Profitability in percent[g]	Newbuilding ship type
Tanker												
Product	13 600	8 740	4 860	36 100 000	3 956	1 978	5 934	14 674	40.4%	-1,074	-7.3%	50 000 dwt
Panamax	13 800	8 872	4 928	44 500 000	4 877	2 438	7 315	16 187	45.2%	-2,387	-14.7%	75 000 dwt
Suezmax	19 700	10 102	9 598	64 100 000	7 025	3 512	10 537	20 639	51.1%	-939	-4.5%	160 000 dwt
VLCC	24 650	11 342	13 308	101 300 000	11 101	5 551	16 652	27 994	59.5%	-3,344	-11.9%	300 000 dwt
Bulker												
Handysize	12 596	5 589	7 007	24 800 000	2 718	1 359	4 077	9 666	42.2%	2,930	30.3%	30 000 dwt
Handymax	14 888	6 318	8 570	30 000 000	3 288	1 644	4 932	11 250	43.8%	3,638	32.3%	55 000 dwt
Panamax	14 863	6 854	8 009	32 600 000	3 573	1 786	5 359	12 213	43.9%	2,650	21.7%	75 000 dwt
Capesize	16 354	7 876	8 478	51 600 000	5 655	2 827	8 482	16 358	51.9%	-4	0.0%	170 000 dwt
Container ships												
Feedermax (100–1,000 TEU)	4 250	4 656	-406	11 400 000	1 249	625	1 874	6 530	28.7%	-2,280	-34.9%	500 TEU (geared)
Container ship (1,000–2000 TEU)	9 825	5 522	4 303	27 400 000	3 003	1 501	4 504	10 026	44.9%	-201	-2.0%	1 500 TEU (geared)
Main Liner (2,000–6,000 TEU)	14 479	8 040	6 439	45 600 000	4 997	2 499	7 496	15 536	48.2%	-1,057	-6.8%	3 500 TEU (gearless)

Ship type	Daily time charter rate in 2011, daily rate in $ [a]	Costs for operations in 2006, daily costs in $ [b]	Contribution margin I [c]	Newbuilding prices 2006, in $	Linear vessel depreciation costs, daily in $ [d]	Costs for capital employed, daily in $ [e]	Total vessel procurement costs, daily in $	Total costs (opera-tions + vessel), daily in $	Percentage share, procurement costs of total vessel costs	Contribution margin II, daily in $ [f]	Profitability in percent [g]	Newbuilding ship type
Tanker												
Product	26 792	6 541	18 570	46 800 000	5 129	2 564	7 693	15 915	48.3%	10,877	68.3%	50 000 dwt
Panamax	23 225	6 640	14 879	48 000 000	5 260	2 630	7 890	16 236	48.6%	6,989	43.0%	75 000 dwt
Suezmax	42 667	7 560	33 164	75 500 000	8 274	4 137	12 411	21 914	56.6%	20,753	94.7%	160 000 dwt
VLCC	55 992	8 489	45 322	124 900 000	13 688	6 844	20 532	31 202	65.8%	24,790	79.5%	300 000 dwt
Bulker												
Handysize	15 860	4 048	10 582	22 300 000	2 444	1 222	3 666	8 944	41.0%	6,916	77.3%	30 000 dwt
Handymax	21 800	4 576	15 834	31 500 000	3 452	1 726	5 178	11 144	46.5%	10,656	95.6%	55 000 dwt
Panamax	22 475	4 964	16 003	35 700 000	3 912	1 956	5 868	12 340	47.6%	10,135	82.1%	75 000 dwt
Capesize	45 645	5 705	38 208	62 100 000	6 805	3 403	10 208	17 645	57.9%	28,000	158.7%	170 000 dwt
Container ships												
Feedermax (100-1,000 TEU)	6 871	3 567	2 499	15 800 000	1 732	866	2 597	6 969	37.3%	-98	-1.4%	500 TEU (geared)
Container ship (1,000-2000 TEU)	16 492	4 231	11 307	33 400 000	3 660	1 830	5 490	10 675	51.4%	5,817	54.5%	1 500 TEU (geared)
Main Liner (2,000-6,000 TEU)	24 233	6 160	16 684	54 500 000	5 973	2 986	8 959	16 508	54.3%	7,725	46.8%	3 500 TEU (gearless)

Sources: UNCTAD calculations. Newbuilding prices and daily time charter rates from Drewry's *Shipping Insight*. Operating cost data from Moore Stephens' report *OptCost 2011*.

a   The assumption is made that the vessel is 100 per cent utilized.

b   Based on operating cost data from Moore Stephens for the year 2010. Data for 2011 are forward projections achieved by multiplying 2010 data by the average operating cost growth rate over the last 10 years. Data for 2006 data are backward projections of the 2010 data based on Moore Stephens' operating costs index. Operating costs include crew costs, spares, repairs and maintenance, insurance and administration.

c   Contribution margin I = (one year time charter rate) – (costs for operations).

d   Depreciation costs determined on the basis of a period of 25 years depreciation.

e   Costs determined by multiplying half of the procurement costs by an assumed interest rate of 4.0 per cent.

f   Contribution margin II = (contribution margin I) – (costs for capital employed) – (vessel depreciation costs).

g   Profitability = (time charter rate / total vessel operating costs) – 1.

than smaller vessels. The reason for this is that, in 2011, the advantage of economies of scale has been offset by a pronounced oversupply of larger vessels, particularly in the bulker segment. When interpreting these numbers, it should to be taken into consideration that the calculations are based on the assumption that vessels have been 100 per cent utilized. However, among most operators utilization rates were much lower in 2011, which would translate into even lower profitability rates.

Results for 2006

The calculations for 2006 illustrate that the cost and revenue structures have changed significantly over the last five years. Freight rates have been considerably higher. The yearly time charter rate for a Capesize tanker stood at an average of $45,645 in 2006 and reached only $16,354 in 2011. Operators also benefited from lower operating costs, which demonstrated moderate and stable growth rates in the last five years. Therefore, profitability rates were much higher in 2006, varying from -1.4 per cent for Feedermax containerships to 158.7 per cent for Capesize bulkers. The promising revenue figures led to massive investment in additional tonnage, pushing up vessel prices. Hence, the share of ship procurement costs as a percentage of the total vessel expenses was considerably higher in 2006. The

indicator reached 57.9 per cent in 2006 for a Capesize bulker, in comparison to 51.9 per cent in 2011 for the same type of vessel.

Second-hand prices were exposed to even higher volatilities as there is usually no significant time gap between the ship being sold and handed over. Buyers can benefit directly from high profitability rates in a positive business environment, making them willing to accept elevated second-hand prices. A contrary effect occurs if freight rates are low: second-hand prices will then drop due to a lack of investors who are willing to operate a ship in an unprofitable market. Prices for second-hand vessels are illustrated in table 3.6. Along with freight rates, second-hand values have been exposed to losses – the price for a Capesize ship, for example, dropped from an average $54 million in 2010 to $43 million in 2011.

The calculations within this section have quantified the effect of economies of scale on freight rates. In addition, the potential fluctuations of new building costs and their impact on the overall vessel expenses have been evaluated. The figures also illustrate that ship operating costs fluctuate only moderately over time. Finally, the pronounced profitability volatility between the years observed underlines the large impact of structural changes in demand and supply on the maritime shipping

Table 3.6.	Second-hand prices, 2003–2011 (Millions of dollars, end-of-year figures)									
Type and size of vessel	2003	2004	2005	2006	2007	2008	2009	2010	2011	Percentage change 2011/2010
Oil tanker – Handy, 45 000 dwt, 5 years old	25	35	44	47	40	51	30	26	28	7.7
Oil tanker – Suezmax, 150 000 dwt, 5 years old	43	60	72	76	87	95	59	62	54	-12.9
Oil tanker – VLCC, 300 000 dwt, 5 years old	60	91	113	116	124	145	84	86	77	-10.5
Chemical tanker – 12 000 dwt, 10 years old	9	11	12	14	23	23	20	13	11	-15.4
LPG carrier – 15 000 m³, 10 years old	21	23	30	39	40	39	30	25	26	4.0
Dry bulk – Handysize, 28 000 dwt, 10 years old	10	15	20	20	28	31	17	20	17	-16.5
Dry bulk – Panamax, 75 000 dwt, 5 years old	20	35	40	39	83	70	31	25	31	24.0
Dry bulk – Capesize, 150 000 dwt, 5 years old	..	..	..	..	..	..	47	54	43	-20.4
Container – geared, 500 TEUs, 10 years old	5	7	11	10	9	13	4	6	7	16.7
Container – gearless, 2 500 TEUs, 10 years old	20	29	39	41	24	36	18	23	30	30.4
Container – gearless, 3 500 TEUs, 10 years old	25	34	43	44	43	45	24	28	34	21.4

Source: Compiled by the UNCTAD secretariat on the basis of data from Drewry's *Shipping Insight*.

business, as discussed in the following section, when commensurate demand is present.

3. Transport demand and supply

During different stages in the shipping market cycle, diverging demand and supply lead to substantial fluctuations in freight rates. It can be observed that freight rates and the volume of new ship orders often evolve in parallel. In times of high freight rates, ship owners tend to invest in new vessel capacity, this being also due to an increased willingness of banks to lend money, thus expanding the orderbook. With an increasing supply of capacity, freight rates fall and less efficient ships line up for cargo, thus reducing the industry's appetite to invest in new vessel capacity.[50] With this interplay between supply and demand in mind, this section will assess selected indicators for the two elements.

Growth rates of both supply (vessel capacity) and demand (shipped volumes) are illustrated in table 3.7. In all three segments, vessel capacity has grown faster than the seaborne trade volume. Between 2000 and 2011, bulk carrier supply expanded almost two times faster than the transport demand. In the tanker segment, this gap was even larger, with a vessel capacity increasing 2.3 times faster than the transported volume of goods. In the coming years, the dry bulk sector in particular will experience high fleet growth rates. The orderbook to current fleet

size ratio of the dry bulk segment stands at 27.8 per cent, compared with 13.1 per cent for tankers and 21.3 per cent for container ships. This will put freight rates under additional pressure within an already oversupplied bulk shipping segment.

The supply side can also be assessed through a comparison of indicators that describe the structure of the fleet. The analysis of market concentration levels, for example, reveals the degree of competition in the market, which may influence the pricing mechanism. Container shipping reaches the highest market concentration levels out of all the three segments. The 10 largest companies account for more than 50 per cent of the world's containerized shipping market. On routes to remote regions with low trade volumes in particular, this may lead to higher freight rates and less volatile price reactions to changes in transport demand. Market concentration levels are significantly lower in the bulk trade business, with the 19 largest operators sharing only 22 per cent of the world transport supply.

4. Freight costs in developing countries

Figure 3.8 shows the maritime freight costs as a percentage of the total value of imported goods. The results illustrate that although volatilities occur over time, in the long term a tendency towards a lower ratio

Table 3.7.		Comparison of maritime transport segments			
			Container ships	Bulk carriers	Tankers
Demand and supply		Ø Transport supply growth per year (2000–2011, based on fleet growth in dwt)	10.1%	6.1%	4.9%
		Ø Transport supply growth per year (2009–2011, based on fleet growth in dwt)	6.6%	12.8%	6.6%
		Ø Transport demand growth per year (2000–2011, based on tons loaded)	7.2%	3.3%	2.2%
		Ø Transport demand growth per year (2009–2011, based on tons loaded)	5.9%	6.8%	2.1%
		Ratio of orderbook to fleet size (April 2012, based on dwt)	21.3%	27.8%	13.1%
Market concentration (supply side)		Market share of the the top 3 companies	28.6%a	n.a.	11.8%b
		Market share of the the top 10 companies	50.8%a	22.0%c	26.7%b
		Market share of shipping business (2012, based on fleet capacity in dwt)	14.9%	46.9%	38.2%

Sources: Growth in transport supply, transport demand and market shares from UNCTAD's *Review of Maritime Transport 2011*; ratio of orderbook to fleet size from *Lloyd's List Intelligence*.

a   Data for 2010 from *Review of Maritime Transport 2011*, based on the number of containers shipped.

b   Data for 2008 from *Tanker Operator Annual Review March 2009*, based on fleet size in dwt.

c   Data for 2006. figure includes the 19 largest operators, based on dwt.

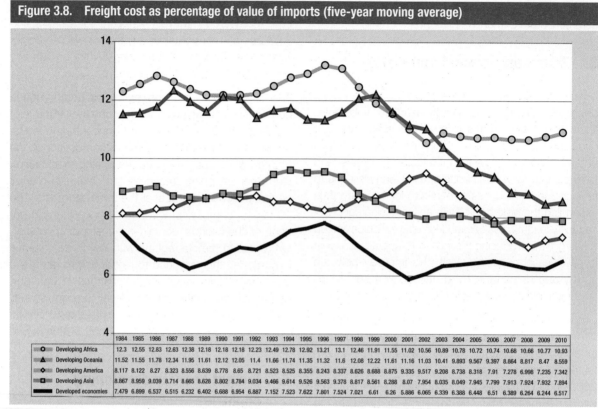

Figure 3.8.   Freight cost as percentage of value of imports (five-year moving average)

	1984	1985	1986	1987	1988	1989	1990	1991	1992	1993	1994	1995	1996	1997	1998	1999	2000	2001	2002	2003	2004	2005	2006	2007	2008	2009	2010
Developing Africa	12.3	12.55	12.83	12.63	12.38	12.18	12.18	12.18	12.23	12.49	12.78	12.92	13.21	13.1	12.46	11.91	11.55	11.02	10.56	10.89	10.78	10.72	10.74	10.68	10.66	10.77	10.93
Developing Oceania	11.52	11.55	11.78	12.34	11.95	11.61	12.12	12.05	11.4	11.66	11.74	11.35	11.32	11.6	12.08	12.22	11.61	11.16	11.03	10.41	9.893	9.567	9.397	8.864	8.817	8.47	8.559
Developing America	8.117	8.122	8.27	8.323	8.556	8.639	8.778	8.65	8.721	8.523	8.525	8.355	8.243	8.337	8.626	8.688	8.875	9.335	9.517	9.208	8.738	8.318	7.91	7.278	6.998	7.235	7.342
Developing Asia	8.867	8.959	9.039	8.714	8.665	8.628	8.802	8.784	9.034	9.466	9.614	9.526	9.563	9.378	8.817	8.561	8.288	8.07	7.954	8.035	8.049	7.945	7.799	7.913	7.924	7.932	7.894
Developed economies	7.479	6.899	6.537	6.515	6.232	6.402	6.688	6.954	6.887	7.152	7.523	7.622	7.801	7.524	7.021	6.61	6.26	5.886	6.065	6.339	6.388	6.448	6.51	6.389	6.264	6.244	6.517

Source: UNCTAD.

between freight costs and value of goods has occurred among all country groupings. Furthermore, the freight rates share of developing countries tend to converge to those of developed economies. Developing Oceania achieved a transport cost share reduction from 11.7 per cent in 1994 to 8.6 per cent in 2010, while the developing nations of America and Asia have already reached a transport cost share approximately 1 per cent above that of developed economies. An exception from this trend of convergence is developing Africa, with a stable ratio of freight costs to import value of 10.9 per cent between 2003 and 2010.

Low productivity, high charges and congestions in many African ports are some of the factors explaining these discrepancies.[51] Vessel operators tend to pass these costs on to shippers when calculating their freight rates. In addition, African ports are often difficult to access from the hinterland due to a lack of transport infrastructure.[52]

On the shipping side, the UNCTAD Liner Shipping Connectivity Index (LSCI) (see also chapter 4) reveals a lack of economies of scale and competition in many African countries. African ports cannot host the largest ships that offer the most competitive freight rates. The relatively small number of alternative operators serving

most African ports results in low competitive pressure, thus keeping freight rates high. Trade imbalances are another factor contributing to higher freight rates in Africa. With an import surplus for containerized cargo, and exports that mostly comprise bulk goods, which are transported by tankers and dry bulk carriers, vessels can often only be fully utilized on one route.[53] Consequently, ship operators have to charge a freight rate for a single trip that compensates their expenditures for both the fronthaul and the backhaul lanes.

C.   POLICY OPTIONS TO REDUCE MARITIME TRANSPORT COSTS

Transport costs remain an important component of the price of the goods when purchased by the final consumer. High maritime transport costs for imported goods impact the price level of the basket of consumer goods. Conversely, excessive freight rates for exports affect the trade competitiveness of the products of a country in the global markets. Hence, countries may want to define approaches to reduce inbound and outbound maritime transport costs in their trade with partners, as discussed below.

The freight rate cost analysis, conducted for the case of a 10,000 dwt tanker (figure 3.7), illustrates major cost elements of freight rates and can assist when identifying policy measures aimed at reducing individual cost drivers. The policy options available to a single country that could produce a substantial reduction of freight rates are, nonetheless, limited. Vessel operators can choose worldwide between many alternative suppliers when procuring the goods and services they need for their vessel operations, thus levelling comparative cost advantages of individual destinations. In most large ports, for instance, cheap fuelling services are offered and, even if these services are not provided, a ship can choose to use bunkering services at an alternative destination. If one country alone were able to offer goods and services at costs significantly below the level of other nations, these competitive advantages would probably not be reflected in the freight rate to or from that country. Hosting competitive insurance service providers, for example, will not assist a country to reduce its maritime transport costs. These cost advantages are likely to be passed on equally to the freight rates for all routes a vessel operator serves within his shipping network.

When evaluating the elements comprising freight rate costs, three major strategic options remain that countries can choose from, and by which maritime freight rates from and to that country can be influenced. Figure 3.9 summarizes these options and their potential effect on ship operating costs and freight rates.

Option 1 – developing coastal shipping

Individual countries can exercise only a limited influence on international maritime shipping, which operates as an open market with very little regulation other than relevant international rules on carrier liability, security and safety. An exception to this is coastal shipping and specifically cabotage, which lies completely within the jurisdiction of a single nation. Countries can directly influence the price level for these services through the design of ship registration requirements, industry development policies and infrastructural investments such as the development of a feeder port network.

In a market where cabotage is restricted to domestic carriers only, ship operators have no choice but to comply with the country's regulatory set up. An improvement of the ship registration requirements will therefore directly affect operating costs. The potential monetary impact has been quantified by a study of the United States Department of Transportation. It

estimates, for example, that the costs for United States-flag vessels in 2010 were around 2.7 times higher than those of foreign flag equivalents.[54]

Opening cabotage to international shipping lines is another policy option. The entrance of new market players may reduce freight rates for shippers and lead to better and more diverse services. However, most countries often give cabotage rights exclusively to domestic carriers with the aim of protecting and promoting the national shipping industry.

Another measure to support cabotage is the expansion of a country's feeder port network. This will facilitate access of traders to coastal shipping and encourage them to shift from land to maritime transport. The increased volumes may lead to higher utilization rates and lower freight rates.

Option 2 – developing port competitiveness

Countries with sea access can apply a wide range of policies that aim at increasing the operational and administrative efficiency of their port network. This includes decisions on the legal and institutional framework, the selection of an ownership model or the allocation of funds for infrastructure investments. The reforms should target all entities having a relevant role in the port, such as the landlord, regulator, operator, marketer and cargo handler, thus reducing port charges related to each function.

The negotiation of a balanced concession agreement between the terminal operator and the responsible regulatory institution is a critical element when shaping a performance-orientated port business environment. This should include appropriate incentives that promote a continuous improvement of operations, competitive price setting mechanisms and a comprehensive performance monitoring system. However, considering that port charges only constitute about 10 per cent of the total freight rate, the lever of these measures appears to be limited – according to the figures indicated in the example freight rate breakdown in figure 3.7, a reduction of port handling charges by 50 per cent would only lead to a total freight rate reduction of 5 per cent.

Option 3 – developing port hinterland connections

The first two options contain policy measures targeting directly the improvement of maritime transport chain elements. In contrast, the third option addresses other modes of transport that indirectly affect freight rates of ships through their role within the multimodal transport chain.

Inland transport linkages are the arteries of ports connecting them to regional markets. They enable ports to consolidate exports from the region and distribute imports to their final destination in the hinterland.

As an example, the port of Durban in South Africa offers more modern and extensive rail linkages than the neighbouring port of Maputo in Mozambique, thus giving it an advantage when competing for customers. Another example is the structure of the transport network within Mozambique. It offers well-developed north–south road connections, which specifically serve the transport needs within the country's territory. However, only a few east–west linkages exist that connect domestic entrepreneurs with ports along the country's long coastline, making it difficult for them to present their goods on the international markets.

Improving transport connections to and from markets in the hinterland, therefore, enables ports to attract greater cargo volumes. This does not only lead to economies of scale within the ports. It may also attract larger vessels with lower unit transport costs or more alternative maritime transport service providers.

Figure 3.9. Strategies to reduce maritime freight rates

	Three national policy related generic strategies to reduce maritime freight rates		
Strategy	1. Developing coastal shipping	2. Developing port competitiveness	3. Developing port hinterland connections
Selected field of policy making	▪ Opening cabotage to global competition or restricting it to domestic operators ▪ National ship registration policies ▪ Institutional framework (e.g. maritime authority) ▪ Investment policies and ownership model ▪ Maritime infrastructure (e.g. feeder ports)	▪ Port administration related laws and regulations ▪ Port management structures and ownership model ▪ Institutional framework (e.g. port authority) ▪ Port operations ▪ Port infrastructure (e.g. links to other modes of transport)	▪ Intermodal interface connecting port with national and regional markets (options: Rail, road, waterway and air transport) ▪ Regulatory and institutional framework for land transport modes ▪ Regional transit and transport development agreements ▪ Public private partnerships
Potential impact on freight rates	▪ The compliance with new ship registration requirements may reduce or increase operations costs ▪ Opening cabotage can increase competitive pressure thus reducing freight rates ▪ Improving coastal shipping infrastructure connects remote regions to international trade networks → modal shift to maritime transport and better economies of scale	▪ Reducing port related charges for maritime transport service providers through: a. efficiency gains in port operations and port administration b. reasonable profit margin of port operator in a more competitive business environment → Includes charges for all port functions: Landlord, regulator, operator, marketer and cargo - handler (e.g. cargo handling fees, channel fees)	▪ Improved port connectivity: a. Increases cargo handling volumes in ports → lower unit handling costs b. attracts larger ships → lower unit transport costs c. attracts new transport service providers → lower margins due to increased competition

Source: UNCTAD secretariat.

ENDNOTES

1   The purpose of the coverage of more vessel sizes within the New ConTex index is to give a more comprehensive picture of container shipping market developments. The composition of the index is described in figure 3.1.

2   Drewry (2011). Container Forecaster 4Q11 – Survival of the fittest. http://www.drewrysupplychains.com/news.php?id=108, accessed 20.02.2012.

3   *Lloyd's List* (2011). Rate hikes and capacity reductions fail to lift box freight prices. http://www.lloydslist.com/ll/sector/containers/article385705.ece, accessed 17.02.2012.

4   *Journal of Commerce* (2011). Shipping's New World, Grand Alliance to Merge Asia-Europa Services. http://www.joc.com/container-lines/new-world-grand-alliances-merge, accessed 21.02.2012.

5   *Journal of Commerce* (2011). Shipping's New World, Grand Alliance to Merge Asia-Europa Services. http://www.joc.com/container-lines/new-world-grand-alliances-merge, accessed 21.02.2012. See also *International Freight News* (2011). MSC/CMA CGM alliance will shake up Asia-Europe trade. http://www.ifw-net.com/freightpubs/ifw/article.htm?artid=20017924842&src=rss, accessed 21.02.2012.

6   Drewry (2011). Container Forecaster 4Q11 – Survival of the fittest. http://www.drewrysupplychains.com/news.php?id=108, accessed 20.02.2012.

7   *Lloyd's List* (2011). Youth trumps age for declining reefer fleet. http://www.lloydslist.com/ll/sector/dry-cargo/article173229.ece, accessed 20.02.2012.

8   *Journal of Commerce* (2011). Star Reefers Swings to $124 million Loss in 2011. http://www.joc.com/container-lines/star-reefers-swings-124-million-loss-2011, accessed 20.02.2012.

9   *Shipping Herald* (2012). Star Reefers posts USD 124m net loss. http://www.shippingherald.com/Admin/ArticleDetail/ArticleDetailsFinanceEconomy/tabid/104/ArticleID/2947/Star-Reefers-posts-USD-124m-net-loss.aspx, accessed 06.04.2012.

10 Drewry (2011). Charter rates thaw amid shifting reefer market. http://www.bairdmaritime.com/index.php?option=com_content&view=article&id=11116:charter-rates-thaw-amid-shifting-reefer-market&catid=66:container&Itemid=57, accessed 20.02.2012.

11 *Lloyd's List* (2011). Youth trumps age for declining reefer fleet. http://www.lloydslist.com/ll/sector/dry-cargo/article173229.ece, accessed 20.02.2011.

12 Drewry (2011). Charter rates thaw amid shifting reefer market. http://www.bairdmaritime.com/index.php?option=com_content&view=article&id=11116:charter-rates-thaw-amid-shifting-reefer-market&catid=66:container&Itemid=57, accessed 20.02.2011.

13 For additional information on the development of the oil price and freight rates refer to UNCTAD (2010). *Oil Prices and Maritime Freight Rates: An Empirical Investigation*. Geneva.

14 *Lloyd's List* (2012). Iran conflict rubs salt in tanker industry's wounds. http://www.lloydslist.com/ll/sector/tankers/article390597.ece, accessed 03.02.2012.

15 *Lloyd's List* (2011). Tanker Owners' Exposure to the Strait of Hormuz. http://www.lloydslist.com/ll/incoming/article388221.ece/BINARY/090112_Liz_page2.pdf, accessed 03.02.2012.

16 Steelguru (2012). Iran oil sanctions revive tanker rates around the globe. http://www.steelguru.com/middle_east_news/Iran_oil_sanctions_revive_tanker_rates_around_the_globe/254183.html, accessed 23.05.2012.

17 *Tankeroperator* (2012). VLCC spike to end. http://www.tankeroperator.com/news/todisplaynews.asp?NewsID=3446, accessed 23.05.2012.

18 *Lloyd's List* (2011). Suezmax owners resist falling West Africa rates. http://www.lloydslist.com/ll/sector/tankers/article381146.ece, accessed 29.02.2012.

19 United Nations (2012). Piracy threatens West Africa oil expansion. http://www.google.com/hostednews/afp/article/ALeqM5hOMaiSYBW6-AW085d3tYMhMc8KCQ?docId=CNG.ac1da1d635b0d9e3fc331f672dc85b9d.4c1, accessed 29.02.2012.

20 One Earth Future Foundation (2011). The Economic Cost of Somali Piracy. http://oceansbeyondpiracy.org/sites/default/files/economic_cost_of_piracy_2011.pdf, accessed 12.06.2012.

21 One Earth Future Foundation (2010). The Economic Cost of Maritime Piracy. http://oneearthfuture.org/images/imagefiles/The%20Economic%20Cost%20of%20Piracy%20Full%20Report.pdf, accessed 12.06.2012. The figures only include cots for ransoms, insurances, rerouting and security equipment.

22 United Nations (2012). Gulf of Guinea needs regional anti-piracy strategy, UN official stresses. http://www.un.org/apps/news/story.asp?NewsID=41390&Cr=gulf+of+guinea, accessed 29.02.2012.

23   *GCaptain* (2011). Stability to help boost Mediterranean tanker market. http://gcaptain.com/stability-libya-boost-mediterranean/?30212#, accessed 03.01.2012.

24   *Hellenic Shipping News* (2011). Tanker Market: Modest demand growth and continued oversupply sets the scene. http://www.hellenicshippingnews.com/News.aspx?ElementId=fc2b1429-a5fa-4526-af80-4d11456bd89c, accessed 03.01.2012.

25   *Market Watch* (2011). Hess shutting St. Croix refinery due to losses. http://www.marketwatch.com/story/hess-shutting-st-croix-refinery-due-to-losses-2012-01-18, accessed 03.02.2012.

26   *Lloyd's List* (2012). St Croix refinery closure opens doors for product tankers. http://www.lloydslist.com/ll/sector/tankers/article391040.ece, accessed 23.05.2012.

27   *Lloyd's List* (2011). China must further boss tanker fleet to meet expanding refining capacity. http://www.lloydslist.com/ll/sector/tankers/article375538.ece, accessed 28.02.2012.

28   *Hellenic Shipping News* (2011). Tanker oversupply to hurt larger ships the most says analyst. http://www.hellenicshippingnews.com/News.aspx?ElementId=f5a1616d-b41c-4d97-9619-aab73c890c75, accessed 27.02.2012.

29   Clarkson Research Services Limited (2012). Dry Bulk Trade Outlook from February 2012, p. 2.

30   Lorentzen & Stemoco (2011). Weekly 33.2011. http://www.lorstem.com/Global/Weekly%20reports/Report%2033-2011.pdf, accessed 14.03.2012.

31   *Lloyd's List* (2011). Largest overnight capesize rate drop in two months. http://www.lloydslist.com/ll/sector/dry-cargo/article387492.ece?service=print, accessed 14.03.2012.

32   Lorentzen & Stemoco (2011). Weekly 33.2011. http://www.lorstem.com/Global/Weekly%20reports/Report%2033-2011.pdf, accessed 14.03.2011.

33   *Fish Info & Services* (2011). Capesize freight rates hit the floor. http://www.freightinvestorservices.com/inc/docs/upload/FISUpdateFeb11.pdf, accessed 03.04.2012.

34   *Index Mundi* (2012). Iron ore Monthly price. http://www.indexmundi.com/commodities/?commodity=iron-ore&months=60, accessed 04.04.2012.

35   *Index Mundi* (2012). Coal, Australian thermal coal monthly price. http://www.indexmundi.com/commodities/?commodity=coal-australian&months=60, accessed 04.04.2012.

36   *Fish Info & Services* (2011). Capesize freight rates hit the floor. http://www.freightinvestorservices.com/inc/docs/upload/FISUpdateFeb11.pdf, accessed 03.04.2012.

37   Clarkson (2012). *Dry Bulk Trade Outlook*. 18(2). February 2012.

38   *Lloyd's List* (2012). Size of Capesize ships set to explode. http://www.lloydslist.com/ll/sector/dry-cargo/article393401.ece, accessed 03.04.2012.

39   *Lloyd's List* (2012). Panamax period charters stall. http://www.lloydslist.com/ll/sector/dry-cargo/article391339.ece, accessed 15.03.2012.

40   Clarkson (2010–2012). *Dry Bulk Trade Outlook*. Various issues.

41   *Lloyd's List* (2012). Weak European coal demand sees Atlantic and Pacific rates diverge. http://www.lloydslist.com/ll/sector/dry-cargo/article392634.ece, accessed 15.03.2012.

42   *IHS Fairplay* (2012). Panamax rates keep sliding. http://www.fairplay.co.uk/login.aspx?reason=denied_empty&script_name=/secure/display.aspx&path_info=/secure/display.aspx&articlename=dn0020120516000001, accessed 30.05.2012.

43   GLG Research (2007). Supramax market better protected than larger cousins. https://www.hightable.com/maritime-and-shipping/insight/supramax-market-better-protected-than-larger-cousins-12957, accessed 05.04.2012.

44   *Lloyd's List* (2011). Bigger Supramaxes steal market share. http://www.lloydslist.com/ll/sector/dry-cargo/article359304.ece, accessed 05.04.2012.

45   Drewry (2012). *Shipping Insight*. Various issues.

46   Clarkson (2011). *Dry Bulk Trade Outlook*. December 2011.

47   Figures based on the analysis of the New ConTex index for containerships, the Baltic Exchange Dry Bulk Index for bulkers and the monthly figures of the Baltic Exchange Dirty Tanker Index for tankers. Period evaluated: 28.03.2011–01.04.2012.

48   Data from study conducted by Moore Stephens in 2011 based on data from over 2,600 vessels. http://www.moorestephens.gr/images/OpCost_Seminar.pdf, accessed 09.05.2012.

49   All assumptions are listed in the notes of figure 6.5.

50   Stopford M (2006). *Maritime Economics*. Routledge. Oxford. p. 43.

51   World Bank (2012). Why Does Cargo Spend Weeks in Sub-Saharan African Ports? Washington DC.

52   World Bank (2007). Port and Maritime Transport Challenges in West and Central Africa. Washington DC.

53   World Bank (2007). Port and Maritime Transport Challenges in West and Central Africa. Washington DC.

54   United States Department of Transportation (2011). Comparison of U.S. and Foreign-Flag Operating Costs. http://www.marad.dot.gov/documents/Comparison_of_US_and_Foreign_Flag_Operating_Costs.pdf, accessed 24.04.2012.

4
PORT DEVELOPMENTS

World container port throughput increased by an estimated 5.9 per cent to 572.8 million 20-foot equivalent units (TEUs) in 2011, its highest level ever. This increase was lower than the 14.5 per cent increase of 2010 that was itself a sharp rebound from the slump of 2009. Chinese mainland ports maintained their share of total world container port throughput at 24.2 per cent.

The UNCTAD Liner Shipping Connectivity Index (LSCI) showed a continuation in 2012 of the trend towards larger ships deployed by a smaller number of companies. Between 2011 and 2012, the number of companies providing services per country went down by 4.5 per cent, while the average size of the largest container ships increased by 11.5 per cent. Only 17.7 per cent of country pairs are served by direct liner shipping connections; for the remaining country pairs at least one trans-shipment port is required.

This chapter covers container port throughput, liner shipping connectivity and some of the major port-development projects underway in developing countries. It also assesses how recent trends in ship enlargement may impact ports.

A. PORT THROUGHPUT

Port throughput is usually measured in tons and by cargo type (for example, liquid or dry cargo). Liquid cargo is usually measured in tons or sometimes, in the case of oil, in barrels. Within the dry cargo sector there is bulk (coal, grain, iron ore, and the like) and break bulk (for example, general cargo, timber and containers). The dry cargo sector represents around two-thirds of world seaborne trade. Approximately 25 per cent of the dry cargo sector relates specifically to the five major bulks (coal, grain, iron ore, phosphates and bauxite/alumina) and approximately 40 per cent is other dry cargo. These other dry cargoes (for example, timber, outsized cargo) are carried in general cargo vessels and by container ships. Around 17 per cent of world seaborne trade relates specifically to container trade. The potential for container trade to continue increasing its share of the dry cargo sector is therefore a real possibility. The goods that are shipped in containers represent a variety of products ranging from scrap waste, raw materials and semi-manufactured goods to finished products ready for consumption. The container is popular because it is practical, versatile, ubiquitous and well understood. The standardization of cargo packaging and handling has other benefits, such as ease of movement between modes and reductions in cargo handling time and costs. The share of container cargo within a country's break-bulk trade could also serve as a barometer of how well a country is integrated into the international trade arena. This chapter therefore pays particular attention to developments in container shipping and container ports.

1. Container ports

Container-port throughput is measured in terms of TEUs. It is one of the few units which enable port activity to be compared globally. The latest figures available for world container-port traffic can be seen in table 4.1. Seventy-five developing countries and economies in transition with an annual national throughput of over 100,000 TEUs are listed. (Annex IV shows port throughput figures for 127 countries). In 2010, the container throughput for developing economies grew by an estimated 15.8 per cent to 376.7 million TEUs. This growth is a turnaround in the sharp decline of the previous year that was largely a direct response to businesses reducing their inventories in light of uncertainties surrounding the global economic crisis. The growth rate for container throughput in developing

economies for 2011 is estimated at 6.8 per cent, signifying a return to previous year-on-year growth levels. Developing economies' share of world throughput continues to remain virtually unchanged at approximately 70 per cent. Out of the 75 developing economies and economies in transition listed in table 4.1, only 10 experienced negative growth in port throughput in 2010, signalling that there have not been any sustained affects on container ports as a result of the global economic crisis. Of the top 10 developing countries and countries in transition, nine are located in Asia. Sixteen of the top 20 countries are also in Asia, while two are in Central and South America and two in Africa. The dominance of Asia in container port throughput signifies the importance of the region in producing exports. The 10 countries registering the highest growth were Morocco (68.5 per cent), the Russian Federation (32.6 per cent), Mexico (28.5 per cent), Panama (28.5 per cent), Ukraine (27.7 per cent), Georgia (24.5 per cent), Peru (24.4 per cent), Argentina (24.1 per cent), Brazil (23.5 per cent) and Turkey (22.7 per cent). The country with the largest share of container throughput continues to be China, with eight of its ports amongst the top 20. Chinese ports, excluding Hong Kong (China), experienced a positive growth of 19.4 per cent in 2010 to reach 128.9 million TEUs. Preliminary figures for 2011 show a reduced growth for Chinese port throughput to around 7.3 per cent, at 138.4 million TEUs. Chinese ports, with the exception of Hong Kong (China) and Taiwan, Province of China, accounted for around 25.8 per cent of world container throughput in 2011, down from 27.4 per cent in the previous year. The reduction of Chinese ports' share in world container throughput also corresponds to a reduction in Chinese imports of some raw materials, such as iron ore and thermal coal.[1] In order to boost imports and achieve a more balanced trade with trading partners, China announced in 2012 a series of reductions on import taxes for certain goods.[2] This move could translate into increased manufacture of goods for export, if these are not consumed domestically, and thus help increase container throughput (a more detailed account of international trade demand and supply is given in chapter 1).

Table 4.2 shows the world's 20 leading container ports for the period 2009–2011. The top 20 container ports accounted for approximately 52 per cent of world container port throughput in 2011. Combined, these ports showed a 7.8 per cent increase in throughput in 2011, down from a 15.2 per cent increase in

Table 4.1. Container port throughput for 75 developing countries and economies in transition for years 2009, 2010 and 2011 (TEUs)

Country	2009	2010	Preliminary figures for 2011[a]	Percentage change 2010–2009	Percentage change 2011–2010
China	107 963 180	128 929 895	138 391 031	19.42	7.34
Singapore	26 592 800	29 178 500	30 722 470	9.72	5.29
China, Hong Kong SAR	21 040 096	23 699 242	24 404 000	12.64	2.97
Republic of Korea	15 699 161	18 537 801	20 809 210	18.08	12.25
Malaysia	15 859 938	18 244 650	19 808 658	15.04	8.57
United Arab Emirates	14 425 039	15 174 023	16 752 724	5.19	10.40
China, Taiwan Province of	11 352 097	12 501 107	13 463 919	10.12	7.70
India	8 011 810	9 752 908	9 951 310	21.73	2.03
Indonesia	7 243 557	8 371 058	8 884 888	15.57	6.14
Brazil	6 574 617	8 121 324	8 597 733	23.53	5.87
Thailand	5 897 935	6 648 532	7 170 500	12.73	7.85
Egypt	6 250 443	6 709 053	6 556 189	7.34	-2.28
Panama	4 597 112	5 906 056	6 534 265	28.47	10.64
Viet Nam	4 936 598	5 983 583	*6 282 762*	21.21	*5.00*
Turkey	4 521 713	5 547 447	5 998 820	22.68	8.14
Saudi Arabia	4 430 676	5 313 141	5 694 538	19.92	7.18
Philippines	4 306 941	4 946 882	5 230 909	14.86	5.74
Sri Lanka	3 464 297	4 000 000	*4 200 000*	15.46	*5.00*
Oman	3 768 045	3 893 198	4 089 760	3.32	5.05
South Africa	3 726 313	3 806 427	3 924 059	2.15	3.09
Mexico	2 874 290	3 693 949	3 878 646	28.52	5.00
Russian Federation	2 360 625	3 129 973	3 692 719	32.59	17.98
Chile	2 795 989	3 171 950	3 387 348	13.45	6.79
Iran (Islamic Republic of)	2 206 476	2 592 522	*2 722 148*	17.50	*5.00*
Colombia	2 056 747	2 443 786	*2 565 975*	18.82	*5.00*
Pakistan	2 058 056	2 149 000	*2 256 450*	4.42	*5.00*
Morocco	1 222 000	2 058 430	*2 161 352*	68.45	*5.00*
Argentina	1 626 351	2 018 424	*2 119 345*	24.11	*5.00*
Jamaica	1 689 670	1 891 770	*1 986 359*	11.96	*5.00*
Peru	1 232 849	1 533 809	*1 610 499*	24.41	*5.00*
Dominican Republic	1 263 456	1 382 601	*1 451 731*	9.43	*5.00*
Bangladesh	1 182 121	1 356 099	*1 423 904*	14.72	*5.00*
Ecuador	1 000 895	1 221 849	*1 282 941*	22.08	*5.00*
Venezuela (Bolivarian Republic of)	1 238 717	1 216 208	*1 277 018*	-1.82	*5.00*
Bahamas	1 297 000	1 125 000	*1 181 250*	-13.26	*5.00*
Costa Rica	875 687	1 013 483	*1 064 157*	15.74	*5.00*
Guatemala	906 326	1 012 360	*1 062 978*	11.70	*5.00*
Lebanon	994 601	949 155	1 034 249	-4.57	8.97
Kuwait	854 044	888 206	*932 616*	4.00	*5.00*
Kenya	618 816	696 000	*730 800*	12.47	*5.00*
Uruguay	588 410	671 952	*705 550*	14.20	*5.00*
Ukraine	516 698	659 541	692 069	27.65	4.93
Syrian Arab Republic	685 299	649 005	*681 455*	-5.30	*5.00*
Honduras	571 720	619 867	*650 860*	8.42	*5.00*
Jordan	674 525	619 000	*649 950*	-8.23	*5.00*
Côte d'Ivoire	677 029	607 730	*638 117*	-10.24	*5.00*
Djibouti	519 500	600 000	*630 000*	15.50	*5.00*
Trinidad and Tobago	567 183	573 217	*601 878*	1.06	*5.00*

Table 4.1.   Container port throughput for 75 developing countries and economies in transition for years 2009, 2010 and 2011 (TEUs) (continued)

Country	2009	2010	Preliminary figures for 2011[a]	Percentage change 2010–2009	Percentage change 2011–2010
Ghana	493 958	513 716	*539 402*	*4.00*	*5.00*
Tunisia	418 880	466 375	*489 693*	11.34	*5.00*
Sudan	431 232	439 100	*461 055*	1.82	*5.00*
United Republic of Tanzania	370 401	426 847	*448 189*	15.24	*5.00*
Mauritius	406 862	444 778	439 695	9.32	-1.14
Yemen	382 445	370 382	*388 901*	-3.15	*5.00*
Senegal	331 076	349 231	*366 693*	5.48	*5.00*
Qatar	410 000	346 000	*363 300*	-15.61	*5.00*
Congo	285 690	297 118	*311 973*	*4.00*	*5.00*
Bahrain	279 799	289 956	*304 454*	3.63	*5.00*
Benin	267 000	277 680	*291 564*	*4.00*	*5.00*
Papua New Guinea	262 209	268 649	283 839	2.46	5.65
Algeria	247 986	265 628	*278 910*	7.11	*5.00*
Cameroon	240 300	249 912	*262 408*	*4.00*	*5.00*
Cuba	283 910	228 346	246 773	-19.57	8.07
Georgia	181 613	226 115	*237 421*	24.50	*5.00*
Cambodia	207 577	224 206	*235 416*	8.01	*5.00*
Mozambique	214 701	223 289	*234 453*	*4.00*	*5.00*
Guam	157 096	183 214	*192 375*	16.63	*5.00*
Myanmar	160 200	166 608	*174 938*	*4.00*	*5.00*
Libya	155 596	161 820	*169 911*	*4.00*	*5.00*
El Salvador	126 369	145 774	*153 063*	15.36	*5.00*
Madagascar	132 278	141 093	*148 148*	6.66	*5.00*
Croatia	130 740	137 048	*143 900*	4.82	*5.00*
Gabon	130 758	135 988	*142 788*	*4.00*	*5.00*
Aruba	125 000	130 000	*136 500*	*4.00*	*5.00*
Namibia	265 663	256 319	107 606	-3.52	-58.02
Subtotal	322 916 789	373 174 905	398 093 478	15.56	6.68
Other reported[b]	2 314 458	3 514 451	4 247 444	51.85	20.86
Total reported	325 231 247	376 689 356	402 340 923	15.82	6.81
World total	472 273 661	540 693 119	572 834 421	14.49	5.94

Sources: UNCTAD secretariat, derived from information contained in Containerisation International Online (May 2012), from various Dynamar B.V. publications and from information obtained by the UNCTAD secretariat directly from terminal and port authorities.

[a]   In this list, Singapore includes the port of Jurong.

[b]   The term other reported refers to countries for which fewer than 100,000 TEUs per year were reported. Notes: Many figures, especially for 2011, are estimates (these figures are highlighted in italics). Port throughput figures tend not to be disclosed by ports until a considerable time after the end of the calendar year. Country totals may conceal the fact that minor ports may not be included; therefore, in some cases, the actual figures may be higher than those given.

2010. The list includes 15 ports from developing economies, all of which are in Asia; the remaining five ports are from developed countries, three of which are located in Europe and two in North America. In 2011, 15 of the ports maintained the same ranking as in the previous year, with all of the top 13 maintaining exactly the same position. One North American port (New York and New Jersey) fell out of the top 20 and was replaced by one Asian port (Dalian). Shanghai maintained its top position, widening the gap between itself and the second in position, Singapore, from

600,000 to 1.7 million TEUs. The entry into the top 20 container ports of Dalian comes on the back of a 22 per cent growth in throughput, the highest in the top 20. The ports of Antwerp and Hamburg swapped places, with the latter taking the lead on the back of a 14.2 per cent increase against the former's 2.3 per cent growth. Long Beach moved down two places from eighteenth to twentieth position as container throughput contracted by 3.2 per cent, the only port in the top 20 to experience a negative growth. Xiamen moved up one place from nineteenth to eighteenth

Table 4.2.	Top 20 container terminals and their throughput for 2009, 2010 and 2011 (In TEUs and percentage change)				
Port Name	2009	2010	Preliminary figures for 2011	Percentage change 2010–2009	Percentage change 2011–2010
Shanghai	25 002 000	29 069 000	31 700 000	16.27	9.05
Singapore	25 866 400	28 431 100	29 937 700	9.92	5.30
Hong Kong	21 040 096	23 699 242	24 404 000	12.64	2.97
Shenzhen	18 250 100	22 509 700	22 569 800	23.34	0.27
Busan	11 954 861	14 194 334	16 184 706	18.73	14.02
Ningbo	10 502 800	13 144 000	14 686 200	25.15	11.73
Guangzhou	11 190 000	12 550 000	14 400 000	12.15	14.74
Qingdao	10 260 000	12 012 000	13 020 000	17.08	8.39
Dubai	11 124 082	11 600 000	13 000 000	4.28	12.07
Rotterdam	9 743 290	11 145 804	11 900 000	14.39	6.77
Tianjin	8 700 000	10 080 000	11 500 000	15.86	14.09
Kaohsiung	8 581 273	9 181 211	9 636 289	6.99	4.96
Port Klang	7 309 779	8 871 745	9 377 434	21.37	5.70
Hamburg	7 007 704	7 900 000	9 021 800	12.73	14.20
Antwerp	7 309 639	8 468 475	8 664 243	15.85	2.31
Los Angeles	6 748 994	7 831 902	7 940 511	16.05	1.39
Tanjung Pelepas	6 016 452	6 530 000	7 500 000	8.54	14.85
Xiamen	4 680 355	5 820 000	6 460 700	24.35	11.01
Dalian	4 552 000	5 242 000	6 400 000	15.16	22.09
Long Beach	5 067 597	6 263 399	6 061 085	23.60	-3.23
Total top 20	220 907 422	254 543 912	274 364 468	15.23	7.79

Source: UNCTAD secretariat and *Containerisation International Online* (May 2012).
Note: In this list Singapore does not include the port of Jurong.

position with a growth of 11 per cent. The overall picture that emerges is that most of the demand and growth for container ports is still firmly in Asia. This signals greater intraregional trade in Asia and the importance of the region as a centre of international trade.

2. Liner shipping connectivity

Components of liner shipping connectivity

As regards the deployment of container ships by liner shipping companies, the year 2012 saw a continuation of trends already observed in previous years, that is, an increase in ship sizes and carrying capacity, and a decrease in the level of competition. Between mid-2004 and May 2012, the average number of companies deploying container ships on services from and to coastal countries' seaports decreased from 22 to 17, a decline of 23 per cent. During the same period, the size of the largest vessels deployed continuously increased, from an average vessel maximum of 2,812 TEUs in 2004 to 5,452 TEUs in 2012, an increase of 94 per cent (see figure 4.1). As vessel sizes have increased faster than the available

volume of cargo, there is less space for liner shipping companies in each market, and the average number of companies is consequently decreasing.

Figure 4.2 illustrates another aspect of this trend. The country average of the total TEU carrying capacity increased by 82 per cent between 2004 and 2012, while the number of ships has remained almost constant. Using larger ships, the growing seaborne containerized trade can be transported without the need to increase vessel numbers.

Developing-country connections

Globally, the best-connected country continues to be China. In May 2012, there were 1,765 container ships deployed on liner shipping services to and from Chinese ports, with a total carrying capacity of 8.96 million TEUs; 75 companies operated ships on these services, the largest vessel having a capacity of 15,550 TEUs.[3]

The best-connected country in Latin America is Panama, with 23 companies deploying 342 ships with a total carrying capacity of 1.28 million TEUs, followed by Brazil, with 937,000 TEUs. The position

Figure 4.1. Trends in container-ship fleet deployment: number of companies and size of the largest ships deployed (Averages per country, midyear estimates)

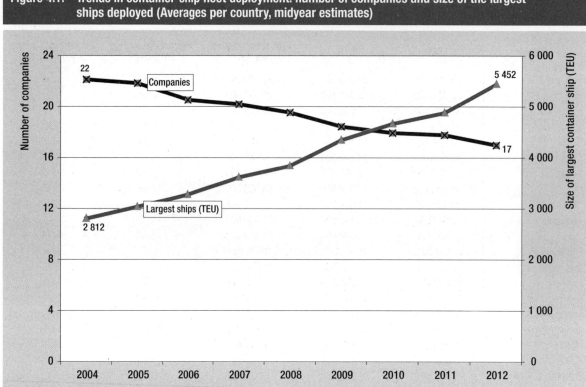

Source: Calculations by the UNCTAD secretariat, on the basis of data supplied by *Lloyd's List Intelligence*.

Figure 4.2. Trends in container-ship fleet deployment: number of ships and their total TEU carrying capacity (Averages per country, midyear estimates)

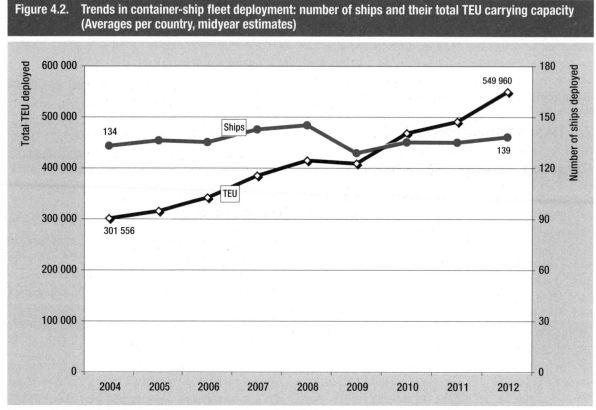

Source: Calculations by the UNCTAD secretariat on the basis of data supplied by *Lloyd's List Intelligence*.

of Panama as a hub in Latin America is made evident by the large number of ships deployed on routes from Panama to China (147 container ships), to the United States (182 ships) and to Colombia (127 ships).

In Africa, the geographical positions of Egypt, Morocco and South Africa at the nodes of the global liner shipping networks contribute to these countries' highest connectivity for this continent. There are more companies that provide services between South Africa and Singapore (15 companies), China (14) and Malaysia (13) than for intra-African connections. For example, there are only eight companies that connect South Africa with Benin and Nigeria.

In South Asia, ports in Sri Lanka cater for larger container ships than ports in India, and the total TEU capacity deployed from and to Sri Lanka (1.14 million TEUs) is higher than the TEU deployed from and to Indian ports (1.06 million TEUs). Singapore and Malaysia are the best-connected countries in South-East Asia, with 5.28 million and 4.21 million TEUs capacity deployed, respectively.

Comparing different regions, the densest network of liner shipping services is within Asia. There are 794 container ships deployed on regular services between China and the Republic of Korea, 718 between China and Singapore, and 600 between China and Malaysia. This compares to just 440 ships deployed between China and the United States, and 111 ships between the United States and Germany.

Characteristics of the global network

An analysis of the structure of the global liner shipping network shows that only 17.7 per cent of country pairs are served by direct liner shipping connections.[4] For the remaining country pairs, at least one trans-shipment is required.

Interestingly, at least in theory (potentially competing shipping companies and ports would need to cooperate) 62.2 per cent of pairs of countries could be connected with only one trans-shipment (for example, Chile to Suriname via Jamaica). Only for 19.9 per cent of country pairs is a second trans-shipment needed; for example, to move a container from Cambodia to Namibia is possible via Singapore and South Africa. A third trans-shipment is required for only 0.2 per cent of country pairs; an example of the latter would be containerized trade between Tuvalu and the Democratic Republic of the Congo via New Zealand, Belgium and the Republic of the Congo. While it is

difficult to envisage demand for a containerized trade transaction between these two countries, thanks to the global liner shipping network and trans-shipment ports, it would be possible.

B. RECENT PORT DEVELOPMENTS

Port developments continue throughout the world at an uneven pace spurred on by national needs to import and export and a chance to seize a share of growing world seaborne trade through trans-shipment opportunities. The following sections are a brief overview of some of these developments organized alphabetically. The list is not exhaustive and the ports mentioned are merely meant to give regional perspective as well as illustrate the variety and type of developments. Other developments mentioned in previous issues of the *Review of Maritime Transport* continue at their pace. Virtually every port or government has a development plan or is presently engaged in infrastructure improvements.

In Cameroon, work continues on the development of the Kribi port complex. The port will enable subregional integration through the Kribi–Bangui (the Central African Republic)–Kasangani (the Democratic Republic of the Congo) transport and development corridor.[5] The port, which is being built as the main export point for oil pumped from Chad via pipeline, will also handle containerised cargo and cargo for Cameroon's mining sector, such as bauxite, iron, nickel and cobalt.

In China, port developments continue at a seemingly relentless pace. The port of Xiamen is planning to invest some RMB 14 billion ($2.2 billion) on upgrading its facilities over the next few years. This is in addition to the $705 million spent to open the new container terminal – Xiamen Ocean Gate Container Terminal – in 2011.[6] For Ningbo-Zhoushan port, plans were announced to build two iron-ore berths of 300,000–400,000 deadweight ton (dwt) capacity, one 100,000 dwt berth and two 50,000 dwt berths. The project, which will cost an estimated of RMB 4.91 billion ($774 million) will give the port a combined handling capacity of 52 million tons of iron ore per year.[7] This suggests that the recent declines in the import of iron ore by Chinese ports is not envisaged to persist into the long term.

In Costa Rica, the Government approved a 33-year concession agreement with APM Terminals (APMT) to construct and operate the Caribbean port at Moin. Located 10 hours sailing time from the Panama Canal, the construction is set to be completed by the end of 2016 and cost $992 million. When complete the port will have an along-side depth of 16 metres and be able to serve the current maximum container vessels.[8] It will be able to attract new clients by accommodating some of the passing traffic transiting the Panama Canal.

In France, the ports of Le Havre, Rouen and Paris, which share access to the River Seine, joined together to form a new entity named HAROPA. The new entity aims to win back some of the trade lost in 2011 due to strikes by port workers in response to nation-wide port reforms. This concept enables synergies in pricing and marketing and if successful could be a concept which may be adopted by other ports in other regions.

In Georgia, transfer of the operations of the Black Sea port of Poti from Ras Al Khaimah Investment Authority (RAKIA), a sovereign wealth fund of the United Arab Emirates, to APMT resulted in the retrenchment of 386 employees, almost one quarter of its labour force. Management of the port had been acquired by RAKIA in 2008, but the company had failed to stimulate local trade through the port.[9] This example illustrates the importance of import/export traffic to a port's success.

In Germany, the port of Wilhelmshaven partially opened for business in 2012. The port has experienced various challenges including, on the operational side, the provision of tug services and, on the infrastructure side, cracks in the quay and weak rail track foundations. The port, which has a depth of 18 metres, is able to serve the world's largest container ships, such as Maersk's Triple E-class vessels. To attract new business the port's management is reportedly offering a 70 per cent rebate on its standard tariff of €0.32 per ton on all ships until December 2013, after which the rebate reduces to 50 per cent until 2018. In addition, the fees payable are only applicable for the first 145,000 tons. This means that, for example, Maersk's E-class vessel the 170,794 gross tonnage (GT) M/V *Emma Maersk* (15,500 TEUs), would pay just €14,000 per call instead of €46,400.[10] Such pricing strategies could also be offered by other ports in order to stimulate demand.

In India, the State of Gujarat has finalized plans for the development of new ports at Dahej, Nargol, Vansi Borsi and Kutchhigarh, which are to be undertaken using public–private partnership (PPP). Plans to develop ports at Dholera and Khambhat have been put on hold in view of the Kalpasar project, which aims to build a dam over the Gulf of Khambhat to establish a huge fresh-water reservoir. These port developments serve to illustrate that the Government of India is committed to undertaking improvements to its transport infrastructure. However, the task is huge and for only 82 of the estimated 276 port projects identified by the government in the past five years has construction commenced, while only 25 have seen completion.[11]

In Indonesia, Perlindo II, the state-owned port operator and port authority, was given permission by the Government to start the construction of Kalibaru port. Phase one of the new port construction will see container-handling capacity of 1.5 million TEUs come online in early 2014, followed by further construction of two more terminals, bringing the total capacity of the port to 4 million TEUs.[12] This development is important for a country which is seeing an average gross domestic product (GDP) growth rate of 6 per cent per year since 2008 and a growing per capita income of $3,000.[13]

In the Democratic People's Republic of Korea, plans were announced to develop the port of Rason in the north-east of the country. Details of the plans are vague but refer to refurbishing three piers, developing an airport, a power station and the construction a 34-mile cross-border railroad linking the port to the Chinese north-eastern city of Tumen.[14] The agreement involves a 45–50 year concession and the $3 billion investment is coming from China.[15] The area around Rason will be a Special Economic Zone. Elsewhere in the country, similar plans are afoot to develop Wihwa Islands located in the north-west and across the Yalu River from the Chinese city of Dandong. Increasing trade between the Democratic People's Republic of Korea and its neighbours allows for greater opportunities and backward linkages into the national economy, which may help raise the country's GDP and living standards.

In Liberia, negotiations with a Dutch dredging company are near completion that will enable better utilization of a previous concession agreement signed between the Government and APMT to develop the port of Monrovia. In 2010, APMT signed a 25-year concession agreement to operate the port and invest $125 million in rebuilding the damaged marginal wharf and improve the port infrastructure.[16] This will help improve market access for both importers and exports and may lead to lower transport costs.

In Morocco, the newly operational container port Tanger Med II is continuing to expand its container capacity with third and fourth terminals, scheduled to be operational in 2015/16. The new terminals will increase the port's capacity to 5 million TEUs per annum. In 2012, Renault opened a new vehicle assembly plant near the port that is expected to boost traffic. This marks a good opportunity for the port, which experienced a labour strike in 2011 over stevedore pay and conditions that then contributed to a reduction in cargo volumes at the port during the later part of 2011 and into 2012. A year-on-year comparison shows that throughput during the first quarter of 2012 was 30 per cent lower than in 2011.[17]

In Nigeria, the Nigerian Ports Authority (NPA) announced plans to develop two new deepwater ports at Lekki, in Lagos State, and Ibaka, near the city of Uyo in Akwa Ibom. The Ibaka port development project is expected to create thousands of jobs.[18] The Lekki port, which will consist of liquid, dry bulk and container terminals, is estimated to have a final capacity of 2.5 million TEUs. The port of Lagos will also benefit from a $124.4 million redevelopment project at the so-called Bull Nose area of Lagos port. The work includes the construction and operation of an oil and gas facility on a 20-year concession basis.[19]

In South Africa, Transnet Port Terminals (TPT) announced plans to spend R 33 billion ($4.2 billion) over seven years on capital expenditure to encourage economic growth and improve efficiencies. The areas marked for investment include container port development at Durban and Ngqura, iron ore bulk facilities at Saldanha, and the creation of additional manganese capacity by relocating cargo from Port Elizabeth to a newly created two-berth manganese facility at the Port of Ngqura. The port of Richards Bay will also receive mobile equipment, quayside equipment and weighbridges, and will be re-engineered to create additional capacity for bulk products.[20] The Port of Ngqura, located just outside Port Elizabeth, officially opened in 2012 after 12 years in construction. The R 10 billion ($1.3 billion) facility upon completion will include four container berths, a liquefied natural gas (LNG) facility and a bulk and break bulk berth. The port has been partially open since the end of 2009 and currently handles around 0.5 million TEUs.[21] Together, these developments help to mark the ascendance of South Africa as one of the world's emerging economies, as described in various press articles under the acronym BRICS (Brazil, Russian Federation, India, China and South Africa).

In Ukraine, the Government gave approval for a new port to be built at Lake Donuzlav in the Crimea. The location is in an area free of ice all year round, has a natural depth of 25 metres and is directly accessible to the Black Sea. The new facilities will focus upon providing ferry, general cargo and container services. The agreement, said to be worth $1.2 billion, was reached between the Ukraine Government and China National Technical Import and Export Corporation (CNTIC).[22] The port will facilitate direct access for trade between Ukraine and Asia.

In the United Kingdom, the Olympic Games and the associated preparation have increased congestion around London resulting in the revival of barge traffic along the River Thames. Two barges normally used for transporting non-containerized cargo on the Thames were deployed from Tilbury to Northumberland wharf – a few kilometres from the Olympic village – to carry 48 40-foot equivalent units (FEUs). If successful, the service could be extended further west along the Thames to Fulham, Battersea or Wandsworth.[23] Elsewhere in the country, barge traffic is also making a comeback, for example between the cities of Liverpool and Manchester.[24] Together, these developments may mark the start of a shift to a more sustainable freight transport.

In the United States, the port of Long Beach is set to invest around $4 billion over the next decade to upgrade its facilities. The project includes, amongst others, $1.2 billion for the upgrading of existing terminals to handle containers and provide rail access, $950 million to replace a bridge providing access to the port, and $650 million for the construction of a new container terminal.[25] The port of New York/New Jersey revealed plans to develop a terminal of 1.7 million TEUs capacity at Bayonne, New Jersey. The new terminal is expected to open in 2014 at a cost of more than $300 million. The location provides an advantage over close neighbours and competitors located west of the height-restricted Bayonne Bridge.[26] These developments coincide with the enlargement of the Panama Canal and provide the opportunity to attract some of the increased traffic that its opening is envisaged to create.

C. PORT DEVELOPMENT OUTLOOK

Port development is closely related to the actual, historical or anticipated volumes of trade that pass through the port, that is, the derived demand of the port's users. Some port development projects are built ahead of demand, typically green field projects, or when congestion at existing ports becomes a problem for one or more parties. Many traditional ports built close to rivers or natural harbours have become constrained over time as cities have grown around them. Port development projects are increasingly subject to lengthy discussions as different interest groups (workers, residents, user groups, business owners, and the like) vie to advocate their concerns and express their needs. These landside users' issues are in stark contrast with those of the seaside users. Landside users are constrained by the physical hinterland and procedural requirements of local or national governments and special-interest groups, whereas the seaside users are often able to make changes which may affect local communities but are not subject to the same procedures. One of these areas concerns the port's maritime customers, the shipowners. Ships are mobile and generally do not operate where they were constructed. Local communities centred around their creation points tend to see their advantages (for example, direct and indirect local employment) and not their operational disadvantages (pollution through emissions of gases, noise and light, among others). Ship construction is a large employer with strong roots in the local community and usually closely associated with other industrial plants, such as smelting. Ports, on the other hand, have lost a lot of their employee-based relations with the local community through retrenchment of labour brought about by mechanisation, streamlined business practices and a concentration on trans-shipment traffic – which seemingly has few direct benefits for the local economy. In addition, port communities are very sensitive to change, because ports rarely move and their facilities usually last for several decades.

In recent times, shipowners have sought to benefit from economies of scale by building ships that are longer, wider and deeper than previous vessels. To service these customers, ports need to undertake a number of upgrades to their infrastructure (quays, turning basins, sea defences, and the like), superstructure (for example, cranes, storage facilities, offices, and the like) and operations (dredging, human resources, software, and the like). Port authorities or governments need to make informed choices about where to invest, the potential return on investment and the cost of each opportunity. Adaptation measures to possible negative impacts of climatic changes, such as sea-level rise and extreme weather events also need to be considered. Infrastructure investments need to be financially sustainable so that countries maintain competiveness in international markets.

The impact of increased ship size upon ports can be substantial. For example, the ports of Rotterdam and Shanghai have, over time, become constrained by the cities which have grown around them. The only route for expansion is to build further into the sea as this satisfies the need for land and for the depth required to accommodate larger ships. Both Rotterdam's new Maasvlakte container terminal and Shanghai's Yangshan container terminals are located at the most extreme outreaches of the ports with the greatest depths, sufficient to cater for the newest generation of container vessels. In addition, some ports (for example, gateway and transit ports)[27] need hinterland connections to facilitate the movement of cargo.

Container terminals

Container trade has grown significantly in the last few decades to represent approximately 17 per cent of world seaborne trade by volume and 52 per cent by value. Containerized trade has grown not just at the expense of the share of general break bulk cargo carried via other means, but also through increased global trade. Many ports have adapted to this changing pattern of trade by undertaking infrastructure development programmes to increase their market share of containerized cargo. Increased port throughput volumes may increase the port's revenue collected through port dues or cargo handling fees. Local government may also see an increase in tax collection through higher trade volumes. However, increased cargo volumes driven by increased competition (between ports, exporters and importers, transport operators, and the like), could greatly improve the chances of return cargoes becoming available. This could lead to improved connectivity and lower transport costs per unit, to the benefit of the end user. The end results for increased trade are well documented and include higher levels of peace, security, health and living standards.[28] While this outcome may seem far removed from ship size, improvements which help lower transport costs could spill over into other areas.

Since the launch of the first post-Panamax vessel, the 6,400 TEU M/V *Regina Maersk,* back in 1996, there has been a trend for ever larger ships. The M/V *Regina Maersk* itself was around 50 per cent larger than its predecessors, but today is dwarfed by the latest class of container ships. In 2006, the M/V *Emma Maersk* was launched with a reported capacity of 15,500 TEUs. Since the start of the recession around 100 ships of more than 10,000 TEUs have been launched, with around one and a half times that number set to be delivered over the next few years.[29] In 2011, the shipping line Maersk ordered 20 vessels reportedly of more than 18,000 TEUs and possibly as large as 22,000 TEUs. These ships are known as super-post-Panamax, ultra-large container ships (ULCSs) or Malaccamax vessels (the maximum size of vessels that are able to transit the Straight of Malacca, a main route for cargo moving between the Far East and Western Asia, Africa and Europe).

Such large vessels require ports with deepwater access channels, alongside berth depths of 18 metres, adequate turning circles and specialised cargo handling equipment. While not every port may be able to accommodate the latest ULCS vessels, their existence has an implication for all ports. Only a few of the world's biggest ports on the East–West trade routes will be served by ULCSs. Displaced ships will, however, operate elsewhere and bring changes to other ports. The first-generation post-Panamax-type vessels (for example, M/V *Regina Maersk*), which are too young to be scrapped, are still operating on the main East–West route.[30] With a draft of 14.5 metres these vessels are still too big for the majority of African ports (excluding those located in South Africa, Egypt, Mauritius and Morocco). However, ports located in Djibouti, Namibia, Nigeria and Sudan all receive vessels greater than 4,000 TEUs, this indicating that displaced East–West vessels are seizing opportunities in South–South trading. This implies that ports in these countries also need to undertake, in their turn, more costly infrastructure works and provide each vessel with a greater provision of equipment.

The implications of ULCSs of 22,000 TEUs for ports are that larger shore-side gantry cranes, with an outreach of 72 metres and a lift height of 52 metres above quay will be needed. The distance between the front and back legs of the cranes may also need to be increased from 30 to 35 metres.[31] This can be problematic as the legs operate on rails built into the quay, making upgrading subject to spatial and underpinning constraints. Some of the challenges with larger cranes include stiffness, weight, corner loads, wind loads, increased power and operational issues including visibility, handling speeds and performance.[32] Another less common implication for ports concerns that of local residents, who may complain about unsightly cranes interrupting their view.[33]

The cost of purchasing new container gantry cranes capable of servicing ULCSs is around $8 million–$10 million each, and a single vessel could theoretically employ 10 to 12 such cranes. These cranes are sometimes called Jumbo 23s, because their outreach stretches to 23 containers width from the quay. However, while ULCSs may be 23 containers wide, the ports of Jebel Ali in Dubai and Felixstowe in the United Kingdom have container gantry cranes with an outreach of 24 containers, and the new port of Wilhelmshaven in Germany reportedly has cranes with an outreach of 25.[34] Adapting existing cranes could, however, prove a solution to some ports, with costs at between 25 to 60 per cent of the cost of new material. In addition, long waiting lists and a limited number of manufacturers often means that the time required to adapt a crane is sometimes half that of procuring a new one.[35] With two of the market leaders in the manufacture of container gantry cranes located in China, and customers located worldwide, the transportation of these cranes via ship can take several months. More than 72 per cent of gantry cranes capable of handling 22 or more rows of containers from the quay are positioned in terminals where global terminal operators have a shareholding.[36] As of 2011, the order book for container gantry cranes with an outreach of greater than 22 container rows totalled 17, two destined for the Caribbean and Central America, four for North America, four for South-East Asia and seven for the Far East. However, the most popular size of cranes on order is for those with an outreach of 18–20 rows. This may imply that smaller ports are upgrading their facilities as the cascading effect of larger ships entering the market pushes smaller vessels to call at other ports.

Container gantry cranes with an outreach of 22 rows and above are 100 per cent controlled by the global terminal operators in the Caribbean, Central America, South Asia and Southern Europe. In Northern Europe the figure is over 97 per cent, in the Middle East and South-East Asia, the figures are close to 95 per cent. This shows that many governments have met the financial challenge of purchasing port equipment through public–private partnerships. According to Drewry Shipping Consultants, of the 1,011 container gantry cranes of between 20 and 22 rows in operation, three are located in South Asia, 48 in the whole of Africa, 99 in South-East Asia and 542 in the Far East. This reflects clearly the source of containerized exports against other destinations, where containerized cargo relates primarily to import trade.

The world's largest crane manufacture is the Chinese firm ZPMC, which holds approximately 75 per cent of the market share and is continually updating its designs.[37] However, as good as each crane design may be, there are limitations to how many can be deployed per vessel and increasingly wider vessels do not necessarily permit more cranes to be deployed unless an indented berth concept is adopted.[38] However, modern technology enables different concepts to be tried and tested. For example, the container terminal operator APMT is working on its own crane concept. This company's FastNet container terminal concept allows gantry cranes to work more closely together, thereby increasing significantly the number of cranes deployed per vessel. The FastNet crane concept enables cranes to work adjacent rows, whereas the present container gantry cranes are too wide to allow this. With ULCSs capable of holding 24 FEUs from fore to aft and 23 containers across their beams, employing more container gantry cranes is imperative to improving port efficiency.

One area often overlooked when considering port development is insurance. According to one survey by the TT Club on accidents in ports, 79 per cent of accidents were caused by human error.[39] Maintenance of complex port equipment in an environment where equipment downtime can be costly may also be a factor in increased claims.[40] In an analysis of its claims, the TT Club revealed that 34 per cent of the cost of asset-related claims was directly related to container gantry cranes. The main causes of damage to container gantry cranes cited were:

• Wind damage – with ports being built further out to sea to cater for larger ships, there are fewer natural wind deflectors available;

• Hoist, spreaders and ropes – better preventative maintenance is needed;

• Structural integrity issues – again better maintenance or design could help;

• Operational issues – boom-to-ship collisions, spreaders, ship-cell guides and ropes all caused significant damage, which could be reduced by retrofitting avoidance systems.[41]

Dry bulk terminals

In the dry bulk sector ships are also increasing in size. The dry bulk sector represents almost one quarter of world seaborne trade by volume but, because these vessels often carry cheap raw materials, a mere 6 per cent by value. The dry bulk sector is dominated by the need to transport the five major bulk cargoes (coal, grain, iron ore, bauxite/alumina and phosphates). Two

of the biggest mining companies are the Australian BHP Billiton and the Brazilian Vale, which compete on many fronts including shipments of iron ore to China, the world's single biggest importer. In 2011, China imported 634 million tons of iron ore.

Because of the greater distance from Brazil to China compared with that of Australia to China, more of the final price of Brazilian iron ore goes towards transport costs. The vessels plying a trade between Brazil and China, usually Capesize vessels of 150,000 dwt, can perform approximately five round trips a year, including loading and unloading time, whereas on the Australia to China route the same vessel can perform an average of 12 voyages. Australian iron ore can thus command a higher price, grading excluded.

In 2008, at the height of the commodity boom and just prior to the global financial crisis, Vale made an order for 12 very large ore carriers (VLOCs) of 400,000 dwt. Termed Valemax vessels, they are the world's largest dry bulk ships. The Valemax vessels are an attempt by the Brazilian firm to lower its geographical disadvantage over its closest competitor, BHP Billiton, for its largest customer market, China. In terms of iron ore alone, Brazil exported over 326 million tons and Australia 437 million tons in 2011. The total iron ore imports by China from Brazil equalled 140 million tons in 2011, significantly below the 295.7 million tons of BHP Billiton, and enough to theoretically keep 70 Valemax vessels in full employment. Presently, it is reported that Vale have 35 Valemax vessels on order (see chapter 2).

The Valemax vessels have, however, caused some controversy, generated especially by Chinese owners of smaller dry bulk vessels concerned about a lack of cargo to carry. As a consequence, in early 2012 the Chinese Government announced that dry bulk vessels of over 350,000 dwt, and tankers of over 450,000 dwt, would no longer be permitted to call at Chinese ports.[42] This decision was apparently superseded by another decision from the Chinese Government that stated that approval would be given to the port of Ningbo-Zhoushan to build two berths of 300,000 dwt capacity, which could receive Valemax vessels.

Vale, in an attempt to overcome Chinese port restrictions, is undertaking an innovative solution using floating storage centres based in countries nearby to China. In 2012, Vale took delivery of the world's largest trans-shipment vessel, the M/V *Ore Fabrica* of 284,000 dwt. The vessel will serve as a platform

Table 4.3.	The relationship between vessel size and terminal type		
	Terminal Type		
	Container terminal	**Dry-bulk terminal**	**Tanker terminal**
Maximum vessel carrying capacity	ULCSs (maximum 18,000–22,000 TEUs; 165,000 dwt)	VLOCs (maximum 400,000 dwt)	Ultra large crude carriers (ULCCs) (maximum 440,000–550,000 dwt)
Maximum vessel dimensions	Length: 400 metres Beam: 59 metres Draught: 14.5 metres	Length: 362 metres Beam: 65 metres Draught: 23 metres	Length: 458 metres Beam: 69 metres Draught: 24.6 metres
Alongside berth depth needed	15 metres	23.5 metres	25 metres
Berth length	1 000 metres. The whole vessel needs to be adjacent to the quay area to allow maximum unloading/loading and further berths needed at the same quay for feeder vessels.	Access to the vessel can be via a pier extended out into deeper water and cargo moved via conveyor.	Access to the vessel can be via a pier extended out into deeper water and cargo moved via pipeline.
Pilotage	Increased assistance likely	Increased assistance likely	Increased assistance likely
Terminal area	Two-way (import/export) cargo movement means increased storage space is needed to discharge and load cargo. Container yard depth should be at least 500 metres. Approximately 25–30 ha is needed for a terminal with an annual throughput of 1 million TEUs.	As cargo tends to move in one way (export to import) the increase storage space needed is minimal and tends to be open air, i.e. requiring only land surface. One million tons of iron ore occupy approximately 12–15 ha.	Although cargo tends to move in one direction, costly storage facilities and land surface are needed. One million barrels of storage occupy an area of 5 ha.
Quayside cargo-handling equipment	8–10 gantry cranes per berth with an outreach of 23 TEUs, $8 million–10 million each.	No significant difference	No significant difference
Onshore cargo-handling equipment	Increased number of vehicles needed to transport containers to stacking yard, automated guidance vehicles, higher reach stackers (possibly up to 7 high), rail-mounted gantry cranes, straddle carriers, etc.	No significant difference	No significant difference
IT equipment	More advanced IT systems needed to monitor increased number of containers.	No significant difference	No significant difference
Customs/security checks	Increased volume of containers and number of individual shippers could significantly increase the number of security checks.	No significant difference	Extra security may be needed to deter terrorist attacks.
Inland congestion	With most containers arriving/leaving ports on trucks, congestion could be severe and affect local residents.	Bulk cargo tends to arrive/leave port via trains/barges. Congestion depends upon other infrastructure.	Congestion within pipelines tends not to be noticeable.
Seaside congestion	A restrictive access channel may cause delays to other vessels.	A restrictive access channel may cause delays to other vessels.	A restrictive access channel may cause delays to other vessels.
Environment	Increased trucks on roads will raise levels of CO_2 pollution. Noise and light pollution may also affect local residents. There may also be ballast water issues for loading ports.	Increased dust affecting the health of local residents is to be expected, as well as possible ballast water issues for loading ports.	In the absence of any spillage, environmental costs will be low. There may also be ballast water issues for loading ports.
Employment	More skilled workers (for example, cranes and IT-systems operators) will be required. Increased potential for employment within supporting industries.	Minimal increase to port workers but a higher potential for employment within supporting industries.	Minimal increase to port workers but a higher potential for employment within supporting industries.

Source: UNCTAD secretariat.

to transfer iron ore from Vale's VLOCs to smaller ships for transport to Asian markets, including China.[43] The locations where these VLOCs will be based include the Philippines, the Republic of Korea and possibly Malaysia.[44] Also in Malaysia, Vale has spent $600 million on the order of port equipment including loaders, ultra-large unloaders, bucket-wheel stackers and reclaimers for its break bulk trans-shipment centre at Teluk Rubiah.[45] With the deployment of both floating and regional trans-shipment centres, large iron ore shipments can be transported from Latin America to Asia at optimum economies of scale and cost savings passed on, allowing Vale to obtain the sought-after market share.

Trans-shipment in dry bulk differs from container trans-shipment, the former being performed at sea and the latter on land. This is possible because, unlike containers, dry bulk cargo is homogenous and can be split and sold en route, whereas containers contain very specific cargos sometimes with multiple owners. Furthermore, the trend of larger vessel sizes in the dry bulk sector does not affect ports in the same way as the increased sizes of container ships, as indicated by the comparison shown in table 4.3. Larger dry bulk or tanker vessels can still be loaded and unloaded with the same equipment needed for smaller vessels. All, however, require deeper alongside berths, but with dry bulk and tanker vessels, extending the reach of conveyor belts or pipelines and power is not technically as challenging.

Tanker terminals

The tanker sector has traditionally benefited from large vessels with the first very large crude carriers (VLCCs) appearing in the 1970s. The tanker sector represents around one third of international seaborne trade by volume and 22 per cent by value. The tanker market is generally concerned with the transportation of crude oil and petroleum products which are mainly used to manufacture other goods. The growth potential of this sector is enormous due to the increases in demand for carbon energy as a result of the growing middle classes in developing countries.

Ports have dealt with the challenges of receiving VLCCs by extending piers with pipelines further out to sea. The port infrastructure needed to service these vessels relates primarily to storage tanks within the port area. However, most oil importing countries would probably benefit from better inland storage facilities closer to the consumer, depending on the geographic characteristics of the country, rather than to rely upon shore-side storage, which better benefits oil-exporting countries. Thus, the role of ports in tanker storage should primarily be a buffer role to help balance inflows and outflows rather than storage per se.

The trend for larger vessels and the concept of floating storage centres to act as trans-shipment hubs could be a competitor to ports which traditionally make their revenue from cargo handling. Floating storage centres already exist in the tanker sector, but their use is mainly by oil refineries to absorb surplus capacity. The largest vessel ever built was the tanker M/V *Seawise Giant* that, along with many other ULCCs, ended her last days as a floating storage platform in the Persian Gulf.[46] Some vessels may be used by oil traders as temporary storage but these vessels do not trans-ship and tend only to be laid up as floating storage until there is an upward movement in the price of oil.

Conclusions

One of the consequences of increasing vessel size to transport cargo more efficiently is that inefficiencies are simply moved to elsewhere in the logistics chain. The quayside (crane handling in particular) continues to be a problem area, together with the landside entrance/exit point where trains or trucks enter or leave the port. Unloading vessels tends to be more time consuming than loading (in container shipping) as boxes often originate from one country specializing in manufacture (for example, China) but are unloaded at many places in lower volumes, making it difficult to achieve the same operational efficiencies. In addition, receiving countries often need to shuffle containers in order to gain access to those underneath. While computer software can make the process easier, space is still needed to perform the movement and thus the areas where work can be performed are reduced. One of the key challenges facing ports working with container shipping is the reduction in frequency of port calls by individual vessels, as highlighted in the LSCI. With larger ships calling at fewer hub ports the frequency of cargo arrival will put many ports to the test. The rate at which cargo flows into a port must match the rate at which it leaves for the port not to occupy large tracks of land or for congestion not to occur. As with most businesses, port operators prefer steady streams of traffic. Cargo surges combined with time constraints and perhaps unfamiliarity of heavy equipment can increase pressure that may translate into a slip in safety standards. With larger vessels and more specialised cargo handling equipment tied up with each vessel, any port downtime could significantly affect the ability of the port to earn enough revenue to make infrastructure investment financially sustainable.

ENDNOTES

1   http://www.ft.com/cms/s/0/a1f5ddda-a26b-11e1-a605-00144feabdc0.html#axzz1zC3LoF6K, accessed 29 June 2012.

2   http://www.china.org.cn/business/2012-03/31/content_25029628.htm, accessed 29 June 2012.

3   Data provided by *Lloyds List Intelligence*, May 2012.

4   Calculations undertaken by UNCTAD on the basis of data provided by *Lloyds List Intelligence*, May 2012. The data cover a total of 159 coastal countries.

5   http://www.worldfolio.co.uk/region/africa/cameroon/paul-biya, accessed 7 May 2012.

6   *WorldCargo News* (2011). Xiamen investing for the future. November, p. 33.

7   http://www.metalbulletin.com/Article/3038980/Chinas-transport-ministry-approves-Ningbo-Zhoushan-Port-upgrade.html, accessed 1 June 2012.

8   *WorldCargo News* (2012). Green light for Moin terminal. March, p. 6.

9   *WorldCargo News* (2012). APMT cuts Poti staff. February, p. 8.

10   http://www.lloydslist.com/ll/sector/ports-and-logistics/article390593.ece, accessed 9 May 2012.

11   http://www.maritimeprofessional.com/Blogs/PFI-sees-India-taking-big-strides-in-port-deve-(4)/March-2012/PFI-sees-India-taking-big-strides-in-port-developm.aspx, accessed 29 June 2012.

12   *WorldCargo News* (2012). Perlindo to build new Jakarta terminal. February, p. 4.

13   http://www.thejakartapost.com/news/2012/01/29/indonesian-economy-2012-bright-can-it-be-sustained.html, accessed 29 June 2012.

14   http://www.joc.com/portsterminals/china-spend-3-billion-expand-port-bordering-north-korean, accessed 1 June 2012.

15   http://larouchepac.com/node/21600, accessed 1 June 2012; and http://theworldnet.info/en/2012/04/north-korea-and-china-attracting-investors-for-rajin-port-development/, accessed 1 June 2012.

16   http://www.pmawca-agpaoc.org/news.php/13/liberian-npa-in-talks-with-van-oord.html, accessed 29 May 2012.

17   *Containerisation International* (2012). Tanger Med well down year-on-year. 11 May.

18   http://www.vanguardngr.com/2011/12/ibaka-seaport-%E2%80%99ll-create-100000-jobs-gov-akpabio/, accessed 7 May 2012.

19   http://www.pmawca-agpaoc.org/news.php/14/nigeria-ports-authority-to-develop-lagos-bull-nose-area.html, accessed 29 May 2012.

20   http://www.pmaesa.org/information/news/news.htm?nid=55, accessed 29 May 2012.

21   http://www.pmaesa.org/information/news/news.htm?nid=54, accessed 29 May 2012.

22   *WorldCargo News* (2012). Chinese aid for new port in Crimea. February, p. 4.

23   http://www.ci-online.co.uk/default.asp?URL=news/showNews.asp?News_ID=32908, accessed 29 May 2012.

24   *Containerisation International* (2012). Manchester Ship Canal service improved. 22 June.

25   *WorldCargo News* (2012). Long Beach builds for the future. February, p. 31.

26   http://www.fairplay.co.uk/secure/display.aspx?path_info=/secure/display.aspx&articlename=dn0020120510000005, accessed 10 May 2012.

27   A gateway port relates to the import and export of cargo (usually national) into or from the hinterland, whereas transit ports refer to the same cargo destined or originating from or to other nearby countries. Trans-shipment cargo, however, stays within the port and thus does not need hinterland connections.

28   For example, see: Intriligator, MD (2003). *Globalization of the World Economy: Potential Benefits and Costs and a Net Assessment*. Milken Institute. January No. 33; Lee, J-W and Ju HP (2008). *Does Trade Integration Contribute to Peace?* ADB Working Paper Series on Regional Economic Integration No. 24. Asian Development Bank. December.

29   *Seatrade* (2011). The 'Valemax' Saga, No. 4, September, p. 5.

30   The M/V *Regina Maersk* was renamed the M/V *Maersk Kure* in 2007, when she was sold and charted back by Maersk Line. The ship still operates along the East–West trade route linking China and Europe.

31   http://www.portstrategy.com/features101/port-operations/cargo-handling/ship-to-shore-cranes/qsgc, accessed 30 May 2012.

32   http://www.worldcargonews.com/htm/n20120414.255863.htm, accessed 29 May 2012.

33   http://www.worldcargonews.com/secure/assets/nf20060905.596033_44fd399113039.pdf, accessed 30 May 2012.

34   http://www.porttechnology.org/blogs/wilhelmshaven_orders, accessed 30 May 2012; http://www.portstrategy.com/features101/port-operations/cargo-handling/ship-to-shore-cranes/qsgc, accessed 30 May 2012.

35   http://www.porttechnology.org/technical_papers/the_new_panamax_and_jumbo_ships_are_coming, accessed 30 May 2012.

36   Drewry (2011). *Global Container Terminal Operators*.

37   http://www.zpmc.com/about.php?act=jtjs, accessed 29 May 2012.

38   Ceres Paragon indented berth terminal in Amsterdam allows the unloading of a container ship from both sides of the vessel, unlike traditional berths that utilize one side only.

39   The world's largest insurer of ports is the TT Club, with a membership of around 400 ports and terminals.

40   http://www.portstrategy.com/features101/legal-and-insurance/drama-or-day-to-day, accessed 30 May 2012.

41   http://www.ttclub.com/fileadmin/uploads/tt-club/Publications___Resources/Annual_Reports/Recommended%20 minimum%20safety%20specifications%20for%20quay%20cranes%2020110607.pdf, accessed 30 May 2012.

42   The world's largest dry bulk carrier, M/V *Berge Stahl*, at 364,767 dwt, had previously called at Chinese ports, indicating that the physical size of the ship was not necessarily the main issue in the Chinese Government's decision.

43   http://www.chamber-of-shipping.com/index.php?option=com_content&task=blogsection&id=1&Itemid=59&limitsta rt=9, accessed 7 May 2012.

44   http://www.lloydslist.com/ll/sector/ports-and-logistics/article399410.ece, accessed 30 May 2012.

45   http://www.lloydslist.com/ll/sector/ports-and-logistics/article400912.ece, accessed 19 June 2012.

46   The world's largest ULCC, the M/V *Seawise Giant*, built in 1979, which underwent several name changes and an enlargement process to reach 564,763 dwt, 4,240,865 barrels or 674,243,676 litres, was scrapped in 2010. The present largest vessel is the TI Class, built in 2002, with a capacity of 441,585 dwt, 3,166,353 barrels or 503,409,900 litres. Its dimensions are: length 380 metres, breadth 68 metres, draught 24.5 metres.

5

LEGAL ISSUES AND REGULATORY DEVELOPMENTS

This chapter provides information on legal issues and recent regulatory developments in the fields of transport and trade facilitation, and on the status of the main maritime conventions. Important issues include the recent adoption of amendments to the 1996 Convention on Limitation of Liability for Maritime Claims (1996 LLMC), as well as a range of regulatory developments relating to maritime and supply-chain security, maritime safety and environmental issues.

Among the regulatory measures worth noting is a set of technical and operational measures to increase energy efficiency and reduce greenhouse gas (GHG) emissions from international shipping that was adopted under the auspices of the International Maritime Organization (IMO) in July 2011 and is expected to enter into force on 1 January 2013. To assist in the implementation of these new mandatory measures, four sets of guidelines were also adopted at IMO in March 2012. Discussions on possible market-based measures for the reduction of GHG emissions from international shipping continued and remained controversial. In respect of liability and compensation for ship-source oil pollution, a new UNCTAD report provides an overview of the international legal framework as well as some guidance for national policymaking.

At the World Trade Organization (WTO), negotiations continued on a future Trade Facilitation (TF) Agreement. While negotiators advanced on the draft negotiating text, it has been suggested that an agreement in TF might be reached earlier than in other areas of the Doha Development Round of negotiations.

A. IMPORTANT DEVELOPMENTS IN TRANSPORT LAW

Adoption of amendments to the 1996 Convention on Limitation of Liability for Maritime Claims

National legislation or international legal instruments may give shipowners and others linked with the operation of a ship the right to limit their liability in respect of certain claims, whatever the basis of liability may be. Under these so-called global limitation regimes, limits of liability are calculated using either the ship's value or a value calculated on the basis of the size of the ship and in particular on the basis of the ship's tonnage.[1] The most important global limitation regimes are the Convention on Limitation of Liability for Maritime Claims, 1976 (1976 LLMC),[2] and the 1976 LLMC as amended by its 1996 Protocol[3] (hereafter 1996 LLMC).

Both the 1976 LLMC and the 1996 LLMC set specific limits of liability for two types of claims against shipowners (and certain other persons),[4] namely, claims for loss of life or personal injury, and claims for property damage, as further defined.[5] In each case, the shipowner is entitled to limitation of liability except in certain cases of wilful misconduct.[6] While the approach to limitation is the same under both regimes, there are important differences. In particular, the actual amounts to which the limitation is limited are higher under the 1996 LLMC.

An important development, of interest to parties engaged in international trade, was the adoption at IMO, in April 2012, of amendments increasing the compensation limits set by the 1996 LLMC.[7] In light of experience with relevant incidents, as well as inflation, the limitation amounts specified in the 1996 Protocol were considered inadequate to cover the costs of claims, especially those arising from incidents involving bunker fuel spills. The new compensation limits, representing an increase of 51 per cent over previous limits, are expected to enter into force for Contracting States to the 1996 LLMC on 19 April 2015, 36 months from the date of adoption, under the tacit acceptance procedure.[8] In outline, the amendments may be summarized as follows: with respect to claims for loss of life or personal injury on ships with a tonnage not exceeding 2,000 tons, the limit of liability is 3.02 million Special Drawing Rights (SDR) (up from 2 million SDR).[9] For larger ships, the following additional amounts apply when calculating the limit of liability:

- For each ton from 2,001 to 30,000 tons, 1,208 SDR (up from 800 SDR);

- For each ton from 30,001 to 70,000 tons, 906 SDR (up from 600 SDR);

- For each ton in excess of 70,000 tons, 604 SDR (up from 400 SDR).[10]

The limit of liability for property claims for ships not exceeding 2,000 tons is 1.51 million SDR (up from 1 million SDR).[11] For larger ships, the following additional amounts apply when calculating the limit of liability:

- For each ton from 2,001 to 30,000 tons, 604 SDR (up from 400 SDR);

- For each ton from 30,001 to 70,000 tons, 453 SDR (up from 300 SDR);

- For each ton in excess of 70,000 tons, 302 SDR (up from 200 SDR).[12]

With the adoption of increased limits of liability, the protection of maritime claimants has been strengthened. However, it should be noted that the amendments affect limitation of liability only under the 1996 LLMC.[13] While many States have adopted the 1996 LLMC, some continue to adhere to the unamended 1976 LLMC, or the earlier International Convention Relating to the Limitation of the Liability of Owners of Seagoing Ships, 1957.[14] Few States now continue to adhere to the first international convention in the field, the International Convention for the Unification of Certain Rules relating to the Limitation of Liability of Owners of Seagoing Vessels, 1924. While each of the relevant Conventions deals with the issue of limitation of liability for maritime claims, there are substantive differences. Limitation of liability amounts vary significantly, with the highest amounts, that is, those most favourable to claimants, under the 1996 LLMC.[15] In view of the most recent amendments, policy makers in States that are not yet Contracting States to the 1996 LLMC may wish to consider afresh the merits of accession.

B. REGULATORY DEVELOPMENTS RELATING TO THE REDUCTION OF GREENHOUSE GAS EMISSIONS FROM INTERNATIONAL SHIPPING AND OTHER ENVIRONMENTAL ISSUES

1. Reduction of greenhouse gas emissions from international shipping

For several years, efforts aimed at establishing a regulatory regime to control and reduce emissions of

GHGs from ships have been dominating substantive discussions at the Marine Environment Protection Committee (MEPC) of IMO.[16] Relevant discussions focus on technical and operational measures, which, according to an IMO study published in 2009,[17] have a significant potential for reduction of GHG emissions from international shipping,[18] but also on the more controversial issue of potential market-based measures (MBMs).[19]

An overview of relevant recent developments at IMO is provided in the following sections. Attention should also be drawn to an UNCTAD-edited volume *Maritime Transport and the Climate Change Challenge*, published in May 2012, which provides detailed insight into a range of the potential implications of climate change for this key sector of global trade.[20]

(a) Adoption of new regulations on energy efficiency for ships and guidelines for their implementation

A key development under the auspices of IMO includes the finalization and adoption of mandatory regulatory measures for GHG emissions control. A set of technical and operational measures[21] to increase energy efficiency and reduce emissions of GHGs from international shipping were adopted during the sixty-second session of the MEPC, which was held from 11 to 15 July 2011. The package of measures – adopted by roll-call vote rather than by consensus – was added by way of amendment to the International Convention for the Prevention of Pollution from Ships, 1973 as modified by the Protocol of 1978 (MARPOL), Annex VI[22] Regulations on the Prevention of Air Pollution from Ships, as a new chapter (chapter 4) entitled "Regulations on energy efficiency for ships". The amendments are expected to enter into force on 1 January 2013.[23]

Four sets of guidelines[24] intended to support the uniform implementation of these mandatory regulations were subsequently adopted during the sixty-third session of MEPC, which was held from 27 February to 2 March 2012. At the same session, the discussion continued on proposed MBMs that would complement the technical and operational measures already adopted.

Regulations on energy efficiency for ships

The Regulations make the Energy Efficiency Design Index (EEDI) mandatory for new ships and the Ship Energy Efficiency Management Plan (SEEMP)

mandatory for all ships.[25] The EEDI establishes a minimum energy efficiency requirement (CO_2 emissions per capacity mile) for new ships, depending on ship type and size. This required level will be reduced every five years, with ships required to be increasingly efficient through technical improvements to elements of design and components influencing fuel efficiency. Reduction rates are set until 2025, when a 30 per cent reduction is mandated over the average efficiency for ships built between 1999 and 2009. The EEDI is a performance-based mechanism, and as long as the required energy-efficiency level is attained, the industry is free to use the most cost-efficient technology for their ships to comply with the relevant Regulations. The current EEDI will cover about 70 per cent of emissions from new oil tankers, gas tankers, bulk carriers, general cargo, refrigerated cargo and container ships, as well as combination carriers (liquid/dry bulk).[26]

Under the Regulations, it will also become mandatory for ships to carry a SEEMP after 1 January 2013. The SEEMP is intended to be a practical tool to help shipowners manage their environmental performance and improve and monitor ship and fleet efficiency over time. It establishes a mechanism for operators to improve the energy efficiency of ships through use of the Energy Efficiency Operational Indicator (EEOI) as a monitoring tool.[27] International Energy Efficiency (IEE) Certificates for ships subject to the Regulations will be issued by the respective Governments.[28]

As of 1 January 2013, the new Regulations shall apply to all ships of 400 tons and above. However, administrations may waive the requirement for such ships to comply with the EEDI requirements. According to the Regulations, this waiver may not be applied to ships above 400 tons:

> "1. for which the building contract is placed on or after 1 January 2017; 2. in the absence of a building contract, the keel of which is laid or which is at a similar stage of construction on or after 1 July 2017; 3. the delivery of which is on or after 1 July 2019; or 4. in cases of a major conversion of a new or existing ship, ... on or after 1 January 2017."[29]

The required EEDI and the attained EEDI shall be calculated for:

> "1. each new ship; 2. each new ship which has undergone a major conversion; and 3. each new or existing ship which has undergone a major conversion that is so extensive that the ship

is regarded by the Administration as a newly constructed ship ...."

In addition:

"the attained EEDI shall be specific to each ship and shall indicate the estimated performance of the ship in terms of energy efficiency. It will be accompanied by the EEDI technical file that contains the information necessary for the calculation of the attained EEDI and that shows the process of calculation."[30]

The calculation shall be done taking into account guidelines developed by IMO.

Guidelines for implementation of energy efficiency measures

Four sets of guidelines intended to assist in the implementation of the mandatory Regulations on energy efficiency for ships in MARPOL Annex VI were adopted by MEPC during its sixty-third session from 27 February to 2 March 2012.[31] They are:

- *2012 Guidelines on the Method of Calculation of the Attained Energy Efficiency Design Index (EEDI) for New Ships*;

- *2012 Guidelines for the Development of a Ship Energy Efficiency Management Plan (SEEMP)*;

- *2012 Guidelines on Survey and Certification of the Energy Efficiency Design Index (EEDI)*;

- *Guidelines for Calculation of Reference Lines for use with the Energy Efficiency Design Index (EEDI)*.[32]

Administrations were invited to take these Guidelines into account when developing and enacting national laws which give force to and implement provisions set forth in the respective Regulations of MARPOL Annex VI, as amended, as well as to bring SEEMP to the attention of masters, seafarers, shipowners, ship operators and any other interested groups.

The 2012 Guidelines address some of the concerns that had been raised regarding the safety of the EEDI, both in debates among States at IMO discussions[33] and within the shipping industry.[34] The key concern in this respect had been that while the EEDI formula value can easily be met by using vessels with smaller, lower-power engines, these are potentially dangerous since they do not have enough reserve power available for emergency conditions, such as extreme weather or special manoeuvring in ports when necessary.

The 2012 Guidelines on the method of calculation of the attained EEDI for new ships contain a provision which allows vessels to be built with whatever engine power the owner thinks necessary, as long as it is limited to provide a suitable shaft power to give the required EEDI value. In an emergency, the limiter will be deactivated or overridden so that more power can be used.[35]

An updated work plan[36] was also agreed upon, for the development of further guidelines and energy-efficiency frameworks for those ships not covered by the current EEDI regulations. According to the work plan, these guidelines are set to be finalized by the end of the sixty-fifth session of the MEPC, to be held in 2013.

Draft MEPC resolution on promotion of technical cooperation and transfer of technology relating to the improvement of energy efficiency of ships

Another new Regulation in chapter 4 of MARPOL Annex VI is that concerning "Promotion of technical cooperation and transfer of technology relating to the improvement of energy efficiency of ships." Under this Regulation, administrations, in cooperation with IMO and other international bodies, are required to promote and provide as appropriate – directly or through IMO – support to States, especially developing States, that request technical assistance. The Regulation also requires administrations to cooperate actively with one another, and, subject to their national laws, regulations and policies, "to promote the development and transfer of technology and exchange of information to States which request technical assistance, particularly developing States, in respect of the implementation of measures to fulfil the requirements of chapter 4 [of MARPOL Annex VI]."[37]

Linked to the implementation of this Regulation, and of the other energy efficiency measures, a draft resolution on the "Promotion of technical co-operation and transfer of technology relating to the improvement of energy efficiency of ships"[38] was discussed during the sixty-third session of MEPC. A group of member States submitted an informal paper during the session, providing comments and proposing additional amendments to the draft resolution, on:

"a methodology for assessing implementation, the necessary financial, technological and capacity-building support for developing countries by developed countries, taking into account the principles of common but differentiated responsibilities and respective capabilities under the UNFCCC [United Nations Framework Convention on Climate Change] and its Kyoto Protocol."[39]

A working group was established to finalize the draft resolution, but could not reach consensus on some of the proposals. Work on the draft resolution will continue during the sixty-fourth session of the MEPC, to be held from 1 to 5 October 2012.

Three other categories of issues relating to GHGs were considered during the sixty-third session of MEPC, namely the application of EEDI to existing ships, uncertainty in emission data, and a performance standard for fuel consumption measurement. Following concerns expressed by industry and supported by a large number of parties, the Committee confirmed that EEDI had been developed as a regulatory tool for new ships only; as a design index, extension of its application to the existing fleet would be inappropriate.[40] The MEPC took note of concerns that the reduction effects of the EEDI and SEEMP may have been overestimated, and noted that uncertainty existed in the estimates and projections of emissions from international shipping.[41] The Committee agreed that further work should take place "to provide the Committee with reliable and up-to-date information to base its decisions on and requested the secretariat to investigate possibilities and report to future sessions."[42] The Committee also agreed that development of an IMO performance standard for fuel consumption measurement for ships could be a useful tool and should be considered further.

(b) Market-based measures, and related matters

While a set of technical and operational measures to increase energy efficiency of ships has now been adopted, discussions on possible MBMs for the reduction of GHG emissions from international shipping continue, and remain highly controversial.[43] As reported in the *Review of Maritime Transport 2011*, an extensive debate on how to progress in the development of an MBM had been held during the sixty-first session of MEPC.[44] The MBM proposals under review ranged from those envisaging a contribution or levy on all CO_2 emissions from all ships, or only for those generated by ships not meeting the EEDI requirement, to emissions trading schemes and to schemes based on a ship's actual efficiency both by design (EEDI) and operation (EEOI).[45] Subsequently,

the third Intersessional Meeting of the Working Group on GHG Emissions from Ships (GHG-WG3), which was dedicated to further work on MBMs, was held from 28 March to 1 April 2011.[46] Due to time constraints, MEPC had been unable to address the issue of MBMs during its sixty-second session, held from 11 to 15 July 2011, and agreed to defer consideration of relevant submissions to its sixty-third session.

During its sixty-third session, MEPC continued its discussion of proposed MBMs, which would complement the technical and operational measures already adopted. It was agreed that the focus should be on a more comprehensive impact assessment of the possible consequences of introducing an MBM from international shipping under IMO. The discussions on MBMs covered a number of different topics which are briefly summarized below.

The sixty-third session of MEPC adopted the report of GHG-WG3, *Reduction of GHG Emissions from Ships*,[47] and, in this respect, noted that the third Intersessional Meeting had completed, as far as possible, the terms of reference given to it by the Committee and had placed the MBM proposals into two groups: (1) focus on in-sector and, (2) in-sector and out-of-sector, based on the emission reduction mechanism used by the MBM proposals.[48] Inter alia, MEPC further noted:

- That there were two opinions as to whether a compelling "need and purpose of an MBM" for international shipping under IMO had been clearly demonstrated, and agreed to return to the issue in due course;

- The debate on the "relation to relevant conventions and rules", and agreed to consider the issue further, partly based on a submission by one delegation;

- The debate on "strengths and weaknesses" and that, for the MBM proposals identified under each group, the proponents had identified and listed strengths and weaknesses[49] and that other delegations which were not proponents of MBMs had identified additional weaknesses for all the MBM proposals;[50]

- That the Intersessional Meeting acknowledged the findings and conclusions of the study of the Expert Group on Feasibility Study and Impact Assessment of Possible Market-based Measures (MBM-EG),[51] including its identification that there would be a need for further study of both the "direct and indirect impacts on developing countries" due to the introduction and non-introduction of an MBM for international shipping under IMO;

• That two documents submitted by delegations,[52] or relevant parts thereof, should be considered further at its current session.

The debate continued on the issue of further impact assessment of proposed MBMs for international maritime transport. Two documents prepared by the Chairperson were considered as part of this debate. The first document[53] set out proposals on how an impact assessment may be undertaken to determine the possible effects of introduction of an MBM for international shipping, including the method and criteria for the assessment. The second document[54] contained proposed draft terms of reference for a steering committee for the impact assessment of MBM proposals, to be established in order to supervise the impact assessment and to assist and provide advice to the IMO secretariat. The MEPC also noted that the feasibility study called for by the work plan for further consideration of MBMs had been successfully completed by the MBM-EG, which had concluded that all MBM proposals under review could be implemented, notwithstanding the challenges associated with the introduction of new measures.[55]

To illustrate the controversial nature of issues related to the introduction of MBMs, especially from the perspective of some developing countries, two submissions by national delegations are particularly pertinent, as detailed below.

A document submitted by India presented the findings of an MBM impact study on the country's shipping sector and trade.[56] According to the study, the adoption of an MBM would lead to adverse impacts on trade and growth and create an inequitable burden on Indian consumers. Moreover, it could have "a deleterious impact on the environment as consumers of coal in India may resort to use of poor quality Indian coal."[57] Based on the results of the study, India reiterated its concerns about the economic implications of MBMs on consumers in developing countries, whose contribution to GHG emissions per capita, were minimal.

Another document submitted by China[58] highlighted the need to carry out further impact assessment on developing countries, and proposed a list of revised criteria to be taken into account for the assessment. Nine criteria were proposed, namely:

(i) The "environmental effectiveness" of the proposed MBMs, particularly in limiting GHG emissions from international shipping;

(ii) The "cost-effectiveness" of the proposed MBMs and the direct and indirect socio-economic impacts on trade, consumers and industries in developing countries, particularly in least developed countries (LDCs) and small island developing states (SIDSs);

(iii) The "potential of the proposed MBMs to provide incentives to technological reform and innovation";

(iv) The "economic, technical and operational feasibility" of implementing the proposed MBMs;

(v) The "potential additional financial, workload and technical burden" for the shipbuilding industry and the maritime sector in developing countries of implementing and enforcing the proposed MBMs, and the "need for financial support, technology transfer and capacity-building";

(vi) The "consistency of the proposed MBMs with other relevant conventions", such as UNFCCC, Kyoto Protocol and World Trade Organization (WTO) rules, "especially the principle of [common but differentiated responsibilities and respective capabilities] CBDR, as well as its compatibility with customary international law, as depicted in the [United Nations Convention on the Law of the Sea] UNCLOS";

(vii) When there is a potential to raise funds, the "costs borne by and benefits for developing countries";

(viii) The "potential additional administrative burden", and the legal aspects for national administrations relating to the implemention and enforcement of the proposed MBMs;

(ix) The "compatibility of the proposed MBMs with the existing enforcement and control provisions" under the IMO legal framework.

It was agreed by consensus that there was a need for a continued impact assessment and that its focus should be on possible impacts on consumers and industries in developing countries. Despite the efforts made to develop the draft terms of reference for further impact assessment of proposed MBMs, including the methodology and criteria for the assessment, a number of issues were still pending. One issue concerned whether the methodology for the impact assessment should be carried out by an expert group or by commissioned research institutes. Another issue concerned the scope of impact assessment. It was agreed to consider the terms of reference further at the next session of MEPC.

As part of the discussions on consideration and possible consolidation of MBM proposals, various submissions by delegations were considered.[59] It was agreed that MBM proposals that would be subject to the impact assessment were those set out in the report of the GHG-WG3.[60] Regarding consolidation of proposals, it was noted, inter alia, that:

- "A number of delegations felt it desirable to carry out the analysis with a reduced number of MBM proposals, but also recognized that, in so doing, vital information could be lost which could be used at a later stage when the final MBM had been advanced in its development; the resultant MBM could be a combination of elements of different MBMs or some compromise solution rather than any of the proposals in their initial form";[61]

- "Some delegations opposed further consideration of MBM, stating that IMO should focus on technical and operational measures";[62]

- A large number of delegations were not ready to select a possible MBM proposal at this time; the presence or absence of draft legal text associated with proposals "[was] not directly linked to the maturity of the proposals and should not be used as the benchmark for selection."[63]

No proposal was eliminated at the session. All proposals should be further developed and finalized in time for the sixty-fourth session of the Committee, where they were expected to be considered further in order to determine whether they could be analysed against all criteria.

The issue of climate finance and possible use of MBM revenues was also considered, including its relation to the wider efforts of the international community to mobilize climate finance for use in developing countries.[64] Once again, as is illustrated by the summary of the discussions in the report of the meeting, the issue is one where consensus has not yet been achieved. The Committee noted, inter alia, that:

- "Divergent views were expressed on the use of revenues and the relation between an IMO MBM and climate finance, with a number of delegations advocating disbursement of revenues as a way to accommodate (reconcile) both CBDR and the IMO principles,[65] while others opposed this, if applied universally to all ships, and advocated an approach that would ensure no net incidence on developing countries";[66]

- "A large number of delegations expressed the view that the greater part of any MBM revenues should be used for climate finance in developing countries";[67]

- "A number of delegations expressed the view that an MBM for international shipping under IMO should not be used as a source for general climate finance in the context of the Green Climate Fund where funding should be provided by developed countries";[68]

- "A number of delegations stated that the Rebate Mechanism (RM)[69] – which aims to reconcile different principles of shipping and climate change conventions – "[was] an innovative and constructive proposal that addresses the CBDR principle and should be analysed and considered further."[70]

The Committee also noted:

(i) The ongoing work under UNFCCC on climate finance;

(ii) The *Report of the Secretary-General's High-level Advisory Group on Climate Change Financing (AGF)*;[71]

(iii) The G20 report by the World Bank and the International Monetary Fund on mobilizing funding sources for the Green Climate Fund,[72] which had identified international shipping as one possible source of finance.

It is also pertinent that the international shipping industry – which, in respect of potential MBMs, has indicated a preference for a fuel levy rather than an emissions trading scheme – has expressed the view that potential revenues should, inter alia, be used for the purposes of adapting ports in developing countries to the impacts of climate change.[73]

Regarding the relation of an MBM to WTO rules, it was recalled that a large number of delegations at GHG-WG3 had concluded that no incompatibility existed between a potential MBM for international shipping under IMO and the WTO rules. However, the view was also expressed that a WTO presentation on this matter at GHG-WG3[74] had to be viewed with caution, as it expressed the position of the WTO secretariat, and some delegations continued to remain concerned about inconsistency issues between an MBM and the WTO rules.[75] The MEPC agreed to continue the debate at its sixty-fourth session, and further submissions and contributions were invited.

(c) Matters concerning the United Nations Framework Convention on Climate Change

With respect to matters concerning UNFCCC, it was noted that the United Nations Climate Change Conference held in Durban from 28 November to 11 December 2011 resulted in the adoption of a number of decisions and conclusions,[76] including those relevant to the control of GHG emissions from international transport,[77] to IMO as the custodian of the London Convention and the London Protocol,[78] and to the next annual Climate Change Conference, planned to take place from 26 November to 7 December 2012 in Doha, Qatar.[79] The MEPC requested the IMO secretariat "to continue its well-established cooperation with the UNFCCC secretariat, to attend relevant UNFCCC meetings, including the meetings concerning the identification of possible funding sources for the Green Climate Fund, and to bring the outcome of IMO's work to the attention of appropriate UNFCCC bodies and meetings."[80]

2. Ship-source pollution and protection of the environment

(a) Developments at the United Nations Conference on Trade and Development

Based on its mandate in the Accra Accord[81] and in the outcome documents adopted at the conclusion of the thirteenth session of the United Nations Conference on Trade and Development (UNCTAD XIII), held from 21 to 26 April 2012 in Doha, Qatar, UNCTAD, as part of its work in the field of transport, has recently published an analytical report with a focus on ship-source oil pollution. The report, entitled *Liability and Compensation for Ship-Source Oil Pollution: An Overview of the International Legal Framework for Oil Pollution Damage from Tankers,*[82] has been prepared to assist policy makers, particularly in developing countries, in their understanding of the complex international legal framework and in assessing the merits of accession to the relevant international legal instruments.

By way of background, it should be noted that approximately half the global crude oil production is carried by sea. Much of this navigation is taking place in relative proximity to the coasts of many countries, in some cases transiting through constrained areas or chokepoints, such as narrow straits or canals. At the same time, the steady increase in the size and carrying capacity of ships transporting cargo of any type means that significant quantities of heavy bunker fuel are carried across the oceans and along coastal zones. While the number and extent of large oil pollution incidents has decreased over time, exposure to ship-source oil pollution remains a potentially significant economic threat for coastal States, in particular for developing countries and SIDS with economies heavily dependent on income from fisheries and tourism.

The international legal framework concerning oil pollution from tankers is very robust and provides significant compensation for loss due to oil pollution incidents. Relevant legal instruments, collectively known as the Civil Liability Convention–International Oil Pollution Compensation Fund (CLC–IOPC Fund) regime,[83] enjoy broad support and have been widely adopted at the international level. However, a considerable number of coastal States, including developing countries that are potentially exposed to ship-source oil pollution incidents, are not yet Contracting Parties to the latest legal instruments in the field and, as a result, would not benefit from significant compensation in the event of an oil-spill affecting their coasts or other areas under their marine jurisdiction (territorial waters and exclusive economic zones). It is against this background that the report has been prepared, to assist policy makers, particularly in developing countries, in their understanding of the relevant legal instruments and in assessing the merits of accession.

The report highlights central features of the international legal framework and provides an analytical overview of key provisions of the most recent of the international legal instruments in force. It also offers considerations for national policymaking, focusing, inter alia, on:

- The relative benefits of adherence to the latest of the relevant international legal instruments;

- The relevant financial burden associated with such adherence;

- Levels of protection available to victims of tanker oil pollution depending on which of the different legal instruments have been adopted.

In conclusion, the report suggests that accession to relevant legal instruments could offer considerable benefits to a number of coastal developing States that may be vulnerable to oil pollution from tankers.

While the report focuses on the international liability and compensation framework for oil pollution from tankers, it also highlights some of the key features of two important related international Conventions that cover other types of ship-source oil pollution. These are:

- The 2001 Bunker Oil Pollution Convention,[84] providing for liability and compensation in the event of bunker oil spills from ships other than oil tankers (for example, container vessels, reefers, chemical tankers, general cargo ships, cruise ships and ferries);

- The 1996 Hazardous and Noxious Substances (HNS) Convention[85] and its 2010 amending Protocol[86] (2010 HNS Convention), which provides for compensation relating to incidents arising in connection with the carriage of a broad range of hazardous and noxious substances, including non-persistent oil.

(b) Developments at the International Maritime Organization

During its sixty-third session, MEPC also adopted amendments to MARPOL relating to regional arrangements for port reception facilities, and adopted guidelines related to the implementation of the revised MARPOL Annex V (Garbage), and the Hong Kong International Convention for the Safe and Environmentally Sound Recycling of Ships, 2009 (Hong Kong Convention).[87] The Committee also granted basic and final approval to a number of ballast water management systems that make use of active substances.

Air pollution from ships: establishment of new emission control areas (ECAs)

While CO_2 is the main GHG emitted by ships, other relevant substances include sulphur oxides (SOx) and nitrogen oxides (NOx). These significantly contribute to air pollution from ships and are covered by MARPOL Annex VI,[88] which had been amended in 2008 to introduce more stringent emission controls.[89] With effect from 1 January 2012, Annex VI establishes reduced SOx thresholds for marine bunker fuels, with the global sulphur cap reduced from 4.5 per cent (45,000 ppm) to 3.5 per cent (35,000 ppm). The global sulphur cap will be reduced further to 0.50 per cent (5,000 ppm) from 2020 (subject to a feasibility review in 2018).[90] Annex VI also contains provisions allowing for special SOx emission control areas (ECAs) to be established where even more stringent controls on sulphur emissions apply. Since 1 July 2010, these ECAs have SOx thresholds for marine fuels of 1 per cent (from the previous 1.5 per cent); from 1 January 2015, ships operating in these areas will be required to burn fuel with no more than 0.1 per cent sulphur. Alternatively,

ships must fit an exhaust gas cleaning system or use any other technological method to limit SOx emissions.

The first two SOx ECAs, the Baltic Sea and the North Sea areas, were established in Europe, and took effect in 2006 and 2007 respectively. The third area established was the North American ECA, taking effect on 1 August 2012. In addition, in July 2011, a fourth ECA, the United States Caribbean Sea ECA, was established, covering certain waters adjacent to the coasts of Puerto Rico (United States) and the United States Virgin Islands, and will take effect on 1 January 2014.[91]

Progressive reductions in NOx emissions from ship engines have also been agreed. For ships that operate in ECAs, the strictest controls are applicable to ships constructed on or after 1 January 2016.

It should be noted that the shipping industry, while supportive of the 2008 amendments, has expressed concerns about some aspects of the implementation of the requirements. This includes, in particular, the availability of compliant low sulphur fuel to meet the new demand.[92]

Port reception facilities, sewage from ships and garbage management

Garbage from ships can be just as dangerous to marine life as oil or chemicals. At its sixty-second session in July 2011, MEPC adopted amendments to MARPOL Annex V[93], and these are expected to enter into force on 1 January 2013. The revised Annex V prohibits the discharge of all garbage into the sea, except as provided otherwise. An overview of the revised MARPOL Annex V discharge provisions is provided in table 5.1.

At its sixty-third session, MEPC also adopted:

- Amendments to MARPOL Annexes I, II, IV, V and VI,[94] which are aimed at enabling SIDS to comply with requirements for port States to provide reception facilities for ship waste through regional arrangements. These amendments are expected to enter into force on 1 August 2013;[95]

- A resolution[96] calling for the development, without delay, of proven, adequate and cost-effective technical on-board equipment to make it possible to meet the discharge standards for passenger ships operating in the Baltic Sea (designated a Special Area under MARPOL Annex IV Regulations for the Prevention of Pollution by Sewage from Ships);[97]

Table 5.1.   Simplified overview of the discharge provisions of the revised MARPOL Annex V (resolution MEPC.201(62)) which will enter into force on 1 January 2013 (for more detailed guidance regarding the respective discharge requirements please refer to the text of MARPOL Annex V or to the 2012 Guidelines for the Implementation of MARPOL Annex V)

Type of garbage	Ships outside special areas	Ships within special areas	Offshore platforms (more than 12 nm from land) and all ships within 500 m of such platforms
Food waste comminuted or ground	Discharge permitted ≥3 nm from the nearest land, en route and as far as practicable	Discharge permitted ≥12 nm from the nearest land, en route and as far as practicable	Discharge permitted
Food waste not comminuted or ground	Discharge permitted ≥12 nm from the nearest land, en route and as far as practicable	Discharge prohibited	Discharge prohibited
Cargo residues[1] not contained in wash water	Discharge permitted ≥12 nm from the nearest land, en route and as far as practicable	Discharge prohibited	Discharge prohibited
Cargo residues[1] contained in wash water		Discharge permitted ≥12 nm from the nearest land, en route, as far as practicable and subject to two additional conditions[2]	Discharge prohibited
Cleaning agents and additives1 contained in cargo hold wash water	Discharge permitted	Discharge permitted ≥12 nm from the nearest land, en route, as far as practicable and subject to two additional conditions[2]	Discharge prohibited
Cleaning agents and additives[1] in deck and external surfaces wash water		Discharge permitted	Discharge prohibited
Carcasses of animals carried on board as cargo and which died during the voyage	Discharge permitted	Discharge prohibited	Discharge prohibited
All other garbage including plastics, synthetic ropes, fishing gear, plastic garbage bags, incinerator ashes, clinkers, cooking oil, floating dunnage, lining and packing materials, paper, rags, glass, metal, bottles, crockery and similar refuse	Discharge prohibited	Discharge prohibited	Discharge prohibited
Mixed garbage	When garbage is mixed with or contaminated by other substances prohibited from discharge or having different discharge requirements, the more stringent requirements shall apply		

Source: www.imo.org.

[1]   These substances must not be harmful to the marine environment.

[2]   According to regulation 6.1.2 of MARPOL Annex V the discharge shall only be allowed if: (a) both the port of departure and the next port of destination are within the special area and the ship will not transit outside the special area between these ports (regulation 6.1.2.2); and (b) if no adequate reception facilities are available at those ports (regulation 6.1.2.3).

• The *2012 Guidelines for the Implementation of MARPOL Annex V*[98] and the *2012 Guidelines for the Development of Garbage Management Plans*.[99] These guidelines are intended to assist in the implementation of the revised MARPOL Annex V Regulations for the Prevention of Pollution by Garbage from Ships, which was adopted at the sixty-second session of MEPC in July 2011 and is expected to enter into force on 1 January 2013.

Ship recycling

At its sixty-third session, MEPC also adopted the *2012 Guidelines for Safe and Environmentally Sound Ship Recycling*[100] and the *2012 Guidelines for the Authorization of Ship Recycling Facilities*.[101] These guidelines, along with the *2011 Guidelines for the Development of the Inventory of Hazardous Materials*[102] and the *2011 Guidelines for the Development of the*

Ship Recycling Plan[103] that were adopted during the sixty-second session of the MEPC, are intended to assist ship-recycling facilities and shipping companies to commence introducing voluntary improvements to meet the requirements of the Hong Kong Convention,[104] which had been adopted in May 2009.

Ballast water management

After considering the reports of the 18th, 19th and 20th meetings of the Joint Group of Experts on the Scientific Aspects of Marine Environment Protection (GESAMP), the Committee granted basic approval to three,[105] and final approval to five, [106] ballast water management systems that make use of active substances.

Even though ballast water is essential to ensure safe operating conditions and stability for vessels at sea, it often carries with it a multitude of marine species that may survive to establish a reproductive population in the host environment, becoming invasive, out-competing native species and multiplying into pest proportions. In February 2004, under the auspices of IMO, the International Convention for the Control and Management of Ships' Ballast Water and Sediments (BWM) was adopted to prevent, minimize and ultimately eliminate the risks to the environment, human health, property and resources arising from the transfer of harmful aquatic organisms carried by ships' ballast water from one region to another.[107]

With regard to the availability of ballast water management systems, MEPC at its sixty-third session noted that there were already 21 type-approved systems available. While some delegations[108] expressed concerns regarding the implementation of the BWM Convention due to lack of approved technologies, limited shipyard capacity, time availability and costs involved, other delegations[109] were of the view that there are sufficient ballast water treatment technologies and shipyard capacity, and encouraged shipowners to start installing ballast water management systems on their ships in order to avoid possible bottlenecks at a later stage. It was noted that despite some differences in views there was consensus regarding the need for additional information on the pace of implementation, and the availability of technologies and shipyard facilities and member States were invited to provide updated information regarding the status in their respective countries, according to an agreed template.[110]

The MEPC also adopted a number of amendments to BMW-related guidelines, including the *2012*

Guidelines on Design and Construction to Facilitate Sediment Control on Ships (G12).[111] These are one of the 14 sets of guidelines developed to assist in the implementation of the BWM Convention – G12 updates the previous version adopted in 2006. The MEPC also urged those countries that had not already done so to ratify the BWM Convention, at their earliest possible opportunity, so that it could enter into force.[112]

Dangerous chemicals and oil spill response

In an effort to develop further measures to prevent pollution from ships, the International Convention on Oil Pollution Preparedness, Response and Cooperation (OPRC) was adopted in 1990. The OPRC requires Contracting States to establish measures for dealing with pollution incidents, either nationally or in cooperation with other countries. A Protocol to the OPRC relating to hazardous and noxious substances (OPRC-HNS Protocol) was adopted in 2000. To assist States in implementing the Convention, the OPRC-HNS Technical Group of MEPC was set up. At its sixty-third session, MEPC approved the following guidance manuals, which were developed by the OPRC-HNS Technical Group:

- *IMO/IPIECA Guidance on Sensitivity Mapping for Oil Spill Response*;

- *Guideline for Oil Spill Response in Fast Currents*;

- *Operational Guide on the Use of Sorbents;*

- *Oil Spill Waste Management Decision Support Tool*.

For the finalized drafts of the four guides, see MEPC annexes 62/8, 62/8/1, 62/8/2 and 62/8/3, respectively.

C. OTHER LEGAL AND REGULATORY DEVELOPMENTS AFFECTING TRANSPORTATION

This section highlights some key issues in the field of maritime security and safety, which may be of particular interest to parties engaged in international trade and transport. These include developments relating to maritime and supply chain security, as well as the entry into force of the International Convention on Standards of Training, Certification and Watchkeeping for Fishing Vessel Personnel, 1995. Issues related to piracy will, for reasons of space, not be covered. However, a separate document on issues related to piracy is in preparation by the secretariat.

1.   Maritime and supply-chain security

There have been a number of developments in relation to existing maritime and supply-chain security standards that had been adopted under the auspices of various international organizations such as the World Customs Organization (WCO), IMO and the International Organization for Standardization (ISO), as well as at the European Union (EU) level and in the United States, both important trade partners for many developing countries.

(a) World Customs Organization–SAFE Framework of Standards

As noted in previous editions of the *Review of Maritime Transport*, in 2005, WCO had adopted the Framework of Standards to Secure and Facilitate Global Trade (the SAFE Framework),[113] with the objective of developing a global supply-chain framework. The SAFE Framework provides a set of standards and principles that must be adopted as a minimum threshold by national customs administrations. These standards are contained within two pillars – pillar 1: customs-to-customs network arrangements, and pillar 2: customs–business partnerships.[114] The SAFE Framework has fast gained widespread international acceptance and as of 1 March 2011, 164 out of 177 WCO members had expressed their intention to implement it.[115]

An important feature of the SAFE Framework is the concept of Authorized Economic Operators (AEOs),[116] which are essentially parties that have been accredited by national customs administrations as compliant with WCO or equivalent supply-chain security standards. Special requirements have to be met by AEOs in respect of physical security of premises, hidden camera surveillance and selective staffing and recruitment policies. In return, AEOs are typically rewarded by way of trade facilitation benefits, such as faster clearance of goods and fewer physical inspections.

In recent years, a number of agreements on mutual recognition of AEO programmes have been concluded, mainly on a bilateral level.[117] However, there still appears to be a lack of consensus on what mutual recognition means in practice. According to the SAFE Framework, for a system of mutual recognition to work it is essential that:

- There is an agreed set of common standards that include sufficiently robust action provisions for both customs and AEOs;

- Standards are applied in a uniform manner so that one customs administration may have confidence in the authorization of another;

- If the certification process is delegated to a designated authority by an authorizing customs administration, that there is an agreed-upon mechanism and standards for that authority;

- Legislation to enable the implementation of a mutual recognition system is in place.[118]

In June 2010, WCO issued its SAFE Package, bringing together all WCO instruments and guidelines that support its implementation.[119] A number of updates have recently been made to this package. This includes the 2011 version of the SAFE Framework, providing a separate annex for data elements for security purposes and incorporating the remaining 10 + 2 data elements into those that were listed in the previous version of 2007, with the aim of improving WCO members' risk assessment capabilities in this area. The 2011 version of the SAFE Framework also includes definitions of the terms scanning and screening to clarify their use in day-to-day customs work. Other updates include 2011 versions of the *Compendium of Authorized Economic Operator (AEO) Programmes*, reflecting relevant data as of June 2011, and of the *WCO Guidelines for the Procurement and Deployment of Scanning/NII Equipment*.

In addition, a new set of *Guidelines for Developing a Mutual Recognition Arrangement/Agreement* was added to the SAFE Package. As noted above, mutual recognition is a broad concept embodied within the WCO SAFE Framework, and its interpretation might still be unclear. Therefore, the issuance of the new Guidelines aims to assist States and industry in this respect. According to the Guidelines, mutual recognition is a concept "whereby an action or decision taken or an authorization that has been properly granted by one customs administration is recognized and accepted by another customs administration" – based on a formalized document generally termed Mutual Recognition Agreement (MRA) or Mutual Recognition Arrangement. As concerns the objective of mutual recognition, the Guidelines note: "one customs administration recognizes the validation findings and authorizations by the other customs administration issued under the other programme and agrees to provide substantial, comparable and, where possible, reciprocal benefits/facilitation to the mutually recognized AEOs. This recognition is generally premised on the existence (or creation) of both relevant legislation (where applicable) and operational compatibility of both or more programmes."[120]

The issue of mutual recognition is also addressed in a WCO research paper,[121] where the concept is clarified, in line with the general WCO approach, as follows:

> "Mutual recognition of AEOs is perceived as an arrangement or agreement between two or more customs administrations (or governments) that recognize each other's audits, controls and authorizations as equivalent and therefore provide reciprocal benefits to AEOs. In practice, this means that AEOs authorized by the partner country are recognized as being as secure and reliable as AEOs authorized by their own administration and will, therefore, receive benefits such as reduced risk score and reduced controls when importing into the customs territory."

The research paper also suggests, however, that some advocate a more expansive interpretation. Some assert that an AEO accredited by one mutual recognition agreement party should have exactly the same status and be recognized as an AEO by the other party or parties to that agreement, and thus need not apply in the country of the other party. It is unclear whether this last interpretation is significant or necessary, considering that international trade is dominated by SMEs with a limited geographic range of trade compared to multinationals.[122]

In recent years, a number of MRAs have been adopted by customs administrations, usually on a bilateral basis. However, it is hoped that these will, in due course, form the basis for multilateral agreements at the subregional and regional levels. The first MRA was concluded between the United States and New Zealand in June 2007. As of 30 June 2012, 19 bilateral MRAs have been concluded and a further 10 are being negotiated between the following: China-EU, China-Japan, Japan-Malaysia, China-Republic of Korea, Hong Kong (China)-Republic of Korea, India-Republic of Korea, Israel-Republic of Korea, New Zealand-Singapore, Norway-Switzerland and Singapore-United States. Many countries already having customs compliance programmes[123] are also in the process of adopting legislative measures and taking other steps necessary to establish their own AEO programmes. As of 30 June 2012, 23 AEO programmes have been established in 49 countries[124] and eight more countries plan to establish them in the near future.[125]

(b) Developments at the European Union level and in the United States

At the regional level, EU and the United States have continued to develop measures to improve maritime and supply-chain security. Given the particular importance for many developing countries of trade with EU and the United States, it is pertinent to mention certain developments in this context.

As regards EU, previous editions of the *Review of Maritime Transport* have provided information on the security amendment to the Customs Code (Regulation 648/2005 and its implementing provisions), which aims to ensure an equivalent level of protection through customs controls for all goods brought into or out of the customs territory of EU. The *Review of Maritime Transport 2011*[126] provided an analysis of the major changes this amendment introduced to the Customs Code, and related developments.

Part of these changes involved the introduction of provisions regarding AEOs, a status that reliable traders may be granted and which entails benefits in terms of trade facilitation measures. Subsequent relevant developments, such as the recommendation for self-assessment of economic operators to be submitted together with their application for AEO certificates,[127] and the issuance of a revised self-assessment questionnaire,[128] to guarantee a uniform approach throughout all EU member States, are also worth mentioning.

The EU is in the process of negotiating MRAs with third countries, including major trading partners[129] such as the United States.[130] In this respect, it is worth noting that EU and the United States signed a decision on mutual recognition of their "secure traders" programmes, namely the EU AEO and the United States Customs–Trade Partnership Against Terrorism (C-TPAT)[131] programmes, on 4 May 2012.[132] The decision represents a formal agreement on mutual recognition of safe traders, allowing these companies to benefit from faster controls and reduced administration for customs clearance, enjoy lower costs, simplified procedures and greater predictability in their transatlantic activities. Importantly, mutual recognition is also expected to improve security on imports and exports by enabling customs authorities to focus their attention on genuine areas of risk. The joint decision started to be implemented from 1 July 2012.[133]

As noted in previous editions of the *Review of Maritime Transport*, a legislative requirement was introduced into United States law in 2007[134] to provide, by July 2012, for 100 per cent scanning of all United States-bound cargo containers before being loaded at a foreign port. In October 2009, the United States Department of Homeland Security (DHS) had acknowledged that the implementation of this scanning requirement was unlikely to be met, and that the target date would be postponed until July 2014.[135] Relevant concerns relating to the feasibility of implementing the legislation appear, however, to remain,[136] as is illustrated by the conclusions of a recent United States Government Accountability Office (GAO) report.[137] On 2 May 2012, an official notification letter was submitted by the DHS Secretary to the US Congress, thus giving effect to the anticipated deferral of the requirement for 100 per cent scanning of United States-bound maritime containers at foreign ports for two years until 1 July 2014.[138] Inter alia, the letter states that 100 per cent scanning of containers was neither the most efficient nor a cost-effective way to secure the supply chain against terrorism. In addition, diplomatic, financial and logistical challenges of such a measure would cost an estimated $16 billion.[139]

(c) International Maritime Organization

(i) Measures to enhance maritime security

Both the Maritime Safety Committee (MSC) and the Facilitation Committee (FAL) of IMO consider measures to enhance maritime security as part of their agenda. In this respect, certain developments at the most recent sessions of these Committees over the past year, relating to the effective implementation of the International Convention for the Safety of Life at Sea (SOLAS) chapter XI-2 and the International Ship and Port Facilities Security (ISPS) Code, to voluntary self-assessment for port facilities and ship security, as well as to the search for solutions to stowaway cases, are relevant to the present Review.

At its ninetieth session, held from 16–25 May 2012, MSC recalled that it had previously urged SOLAS Contracting Governments and international organizations to bring to its attention, at the earliest opportunity, the results of the experience gained from the use of the relevant maritime security guidance[140] for consideration of action to be taken. One country informed the Committee that it had, in early 2012, conducted and completed a voluntary self-assessment of its port facilities and ship security using the guidance provided in the above circulars, which had demonstrated to it the value of these self-assessment tools.[141]

A number of maritime security-related measures were considered during the thirty-seventh session of FAL, held from 5–9 September 2011. During the session the Committee adopted resolution FAL.11(37), *Revised Guidelines on the Prevention of Access by Stowaways and the Allocation of Responsibilities to Seek the Successful Resolution of Stowaway Cases*.[142] Finding a solution to stowaway cases can be challenging because of differences between the national legislation of, potentially, several involved States: the State of embarkation, the State of disembarkation, the flag State of the ship, the State of apparent, claimed or actual nationality/citizenship or right of residence of the stowaway, and States of transit during repatriation. The revised Guidelines outline comprehensive strategies to improve access control and prevent intending stowaways from gaining access to ships. They also provide guidance for public authorities, port authorities, shipowners and masters, to enable them to cooperate to the fullest extent possible in order to resolve stowaway cases expeditiously and ensure that an early return or repatriation of the stowaway will take place.

The Committee also endorsed the inclusion, in the Global Integrated Shipping Information System (GISIS), of a module on stowaways, and urged member States to make as much use as possible of the GISIS reporting facilities. In 2008, 494 reports of stowaway cases were received by IMO, 314 in 2009, 253 in 2010 and 47 in 2011 (up to August 2011). The reported cases involved 2,052 stowaways in 2008, 1,070 in 2009, 721 in 2010 and 147 in the first eight months of 2011. However, the low number of reporting sources meant that meaningful analysis of the reports was difficult.[143] Associating the increasing problem of stowaways with a lack of proper implementation of physical security measures and access controls on board ships and within port facilities, member States' obligations to implement fully the provisions of SOLAS chapter XI-2 and the ISPS Code were recalled and, in particular, the requirement for flag States to assess, on a continuous basis, all threats to ships entitled to fly their flag, to set the security level accordingly, and to ensure that ships implement fully the security procedures appropriate to the security level as detailed in the ship security plan.[144]

(ii) Measures to improve security and facilitation of international trade and transport

A number of developments aimed at improving security and facilitation of international trade and transport are also relevant. In particular, FAL, at its thirty-seventh session, adopted a set of *Guidelines for Setting up a Single Window System in Maritime Transport*.[145] Single window systems enable information to be provided to multiple users through a single report. Hence they facilitate trade and decrease the administrative burden on the shipmaster, while at the same time improving the information flow to both individual port authorities and government agencies concerned. The Committee also adopted a revised *IMO Compendium on Facilitation and Electronic Business*.[146] The compendium provides updated information, guidance and recommended formats for electronic exchange of information required by public authorities for the arrival, stay and departure of the ship, persons and cargo in order to facilitate clearance processes.

At its ninetieth session, MSC adopted *Amendments to the International Maritime Dangerous Goods (IMDG) Code*[147] which are intended to harmonize the IMDG Code with the amendments to the United Nations Economic Commission for Europe (UNECE) *Recommendations on the Transport of Dangerous Goods* (17th revised edition). The Committee also issued a circular, *Interim Measures for Early Implementation of the Draft Amendments to the International Maritime Solid Bulk Cargoes (IMSBC) Code*;[148] these measures are set to be adopted in 2013, following recent incidents associated with the liquefaction of cargoes.

(d) International Organization for Standardization

During the last decade, ISO has been actively engaged in matters of maritime transport and supply chain security. Shortly after the release of the ISPS Code, and to facilitate its implementation by the industry, the

---

Box 5.1.   The current status[149] of the ISO 28000 series of standards

Published standards:

- **ISO 28000:2007** – *Specification for Security Management Systems for the Supply Chain*. This provides the overall umbrella standard.

- **ISO 28001:2007** – *Security Management Systems for the Supply Chain – Best Practices for Implementing Supply Chain Security, Assessments and Plans*. This standard is designed to assist the industry meet the requirements for AEO status.

- **ISO 28002:2011** – *Security Management Systems for the Supply Chain – Development of Resilience in the Supply Chain – Requirements with Guidance for Use*. This standard provides additional focus on resilience, and emphasizes the need for an ongoing, interactive process to prevent, respond to and assure continuation of an organization's core operations after a major disruptive event.

- **ISO 28003:2007** – *Security Management Systems for the Supply Chain – Requirements for Bodies Providing Audit and Certification of Supply Chain Security Management Systems*. This standard provides guidance for accreditation and certification bodies.

- **ISO 28004:2007** – *Security Management Systems for the Supply Chain – Guidelines for the Implementation of ISO 28000*. The objective of this standard is to assist users to implement ISO 28000.

- **ISO 28005-2:2011** – *Security Management Systems for the Supply Chain – Electronic Port Clearance (EPC) – Part 2: Core Data Elements*. This standard contains technical specifications that facilitate efficient exchange of electronic information between ships and shore for coastal transit or port calls, as well as definitions of core data elements that cover all requirements for ship-to-shore and shore-to-ship reporting as defined in the ISPS Code, FAL Convention and relevant IMO resolutions.

Standards under development:

- **ISO 28004-Addenda** – *Additional Guidance for Adopting and Certifying ISO 28000:*
    - – For use in medium & small seaport operations;
    - – Adopting ISO 28000 for small–medium-sized businesses (SME);
    - – For security requirements for AEOs.

- **ISO 28005-1** – *Security Management Systems for the Supply Chain – Electronic Port Clearance (EPC) - Part 1: Message Structures*. Provides for computer-to-computer data transmission.

- **ISO 28006** – *Security Management Systems for the Supply Chain – Security Management of RO-RO Passenger Ferries*. Includes best practices for application of security measures.

- **ISO 20858** – *Uniform Implementation of ISPS Code*. If IMO revises the ISPS Code, ISO 20858 may also need revision.

ISO Technical Committee ISO/TC 8 published ISO 20858:2007, *Ships and Marine Technology – Maritime Port Facility Security Assessments and Security Plan Development*.

Another important contribution is the ongoing development of the ISO 28000 series of standards, *Security Management Systems for the Supply Chain,* which are designed to help the industry successfully plan for, and recover from, any disruptive event (see box 5.1). These standards promote a holistic, risk-based approach to managing risks associated with any disruptive incident in the supply chain, before, during and after the event.

The core standard, ISO 28000:2007, *Specification for Security Management Systems for the Supply Chain*, serves as an umbrella management system that enhances all aspects of security: risk assessment, emergency preparedness, business continuity, sustainability, recovery, resilience and/or disaster management, whether relating to terrorism, piracy, cargo theft, fraud, and many other security disruptions. The standard also serves as a basis for AEO and C-TPAT certifications. Various organizations adopting such standards may tailor an approach compatible with their existing operating systems.

2. Maritime safety: entry into force of the International Convention on Standards of Training, Certification and Watchkeeping for Fishing Vessel Personnel, 1995 (STCW-F)

A Convention containing special rules on standards of training, certification and watchkeeping applicable to fishing vessel personnel was adopted on 7 July 1995.[150] The STCW-F Convention, consisting of 15 articles and an annex containing technical regulations, sets the certification and minimum training requirements for crews of seagoing fishing vessels of 24 metres in length and above. Seventeen years after its adoption, the Convention finally entered into force on 29 September 2012, having reached the required number of ratifications twelve months earlier on 29 September 2011.[151] The entry into force of the STCW-F Convention coincided with a diplomatic conference, held from 9 to 11 October 2012, in South Africa for the purpose of adopting an international agreement on the implementation of the 1993 Protocol[152] relating to the 1977 Torremolinos International Convention for the Safety of Fishing Vessels.

The safety of fishermen and fishing vessels constitutes an important part of the mandate of IMO. However, the two instruments on fishing vessel safety mentioned above, that is, the 1977 Convention and its 1993 Protocol, have not come into force due to a variety of technical and legal obstacles and unfortunately many lives continue to be lost in accidents involving fishing vessels every year. With the entry into force of the STCW-F Convention on 29 September 2012, and the renewed efforts to reach agreement at the diplomatic conference held from 9 to 11 October 2012, it is expected and hoped that the Torremolinos Protocol will also meet its entry force requirements as soon as possible.[153]

D. STATUS OF CONVENTIONS

A number of international Conventions in the field of maritime transport have been prepared or were adopted under the auspices of UNCTAD. Box 5.2 provides information on the status of ratification of each of these Conventions, as at 19 September 2012.

Box 5.2.	Contracting States to selected international conventions on maritime transport, as at 19 September 2012	
Title of Convention	**Date of entry into force or conditions for entry into force**	**Contracting States**
United Nations Convention on a Code of Conduct for Liner Conferences, 1974	Entered into force 6 October 1983	Algeria, Bangladesh, Barbados, Belgium, Benin, Burkina Faso, Burundi, Cameroon, Cape Verde, Central African Republic, Chile, China, Congo, Costa Rica, Côte d'Ivoire, Cuba, Czech Republic, Democratic Republic of the Congo, Egypt, Ethiopia, Finland, France, Gabon, Gambia, Ghana, Guatemala, Guinea, Guyana, Honduras, India, Indonesia, Iraq, Italy, Jamaica, Jordan, Kenya, Kuwait, Lebanon, Liberia, Madagascar, Malaysia, Mali, Mauritania, Mauritius, Mexico, Montenegro, Morocco, Mozambique, Niger, Nigeria, Norway, Pakistan, Peru, Philippines, Portugal, Qatar, Republic of Korea, Romania, Russian Federation, Saudi Arabia, Senegal, Serbia, Sierra Leone, Slovakia, Somalia, Spain, Sri Lanka, Sudan, Sweden, Togo, Trinidad and Tobago, Tunisia, United Republic of Tanzania, Uruguay, Venezuela (Bolivarian Republic of), Zambia. **(76)**
United Nations Convention on the Carriage of Goods by Sea, 1978 (Hamburg Rules)	Entered into force 1 November 1992	Albania, Austria, Barbados, Botswana, Burkina Faso, Burundi, Cameroon, Chile, Czech Republic, Dominican Republic, Egypt, Gambia, Georgia, Guinea, Hungary, Jordan, Kazakhstan, Kenya, Lebanon, Lesotho, Liberia, Malawi, Morocco, Nigeria, Paraguay, Romania, Saint Vincent and the Grenadines, Senegal, Sierra Leone, Syrian Arab Republic, Tunisia, Uganda, United Republic of Tanzania, Zambia. **(34)**
International Convention on Maritime Liens and Mortgages, 1993	Entered into force 5 September 2004	Albania, Benin, Ecuador, Estonia, Lithuania, Monaco, Nigeria, Peru, Russian Federation, Spain, Saint Kitts and Nevis, Saint Vincent and the Grenadines, Serbia, Syrian Arab Republic, Tunisia, Ukraine, Vanuatu. **(17)**
United Nations Convention on International Multimodal Transport of Goods, 1980	Not yet in force – requires 30 contracting parties	Burundi, Chile, Georgia, Lebanon, Liberia, Malawi, Mexico, Morocco, Rwanda, Senegal, Zambia. **(11)**
United Nations Convention on Conditions for Registration of Ships, 1986	Not yet in force – requires 40 contracting parties with at least 25 per cent of the world's tonnage as per Annex III to the Convention	Albania, Bulgaria, Côte d'Ivoire, Egypt, Georgia, Ghana, Haiti, Hungary, Iraq, Liberia, Libya, Mexico, Morocco, Oman, Syrian Arab Republic. **(15)**
International Convention on Arrest of Ships, 1999	Entered into force 14 September 2011	Albania, Algeria, Benin, Bulgaria, Ecuador, Estonia, Latvia, Liberia, Spain, Syrian Arab Republic. **(10)**

Source: For official status information, see http://www.un.org/law.

E. TRADE FACILITATION IN INTERNATIONAL AGREEMENTS

1. Towards multilateral rules on trade facilitation at the World Trade Organization: the early or only harvest of the Doha Round?

Eight years since their official start in 2004, the WTO negotiations on trade facilitation (TF) may be close to delivering what could be the early – if not the only – harvest of the Doha Round. Indeed, while the Round itself is now largely considered to be failing,[154] TF is increasingly seen as a rare success story of the negotiations. At the same time, the WTO Negotiating Group on Trade Facilitation (NGTF) has yet to finalize the draft consolidated negotiating text on the individual TF measures. What is also lacking at this stage of the negotiations is an agreement on the degree of commitment of the developed members to delivering technical assistance and capacity building (TACB) to developing and least developed countries in exchange for their commitments to implement TF.

The fate of the future WTO agreement, therefore, hinges on two elements: delinking TF from the WTO Doha Round, and finalizing the TF agreement itself and, in particular, its provisions on special and differential treatment (SDT).

2. Delinking trade facilitation from the WTO Doha Round

In the climate of uneasiness and scepticism surrounding the Doha Round and its unsuccessful last ministerial meeting in December 2011, some WTO members, representatives of the business community and high-level WTO officials issued official statements where they singled out TF as one of the very few areas where an agreement was within the reach.[155]

The support expressed by G20 Ministers in Mexico, April 2012, for breaking up the Doha Round into its component parts, with an emphasis on TF, fuelled the appeals for the delinking of TF from the rest of the Doha issues. The idea is widely discussed and supported by such countries or groups of countries as Australia, Canada, Chile, the United States, and the European Union and their business communities. In June 2012, the World Bank and Regional Development

Bank Presidents issued a personal press article, published later in the press around the world and in developing countries. In the article they urged, in particular, the countries to conclude the TF Agreement and reiterated the commitment for capacity-building projects and technical assistance to address the needs of developing countries so that they may be able to fully implement the Agreement.[156]

The proponents of de-linking TF from the Doha Round emphasize that the expected benefits from a TF Agreement in WTO represent more than 40 per cent of the expected benefits of the entire Round, with two thirds of these gains benefiting developing and the least developed countries.[157] They also consider that the current negotiating text on TF is close to receiving the overall consensus. In his speech at the UNCTAD Multi-year Expert Meeting on Transport and Trade Facilitation in December 2011, the Ambassador and Permanent Representative of Sweden to the WTO voiced strong support for the WTO TF Agreement in 2012, presenting the Agreement as a "win–win", especially in the light of its benefits for developing countries and LDCs. He argued that this was a unique opportunity to muster a much-needed boost to world economy and the best way to address the key legitimate concern of poorer developing countries, that is, getting adequate and sustained support for their TF reforms, through the mechanism of SDT.[158]

The opponents of the idea of de-linking TF from the Doha Round include major emerging economies, such as Argentina, Brazil, China, India and South Africa. They stress the importance of the rest of the Doha package (agriculture subsidies, duty-free/quota-free market access and a services waiver for LDCs) for the developing countries. For them an agreement on TF could not and should not be separated from the rest of the negotiations and, therefore, should share the final fate of the other major elements of the Doha Round. They also reiterate that implementing TF commitments would be much more onerous for developing countries, as opposed to the industrialized countries, who have already implemented most of the TF measures under consideration.[159] In their eyes, agreeing on other Doha issues that would be of benefit to developing countries would tip the overall balance in favour of signing up to legal obligations in the TF area.

The idea of TF as an early harvest, which has emerged timidly over the last two years, is now a frequent feature of the trade talks, media reports and speeches of the high level officials from WTO, the World Bank and other major financial institutions. It remains to be seen whether the economic and political benefits of agreeing on TF would sway the opposition, leading to the signature of the agreement in the near future. But, while the debates on delinking TF from the Doha Round are intensifying and gaining prominence, some work remains to be done to finalize the TF Agreement itself.

3. Finalizing the TF provisions, including the commitments on the special and differential treatment

The draft consolidated negotiating text, currently in its 12th revision, released on 8 May 2012 (TN/TF/W/165/12), contains a total of 26 articles[160] with 675 pairs of square brackets, denoting provisions or parts of provisions yet to be finalized. Only one substantial provision (draft article 14 on the National Committee on Trade Facilitation) contains no such brackets.

The provisions of the current draft consolidated negotiating text can be divided into three sets:[161]

(a) Provisions on the individual TF measures;

(b) Institutional arrangements;

(c) Provisions on the special and differential treatment.

(a) Provisions on individual measures – codifying the best practices in trade facilitation

The individual TF measures currently included in the draft consolidated negotiating text constitute what can generally be seen as a set of the TF best practices (box 5.3).

Many of these measures are present in such classical TF instruments as the Revised International Convention on the Simplification and Harmonization of Customs Procedures (Revised Kyoto Convention) of the World Customs Organizations, the 1982 Convention on the Harmonization of Frontier Controls of Goods, and the United Nations trade facilitation recommendations.[162] In addition, the draft article 10 paragraph 4 – in its more binding version – aims to establish the obligation to use relevant international standards or parts thereof for their importation, exportation or transit formalities and procedures. This potentially includes in the scope of the agreement international TF standards, so far used on

a voluntary basis, such as the United Nations Layout Key (UNLK)[163], the United Nations Trade Data Element Directory and the WCO Data Model. Furthermore, as documented by UNCTAD in the *Review of Maritime Transport 2011* and in a special technical note on *Trade Facilitation in Regional Trade Agreements*, the TF measures being negotiated by WTO are increasingly part of the regional and bilateral trade agreements, reinforcing their status as generally recognized and promoted measures of trade facilitation.[164]

The draft negotiating text, therefore, constitutes already at this stage a framework of reference on TF best practices and is already used as a basis for the national and/or regional TF strategies, bilateral and regional trade cooperation, as well as in TF technical and financial assistance delivered by the international organizations.[165] At the same time, almost all provisions on TF measures need significant fine tuning of the exact language and, thus, of the scope and the strictness of the measure. The objective of the negotiations, as reported by some countries, is to identify the elements of the substantial disagreement so that a political decision can be taken, and to make a decision on the desired degree of precision in the legal wording.[166]

(b) Institutional arrangements – coordinating at the World Trade Organization and the national levels

The draft consolidated negotiating text also addresses the issue of creating and maintaining institutional arrangements at both WTO and national levels.

The draft article 13 establishes a WTO TF Committee, which is to carry out specific responsibilities as assigned to it by agreement or by the members, such as receiving notifications on the modalities of the implementation of certain obligations (publication, Internet publication, implementation categories and schedules), overseeing the implementation of SDT, identifying relevant international standards on export, import and transit procedures and, possibly, carrying out dispute settlement during a transitional period. The mandate of the Committee is potentially vast, as, according to the current draft, it can address "any matters related to the operation of this Agreement or the furtherance of its objectives", which it is expected to do in close contact with other international organizations dealing with TF to avoid duplication of efforts.

At the national level, the draft negotiating text of article 14 of the Agreement contains a future obligation

Box 5.3.   Individual measures currently included in the draft negotiating text

TF measures currently included in the draft consolidated negotiating text		
1. Publication	21.	[Authorized operators]
2. Information available through Internet	22.	Expedited shipments
3. Enquiry points	23.	Prohibition of consular transaction requirement
4. Notification	24.	Border agency cooperation
5. Interval between publication and entry into force	25.	[Declaration of trans-shipped or in transit goods] [domestic transit]
6. Opportunity to comment on new and amended rules	26.	Review of formalities and documentation requirements
7. Consultations	27.	Reduction/limitation of formalities and documentation requirements
8. Provision of advance ruling	28.	Acceptance of copies
9. Right of appeal	29.	Use of international standards
10. Appeal mechanism [in a custom union] [that is a WTO Member]	30.	Single window
11. Import alerts/rapid alerts	31.	[Elimination of] [Mandatory] Pre-shipment [and Post-shipment inspections]
12. Detention	32.	Use of customs brokers
13. Test procedures	33.	Common border procedures [and requirements]
14. Disciplines on fees and charges imposed on or in connection with importation and exportation	34.	Uniform forms and documentation requirements relating to clearance
15. Penalty disciplines	35.	Option to return rejected goods to the exporter
16. Pre-arrival processing	36.	Temporary admission of goods
17. Separation of release from final determination and payment of customs duties, taxes, fees and charges	37.	Inward and outward processing
18. Risk management	38.	Freedom of transit
19. Post-clearance audit/customs audit	39.	Customs cooperation
20. Establishment and publication of average release times	40.	National committee on Trade Facilitation

for all members to establish a national committee on TF to facilitate both domestic coordination and implementation of the agreement. This proposal is based on a particular set of TF best practices traditionally promoted by the United Nations (UNCTAD and the United Nations regional commissions) and international financial institutions, such as the World Bank and the Asian Development Bank (ADB).[167] The usefulness of such a mechanism is widely recognized and in many countries the WTO negotiations on TF created the momentum and the political support for such bodies. Setting up and, much more importantly, maintaining such a committee is not an easy task, especially for developing countries and LDCs, where ensuring the domestic coordination and cooperation on TF is often very difficult in the absence of a clear legal basis, the strong political support and regular technical assistance. Article 14 may, therefore, provide the much needed legal basis and, where appropriate,

solid grounds for requesting and receiving long-term technical assistance, ensuring the viability and the adequate performance of such a mechanism.

(c) Provisions on the special and differential treatment – overcoming the stumbling block of the commitment on technical assistance and capacity building?

While progress has been made on identifying and fleshing out the legal text for individual TF measures, achieving the agreement between all the negotiators on SDT for developing countries and LDCs is still seen as problematic and far from guaranteed.

Special and differential treatment is built into the draft negotiating text and is embodied in the introduction of three categories of commitments for developing country and LDC members, using which these countries can delay the implementation of some measures and/or make it conditional upon receiving the appropriate TACB.[168] Special and differential treatment is also expressed in other elements, such as the proposed "grace period" for the application of the WTO dispute settlement mechanism (the period of time for which has yet to be agreed on).

Setting aside the technicalities of making this differentiated speed of the implementation of the TF measures possible, which are yet to be finalized, the stumbling block in the eyes of many negotiators and analysts is the reticent attitude of the developed members vis-à-vis the inclusion of a clear legal commitment to provide TACB to developing countries and LDCs and to report on the assistance provided individually or through international aid agencies.

It is true that, to date, linking implementation flexibilities to technical assistance delivery, and introducing the mandatory reporting obligations on the TACB provided is unprecedented in the WTO.[169] Furthermore, the developed countries explain their reservations by pointing out the fact that the global TF-related assistance is booming and, therefore, the needed TACB is already available to the countries in need of the assistance and in sufficient quantity.[170] In the course of the negotiations, some developed country WTO members submitted several comprehensive reports to NGTF either on their financing of the projects in the area of TF, or with TF illustrating this point.[171] The overall share of TACB assigned to TF has, in fact, been increasing significantly over the last years. At the same time, the UNCTAD calculations, based on data provided by OECD, also show a difference between the middle-income developing countries and the LDCs. The share of technical assistances assigned to TF is much lower in LDCs than in middle-income developing countries.[172] This element, coupled with

the reasonable expectations that the costs of TF implementation will be the highest in LDCs, lends grounds to the concern of the developing countries regarding a legally binding promise of TACB. Linking TF commitments to a technical assistance was already incorporated in some bilateral trade agreements more than a decade ago, as illustrated by the 2001 Canada–Costa Rica Free Trade Agreement, and references to technical assistance are increasingly included in the new bilateral and regional trade agreements.[173]

4. Conclusion: Window of opportunity for the World Trade Organization trade facilitation agreement?

Eight years after their official launch, TF negotiations in WTO have gained sufficient technical and political momentum to deliver, perhaps, multilateral legally binding rules and the institutional setting for their implementation. While the speed of the negotiations may appear relatively moderate, it is important to bear in mind that drafting technical agreements on trade and transport facilitation issues usually requires several years even at the regional level. Already at this stage, the WTO negotiations on TF have an impact on the current regional and bilateral trade agreements, on the TF-related TACB and national TF strategies.[174]

At present, TF seems to have a definite window of opportunity in WTO. What, in the end, will dictate the ultimate fate of the agreement is the negotiators' willingness and ability to meet each other halfway both in delinking TF from Doha and in finalizing the text of the agreement. Whatever their final outcome, the WTO TF negotiations are already a definite and important chapter of the international regulatory and legal framework of TF.

ENDNOTES

1   For further detail on relevant international regimes, see Reynolds, BWB and Tsimplis MN (2012) *Shipowners' Limitation of Liability*, AH Alphen aan den Rijn, Wolters Kluwer, Part II.

2   1976 LLMC entered into force on 1 December 1986. As at 30 June 2012 it had 53 States Parties representing 53.75 per cent of world tonnage.

3   The 1996 Protocol to the Convention on Limitation of Liability for Maritime Claims, 1976. It entered into force on 13 May 2004. As at 30 June 2012 this Protocol had 46 States Parties representing 45.95 per cent of world tonnage.

4   For further detail on persons entitled to invoke limitation and on the types of vessel in respect of which limitation is available, see Reynolds, BWB and Tsimplis, MN (2012), fn 1 above, chapters 3 and 4. See also fn 13, below.

5   See Arts. 2 and 3 of the 1976 LLMC and 1996 LLMC. Art. 2 lists a set of broad categories of claims subject to limitation and Art. 3 provides for a subset of claims that is excluded from limitation of liability (e.g. claims covered by specialized international liability regimes). For detailed commentary, see Reynolds, BWB and Tsimplis, MN (2012), fn 1 above, chapter 5.

6   See Art. 4 of the 1976 LLMC and 1996 LLMC: "A person liable shall not be entitled to limit his liability if it is proved that the loss resulted from his personal act or omission, committed with the intent to cause such loss, or recklessly and with knowledge that such loss would probably result".

7   The IMO Legal Committee (LEG) during its ninety-ninth session held from 16 to 20 April 2012, adopted amendments to increase the limits of liability in the 1996 Protocol. See Resolution LEG.5(99), *Report of the Legal Committee on the work of its ninety-ninth session*, LEG 99/14, Annex 2.

8   Under the "tacit acceptance" procedure, amendments enter into force on a specified date unless an agreed number of States Parties object before that date.

9   9 Article 3(a)(i).

10   Article 3(a)(ii).

11   Article 3(b)(i).

12   Article 3(b)(ii). The daily conversion rates for Special Drawing Rights (SDRs) can be found on the International Monetary Fund (IMF) website, www.imf.org.

13   The 1996 LLMC applies in respect of proceedings before the courts of a Contracting State (see Art. 15); however, a State may choose not to apply the limits of the Convention in relation (a) to a person who does not have his habitual residence in a State Party, or does not have his principal place of business in a State Party or (b) any ship in relation to which the right of limitation is invoked or whose release is sought and which does not at the time specified above fly the flag of a State Party. See also fn 4, above.

14   The 1957 Limitation of Liability Convention entered into force in 1968, and still has 14 States Parties.

15   The scope of application of the 1976 LLMC is identical to that of the 1996 LLMC (see fn 13 above). The 1924 Limitation of Liability Convention and the 1957 Limitation of Liability Convention also apply in principle to proceedings before the courts of a Contracting State. However, under each of the Conventions a State may choose not to apply the limits to certain categories of person or ship that lack a nexus to the Contracting State.

16   An overview of the deliberations on the reduction of GHG emissions form shipping, during the sixty-first session of the MEPC held from 27 September to 1 October 2010 was provided in chapter 5 of the *Review of Maritime Transport 2011*.

17   See the Second IMO GHG Study 2009, available at http://www.imo.org/blast/blastDataHelper.asp?data_id=27795&filename=GHGStudyFINAL.pdf . The study suggests that if implemented, relevant measures could increase energy efficiency and reduce the emissions rate by 25-75 per cent below the current levels.

18   For an overview of the discussions on the different types of measures, see the *Review of Maritime Transport 2010*, p.118-119 and *2011,* p.114-116.

19   In respect of market-based measures, see particularly the *Review of Maritime Transport 2011*, p.114 and 117-119.

20   The book, a UN co-publication with Earthscan/Routledge, includes contributions from experts from academia, international organizations - such as the IMO, the UNFCCC secretariat, OECD, IEA and the World Bank - as well as the shipping and port industries. Issues covered include the scientific background; greenhouse gas emissions from international shipping and potential approaches to mitigation; the state of play in terms of the relevant regulatory and institutional framework; potential climate change impacts and approaches to adaptation in maritime transport; and relevant cross-cutting issues such as financing and investment, technology and energy. For further information, see the UNCTAD website at www.unctad.org/ttl/legal.

21   For the text of the new Regulations, see the *Report of the Marine Environment Protection Committee at its Sixty-Second Session*, MEPC 62/24/Add.1, Resolution MEPC.203(62), Annex 19.

22   The International Convention for the Prevention of Pollution From Ships, 1973 as modified by the Protocol of 1978 (MARPOL 73/78), Annex VI (MARPOL Annex VI), sets limits on sulphur oxide and nitrogen oxide emissions from ship

exhausts and prohibits deliberate emissions of ozone depleting substances. It also contains provisions allowing for special SOx Emission Control Areas (SECAS) to be established with more stringent controls on sulphur emissions. MARPOL Annex VI entered into force on 19 May 2005 and as of 30 June 2012 had 70 States Parties representing 93.29 per cent of world tonnage.

23   The Regulations were formally voted on and adopted by a majority of the States Parties to MARPOL Annex VI that were represented in the sixty-second session of the MEPC, by a roll-call vote, rather than by consensus. The results of the vote were: 49 parties of MARPOL Annex VI in favour, 5 against and 2 abstained. The Regulations are expected to enter into force for the States Parties to MARPOL Annex VI as of 1 January 2013.

24   For the text of the Guidelines see the *Report of the Marine Environment Protection Committee on its sixty-third session*, MEPC 63/23 and MEPC 63/23 Add.1, Resolutions MEPC.212-215(63), Annex 8-11.

25   For a brief description of these measures, see *Review of Maritime Transport 2011,* p.114-116.

26   The current regulations cover ships with conventional diesel propulsion. Other ship types such as Ro/Ros, passenger ships and ships with diesel-electric propulsion, turbine propulsion or hybrid propulsion will be subject to the energy efficiency requirements later.

27   For detailed requirements regarding EEDI and SEEMP see Regulations 20-22. See also *Objectives of IMO's strategies on GHG emissions*, http://www.imo.org/OurWork/Environment/PollutionPrevention/AirPollution/Documents/GHG%20Flyer%20WEB.pdf.

28   See Regulations 5-10 and Appendix VIII.

29   See Regulation 19.

30   See Regulation 20.

31   The guidelines were prepared by the *Second Intersessional Meeting of the Working Group on Energy Efficiency Measures for Ships* (EE-WG 2). EE-WG 2 also considered guidelines for determining minimum propulsion power and speed to enable safe manoeuvring in adverse weather conditions, and other important issues, such as EEDI requirement for large tankers and bulk carriers, and EEDI frameworks for ships not covered by the current EEDI, for further development at future sessions. For more information see the report of the intersessional meeting, MEPC/63/4/11.

32   See the *Report of the Marine Environment Protection Committee on its sixty-third session*, MEPC 63/23 and MEPC 63/23 Add.1, Resolutions MEPC.212-215(63), Annex 8-11.

33   For most recent IMO discussions, see MEPC 63/23, p.23-26.

34   For discussions in the context of BIMCO for instance, see *It has taken three years of often debate at the International Maritime Organization to finalize EEDI*, Lloyd's List, 23 March 2012.

35   See *2012 Guidelines on the method of calculation of the attained Energy Efficiency Design Index (EEDI) for new ships, Report of the Marine Environment Protection Committee on its sixty-third session*, MEPC 63/23, Annex 8.

36   MEPC 63/23 Add.1, Annex 12.

37   See Regulation 23.

38   For the text of the draft resolution see document MEPC 63/5/4.

39   See MEPC 63/23, p.32.

40   MEPC 63/23 at para. 5.54. Proponents of MBM proposals which rely on design benchmarks/parameters were invited to "clarify in their proposals the relation between such design benchmarks/parameters and the EEDI set out in the new chapter 4 to MARPOL Annex VI".

41   The concerns had been expressed in respect of an IMO commissioned study by Lloyd's Register (LR) in partnership with Det Norske Veritas (DNV) which had been finalized in October 2011 (*Air pollution and energy efficiency, Estimated CO_2 emissions reduction from introduction of mandatory technical and operational energy efficiency measures for ships*, see MEPC 63/INF.2 and MEPC 63/4/1). Concerns regarding the study related in particular to significant uncertainties regarding future emission projections, accuracy of the database used, as well as the fleet growth and scrapping rate scenarios. Moreover, it was argued, the study was optimistic in its estimate of the cost of complying with the EEDI requirements and there was a lack of transparency in terms of the calculation process. See MEPC 63/23, p.27.

42   MEPC 63/23 at para. 5.58. Member States were encouraged to submit documents to MEPC 64.

43   It should be noted that a range of concerns on matters of principle and policy concerning reduction of GHG emissions and in respect of potential MBMs have been expressed by a number of developing countries' delegations, including in particular the delegations of Brazil, China and India. For further details, see also the statements by several delegations, set out in Annexes 14-17 to the *Report of the Marine Environment Protection Committee on its sixty-third session*, MEPC 63/23 Add.1.

44   See the *Review of Maritime Transport 2011*, p.114 and 117-119.

45   For a summary of the MBM proposals submitted at the MEPC, see *Review of Maritime Transport 2010*, p.119-122.

46   For a summary of the discussions, see the *Review of Maritime Transport 2011*, p.117-119.

47   Document MEPC 62/5/1.

48   MEPC 62/5/1, Annex 3.

49   Ibid., Annex 4.

50   Ibid., Annex 5.

51   Study of the *Expert Group on Feasibility Study and Impact Assessment of Possible Market-based Measures (MBM-EG)*, MEPC 61/INF.2. For a brief summary see *Review of Maritime Transport 2010*, p.122-123.

52   GHG-WG 3/3/4 (Cyprus, Denmark, Marshall Islands and Nigeria) and GHG-WG 3/3 (Greece).

53   MEPC 63/5/2 (Note by the Chairman).

54   MEPC 63/WP.12 (Note by the Chairman).

55   Comments on the impact assessment and highlighting the need for further impact studies on developing countries, were provided as part of the discussion in documents MEPC 63/5/8 (India) presenting the findings of an MBM impact study on India's shipping sector and trade, and MEPC 63/5/11 (China).

56   Document MEPC 63/5/8 (India). The study assessed the potential impact of MBMs on freight rates and export/import prices of three essential commodities (capesize iron ore exports from India to China, imports of coal to India from Australia and imports of crude oil to India from Saudi Arabia).

57   It is to be noted that coal accounts for nearly 65% of India's CO_2 emissions. This will defeat the basic purpose of "Reduction of GHG emissions".

58   Document MEPC 63/5/11 (China).

59   See MEPC 63/23, p.34-44. The following documents were considered under this topic: MEPC 63/5/1 (Bahamas) and relevant parts of MEPC 62/5/13; MEPC 63/5/3 (Japan and WSC); MEPC 63/5/9 (Germany); MEPC 63/5/10 (Russian Federation); MEPC 62/5/7 (Greece); GHG-WG 3/3 (Greece); MEPC 62/5/8 (United States); MEPC 62/5/33 (Cyprus, Denmark, the Marshall Islands, Liberia, Nigeria, the Republic of Korea and IPTA); and GHG-WG 3/3/4 (Cyprus, Denmark, Marshall Islands and Nigeria). Documents related to climate finance were discussed subsequently. For discussions on earlier proposals under consideration see *Review of Maritime Transport 2010 and 2011*.

60   Annex 3 of MEPC 62/5/1, see fn 47, above, and accompanying text.

61   MEPC 63/23 at para. 5.25.

62   Ibid.

63   Ibid.

64   The MEPC had the following documents for consideration on this issue: MEPC 62/5/15 (Germany), MEPC 63/5/7 (France), MEPC 62/5/34 (France), MEPC 63/5/6 (WWF), and MEPC 62/5/14 (WWF).

65   The UNFCCC regime is based on the principle of "Common but Differentiated Responsibilities and Respective Capabilities" (CBDR) of States, whereas policies and measures adopted under the auspices of IMO are guided by its major principle of non-discrimination and equal treatment of ships (flag neutrality).

66   MEPC 63/23 at para. 5.34.

67   Ibid.

68   Ibid.

69   The "Rebate Mechanism" refers to a MBM proposal submitted by the International Union for the Conservation of Nature (IUCN), with further details submitted by the WWF; see MEPC 60/4/55, MEPC 61/5/33, MEPC 62/5/14, and MEPC 63/5/6. See also Stochniol A, "A rebate mechanism for an equitable maritime emission reduction scheme". In: Asariotis R and Benamara H. (2012) *Maritime Transport and the Climate Change Challenge*. London: Earthscan (Routledge/Taylor & Francis), chapter 7.

70   MEPC 63/23 at para. 5.34.

71   *Report of the Secretary-General's High-level Advisory Group on Climate Change Financing*, 5 November 2010, available at http://www.un.org/wcm/webdav/site/climatechange/shared/Documents/AGF_reports/AGF_Final_Report. pdf. See also MEPC 62/INF.2 (secretariat).

72   See *Mobilizing Climate Finance*. 6 October 2011, available at http://www.g20-g8.com/g8-g20/root/bank_objects/ G20_Climate_Finance_report.pdf. The report's Annex 2, entitled "Market-based Instruments for International Aviation and Shipping as a Source of Climate Finance" is available at http://www.imf.org/external/np/g20/pdf/110411a.pdf. Information on and a request to consider the G-20 report and its Annex 2 was provided to the Committee in document MEPC 63/5/7, submitted by France.

73   See the remarks of a speaker from the International Chamber of Shipping (ICS) at an UNCTAD Ad-Hoc Expert Meeting on "Climate change impacts and adaptation: a challenge for global ports", held in September 2011. Audio-files of presentations at the meeting and a document presenting main outcomes and summary of discussions (UNCTAD/DTL/ TLB/2011/3) are available on the UNCTAD website at www.unctad.org/ttl/legal. The ICS comments were widely reported in the press, see e.g. http://www.worldbunkering.com/news/industry-news/0730-ics-sells-levy-idea-at-unctad.html. For further information on the position of the ICS in respect of GHG emissions control, see www.marisec.org.

74   See document GHG-WG 3/WP.6.

75   On this matter, see also document MEPC 62/5/27 (India), *On possible incompatibility between WTO Rules and a Market-Based Measure for international shipping*. The delegation of India reiterated its concerns in a statement at the sixty-third session of the MEPC, see MEPC 63/23/Add.1, Annex 17.

76   These decisions and conclusions are summarised in MEPC 63/23 at paras 5.43-5.48. For further information on the outcome of the Durban Conference, see MEPC 63/5/5 (Note by the secretariat).

77   See the conclusion by SBSTA 35, which can be found in MEPC 63/5/5 at paras 23 to 26, as well as the continued consideration of issues related to addressing emissions from international aviation and maritime transport under AWG-LCA, which can be found in MEPC 63/5/5 at paras 18 to 21, and alternative sources.

78   See the decision referred to in MEPC 63/5/5 at para 8.5 to include carbon dioxide capture and storage in geological formations as a Clean Development Mechanism activity.

79   The Conference will be preceded by a two-week session in Bonn, Germany, and it is expected that additional intersessional meetings of the three ad hoc working groups will be held, as well as workshops related to further work on the Green Climate Fund, in accordance with the decision reproduced in MEPC 63/5/5 at para 8.4. See also MEPC 63/23, paras 5.35-5.44.

80   See MEPC 63/23, para. 5.47.

81   UNCTAD, as part of its mandated work programme in the field of transportation, carries out research and analysis "to help developing countries make informed policy choices to address the environmental challenges in relation to transport strategy and to help identify associated capacity-building needs and appropriate regulatory responses" (Accra Accord, para. 168).

82   Document UNCTAD/DTL/TLB/2011/4, available at www.unctad.org/ttl/legal.

83   These include the *International Convention on Civil Liability for Oil Pollution Damage*, 1969; *International Convention on Civil Liability for Oil Pollution Damage* 1992; *International Convention on the Establishment of an International Fund for Compensation for Oil Pollution Damage*, 1971 (no longer in force); *International Convention on the Establishment of an International Fund for Compensation for Oil Pollution Damage* 1992; and the *Protocol of 2003 to the International Convention on the Establishment of an International Fund for Compensation for Oil Pollution Damage*, 1992.

84   *International Convention on Civil Liability for Bunker Oil Pollution Damage 2001*. The Convention entered into force on 21 November 2008 and as of 30 June 2012 had 66 States Parties representing 90 per cent of world tonnage.

85   *International Convention on Liability and Compensation for Damage in Connection with the Carriage of Hazardous and Noxious Substances by Sea (HNS) 1996*. The Convention has not yet entered into force.

86   *2010 Protocol to the International Convention on Liability and Compensation for Damage in Connection with the Carriage of Hazardous and Noxious Substances by Sea, 1996*. The Protocol has not yet entered into force. See also *Review of Maritime Transport 2010* p.124-125.

87   The Convention has not yet entered into force. For more information on the Hong Kong Convention, see *Review of Maritime Transport 2010* p.123.

88   MARPOL annex VI came into force on 19 May 2005, and by 30 June 2012 it had been ratified by 70 States, representing approximately 93.29 per cent of world tonnage. Annex VI covers air pollution from ships, including SO_x and NO_x emissions and particulate matter.

89   See *Review of Maritime Transport* 2008 p.119.

90   In case of a negative conclusion of the review the new global cap should be applied from 1 January 2025.

91   See MEPC 62/24, Resolution MEPC.202(62), Annex 14.

92   See ICS http://www.marisec.org/2012_Text.htm#low sulphur fuel.

93   See resolution MEPC.201(62).

94   See resolutions MEPC.216(63) and MEPC.217(63), MEPC 63/23, Annex 20 and 21.

95   Resolution MEPC.221(63), MEPC 63/23, Annex 26.

96   Resolution MEPC.218(63), MEPC 63/23, Annex 22.

97   This resolution follows the adoption by MEPC 62 of amendments to MARPOL Annex IV designating the Baltic Sea as a "Special Area" under this Annex. Those amendments are expected to enter into force on 1 January 2013.

98   Resolution MEPC.219(63), MEPC 63/23, Annex 24.

99   Resolution MEPC.220(63), MEPC 63/23, Annex 25.

100   Resolution MEPC.210(63), MEPC 63/23, Annex 4.

101   MEPC.211(63), MEPC 63/23, Annex 5.

102   Resolution MEPC.197(62), MEPC 62/24, Annex 3.

103   Resolution MEPC.196(62), MEPC 62/24, Annex 2.

104   The Hong Kong Convention was open for accession since 1 September 2010, and it is not yet into force. It will enter into force 24 months after the date on which 15 States, representing 40 per cent of the world's merchant fleet tonnage have become Parties to it.

105   These were "Smart Ballast" Ballast Water Management System proposed by the Republic of Korea in document MEPC 62/2/8; DMU OH Ballast Water Management System proposed by China in document MEPC 63/2; and EcoGuardian™ Ballast Water Management System proposed by the Republic of Korea in document MEPC 63/2/4.

106   1These were: SiCURE™ Ballast Water Management System proposed by Germany in document MEPC 62/2/10; ERMA FIRST Ballast Water Management System proposed by Greece in document MEPC 63/2/1; MICROFADE™ Ballast Water Management System proposed by Japan in document MEPC 63/2/2; AquaStar™ Ballast Water Management System proposed by the Republic of Korea in document MEPC 63/2/3; and Neo-Purimar™ Ballast Water Management System proposed by the Republic of Korea in document MEPC 63/2/6.

107   See *The 2004 Ballast Water Management Convention with international acceptance growing, the Convention may soon enter into force,* UNCTAD, *Transport Newsletter No.50*, Second Quarter 2011, p.8.

108   The delegations of Brazil; Liberia; Malaysia; Malta; Panama; Singapore; Hong Kong, China and ICS.

109   The delegations of Germany, Ireland, Italy, Norway, the Republic of Korea and Spain.

110   See the *Report of the Marine Environment Protection Committee on its sixty-third session*, MEPC 63/23, p.12.

111   See Resolution MEPC.209(63), MEPC 63/23, Annex 3.

112   The BWM Convention has been open for accession by any State since 31 May 2005, and as of 30 June 2012, it had 35 Parties, representing 27.95 per cent of the world's merchant fleet tonnage. According to Article 18 of the BWM, the Convention will enter into force twelve months after the date on which not fewer than 30 States, the combined merchant fleets of which constitute not less than 35 per cent of the gross tonnage of the world's merchant shipping, have become Parties to it.

113   A June 2011 updated version of the SAFE Framework is available at: http://www.wcoomd.org/files/1.%20Public%20 files/PDFandDocuments/Procedures%20and%20Facilitation/safe_package/safe_package_I_2011.pdf.

114   Pillar 1 is based on the model of the Container Security Initiative (CSI) introduced in the U.S. in 2002. Pillar 2 is based on the model of the Customs-Trade Partnership against Terrorism (C-TPAT) programme introduced in the U.S. in 2001. For more information on these as well as for an analysis of the main features of the customs supply chain security, namely advance cargo information, risk management, cargo scanning and Authorized Economic Operators (AEOs), see "WCO research paper No.18, *The Customs Supply Chain Security Paradigm and 9/11: Ten Years On and Beyond*", September 2011, available at www.wcoomd.org. For a summary of the various U.S. security programmes adopted after Setpemeber 11 see UNCTAD report *Container Security: Major initiatives and related international developments*, UNCTAD/SDTE/TLB/2004/1, available at http://r0.unctad.org/ttl/ttl-docs-legal-reports+docs.htm.

115   For the list of WCO members who have expressed their intention to implement the SAFE Framework, see http://www. wcoomd.org/files/1.%20Public%20files/PDFandDocuments/Enforcement/FOS_bil_05.pdf.

116   The SAFE Framework AEO concept has its origins in the revised Kyoto Convention which contains standards on "authorized persons", and national programmes.

117   See text to fn. 122 below.

118   *WCO Safe Framework of Standards*, June 2011, p.49.

119   See also *Review of Maritime Transport 2011*, p.121-122. The Package included the *SAFE Framework of Standards*, *Customs Guidelines on Integrated Supply Chain Management*, *AEO Implementation Guidance*, *AEO Compendium*, *Model AEO Appeal Procedures*, *AEO Benefits: A contribution from the WCO Private Sector Consultative Group*, *Guidelines for the Purchase and Deployment of Scanning/Imaging Equipment*, *SAFE Data Element Maintenance Mechanism*, *Trade Recovery Guidelines*, and *FAQ for Small and Medium Enterprises*. The SAFE package is available at: www.wcoomd.org/home_pfoverviewboxes_safepackage.htm.

120   See *Guidelines for developing a mutual recognition arrangement/agreement, 2011,* p.2.

121   See WCO research paper No.18, *The Customs Supply Chain Security Paradigm and 9/11: Ten Years On and Beyond*, September 2011, available at http://www.wcoomd.org/files/1.%20Public%20files/PDFandDocuments/ research/18_CSCSP_911.pdf.

122   Ibid.

123   Customs compliance programmes are mainly focused on traditional fiscal rather than security criteria.

124   Due to the fact that 27 EU countries have one common uniform AEO programme.

125   According to information provided by the WCO secretariat. For more information see *Compendium of AEO Programmes, 2012 Edition*, available at www.wcoomd.org/home_research_researchseries.htm.

126   See p.122-123.

127   There are three types of certificate that may be applied for: Customs Simplifications (AEO-C), Security and Safety (AEO-S) and Customs Simplifications/Security and Safety jointly (AEO-F). According to information provided by the European Commission's Directorate General for Taxation and Customs Union, as of 8 February 2012, a total of

13,027 applications for AEO certificates had been submitted, and a total of 9,894 certificates had been issued. The total number of applications rejected up until that date was 1,201 (13 per cent of the applications received), and the total number of certificates revoked was 289 (3 per cent of certificates issued). The number of applications received in the space of one year from 1 January to 31 December 2011 was 5,533. The number of certificates issued during that same period was 4872 (an average of 406 per month). The breakdown reported per certificate type issued was: AEO-F 4700 (49 per cent); AEO-C 4531 (48 per cent); and AEO-S 258 (3 per cent).

128   For the self-assessment questionnaire, see http://ec.europa.eu/taxation_customs/resources/documents/customs/policy_issues/customs_security/aeo_self_assessment_en.pdf . Explanatory notes are also available at http://ec.europa.eu/taxation_customs/resources/documents/customs/policy_issues/customs_security/aeo_self_assessment_explanatory_en.pdf.

129   MRAs have already been concluded with Switzerland, Norway and Japan. A similar agreement is also being explored with China.

130   The EU and the USA are strategic trade partners, with imports and exports accounting for almost €500 billion in 2011.

131   Membership in the C-TPAT has reached 10,221 companies as of January 12, 2012. CBP currently has signed MRAs with the European Union, New Zealand, Canada, Jordan, Japan and the Republic of Korea and is continuing to work towards similar recognition with Singapore, Taiwan and other countries.

132   Preparatory work on mutual recognition was completed in November 2011, when they came to an agreement to mutually recognize each others secure traders programmes. A copy of the decision is published in the Official Journal of the European Union, L 144/44, 5 June 2012, p.44-47, at http://eur-lex.europa.eu.

133   See *Customs: EU and USA agree to recognize each other's "trusted traders"*, EU Press Release IP/12/449, 4 May 2012.

134   *Implementing Recommendations of the 9/11 Commission Act of 2007*. Public Law 110-53, 3 August 2007. For an analysis of the respective provisions, see UNCTAD's *Transport Newsletter* no.45, first quarter 2010, available at www.unctad.org/ttl.

135   See *Review of Maritime Transport 2010*, p.128.

136   See also *"Balancing maritime security and trade facilitation: Protecting our ports, increasing commerce and securing the supply chain"*, Joint Statement by DHS before the House Committee on Homeland Security Subcommittee on Border and Maritime Security, 7 February 2012, available at: http://homeland.house.gov/sites/homeland.house.gov/files/Testimony%20Heyman%2C%20Zunkunft%2C%20McAleenan.pdf.

137   *Container Security Programs Have Matured, but Uncertainty Persists over the Future of 100 Percent Scanning*, Statement of Stephen L. Caldwell, Director Homeland Security and Justice, 7 February 2012, GAO-12-422T, available at: www.gao.gov/products/GAO-12-422T. The report states that "uncertainty persists over how the Department of Homeland Security (DHS) and the United States Customs and Border Protection (CBP) will fulfil the mandate for 100 per cent scanning given that the feasibility remains unproven in light of the challenges the CBP has faced implementing a pilot program for 100 per cent scanning. In response to the SAFE Port Act requirement to implement a pilot program to determine the feasibility of 100 per cent scanning, CBP, the Department of State, and the Department of Energy announced the formation of the Secure Freight Initiative (SFI) pilot program in December 2006. However, logistical, technological, and other challenges prevented the participating ports from achieving 100 per cent scanning and CBP has since reduced the scope of the SFI program from six ports to one. In October 2009, GAO recommended that CBP perform an assessment to determine if 100 per cent scanning is feasible, and if it is, the best way to achieve it, or if it is not feasible, present acceptable alternatives".

138   In order for a two-year extension to take effect, the Secretary of the Department for Homeland Security (DHS) was required to provide a report to Congress 60 days before 1 July 2012 (i.e. by 2 May 2012). See Section 1701 (b)(2) of the *Implementing Recommendations of the 9/11 Commission Act of 2007 (9/11 Act)* which amends the *SAFE Port Act*.

139   For the full text of the letter, see www.brymar-consulting.com/wp content/uploads/security/Scanning_deferral_120502.pdf.

140   MSC.1/Circ.1192 on Guidance on voluntary self-assessment by SOLAS Contracting Governments and by port facilities; MSC.1/Circ.1193 on Guidance on voluntary self-assessment by Administrations and for ship security; and MSC.1/Circ.1194 on Effective implementation of SOLAS chapter XI-2 and the ISPS Code.

141   See document MSC 90/4/1 (Australia).

142   Resolution FAL.11(37), *Report of the Facilitation Committee on its thirty-seventh session*, FAL 37/17 Annex 1.

143   See FAL 37/17, p.18. Reports on stowaway incidents were received by the IMO from nine Member States; one Associate Member and one NGO in 2008; from eight Member States, one Associate Member and one NGO in 2009, from five Member States and one Associate Member in 2010, and one Member State in 2011.

144   Ibid., p.21.

145   FAL.5/Circ.36.

146   FAL.5/Circ.35.

147 For more information on these amendments adopted during the ninetieth session of the MSC see the report of the MSC on its ninetieth session, document MSC 90/28, Annex 4.

148 MSC.1/Circ.1441.

149 For more information see www.iso.org. See also FAL 37/8/3, *ISO 28000 Series Standards Update, submitted by the International Organization for Standardization (ISO)* reflecting information as of 1 July 2011. The procedure of preparing International Standards at the ISO is as follows: Draft International Standards adopted by the technical committees (TCs) are circulated to the member bodies for voting. Approval by at least 75% of the member bodies casting a vote is requested for an International Standard to be published. When there is an urgent market requirement for such documents, a TC may decide to publish other types of documents, such as an ISO Publicly Available Specification (ISO/PAS) or an ISO Technical Specification (ISO/TS). An ISO/PAS is accepted for publication if it is approved by more than 50% of the members of the parent committee casting a vote, while an ISO/TS is accepted for publication if it is approved by 2/3 of the members of the TC casting a vote. An ISO/PAS or ISO/TS is reviewed after three years in order to decide whether it will be confirmed for a further three years, revised to become an International Standard, or withdrawn. If an ISO/PAS or ISO/TS is confirmed, it is reviewed again for a further three years, at which time it must either be transformed into an International Standard or be withdrawn.

150 For further information see http://www.imo.org/about/conventions/listofconventions/pages/international-convention-on-standards-of-training,-certification-and-watchkeeping-for-fishing-vessel-personnel-.aspx.

151 According to Article 12 of the Convention, it will enter into force 12 months after the date on which not fewer than 15 States have ratified it. On 29 September 2011, the Republic of Palau was the fifteenth State to ratify the Convention, increasing its level of ratification to 4.75 per cent of world tonnage.

152 The 1993 Protocol had been adopted to amend the original Torremolinos Convention of 1977.

153 For information on another related convention of a more general nature, the International Convention on Standards of Training, Certification and Watchkeeping for Seafarers (STCW), 1978, and its subsequent amendments, see *Review of Maritime Transport* 2011, p.126-128.

154 Policy Brief, Global Governance Programme, Issue 2011/1, June 2011; Bridges Weekly Trade News Digest, Volume 15, Number 15, 27 April 2011.

155 See reports on the recent informal ministerial trade talks in Paris on 22 May 2012, as reported by 24 May 2012 issue of Washington Trade Daily and the Wall Street Journal on 23 May 2012; Joint Statement of 13 December 2011 of ANTAD (Mexico), EuroCommerce (Europe), the Conseil québécois du commerce de détail (Canada), FTA (Europe) and NRF (US) and P. Lamy (WTO) on March 19 2012, as reported by Reuters (US Edition) on 19 March 2012.

156 "A Down Payment on Development: Conclude a WTO Trade Facilitation Deal", 27 June 2012, Ahmad Mohamed Ali Al-Madani, President of the Islamic Development Bank, Donald Kaberuka, President of the African Development Bank, Haruhiko Kuroda, President of the Asian Development Bank, Thomas Mirow, President of the European Bank for Reconstruction and Development, Luis Alberto Moreno, President of the InterAmerican Development Bank and Robert B. Zoellick, President of the World Bank Group.

157 Interview with Pablo Longueira, Minister of Economics, Development and Tourism of Chile and Gabriel Duque, Deputy Minister of Trade of Colombia, 19 April 2012, transcribed by the office of the Australian Minister for Trade and Competitiveness.

158 "The Case for a WTO agreement – now", Mr. Joakim Reiter, Ambassador and Permanent Representative of Sweden to the WTO, 8 December 2011, UNCTAD Multi-year Expert Meeting on Transport and Trade Facilitation.

159 For a recent overview, see 4-5 June 2012 talks of the trade ministers from the 21 Asia-Pacific Economic Cooperation (APEC), as reported by Bridges Weekly Trade News Digest, Volume 16 · Number 22, 6 June 2012.

160 Section I contains 16 articles and section II on STD, while not divided in articles, contains 11 distinct provisions.

161 The text also deals with the cross-cutting matters which include relationship to other WTO agreements, dispute settlement, final provisions, implementation schedules and exceptions. Due to the limited space, they are not analysed here.

162 See, for instance, Recommendation No. 18 on Facilitation Measures Related to International Trade Procedures of the United Nations Centre for Trade Facilitation and Electronic Business (UN/CEFACT).

163 In some trade and transport agreements, however, such as the abovementioned Harmonization Convention, however, the Contracting Parties commit to align their documents on UNLK.

164 UNCTAD, Transport and Trade Facilitation, Series No.3, "Trade Facilitation in Regional Trade Agreements", UNCTAD/DTL/TLB/2011/1.

165 In several of its ongoing capacity-building projects and regional workshops on TF, UNCTAD is using the draft negotiating text of WTO as a reference for assessing the state of TF in the participating countries. For more information, see http://unctad.org/en/Pages/DTL/Trade-Logistics-Branch.aspx.

166 Switzerland, Note on TF negotiations, August 2011.

167 See UNCTAD, Technical Notes on Trade Facilitation Measures UNCTAD/DTL/TLB/2010/1, and UNCTAD, Trade Facilitation Handbook (Part I): National Facilitation Bodies: Lessons from Experience, UNCTAD/SDTE/TLB/2005/1 (currently under revision).

168   The proposed categories are as follows:
Category A: Provisions that a developing country member or a least developed country member has designated for implementation upon entry into force of the agreement.
Category B: Provisions that a developing country member or a least developed country member has designated for implementation on a date after a transitional period of time following the entry into force of the agreement.
Category C: Provisions that a developing country member or a least developed country member has designated for implementation on a date as requiring a transitional period of time after the entry into force of the agreement and technical and/or financial assistance and support for capacity building.

169   See UNCTAD, Reflection on a Future Trade Facilitation Agreement : Implementation of WTO obligations. A comparison of existing WTO agreements, UNCTAD/DTL/TLB/2010/2, p.45.

170   "The Case for a WTO agreement – now", supra, p.5.

171   For the most recent example, see the communication from the European Union, TN/TF/W/149/Rev.3 of 12 May 2012.

172   Challenges and policy options for transport and trade facilitation, Note by UNCTAD secretariat, 28 September 2011, TD/B/C.I/MEM.1/11, pp. 65-68.

173   A detailed analysis of the TF related provisions in bilateral and regional agreements is available in the abovementioned note by UNCTAD on "Trade Facilitation in Regional Trade Agreements".

174   For a recent example, see the presentation by Argentina at the last UNCTAD Multi-year Expert Meeting on Transport and Trade Facilitation on 7-9 December 2011.

SUSTAINABLE FREIGHT TRANSPORT DEVELOPMENT AND FINANCE

The importance of freight transport as a trade enabler, engine of growth and a driver of social development is widely recognized. However, the associated adverse impacts of freight transport activity on the environment, human health and climate are also cause for concern. Overall, transport consumes over 50 per cent of global liquid fossil fuels and is projected to grow by 1.4 per cent per year from 2008 to 2035 and to account for 82 per cent of the total projected increment in liquid fuel use. It is also estimated that freight in tons per kilometre will triple by 2050 and that energy demand of commercial transportation – trucks, aeroplanes, ships and trains – will rise by over 70 per cent by 2040, driven by economic growth particularly in developing countries. At the same time, the transport sector accounts for around 13 per cent of all world greenhouse gases (GHGs), of which 5.5 per cent are related to logistics (with freight transport accounting for 90 per cent of the total share). Nearly 25 per cent of global carbon dioxide (CO_2) emissions are transport related and these are expected to increase by 57 per cent worldwide (or 1.7 per cent a year) between 2005 and 2030.

If left unchecked, unsustainable patterns are likely to intensify, increasing the potential for global energy and environmental crises, and undermining progress being made on sustainable development and growth. This chapter highlights the relevance of sustainability imperatives in the freight transport sector and focuses on the need to reduce the sector's energy consumption and air emissions. Some of the main developments and initiatives undertaken by countries, industry and the international community with a view to promoting sustainable freight transport are also presented, along with a number of financial considerations that can determine the ability to implement a shift towards sustainable freight transport systems.

A. INTRODUCTION

Environmental sustainability is a pressing issue that is gathering momentum globally. This is triggered by the growing needs of an expanding world population and increasing economic activity which are depleting world natural resources and imposing great pressure on the environment, including the climate. In this context, adhering to sustainability principles becomes crucial to enable an effective balancing act between these competing trends and developments.

The need to achieve sustainability objectives has been further moulded by the global economic and financial crisis, highlighting the emergence of so-called green economies. This term is understood to mean an economy which is low carbon, resource efficient and socially inclusive.[1] The green economy is seen as a key policy option that can address the growing economic, environmental and social challenges.

The United Nations General Assembly and several United Nations agencies have called for the development of green economy initiatives as part of the stimulus packages put in place to support recovery and stimulate growth. The green economy concept was also one of the two major themes considered during the United Nations Conference on Sustainable Development (UNCSD), held in June 2012 in Brazil (RIO+20)[2], which included, for the first time, explicit reference to sustainable transport. The Conference recognized the importance of sustainable transport within the framework of global sustainable development and identified measures to promote such transport systems, including, inter alia, by energy efficient multimodal transport systems, clean fuels and vehicles, as well as improved transportation systems in rural areas and the promotion of integrated approaches to policymaking.[3]

Achieving a green economy also implies tackling climate change and accelerating low-carbon green growth. Estimates indicate that by 2050 the world will need 50 per cent more food, 45 per cent more energy and 30 per cent more water.[4] At the same time, these resources are likely to become depleted or scarce, and only available at prohibitive costs due, in particular, to the negative impacts of climate change. Despite international efforts, namely under the United Nations Framework Convention on Climate Change (UNFCCC), which promoted the adoption of an international binding regulatory regime to mitigate climate change, GHG emissions increased by 5 per cent in 2010, taking the total volume of emissions

to 30.6 gigatons (Gt).[5] Thus, immediate and strong action to cut GHG emissions, while at the same time promoting growth and development, is ever more crucial.

Against this background, an appraisal of the transport sector, including freight transport, within the framework of sustainable development is seen as an essential contribution to the present Review. Around 95 per cent of fuels used in the transport sector are fossil based. With transport depending heavily on oil for propulsion, the sector emits large amounts of GHGs (notably CO_2[6]) and other air emissions such as nitrogen oxides (NOx), sulphur oxides (SOx), volatile organic compounds, particulate matter and lead. All these emissions have negative impacts on human health, the environment (water quality, soil quality, biodiversity, land take, land use, congestion and noise)[7] and the climate.

Freight transport activity will continue to grow in tandem with projected growth in business activities, rising incomes and greater movements of goods – both within and between nations. Growing freight transport activity will in turn lead to a commensurate rise in global demand and use of oil and emissions of GHGs, which can lead to unpredictable changes in the global climate.

In addition to GHG emissions and related global climate effects, local and regional emissions of air pollutants are also raising concerns. Worldwide, air pollution from transport is responsible for about 1.1 per cent of all deaths annually.[8] Trucks and ships are a major source of air pollutants, especially particulate matter. For instance, although only 4 per cent of vehicles in China are trucks, they are responsible for 57 per cent of particulate emissions from transport.[9] Also, particular matter contains black carbon and diesel emissions that are now confirmed carcinogens.[10]

Sustainability in freight transport requires a balancing act between economic, social and environmental considerations, and *entails the ability to provide fuel efficient, cost-effective, environmentally friendly, low-carbon, and climate-resilient transport systems.*[11] Governments and industry have now started to mainstream sustainability criteria into their planning processes, policies, and programmes. Specific actions may involve reshaping transport architecture and networks, balancing transport modes, adapting and developing appropriate infrastructure, rethinking supply chain designs and operating procedures of freight logistics, harnessing new technologies, and supporting information and communications technology (ICT) and intelligent transport systems (ITS). Even though there has been significant progress in sustainable freight approaches and practices, meeting effectively and in full the sector's sustainability objectives has yet to be achieved.

While addressing climate change impacts on freight transport through adaptation action is also a key consideration when pursuing sustainability objectives, this issue falls outside the scope of this chapter and is addressed in greater detail in chapter 1. This chapter highlights the importance of achieving sustainability in freight transport and the need to mitigate the sector's emissions and to reduce the sector's energy consumption as well as its heavy reliance on oil. Some key developments and initiatives undertaken by countries, industry and the international community with a view to promoting sustainable freight transport are also discussed in the present chapter, along with a number of financial considerations that may help to determine the ability to implement a shift towards sustainable freight transport systems.

B. TRANSPORT SECTOR ENERGY USE AND EMISSIONS

This section highlights the large energy use and emissions from transport, including freight transport, and underlines the importance of reducing the sector's oil consumption and dependency to achieve greater environmental sustainability, and reduce exposure to rising and volatile energy prices that drive up fuel and transport costs.

1. Energy use

The transport sector is heavily dependent on oil as its main source of fuel. As shown in figure 6.1, transportation consumes more than 50 per cent of global liquid fossil fuels and its share of world consumption has grown by 17 per cent between 1973 and 2010.[12] In comparison, other economic sectors have recorded a declining trend during the same period. World liquid fuel consumption for transportation is expected to grow by 1.4 per cent per

Figure 6.1.   World oil consumption, 1973 and 2010

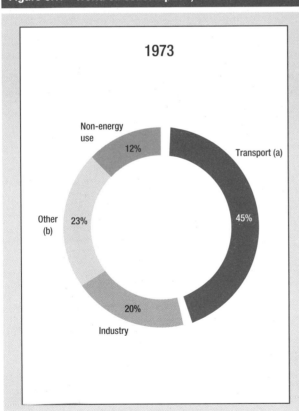
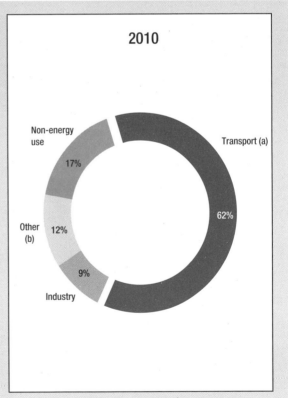

Source: *Key World Energy Statistics 2012*, International Energy Agency (IEA). The oil products comprise refinery gas, ethane, liquefied petroleum gas (LPG), aviation, gasoline, motor gasoline, jet fuels, kerosene, gas/diesel oil fuel, oil, naphtha, white spirit, lubricants, bitumen, paraffin waxes, petroleum coke and other oil products.
(a)   Includes international aviation and international marine bunkers.
(b)   Includes agriculture, commercial and public services.

year from 2008 to 2035 and accounts for 82 per cent of the total projected increment in liquid fuel use.[13]

Freight transport has been growing more rapidly than passenger transport and is expected to continue rising in the future. Some existing forecasts indicate that freight in tons per kilometre will triple between 2010 and 2050, driven by economic growth particularly in developing countries.[14] Energy demand for commercial transportation – trucks, aeroplanes, ships and trains – is projected to rise by more than 70 per cent from 2010 to 2040. Most of this growth will come from heavy duty vehicles, which include freight trucks of all sizes, as well as buses, emergency vehicles and work trucks. [15]

Oil supply and demand and price fluctuation are important considerations for transport and will continue to play a significant role in the future, as uncertainty over global oil reserves, among other issues, become more prevalent. Alternative sources of energy and fuel efficiency in transport may take up a more prominent role, assuming continued research and development, technological advances and strong policies are put in place to ensure their implementation at an affordable cost and on a massive scale. In the meantime, this should not prevent practical steps being taken to gear current operations towards more energy-efficient practices (see section C).

2. Emissions

The transport sector is estimated to have accounted for around 13 per cent of all world GHGs in 2004.[16] Logistics, including freight transport and 'logistics buildings' account for 5.5 per cent of global GHG emissions. Of this total, freight transport accounts for the lion share of 90 per cent or 4.95 per cent of total GHG emissions.[17] In terms of CO_2 emissions, the transport sector is estimated to have accounted for around 23 per cent of global CO_2 emissions in 2009.[18] As shown in figure 6.2, the transport industry is the second largest CO_2-emitting sector after electricity and heat production.

Figure 6.3 compares CO_2 emissions from major freight transport modes. It shows that in terms of grams of CO_2 produced for every ton carried over one kilometre, air transport is the largest emitter, followed by road. It should also be noted that air and road transport are the two most expensive modes of transport in terms of freight rates per volume.

If current trends persist, transport-related CO_2 emissions are estimated to increase by 57 per cent worldwide (1.7 per cent a year) for the period 2005–2030.[20] It is also expected that more than 80 per cent of the predicted growth in transport

Figure 6.2. World CO_2 emissions from fuel combustion by sector, 2009 (a)

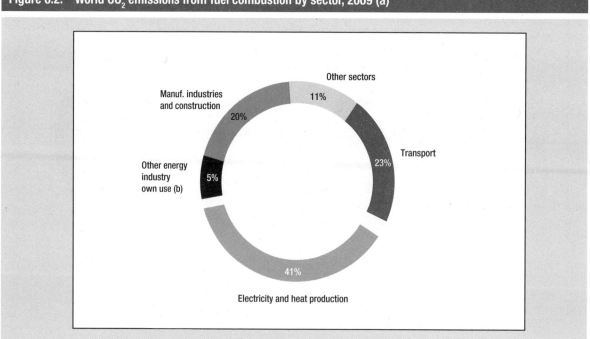

Source: CO_2 Emissions from Fuel Combustion Highlights, 2011, IEA.
(a)   Includes international bunkers in the transport sector.
(b)   Includes emissions from own use in petroleum refining, the manufacture of solid fuels, coal mining, oil and gas extraction and other energy-producing industries.

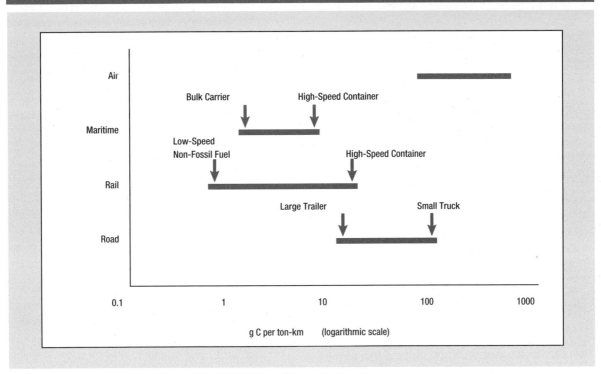

Figure 6.3.   Comparison of CO₂ emissions in freight transport by mode of transport (Grams carbon per ton freight carried per kilometre)

Source: Intergovernmental Panel on Climate Change (IPCC)[19]

emissions would be in developing countries (with China and India alone accounting for more than 50 per cent of the global increase[21]) and with most of the emissions being generated by land transport. Air pollution is also expected to be more intensive in developing countries due to the quality of fuel used for propulsion and the condition of equipment and vehicles, in particular the ageing trucks.

The challenge now is for all countries to promote sustainable transport policies, strategies, planning and investment decisions that balance the economic, environmental and social objectives. This is particularly crucial for developing countries that have the opportunity to consider from inception a sustainable development path. Missing this opportunity may lead to increased costs in the future, as Governments and industries would eventually face additional expenses to adapt to new circumstances and adopt new transport systems, including new technologies and operating practices. Retrofitting existing infrastructure and equipment to shocks, including those caused by climate change impacts, can be burdensome, capital intensive and costly. Thus, timely action at an early stage is

crucial. Any delay in pursuing energy fuel efficiency and low carbon systems will promote false savings. It is estimated that every United States dollar spent on energy efficiency saves $2 through investments in new supply, with the savings being even greater in developing countries.[22]

C. RECENT DEVELOPMENTS IN SUSTAINABLE FREIGHT TRANSPORT

Addressing sustainability in the freight transport sector requires a holistic approach where the perspectives of all private and public stakeholders in the system must be considered and integrated, inclusive of all modes and activities. Institutional, technical and operational measures have to be defined and combined to overcome the various cross-cutting sustainability challenges characteristic of the sector. Some of the salient measures can generally be associated with three main areas for action – also described as the avoid–shift–improve approach[23] – which would encounter cross-cutting issues that can be summarized as follows:

- Avoid inefficient freight transport: avoid or reduce wasteful and unnecessary or empty trips, and duplication of roads, thus optimizing freight transport planning/volume/operations and reducing congestion, and the like.

- Shift to sustainable transport modes and systems: shift to cleaner transport modes (railways and waterways when applicable), to alternative fuels and to appropriate vehicle size, loads and routes, and the like.

- Improve the sustainability of freight transport, logistics, vessels and vehicles: improve infrastructure design and construction; improve fuels efficiency in all modes by improving freight transport operations (for example, by better management of transport system flows and capacities) and freight logistical systems (for example, creating smart logistics network concepts), leveraging technologies capable of improving fuel efficiency and reducing emissions, and improving drivers' behaviour (for example, through training and capacity building).

This section focuses on some of the measures and initiatives undertaken by the sector (maritime and inland) to promote a shift towards sustainable freight transport. These initiatives are expected to produce benefits in terms of improving the competitiveness of environmentally friendly transport modes and systems, increasing fuel efficiency, time and cost-effectiveness, thereby reducing the sector carbon footprint.

1. The maritime sector

As the debate on climate change has been gaining momentum globally, the maritime and shipping sector has been facing pressure to respond to the challenges of increasing GHG emissions (CO_2, SOx, NOx, etc.) and air pollution (especially particulate matter) and possible mitigation and adaptation measures are being considered, both at the regulatory and industry levels.

Although considered to be a relatively energy-efficient and climate-friendly mode of transport, especially in terms of emissions per ton of freight per kilometre, shipping and its environmental footprint is increasingly coming under public scrutiny.

According to the International Maritime Organization (IMO), shipping was estimated to have accounted for 3.3 per cent of the global emissions during 2007. International shipping was estimated to be responsible

for 2.7 per cent of the global emissions of CO_2 in 2007. In the absence of global policies to control emissions from international shipping, ship emissions may increase by 200–300 per cent by the year 2050 (compared to the emissions in 2007) due to the expected continued growth in international seaborne trade.[24]

There does, however, appear to be a consensus within the International community, including the International Maritime Organization (IMO), that some measures affecting the technology of ships and fuels could help achieve some energy efficiency and reduce GHG emission intensity rates (CO_2/ton-mile) by 25–75 per cent below the current levels. Moreover, the international shipping industry is of the view that through joint and combined technical and operational efforts, it should be possible to reduce 15–20 per cent of CO_2 emissions per ton freight per kilometre by 2020.[25]

At the regulatory level, the international shipping industry is adhering increasingly to environmental sustainability principles and is recognizing its important role in maintaining the current international momentum on sustainability and climate change action in maritime transport. In 2011, the IMO (the body entrusted by UNFCCC to develop and enact global regulations to control GHG emissions from ships engaged in international trade) adopted the first global regime that addresses carbon emissions from international shipping, namely the Energy Efficiency Design Index (EEDI) and the Ship Energy Efficiency Management Plan (SEEMP) (see chapter 5 for a more detailed discussion of the new rules). Market-based measures, such as emissions trading or a global levy to help cut further emissions from international shipping are also being considered by IMO, but a number of outstanding issues are holding back a rapid adoption of an international agreement. These include the need to reconcile the principle of common but differentiated responsibilities and respective capabilities (CBDR) under the UNFCCC with the principle of uniform and global application of IMO instruments, as well as the need to determine the level of contribution by shipping into the Green Climate Fund (GCF) (established in December 2011 at the United Nations Climate Change Conference in Durban – see the following section on climate finance). The Fund aims to generate $100 billion per year by 2020 to enable mitigation and adaptation action in developing countries. While the United Nations Secretary-General's High-level Advisory Group on Climate Change Financing (AGF), established in 2010, suggested that some $16 billion per year could be raised from international shipping, the World Bank suggests that instead some $25 billion per year could be generated.[26] The shipping industry is concerned that its potential contribution into the Fund will be disproportionate to its responsibility for global CO_2 emissions, and that it will be doubly charged through the UNFCCC as well as via a potential market-based instrument under the IMO.[27]

At the industry level, the shipping industry is taking important actions, including technological, operational or engineering-based measures to improve the sector's energy efficiency, reduce fuel consumption and emissions. Relevant initiatives include building fuel-saving and environment-friendly ships, promoting the switch to cleaner fuels and increasingly adopting slow steaming. As an example, SinoPacific Shipbuilding Group launched, in May 2012, a new generation of fuel-saving and environment-friendly bulk carriers which aim at the segmented markets for 60,000, 80,000 and 120,000 deadweight ton (dwt) bulk carriers (CROWN 63, CROWN MHI 82 and CROWN 121 Ultimate, respectively). At a service speed of 14.3 knots, the fuel consumption of CROWN 63 Ultramax bulk carriers is reduced to 25.8 tons per day, representing a 13 per cent reduction in fuel consumption compared to equivalent-sized bulk carriers currently operating.

For the ports and terminals, various opportunities have also emerged for improving environmental sustainability. Examples vary from enhanced port infrastructure design, switching to greener modes of transport for hinterland access (e.g. rail, inland waterways), the adoption of energy efficiency programmes and using renewable energy (such as biofuels, solar energy and wind turbines) to cater for port operations in general, including cargo loading, unloading and warehouses, as well as traffic management systems (both for servicing vessels and for cargo handling inside the terminals). In this context, one study has demonstrated that by mixing 30 per cent biofuels with used diesel can lead to a 13–26 per cent reduction of CO_2 emissions per terminal and to a 21 per cent emission reduction of the total container sector.[28] The so-called cold ironing – whereby ships, while in the port, use onshore electricity as energy source instead of running their engines – constitutes another strategy able to reduce emissions in ports and even in some cases completely eliminating, harmful air emissions from diesel engines. Furthermore, ports and terminal operators see a competitive advantage to be gained in integrating technology to their business processes and in using cleaner land-based cargo-

handling equipment such as IT-driven quay cranes and eco-friendly rubber-tyred gantry cranes.

Other port-based measures aiming to achieve greater efficiencies in ports include changing terminal layouts to reduce time and processes required to move containers and cargo. By doing so, a reduction of CO_2 emissions can be generated, as illustrated by the Rotterdam Shortsea Terminal which noted a CO_2 emission reduction of nearly 70 per cent.[29] Another more comprehensive approach consists of incorporating systemic logistics solutions aimed at reducing time and cost into the design and planning of ports and terminals, as shown by the port-centric logistics or cargo hub operating structure.[30] Recent studies[31] have shown that the port-centric model does address the key supply chain challenges of time, cost and carbon emissions. However, in some countries land availability and affordability may be a barrier to delivering fully efficient port-centric solutions. The development of port-centric models have been widely accepted in Europe, where there is a growing shift to the building of logistics centres adjacent to new sea or inland water transport terminals.[32] For example, DP World's London Gateway is developing a large port-centric logistics park connected to a new 3.5 million TEU deep-sea container port located east of London. London Gateway would offer a quicker, more reliable and greener way to transport goods to their destination compared with existing supply chain models. It is estimated that 65 million road-freight miles every year will be saved since goods will no longer need to be transported from deep-sea ports to inland distribution centres.[33] Another scheme to improve sustainability is to investigate how logistics chains can be developed in ways that mitigate empty cargo loads and consolidate shipping journeys via so-called optimization. Enhanced logistics and supply chain management can improve freight loads and storage, thereby reducing the number of trips required for deliveries. Other innovative approaches used by ports to reduce emissions include the so-called low emissions zones or the geographically defined areas that seek to restrict or prevent access to polluting vehicles within and around port areas. Low emissions zones exist in Singapore, Hong Kong (China), Seattle and Antwerp and coast lines such as the West Coast of the United States and the East Coast of China (planned). Together, all these measures can help reduce the carbon footprint and control air pollution in the maritime transport sector while, at the same, improve efficiency in the business.

2. Inland freight transport and logistics

As previously mentioned, the large scale of transport energy consumption and CO_2 emissions is due mainly to land modes, in particular haulage by road. This is likely to grow significantly in the next decades, mostly in developing countries. The travel activity of surface freight transport– including rail, medium-duty truck and heavy truck (in ton-kilometres) worldwide is expected to increase by an average annual rate of 2.3 per cent from 2000 to 2050.[34] In India, this growth will likely be 3.8 per cent over the same period, followed by China at 3.3 per cent, Africa 3.1 per cent and Latin America 2.8 per cent.[35] Therefore, achieving growth and sustainability will become increasingly difficult in the future, without taking into consideration improving fuel efficiency and reducing emission from land transport.

Past experiences, namely from the developed countries, have demonstrated that given the long-lived nature of the transport assets and huge investment implications of the sector, land transport is one of the toughest sectors to switch from or within which to reduce emissions once the systems have been established. For instance, switching to more environmentally friendly modes, such as rail and inland waterways, offers a well-known initially costly alternative that would require long-term planning and appropriate corrective and supportive measures at policy, as well as business and operational levels.

Moreover, there are several challenges, including a fragmented inland freight sector, inadequate policies and institutional arrangements, as well as the limited availability and high cost of technologies that are preventing wide adoption of sustainable strategies.

Yet, there are considerable opportunities to improve sustainability in land freight transport and logistics through a "comprehensive and integrated approach". Subject to a considered cost–benefit analysis and assessment of trade-offs (energy efficiency gains, transport costs, speed and reliability of services, and the like), a number of integrated options have the potential to promote sustainability in land freight transport. This entails, inter-alia, optimizing the performance of multimodal logistics chains, improving the competitiveness of environmentally friendly modes of transport, leveraging technologies capable of improving energy efficiency, logistical efficiency and reducing emissions, as well as creating integrated

transport networks and environmentally -friendly dedicated freight corridors.

An example of an integrated transport planning approach is the European Commission White Paper on transport (adopted in March 2011) that defines a strategy towards competitive and resource-efficient transport systems and sets clear objectives and targets such as:

(a) Optimizing the performance of multimodal logistics chains;

(b) Promoting the use of more energy-efficient modes of transport at a larger scale, facilitated by efficient and environmentally friendly freight corridors;

(c) Instigating a 50 per cent shift in longer-distance freight journeys from road to other modes;

(d) Instigating a 40 per cent use of sustainable low-carbon fuels in aviation;

(e) Achieving at least a 40 per cent cut in shipping emissions.

This has the overall objective of achieving a total of 60 per cent reduction in CO_2 emissions and a comparable reduction in oil dependency.[36]

Another example is provided by the Government of Indonesia, which has introduced comprehensive policies that aim at promoting sustainable freight transport systems and reducing the transport burden on roads, the predominant mode of transport (which accounts for about 70 per cent of freight ton-kilometres). These policies include a shift towards greener modes of transport such as rail and short sea shipping (where ferries can carry out roll-on, roll-off operations) and develop rail-based logistics in Jakarta to relieve traffic congestion caused by freight movements. Improving fuel efficiency and reducing land transport related emissions is crucial, given the recent growth in freight movement in Indonesia (which has increased by 67 per cent in 5 years, i.e. from 9.4 billion tons in 2006 to 15.7 billion tons in 2011) and the significant share of CO_2 emissions from land transport (which represent 89 per cent of total transport emissions and about 20 per cent of total national emissions).[37]

An integrated transport planning strategy aimed at promoting more efficient transport and logistics systems would usually encompass the development of intermodal transport and integrated freight transport networks. These would also require the development of appropriate infrastructure and services, facilitating movement of goods and reducing or eliminating cumbersome procedures along the supply chain, which in turn would enhance efficiency of freight transport systems. One example is the development of multimodal hubs and logistical centres (linked to seaport and freight terminals through railways or waterways) which exist already and are quite advanced in several developed and some developing countries. In Asia, for instance, dry ports with logistics service centres are being developed as an integrating mechanism for regional transport networks. Examples can be found in China, India, Nepal, and Thailand.[38]

Other innovative concepts that countries have developed to promote sustainable freight transport is the establishment of dedicated freight corridors (such as in Australia and India). The purpose of these corridors is to ensure efficient freight movements and shift freight traffic from carbon intensive transport modes such as roads to less carbon intensive transport modes such as rail.[39] Other initiatives have fostered the development of urban logistics centres (such as in Germany and the United Kingdom) to promote efficient delivering and collecting goods in town and city centres while mitigating congestion and environmental externalities. The growing significance of urban freight transport and logistics is related to increased population and sustained economic growth in urban areas. Similarly, in many developing countries, where trade remains largely dependent on primary products and represents a major source of income for a big part of the population, rural transport and logistics networks (such as in China, India and South Africa) are increasingly becoming key for the countries' overall economic development. Many of these countries face significant transport infrastructure

deficits in rural areas, including logistics practices and services which increase their losses and hamper their competitiveness.[40] Promoting such concepts would help countries to reduce important inefficiencies in their value chain systems and introduce sustainable and environmentally-friendly transport solutions.

In general, there is no single unified approach to defining and implementing sustainability measures in freight transport for all countries and regions, particularly when dealing with land-freight transport and logistics. Measures to promote sustainable freight transport have to be consistent with a country's longer-term development plans and objectives. These also need to take into account the relative importance of fuel security, emissions, air pollution and the geographical situation of a country. Furthermore, they have to be compatible with the country's level of infrastructure and logistics development as well as its specific local circumstances, including socio-economic issues. An overview of the nationally appropriate mitigation actions (NAMAs)[41] for non-annex I countries (that is, countries not bound by Kyoto targets) shows that there are no systemic actions presented by countries to promote less energy-intensive and carbon-intensive freight transport systems. Countries actions vary in terms of subsector and objectives as described in table 6.1.[42]

Various studies also demonstrate how a combined package of measures (institutional and technical) relating to inter alia energy efficiency, emission intensity, supply chain structure, modal split and vehicle utilization, can enable the move to sustainable freight logistics, but also underline the relative importance of a country's level of development and geography for the application of these measures. For example, the aerodynamic profiling of trucks, which is a cost-

Table 6.1.   Overview of nationally appropriate mitigation actions in freight transport (2011)

	Country	Subsector	Type of action	Objective
Modernization of freight train infrastructure	Argentina	Rail cargo	Not known	Modernize the infrastructure of the Belgrano Cargas freight rail system and promote a modal shift from trucks to rail for agricultural products
Programme for energy efficiency in the transport sector in Chile	Chile	Road cargo	Strategy/plan	Promotion of energy efficiency in the transport sector to reduce GHG emissions and to secure sustainable cargo and passenger transport
National plan for freight transport: NAMA pilot study	Colombia	Road cargo	Strategy/plan	Build the planning and implementation capacity of the Ministry of Transport and the National Planning Department in Colombia to structure NAMAs in the transportation sector and more specifically in the field of freight transportation
Shifting freight to electric rail	Ethiopia	Rail cargo	Project	Increase in ton-km of freight transported by electric rail as opposed to road transport. Rail transport will be powered by renewable electricity.

Source: NAMA database.

effective measure of cutting fuel consumption and emissions in developed countries possessing good road infrastructure and high speed operations, may be much less beneficial in less developed countries where infrastructure is not adequate and average speeds are much lower.[43]

The role of industry

At the industry level, a large number of sustainable freight transport initiatives have been introduced, such as: promoting energy efficiency in vehicles (in kilometres and ton-kilometres, using simple options such as adjusting tyre pressures and promoting eco-driving, and more advanced use of technologies such as hybrid diesel–electric engine trucks), shifting to cleaner modes of transport, as well as using low-carbon technologies and ICT. The efficiency of logistics operations can be improved in a number of ways using ICT, including for instance the use of software able to improve the design of transport networks and allow the running of centralized distribution networks and management systems. Implementing such solutions will enable the reduction of freight congestion, waiting times in delivery places, unnecessary trips (reducing frequency of vehicles travelling empty or partially loaded), storage needed for inventory, and so lead to a greener and more efficient transportation. It was noted that optimizing logistics using ICT could result in a 16 per cent reduction in transport emissions globally and could achieve a decline in total global emissions of 1.52 Gt CO_2 by 2020.[44]

Some of the successful private-sector led sustainable freight transport initiatives are provided below:

- The German chemical company, BASF, has set a new policy to use inland waterways to transport over 70 per cent of its supplies, and IKEA has a policy of using trains wherever possible;

- The German food company, Kraft Jacobs Suchard, uses trains to carry raw coffee beans from Bremen to its factories in Berlin. The coffee bean trains, which have replaced local delivery trips by road, have saved 40 per cent of the energy previously used for road transport;

- In the Netherlands, EVO, the employers' organization for logistics and transport, organizes courses and training programmes to teach drivers to drive more economically. Drivers who follow these courses can achieve fuel consumption reductions of up to 10 per cent;[45]

- Walmart aims to double the truck fleet's fuel economy by 2015 and reduce CO_2 emissions by 26 billion pounds by 2020. Trucks in Walmart's distribution network drive 900 million miles a year to deliver goods to the retailer's 4,000 stores. Aside from tyre and aerodynamics technologies, auxiliary power units (APUs) were installed in 2006 on all trucks that made overnight trips, reducing CO_2 emissions by an estimated 100,000 tons and fuel use by 10 million gallons;[46]

- FedEx has launched "EarthSmart" Initiative which encompasses various sustainability efforts, including adding more sustainable delivery vehicles, optimizing delivery routes in order to minimize driving time, and maximizing cargo space in fuel-efficient planes to reduce the number of planes in the sky. Fuel efficiency has increased from 5.4% in 2006 to 15.1% in 2010;

- In China, the Henan Anyang Modern Logistics Information Development, a company established in 2006 as an online logistics information platform that provides freight information exchange services and other value-added services, has helped trucking companies in Anyang city (Henan Province) to reduce the empty mile percentage from 53 per cent in 2006 to 38 per cent in 2008. The total freight empty mileage saving in Anyang is about 137.5 million kilometres, which saved 27.5 million litres of fuel (equal to 165 million Chinese yuan (CNY)) during the same period. The platform has since expanded to the entire province, with more than 50,000 deals made per month and with average savings per month of 43.9 million kilometres, 8.8 million litres of fuel and 52.7 million CNY (approximately $8.2 million);[48]

- The European Chemical Industry Council (CEFIC) introduced in 2011 a study – *Guidelines for Measuring and Managing CO_2 Emissions from Freight Transport Operations* – to assist chemical companies understanding how they can assess and improve their transport-related operations and reduce emissions;[49]

- The Green Freight Asia Network, involving global freight logistics companies, manufacturers, freight carriers and industry associations was established in 2011 to support green freight initiatives and programmes in Asia;[50]

- A joint voluntary commitment to promote green freight in Europe and Asia has been reached between the Clean Air Initiative for Asian Cities (CAI-Asia), the Secretariat for Green Freight Europe (European Shippers' Council - ESC and EVO Dutch Shippers' Council), and the Sustainable Supply Chain Centre Asia Pacific (SSCCAP) under the auspice of the Rio+20 conference. The programme, which will be fully operational in Europe and Asia, aims to help countries reduce fossil-fuel dependency, improve air quality and minimize CO_2 emissions that contribute to climate change, without hindering economic development.

Even though there has been significant progress in sustainable freight approaches and practices in recent years, sustainable freight transport is still in its infancy and most stakeholders are still in the learning phase. To ensure the delivery of successful initiatives, combined efforts emanating from both the public and private sectors, including comprehensive approaches that would ensure interdisciplinary and inter-institutional collaborations in areas such as research, data analysis and technology, must be strengthened. Strategic thinking and development related to sustainable freight transport must also be reinforced, with the objective of seeking common institutional and operational benefits and efficiencies in terms of transport decarbonization, energy conservation, cost management and efficient freight logistics movement in support of global trade and development.[51]

D. ENABLING SUSTAINABLE FREIGHT TRANSPORT: FINANCE-RELATED CONSIDERATIONS

Transport is shaped by financial flows from various sources – public and private, national and international. The state of financial resources in 2010 indicates that domestic flows (public and private) are the most important source of finance in the transport sector (representing around $583 billion), followed by foreign direct investment (around $149 billion) and international debt finance ($150 billion). Official development assistance (ODA) has been also available but of much lesser magnitude (around $8 billion). Other sources of finance, such as climate finance, are even less significant, representing around $1.25 billion.[52]

Shifting towards sustainable freight transport will require advanced systems which will necessitate more resources and capacities than are available. A fundamental element in this respect will be the promotion of a collaborative approach between public and private

investment partners to meet the increased investment requirements for more sustainable transport patterns.

This section will provide a brief overview of some of the relevant sources of financing and their role in prompting current and future development of sustainable freight transport. It is by no means comprehensive, but does highlight some of the main considerations that arise in connection with financing a shift towards sustainable freight transport.

1. Domestic public finance

Domestic public finance (using both domestic and international flows, such as ODA) is an essential source of financing for the transport sector, namely for infrastructure construction and maintenance. Countries typically spend 2–13 per cent of their public budgets on transport.[53] For many developing countries, public financing of transport infrastructure faces a number of challenges. These include:

(a) Competition with other high-priority areas for public funds such as health care, education and debt service;

(b) Tightly constrained national budgets and limited ability of Governments to borrow either at home or abroad;

(c) A significant amount of public finance is spent on environmentally harmful subsidies, most notably on fossil fuels.[54]

Nevertheless, the public sector remains a key player. The role of Government can vary from that of an investment provider to a co-sharer of risks and facilitator of transport infrastructure and services development. The Government has a key role to play in providing incentives and market signals to trigger the shift to sustainable freight transport systems. These can take various forms, such as: the phasing out of fuel subsidies as deemed appropriate and supporting greener freight modes; the application of appropriate pricing mechanisms (such as road pricing taking into account actual externalities); the support of investment (through guarantee/funding) appropriate for the development and operation of sustainable freight transport systems.

Other incentives may involve the development of dedicated financing schemes that would support infrastructure development of sustainable freight transport. As an example, the United Kingdom Department for Transport has developed two freight grant funds to promote a shift of freight movement from road to rail or inland water. The two schemes (the Mode Shift Revenue Support Scheme and the Waterborne Freight Grant Scheme) are designed to support environmental and social benefits that result from using rail or water transport.[55]

Another example is provided by South Africa, which in its new policy framework for achieving more inclusive and greener growth, has defined green transport as a key strategy that encompasses a new freight rail transport strategy to accelerate the shift from road. The state-owned transport enterprise, Transnet, will invest about R63 billion ($7 billion) in the freight rail system over a five-year period and continue promoting greater use of rail freight by companies.[56]

2. Private finance and public–private partnerships

Traditionally, Governments have had the main responsibility of financing and managing transport

infrastructure, but with the growing demand for new infrastructure and efficient and cost-effective infrastructure services, many countries have increasingly turned to the private sector. In recent decades, public–private partnerships (PPPs) have emerged as an important mechanism to scale up public contribution with private sector investment and expertise. Today's transport systems require highly specialized managerial and operational skills, as well as cutting-edge technologies. Therefore, the expertise of private partners for building, operating and maintaining transport infrastructure and services is significant, and constitutes an important resource to draw from in addition to finance.

The private sector is a key player to leverage greater investment and most importantly it allows access to specialized skills, innovations and new technologies associated with sustainable freight transport. Public finance alone will not be able to fund the transition to sustainable freight transport, particularly for developing

Figure 6.4.   Number of projects and investment in projects by subsector, 1990–2011

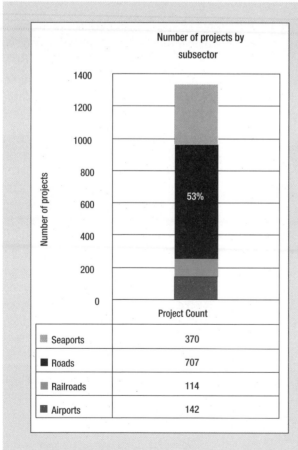
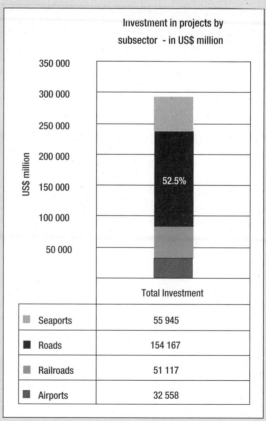

Source: Private Participation in Infrastructure Projects Database – the World Bank and the Public–Private Infrastructure Advisory Facility.

countries, at the speed, scale and expertise required. Private sector participation can enable the required changes and PPPs can serve as an effective means to realize sustainable investments and skills. In many countries, the potential of the private sector still remains largely underutilized and Governments may wish to explore alternative collaboration models of PPPs with appropriate risk-sharing frameworks and administrative and institutional arrangements supported by the necessary legal, regulatory and policy provisions.

Yet, the contribution of private sector investment in the transport industry is greatly influenced by the trends in public finance flows and international support. Observing the investment commitments of private participation in transport infrastructure in the last two decades (figure 6.4), it is clear that the road subsector received a large amount of private investment in developing countries. Of the 1,333 projects with private activities (totalling about $294 billion) carried out in developing countries over the period 1990–2011,

707 (53 per cent) where in the road subsector. Private activity in road projects in developing countries has undergone a resurgence in the past years. Investment commitments to road projects with private participation grew from $7 billion in 2005 to $16.7 billion in 2008.[57]

These trends will have to shift to enable the development of more sustainable and efficient modes of transport. The ability of the public sector to reorient and leverage significant private investment and cooperation into sustainable transport projects and initiatives will therefore be crucial.

3. Climate Finance

Climate finance is an important component that could help the shift towards low-carbon and climate-resilient transport development.

Climate finance relates to funding that can be used to support climate change mitigation and adaptation activities. It encompasses both public and private sources of finance and can be used to support activities

Figure 6.5. Climate finance mechanisms

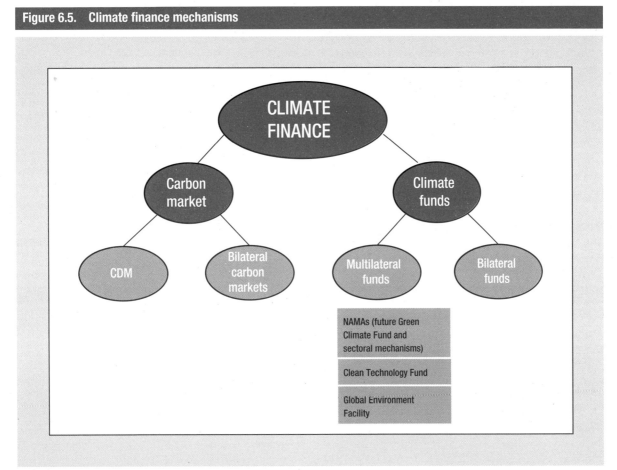

Source: UNCTAD secretariat.

in all sectors of the economy in both developed and developing countries. Consequently, climate finance can be used to help achieve the shift and scale-up of funding for sustainable low-carbon freight transport that directly contributes to the enactment of sustainable development on a larger scale. Yet, climate and environmental concerns are not usually given all the necessary attention when evaluating transport investment projects. Generally, cost–time analysis remains the most significant focus in a project appraisal.

There are, however, several sources and mechanisms of climate finance that can be applied in transport sector today (figure 6.5). These mechanisms can be grouped into two categories: the carbon market and climate funds.

Carbon markets

Carbon markets are mechanisms that provide an incentive to reduce GHG emissions by creating a market for emissions allowances and credits. The carbon market channels financial resources to low-carbon investments through, inter alia, project-based mechanisms such as the clean development mechanism – CDM (regulatory/compliance market) and voluntary markets.[58] The CDM projects are supposed to contribute to sustainable development in developing countries, and also generate real and additional emission savings.

Only 47 out of 7,532 projects in the CDM pipeline were related to transport as of January 2012 (11 of which had been registered).[59] These 47 projects are expected to reduce 5.5 megatons CO_2-equivalents per year up to 2012 – just 0.5 per cent of the total reductions of the current CDM pipeline.[60] The barriers which currently prevent the application of CDM projects in the transport sector relate to the size, scope and complexity of the sector itself. The narrow approach to measuring the mitigation potential of policy actions (and the associated

incremental costs), together with the lack of data to allow for the measurement, reporting and verification of mitigation actions, limits the transport sector's access to this source of finance. Nevertheless, within the context of the ongoing negotiations on climate change, the design of financial instruments is becoming increasingly concentrated on tools that can be applied to the transport sector, something that the existing instruments such as CDM have not succeeded in covering (see box 6.1).

Climate funds for sustainable freight transportation

The term climate funds designates financial resources, investment funds and financing instruments that can be used to address the adaptation and mitigation of the climate change impacts activities. Recently, there has been a proliferation of climate fund initiatives (multilateral and bilateral), which seek to mitigate climate risks and help the most vulnerable adapt to climate change. Although not specifically devoted to transport, several of the existing climate funds can be used for the mitigation of GHG emissions or to reduce the negative effect of impacts activities in the transport sector. These include, for example, the Global Environment Facilities, the Clean Technology Fund, the Global Climate Change Alliance, the Inter-American Development Bank (IDB) Sustainable Environmental Climate Change Initiative, the ADB Climate Change Fund, and the ADB Clean Energy Fund. Many of the funds include a sunset clause that stipulates the necessary steps that will be taken to conclude operations once a new UNFCCC financial architecture takes effect (see box 6.2). It is, however, far from clear what the future funding landscape will look like in the post-2012 regime.

For sustainable freight transport, climate finance can be an important tool to support activities targeted to

---

Box 6.1.   The future role of climate finance in enacting green transport

Within a post-2012 framework, mitigation actions in transport in developing countries are likely to fall under the umbrella of NAMAs, which could be financed through:

- A transport window under a mitigation fund such as the GCF – see box 6.2;

- A scaled-up, programmatic CDM;

- A transport-specific instrument;

- Other potential funds specific to capacity building or technology.

The NAMAs supported by developed countries are likely to be financed by fund-type instruments, whereas actions taken to acquire credits would be enacted through a crediting scheme, such as a scaled-up CDM.

Source: United Nations Environment Programme, http://www.unep.org/greeneconomy/Portals/88/documents/ger/GER_10_
            Transport.pdf.

Box 6.2.   The United Nations Green Climate Fund

The establishment of the GCF was decided at the sixteenth session of the Conference of the Parties (COP) to the UNFCCC, held in Cancun, Mexico, in 2010, with the goal of becoming the main multilateral financing mechanism to support climate action in developing countries.

The GCF is expected to start operating by 2014 and is intended to provide $100 billion each year by 2020 to help the mitigation and adaptation activities of the world's poorest countries. Private sector funds can also contribute to programmes.

The GCF will contribute to the achievement of the ultimate objective of the UNFCCC by providing support to developing countries to limit or reduce their GHG emissions and to adapt to the impacts of climate change. Application of the Fund will take into account the needs of those developing countries particularly vulnerable to the adverse effects of climate change. The Fund will also play a key role in channelling new, additional, adequate and predictable financial resources to developing countries, and will catalyse climate finance, both public and private, and at the international and national levels. It will pursue a country-driven approach and promote and strengthen engagement at the country level through effective involvement of relevant institutions and stakeholders. The financing can be in the form of concessional lending, grants and other types as decided by the board.

The GCF will be a legally independent institution with its own separate secretariat and the World Bank as its interim trustee, but functioning under the guidance of and accountable to the COP. Arrangements between the COP and the GCF are to be concluded at COP 18 (in Doha, December 2012) to ensure that it is accountable to and functions under the guidance of the COP.

The biggest challenge of the GCF is to secure adequate and sustained long-term funding. Substantial financial pledges by contributing countries will be necessary to show broad political support for the GCF and secure its viability.
Source: GCF; for more information please refer to http://gcfund.net/home.html.

reducing GHG emissions. The range of eligible activities is broad and encompasses supporting programmes, policies, projects and enabling measures and strategies. However, given the unpredictable size of climate finance and the conditionality associated with it, direct funding to support large infrastructure, even by way of co-financing, is probably out of range. Yet, climate finance can have a particular impact where sustainable freight transport programmes require funding from a combination of sources and when the availability of climate finance can push an activity beyond the tipping point that determines whether or not a given project can be implemented. Climate finance instruments can also be used as a leveraging device that can help promote sustainable freight transport in several ways, including by awareness raising and capacity building, supporting national assessment and policy reforms, implementing pilot measures, identifying and implementing pilot projects, making marginal projects financially viable, and leveraging other funding flows.

E.   SUMMARIZING THE POINTS

Some key elements appear as outstanding in the preceding discussions regarding the development and finance of sustainable freight transport. These can be summarized as follows:

(a) The transport sector is a major consumer of world fossil fuels and is responsible for an important part

of global GHG emissions and air pollution at local and regional level. To achieve global sustainability and attain the global goal of reducing emissions, urgent actions are needed. These actions must transform the way in which freight transport is growing and address the fuel efficiency and rapid increase in all emissions from the transport sector. This is particularly relevant for developing countries, where freight transport activities will grow substantially and transport systems are being developed. Sustainable freight transport has the potential to increase energy economy and efficiency and thereby address concerns over non-renewable sources, costs and environmental degradation.

(b) Promoting sustainable freight transport systems requires a balancing act between economic, social and environmental considerations, and entails the ability to provide fuel efficient, cost-effective, environmentally friendly, low-carbon, and climate-resilient transport systems. Developing sustainable freight transport systems, based on the avoid–shift–improve approach will help addressing in a systemic fashion different transport and logistics concerns and issues stemming from current and future anticipated economic demands, and climate change and environmental challenges. Reconciling growth imperatives with climate protection and environmental sustainability can be challenging for transport and logistics, but not impossible. Subject to a considered cost–benefit analysis and an assessment of trade-offs (energy efficiency gains, transport costs, speed and reliability of services, and the like) a number of options have the potential to reduce GHG emissions from transport, while at the same time tackling other environmental concerns such as soil, water and air pollution, noise and infrastructure degradation. Relevant options include, for example, including reshaping transport architecture and networks, rethinking supply chain designs and logistics, balancing transport modes, using cleaner technologies and ICT, switching to low-carbon fuel sources, and the like.

(c) Developing sustainable freight transport systems, based on an avoid–shift–improve approach can help developing countries to leapfrog towards a sustainable development path. By investing in sustainable freight transport systems today, developing countries will be better prepared to reap future economic, social and environment benefits. Missing this opportunity may lead to increased costs in the future, as Governments and industries would eventually face additional expenses to adapt to new circumstances and adopt new transport systems, including new technologies and operating practices.

(d) Although global freight transport has over recent years made important progress regarding compliance with sustainability imperatives, including the efforts made to reduce negative externalities, these efforts are still insufficient. More work is needed and should include comprehensive and integrated approaches that will ensure interdisciplinary and inter-institutional collaboration at all levels (local, national, regional and global) as well as a greater involvement of industry. In this respect, coordinated and combined efforts by both public and private sectors in key areas (such as research and analysis, data collection,

policy and regulatory frameworks, technology development) must be reinforced to achieve common institutional and operational benefits and efficiencies. These advances should be in the fields of transport decarbonization, energy conservation, and efficient freight logistics movement in support of global trade and development, and the like.

(e) There is no "one size fits all" standard approach to addressing the challenges associated with the development and the implementation of sustainable freight transport. While it will be important to draw from existing experiences and best practices, each country and region will have to formulate its own approach that will take into account its local-regional circumstances, conditions and opportunities, and that will be consistent with its longer-term strategic development plans and objectives.

(f) Sustainable freight transport requires substantial investments in transport infrastructure, services and equipment. The public sector (as an investment provider, a co-sharer of risk or guarantor, or as facilitator) and the private sectors (through PPPs) have important roles to play to ensure that requisite funding is forthcoming through diversified sources of finance, including climate finance. Climate finance instruments can be used as leveraging devices that can help promote sustainable freight transport in several ways, including by awareness raising and capacity building, supporting national assessment and policy reforms, implementing pilot measures, identifying and implementing pilot projects, making marginal projects financially viable, and leveraging other funding flows. These different sources can be designed to complement each other to drive the change towards sustainable freight transport. Therefore, there is a clear need to take stock of existing transport-relevant financial sources as well as to reorient and structure the sources in accordance with the sustainability criteria.

ENDNOTES

1   United Nations Environment Programme definition, http://www.unep.org/wed/theme/.

2   RIO+20 aimed to reaffirm political commitment to sustainable development and to evaluate the progress on agreed commitments and explore emerging challenges. The conference resulted in the agreed outcome "the future we want", http://www.uncsd2012.org/thefuturewewant.html.

3   With sustainable transport included for the first time, two paragraphs of the agreed outcome were devoted to sustainable transport (paragraphs 132 and 133) and seventeen sustainable transport Voluntary Commitments were presented by various public and private stakeholders in Rio, http://www.uncsd2012.org/index.php?page=view&type=12&menu=153&nr=371&theme=17).

4   Associated Press (2011). United Nations says 2011 disasters were costliest ever. March 6 2011, http://www.newsday.com/news/world/un-says-2011-disasters-were-costliest-ever-1.3590598.

5   International Energy Agency (IEA) (2011). Climate change emissions. Prospect of limiting the global increase in temperature to 2°C is getting bleaker. 30 May 2011.

6   CO_2 is a gas derived from the combustion of fossil energies, which represents the bulk of anthropic GHG emissions (about 55%). http://www.ifpenergiesnouvelles.com/.

7   *The Geography of Transport Systems,* chapter 8: Transport, Energy and Environment, The Environmental Impacts of Transportation, Dr. Jean-Paul Rodrigue and Dr. Claude Comtois.

8   *Air pollution from Ground Transportation: An Assessment of Causes, Strategies and Tactics, and Proposed Actions for the International Community*, by Roger Gorham. The Global Initiative on Transport Emissions: A Partnership of the United Nations and the World Bank Division for Sustainable Development Department of Economic and Social Affairs United Nations, 2002. http://www.un.org/esa/gite/csd/gorham.pdf.

9   http://www.who.int/en/ and http://press.iarc.fr/pr213_E.pdf.

10   *Low Carbon Actions in Chinese Trucking Industry*, Mr. Tan Xiaping, Ministry of Transport, Green Freight China Seminar, May 2011, http://cleanairinitiative.org/portal/node/7313.

11   The broader scope of sustainability in freight includes safety and security, water pollution, HIV/Aids, and the like.

12   Key World Energy Statistics, 2012, IEA.

13   *International Energy Outlook 2011*, The United States Energy Information Administration, http://www.eia.gov/forecasts/ieo/highlights.cfm.

14   http://www.delivering-tomorrow.com/mapping-a-decarbonization-path-for-logistics/.

15   *ExxonMobil Outlook for Energy: a View to 2040* (2012), p.19, http://www.exxonmobil.com/Corporate/energy_outlook_view.aspx.

16   According to the *Fourth Assessment Report of the Intergovernmental Panel on Climate Change (IPCC)* - 2007. Cambridge University Press, Cambridge, United Kingdom and New York, NY, USA.

17   Logistics & Supply Chain Industry Agenda Council Final Report 2010–2011, *Decarbonizing Global Logistics: The Challenges Ahead*, World Economic Forum. p. 10, http://www3.weforum.org/docs/WEF_GAC_LogisticsSupplyChain_Report_2010-11.pdf.

18   According to the *IEA CO_2 Emissions from Fuel Combustion* - 2011 edition.

19   http://www.ipcc.ch/ipccreports/sres/aviation/126.htm#img86.

20   Partnership on Sustainable Low Carbon Transport 2010 Policy Options for consideration by the Commission on Sustainable Development 18th Session, 3-14 May, 2010, http://www.un.org/esa/dsd/resources/res_pdfs/csd-18/csd18_2010_bp12.pdf .

21   Global Environment Outlook5 (GEO 5): Asia and the Pacific, UNEP 2012, http://www.unep.org/geo/pdfs/geo5/RS_AsiaPacific_en.pdf .

22   *World Development Report 2010: Development and Climate Change*. World Bank. Washington DC: 2010.

23   The "avoid, shift and improve" approach to climate change mitigation, as introduced in Dalkmann and Brannigan (2007) and endorsed in the *Common Policy Framework on Transport and Climate Change* (Leather et al, 2009) aims to reduce GHG emissions and energy consumption and promote sustainable transport, also presented in *Rethinking Transport and Climate Change*, by James Leather and the Clean Air Initiative for Asian Cities Centre, ADB, December 2009.

24   International Maritime Organization second GHG study 2009, http://www.imo.org/blast/blastDataHelper.asp?data_id=27012&filename=ExecutiveSummary-CMP5_1.pdf.

25   http://www.shippingandco2.org/CO2%20Flyer.pdf.

26   International Chamber of Shipping (ICS), *Annual Review 2012*. 2012.

27   Ibid. See also Simon Bennett, ICS, presentation at UNCTAD Ad Hoc Expert Meeting 2011.

28   Geerlings H and van Duin R (2010). A new method for assessing CO_2-emissions from container terminals: a promising approach applied in Rotterdam. *J. Cleaner Production*, 11 November 2010.

29   Ibid. The same study emphasizes that one of the most effective measures for CO_2 reduction is undoubtedly the adaptation of the terminal layout as in the example of the Rotterdam Shortsea Terminal. This makes it possible to reduce the CO_2 emissions of the current terminals by nearly 70 per cent.

30   Mangal and Al (2008) defines port-centric logistics as the provision of distribution and other value adding logistics services at a port.

31   Such as the research paper *Time, cost & carbon – does the port-centric model have benefits in the supply chain where goods are imported by suppliers to UK retailers?* conducted by the University of Southampton (summary of findings can be found at http://www.importservices.co.uk/files/PDFFiles/Report%20V3.pdf), and the research project "Decarbonising the Maritime Supply Chain: Assessing the Contribution of the Shippers", being undertaken by the Logistics Research Centre, Heriot-Watt University , by Prof. Alan McKinnon, Dr. Dong-Wook Song, and Mr. Rob Woolford, http://www.fta.co.uk/export/sites/fta/_galleries/downloads/international_supply_chain/decarbonising_the_maritime_supply_chain_heriot_university_research_project.pdf, including article: http://www.portstrategy.com/features101/port-operations/port-services/portcentric-logistics/portcentric-steps-up.

32   *Logistics & supply chain industry agenda council final report 2010-2011*, World Economic Forum.

33   The project has planning consent for a 9.25 million square feet, rail connected to logistics park, adjacent to the new deep-water port, which is on schedule to open in Q4 2013. The vast majority of deep-sea imports enter the United Kingdom through south-east ports yet only 10 per cent of warehousing is in the South East. London Gateway offers significant supply chain savings for global businesses through reduced transport costs created by having warehousing at the port of entry, closer to key United Kingdom consumer markets: http://www.4-traders.com/DP-WORLD-LLC-6500032/news/DP-World-LLC-Europe-s-Largest-Port-Centric-Logistics-Park-Appoints-Property-Agents-14298108/.

34   World Business Council for Sustainable Development (WBCSD) (2004). *Mobility 2030: Meeting the Challenges to Sustainability*. The Sustainable Mobility Project, http://www.wbcsd.org/web/publications/mobility/mobility-full.pdf.

35   Ibid.

36   http://ec.europa.eu/transport/strategies/doc/2011_white_paper/white-paper-illustrated-brochure_en.pdf.

37   "Sustainable Freight Transport Policy in Indonesia", by Bambang Susantonneo Ph.D., Vice Minister for Transportation Republic of Indonesia, at the UNCTAD XIII side event: Paving the Way for Sustainable Freight Transport, Doha, 25 April 2012, http://unctadxiii.org/en/Presentation/uxiii2012sdSFT_SUSANTONNEO.pdf.

38   *Introduction to the Development of Dry Ports in Asia*, United Nations Economic and Social Commission for Asia and the Pacific - UNESCAP, 2010, (http://www.unescap.org/ttdw/common/Meetings/TIS/EGM-DryPorts-Bangkok/TD_EGM_3.pdf), and *Emerging issues in transport: Sustainable transport development,* UNESCAP Ministerial Conference on Transport, Second session Bangkok, 12-16 March 2012, (http://www.unescap.org/ttdw/MCT2011/MCT/MCT2-7E.pdf).

39   For example, the "carbon footprint analysis" conducted by Dedicated Freight Corridor Corporation for the Eastern corridor in India shows that moving goods by rail would be much more environment friendly despite the higher load it would have to handle. The corridor is expected to generate 2.25 times less carbon emissions when compared to a scenario where the freight is transported through existing roads network.

40   "Unlocking Economic Values", Mr. Arvind Mayaram, IAS Additional Secretary Financial Advisor, India, UNCTAD Multi-year Expert Meeting on Transport and Trade Facilitation, Geneva, December 2011, http://archive.unctad.org/sections/wcmu/docs/cimem1_4th_26_en.pdf.

41   Nationally appropriate mitigation action (NAMA) refers to a set of policies and actions that countries undertake as part of a commitment to reduce greenhouse gas emissions. The term recognizes that countries may take different nationally appropriate action on the basis of equity and in accordance with common but differentiated responsibilities and respective capabilities. It also emphasizes financial assistance from developed countries to developing countries to reduce emissions. The policy framework around NAMAs is still being developed but NAMAs are set to become a building block for a future climate agreement.

42   NAMA Database, http://namadatabase.org/index.php/Transport.

43   Examples of relevant studies mainly relate to those conducted by Professor Alan McKinnon, Kühne Logistics University in Hamburg, including: Mapping a Decarbonization Path for Logistics 2012; Green logistics: the carbon agenda, Vol. 6, Issue 3 No 1, logfourm, 2010; The role of Government in promoting green logistics 2010; The present and future land requirements of logistical activities: Land Use Policy, vol. 26S, 2009, etc. For list of publication, please refer http://www.the-klu.org/alan-mckinnon-publications/.

44   *Smart 2020: Enabling the low carbon economy in the information age*, a report by The Climate Group on behalf of the Global eSustainability Initiative (GeSI), 2008, http://www.smart2020.org/_assets/files/02_Smart2020Report.pdf.

45   The above three examples originate from the presentation on "Best European Practice in Freight & Logistics", by Dr. Jürgen Perschon, Executive Director, European Institute for Sustainable Transport (EURIST), Germany, at the Green Logistics Conference Singapore, 31 August 312011 (http://eurist.info/app/download/5782132958/GreenLogisticsSin.pdf) . More examples can be found at http://www.eia-ngo.com/wp-content/uploads/2010/01/Best-Practice_Bestlog.pdf.

46 APUs avoid the need for idling of a truck's base engine and consist of a small diesel engine that provides power for an HVAC system and electrical outlets that service the sleeper cab. Example from "Best practices in green freight for an environmentally sustainable road freight sector in Asia", http://cleanairinitiative.org/portal/sites/default/files/documents/BGP-EST5A_Green_Freight_Best_Practices_CAI-Asia-PunteGotaPeng.pdf.

47 http://esci-ksp.org/?task=energy-efficient-freight-transport-network.

48 Ibid.

49 European Chemical Industry Council (CEFIC). http://www.cefic.org/Documents/IndustrySupport/Transport-and-Logistics/Best%20Practice%20Guidelines%20-%20General%20Guidelines/Cefic-ECTA%20Guidelines%20for%20measuring%20and%20managing%20CO2%20emissions%20from%20transport%20operations%20Final%20 30.03.2011.pdf. A related study was also conducted by Professor Alan McKinnon and Dr Maja Piecyk for CEFIC in 2012 on Measuring and Managing CO2 Emissions of European Chemical Transport, http://cefic-staging.amaze.com/Documents/Media%20Center/News/McKinnon-Report-Final-230610.pdf.

50 The ·network is coordinated by the Sustainable Supply Chain Centre–Asia Pacific and CAI-Asia. See http://cleanairinitiative and http://www.greenfreightandlogistics.org/assets/Uploads/asianconnections.pdf.

51 http://www.uncsd2012.org/index.php?page=view&type=1006&menu=153&nr=517.

52 These figures are extracted from "Paradigm Shift Towards Sustainable Low-carbon Transport: Financing the Vision", by K Sakamoto, H Dalkmann and D Palmer, 2010, http://www.itdp.org/documents/A_Paradigm_Shift_toward_Sustainable_Transport.pdf.

53 International Monetary Fund (2010). Government Finance Statistics. http://www.imf.org/external/pubs/ft/gfs/manual/gfs.htm, from http://www.itdp.org/documents/A_Paradigm_Shift_toward_Sustainable_Transport.pdf.

54 http://www.itdp.org/documents/A_Paradigm_Shift_toward_Sustainable_Transport.pdf.

55 Mode Shift Revenue Support (MSRS) assists companies with the operating costs associated with running rail freight transport instead of road (where rail is more expensive than road). It is designed to facilitate and support modal shift, generating environmental and wider social benefits from reduced lorry journeys on United Kingdom roads. Since September 2009 this scheme has also been open to inland waterway traffic and The Waterborne Freight Grant (WFG) scheme assists companies with the operating costs, for up to three years, associated with running water freight transport instead of road (where water is more expensive than road). http://www.dft.gov.uk/topics/freight/grants.

56 http://www.moneyweb.co.za/mw/view/mw/en/page295023?oid=557289&sn=2009+Detail.

57 http://ppi.worldbank.org/features/October2009/didyouknowOctober2009.aspx.

58 The United Nations Kyoto protocol established binding GHG emission reduction targets for 37 industrialized countries and the European Community. To help achieve these targets, the protocol introduced three "flexible mechanisms" – international emissions trading (IET), joint implementation (JI) and the CDM. The CDM allows developed countries to partially meet their GHG limitation commitments acquiring credits from emission reductions resulting from projects implemented in developing countries (which have no GHG limitation commitments under the Kyoto Protocol). JI allows developed countries to partially meet their targets acquiring emissions reductions credits achieved by projects implemented in other developed countries. IET allows countries to transfer and acquire emissions credit from other countries to help meet their domestic emission reduction targets.

59 Registration is the formal acceptance by the Executive Board of a validated project as a CDM project activity. Registration is the prerequisite for the verification, certification and issuance of Certified Emission Reductions related to that project activity.

60 From UNEP Risoe CDM/JI Pipeline Analysis and Database, http://www.cdmpipeline.org/cdm-projects-type.htm#2.

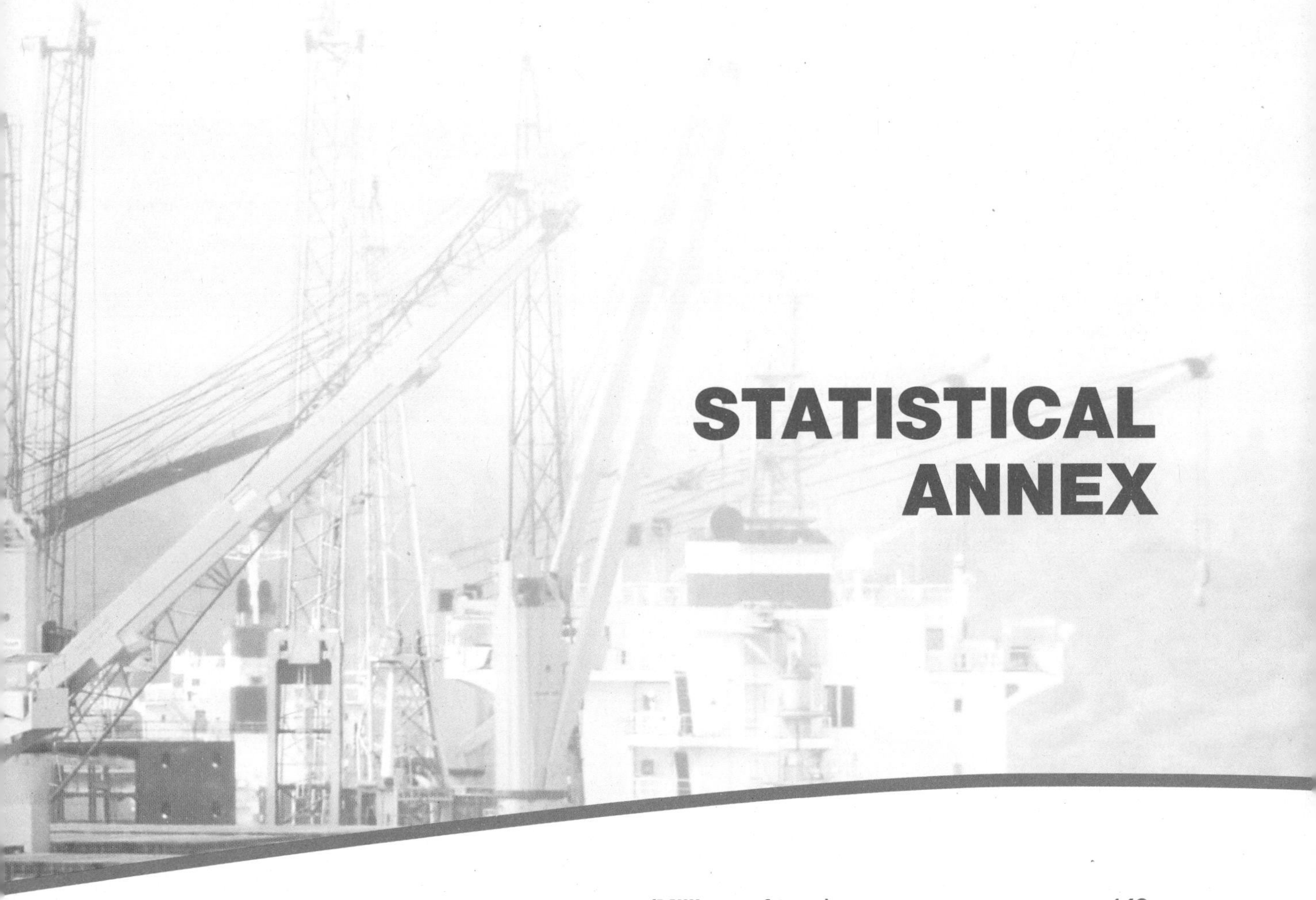

STATISTICAL ANNEX

| Annex I. | | World seaborne trade by country group (Millions of tons) | | | | | | | |

Area	Year	Goods loaded			Total goods loaded	Goods unloaded			Total goods unloaded
		Oil & gas		Dry cargo		Oil & gas		Dry cargo	
		Crude	Petroleum products and gas[a]			Crude	Petroleum products and gas[a]		
Developed economies									
North America	2006	22.2	86.4	436.8	545.4	501.0	155.7	492.1	1 148.7
	2007	24.9	91.3	516.7	632.9	513.5	156.1	453.1	1 122.7
	2008	24.1	119.0	549.4	692.5	481.3	138.9	414.3	1 034.5
	2009	23.9	123.8	498.5	646.1	445.2	132.0	306.4	883.6
	2010	25.5	126.9	530.1	682.5	465.2	113.7	331.0	909.9
	2011	24.0	123.9	590.6	738.6	439.3	113.7	336.4	889.5
Europe	2006	100.9	235.8	768.6	1 105.2	535.6	281.9	1 245.2	2 062.7
	2007	96.9	253.3	776.6	1 126.8	492.2	262.2	1 154.7	1 909.2
	2008	88.2	261.5	751.1	1 100.8	487.9	273.0	1 213.1	1 974.0
	2009	78.1	236.0	693.8	1 008.0	467.9	281.8	935.0	1 684.6
	2010	93.7	266.3	735.1	1 095.1	484.2	280.6	1 044.1	1 808.9
	2011	81.9	275.8	752.5	1 110.2	456.5	312.3	1 067.1	1 835.9
Japan and Israel	2006	0.0	10.0	153.1	163.1	219.3	84.4	559.6	863.3
	2007	0.0	14.4	161.2	175.7	213.3	88.5	560.9	862.6
	2008	0.0	21.0	162.0	183.0	254.7	92.8	548.8	896.2
	2009	0.0	19.3	139.8	159.0	190.7	102.3	417.0	710.0
	2010	0.0	24.7	148.4	173.1	191.1	109.6	480.4	781.2
	2011	0.0	19.1	147.9	166.9	187.1	123.9	466.9	777.9
Australia and New Zealand	2006	9.9	4.2	632.7	646.8	26.2	13.5	50.2	90.0
	2007	13.3	4.0	656.3	673.6	27.0	17.3	51.7	96.0
	2008	16.7	3.8	718.5	739.1	27.3	19.2	56.7	103.2
	2009	12.9	4.8	723.4	741.1	21.5	13.8	60.8	96.1
	2010	16.7	4.3	893.6	914.6	24.8	18.7	60.9	104.5
	2011	17.5	4.5	928.6	950.5	26.6	20.0	65.4	112.0
Subtotal: developed economies	2006	132.9	336.4	1 991.3	2 460.5	1 282.0	535.5	2 347.2	4 164.7
	2007	135.1	363.0	2 110.8	2 608.9	1 246.0	524.0	2 220.5	3 990.5
	2008	129.0	405.3	2 181.1	2 715.4	1 251.1	523.8	2 233.0	4 007.9
	2009	115.0	383.8	2 055.5	2 554.3	1 125.3	529.9	1 719.2	3 374.4
	2010	135.9	422.3	2 307.3	2 865.4	1 165.4	522.6	1 916.5	3 604.5
	2011	123.3	423.3	2 419.5	2 966.2	1 109.6	569.9	1 935.7	3 615.3
Economies in transition	2006	123.1	41.3	245.9	410.3	5.6	3.1	61.9	70.6
	2007	124.4	39.9	243.7	407.9	7.3	3.5	66.0	76.8
	2008	138.2	36.7	256.6	431.5	6.3	3.8	79.2	89.3
	2009	142.1	44.4	318.8	505.3	3.5	4.6	85.3	93.3
	2010	150.2	45.9	319.7	515.7	3.5	4.6	114.0	122.1
	2011	138.7	49.7	322.0	510.4	4.2	4.4	146.1	154.7

| Annex I. | World seaborne trade by country group (Millions of tons) *(continued)* | | | | | | | |

Area	Year	Goods loaded			Total goods loaded	Goods unloaded			Total goods unloaded
		Oil & gas		Dry cargo		Oil & gas		Dry cargo	
		Crude	Petroleum products and gas[a]			Crude	Petroleum products and gas[a]		
Developing economies									
North Africa	2006	117.4	63.8	77.2	258.5	6.0	13.3	142.0	161.3
	2007	116.1	61.8	80.2	258.1	7.5	14.6	155.4	177.4
	2008	113.2	61.3	77.2	251.8	11.3	16.1	151.1	178.5
	2009	101.1	64.9	71.3	237.3	12.2	14.3	156.2	182.7
	2010	94.4	65.5	76.2	236.1	11.3	14.4	171.1	196.8
	2011	72.4	72.4	81.4	226.2	9.2	17.4	129.0	155.6
Western Africa	2006	110.6	12.6	39.8	162.9	5.4	14.2	62.4	82.0
	2007	110.1	10.3	46.5	166.9	7.6	17.1	67.8	92.6
	2008	111.8	9.1	54.2	175.1	6.8	13.5	61.5	81.8
	2009	104.4	10.5	41.4	156.2	6.8	10.8	66.2	83.8
	2010	112.1	13.5	56.0	181.5	7.4	12.8	92.3	112.5
	2011	123.2	21.0	62.3	206.5	6.4	12.8	94.4	113.6
Eastern Africa	2006	11.8	1.1	29.0	42.0	2.1	7.7	18.2	28.0
	2007	13.6	1.2	23.3	38.1	2.1	8.3	19.8	30.3
	2008	19.7	0.8	27.8	48.2	1.8	7.9	23.8	33.5
	2009	19.0	0.6	18.3	37.8	1.7	9.2	24.4	35.3
	2010	19.0	0.5	29.5	49.1	1.9	8.6	26.3	36.8
	2011	22.0	0.6	31.1	53.8	1.4	8.3	28.8	38.6
Central Africa	2006	114.0	2.6	6.3	122.8	2.1	1.7	7.3	11.2
	2007	122.7	2.6	7.8	133.1	2.8	1.9	7.7	12.3
	2008	134.2	5.8	9.0	149.0	1.7	2.8	8.9	13.5
	2009	129.3	2.0	8.5	139.7	1.9	2.7	10.9	15.5
	2010	125.3	7.2	9.7	142.1	1.4	2.3	8.3	12.0
	2011	126.8	12.5	8.7	148.0	1.4	2.3	8.8	12.5
Southern Africa	2006	0.0	5.9	129.9	135.8	25.6	2.6	39.1	67.4
	2007	0.0	5.9	129.9	135.8	25.6	2.6	39.1	67.4
	2008	0.3	6.2	136.0	142.5	23.4	3.1	42.8	69.3
	2009	0.3	5.1	131.5	136.8	22.0	2.7	44.8	69.4
	2010	0.3	5.4	139.5	145.1	20.8	2.3	35.7	58.8
	2011	0.0	2.5	150.7	153.2	21.7	2.5	26.8	51.0
Subtotal: developing Africa	2006	353.8	86.0	282.2	721.9	41.3	39.4	269.1	349.8
	2007	362.5	81.8	287.6	732.0	45.7	44.5	289.8	380.0
	2008	379.2	83.3	304.2	766.7	45.0	43.5	288.1	376.6
	2009	354.0	83.0	271.0	708.0	44.6	39.7	302.5	386.8
	2010	351.1	92.0	310.9	754.0	42.7	40.5	333.7	416.9
	2011	344.5	108.9	334.2	787.7	40.1	43.4	287.8	371.3

Annex I.   World seaborne trade by country group (Millions of tons) *(continued)*

Area	Year	Goods loaded			Total goods loaded	Goods unloaded			Total goods unloaded
		Oil & gas		Dry cargo		Oil & gas		Dry cargo	
		Crude	Petroleum products and gas[a]			Crude	Petroleum products and gas[a]		
Caribbean and Central America	2006	108.4	34.6	73.5	216.6	18.5	42.1	101.5	162.2
	2007	100.4	32.4	75.2	208.1	38.8	44.5	103.1	186.5
	2008	89.1	41.0	84.4	214.5	35.7	47.0	103.5	186.2
	2009	75.1	27.4	71.0	173.4	33.6	46.8	87.2	167.6
	2010	75.9	29.3	81.3	186.5	34.7	51.4	99.4	185.5
	2011	80.1	32.6	100.1	212.8	37.6	53.5	108.9	200.0
South America: northern and eastern seaboards	2006	110.8	49.1	499.5	659.4	16.9	10.3	116.2	143.5
	2007	120.2	47.8	530.7	698.7	19.9	10.8	125.3	156.1
	2008	112.6	40.5	560.2	713.2	22.7	13.9	128.3	165.0
	2009	119.0	38.8	524.4	682.2	19.6	14.5	94.8	128.9
	2010	123.5	42.6	620.6	786.8	17.5	11.4	144.2	173.1
	2011	125.9	43.0	653.6	822.5	21.2	12.4	161.0	194.6
South America: western seaboard	2006	32.1	10.2	112.4	154.8	14.1	7.7	45.9	67.8
	2007	31.6	10.5	118.3	160.4	17.2	8.7	47.5	73.4
	2008	32.9	11.5	136.0	180.4	15.8	9.0	60.9	85.7
	2009	31.7	7.8	134.7	174.2	11.1	12.3	52.0	75.4
	2010	42.1	13.2	144.0	199.3	17.6	12.0	60.6	90.1
	2011	48.1	17.9	158.7	224.7	15.3	13.4	68.2	96.9
Subtotal: developing America	2006	251.3	93.9	685.5	1 030.7	49.6	60.1	263.7	373.4
	2007	252.3	90.7	724.2	1 067.1	76.0	64.0	275.9	415.9
	2008	234.6	93.0	780.6	1 108.2	74.2	69.9	292.7	436.8
	2009	225.7	74.0	730.1	1 029.8	64.4	73.6	234.0	371.9
	2010	241.6	85.1	846.0	1 172.6	69.9	74.7	304.2	448.7
	2011	254.0	93.5	912.4	1 260.0	74.1	79.3	338.1	491.5
Western Asia	2006	729.1	158.1	151.0	1 038.2	27.0	50.3	296.5	373.8
	2007	753.7	155.2	179.5	1 088.5	34.4	51.2	344.4	430.0
	2008	714.0	159.8	181.9	1 055.7	30.6	54.5	349.8	434.9
	2009	717.0	135.8	172.4	1 025.2	22.3	53.1	320.1	395.6
	2010	720.4	152.7	183.8	1 056.9	30.2	55.6	343.7	429.6
	2011	730.4	155.0	195.8	1 081.2	20.1	54.7	366.3	441.1
Southern and Eastern Asia	2006	132.3	102.5	922.6	1 157.3	411.3	104.0	1 482.0	1 997.4
	2007	128.1	104.7	959.7	1 192.5	455.0	106.9	1 674.7	2 236.7
	2008	130.7	103.0	943.0	1 176.7	420.5	124.3	1 811.2	2 356.0
	2009	107.6	115.2	823.7	1 046.5	498.8	126.1	2 034.0	2 659.0
	2010	128.7	111.8	964.0	1 204.5	514.5	143.2	2 198.7	2 856.4
	2011	107.5	119.4	955.4	1 182.2	537.4	151.4	2 390.2	3 078.9

Annex I.		World seaborne trade by country group (Millions of tons) *(continued)*						
Area	**Year**	**Goods loaded**			**Total goods loaded**	**Goods unloaded**			**Total goods unloaded**
		Oil & gas		**Dry cargo**		**Oil & gas**		**Dry cargo**	
		Crude	**Petroleum products and gas**[a]			**Crude**	**Petroleum products and gas**[a]		
South-Eastern Asia	2006	59.8	96.5	721.3	877.6	114.4	94.4	326.8	535.6
	2007	56.4	98.2	779.0	933.6	131.3	102.6	363.0	596.9
	2008	58.1	75.8	837.3	971.2	114.6	108.0	348.5	571.0
	2009	47.7	94.7	840.3	982.7	115.2	90.7	332.0	537.9
	2010	58.4	73.7	701.0	833.2	107.0	134.2	311.0	552.3
	2011	62.2	83.5	807.2	952.9	121.5	131.6	348.9	602.0
Subtotal: developing Asia	2006	921.2	357.0	1 794.8	3 073.1	552.7	248.8	2 105.3	2 906.8
	2007	938.2	358.1	1 918.3	3 214.6	620.7	260.8	2 382.1	3 263.6
	2008	902.7	338.6	1 962.2	3 203.6	565.6	286.8	2 509.5	3 361.9
	2009	872.3	345.8	1 836.3	3 054.3	636.3	269.9	2 686.2	3 592.4
	2010	907.5	338.3	1 848.8	3 094.6	651.8	333.1	2 853.4	3 838.2
	2011	900.1	357.9	1 958.4	3 216.4	679.0	337.7	3 105.3	4 122.0
Developing Oceania	2006	1.2	0.1	2.5	3.8	0.0	6.7	6.2	12.9
	2007	0.9	0.1	2.5	7.1	0.0	7.0	6.5	13.5
	2008	1.5	0.1	2.6	4.2	0.0	7.1	6.7	13.8
	2009	1.5	0.2	4.6	6.3	0.0	3.6	9.5	13.1
	2010	1.5	0.2	4.8	6.5	0.0	3.7	9.7	13.4
	2011	1.6	0.2	5.3	7.1	0.0	3.9	10.6	14.5
Subtotal: developing economies and territories	2006	1 527.5	537.1	2 765.0	4 829.5	643.6	355.1	2 644.3	3 642.9
	2007	1 553.9	530.7	2 932.6	5 020.8	742.4	376.3	2 954.3	4 073.0
	2008	1 518.0	515.1	3 049.6	5 082.6	684.9	407.2	3 097.0	4 189.1
	2009	1 453.5	502.9	2 842.0	4 798.4	745.3	386.9	3 232.1	4 364.2
	2010	1 501.6	515.6	3 010.5	5 027.8	764.4	452.0	3 500.9	4 717.3
	2011	1 500.3	560.5	3 210.3	5 271.2	793.2	464.3	3 741.8	4 999.3
World total	2006	1 783.4	914.8	5 002.1	7 700.3	1 931.2	893.7	5 053.4	7 878.3
	2007	1 813.4	933.5	5 287.1	8 034.1	1 995.7	903.8	5 240.8	8 140.2
	2008	1 785.2	957.0	5 487.2	8 229.5	1 942.3	934.9	5 409.2	8 286.3
	2009	1 710.5	931.1	5 216.4	7 858.0	1 874.1	921.3	5 036.6	7 832.0
	2010	1 787.7	983.8	5 637.5	8 408.9	1 933.2	979.2	5 531.4	8 443.8
	2011	1 762.4	1 033.5	5 951.9	8 747.7	1 907.0	1 038.6	5 823.7	8 769.3

Source: Compiled by the UNCTAD secretariat on the basis of data supplied by reporting countries, as published on the relevant government and port industry websites and by specialist sources. The data for 2006 onwards have been revised and updated to reflect improved reporting, including more recent figures and better information regarding the breakdown by cargo type. Figures for 2011 are estimates based on preliminary data or on the last year for which data were available.

[a] Including l NG, LPG, naphtha, gasoline, jet fuel, kerosene, light oil, heavy fuel oil and others.

Annex II (a). Merchant fleets of the world by flags of registration, groups of economies and types of ship, as at 1 January 2012 (Thousands of GT)						
	Bulk carriers	Container ships	General cargo ships c	Oil tankers	Other types	Grand total
DEVELOPING ECONOMIES OF AFRICA						
Algeria	121	–	66	19	586	792
Angola	–	–	11	6	55	72
Benin	–	–	–	–	2	2
Cameroon	–	–	2	–	14	16
Cape Verde	–	–	9	7	25	41
Comoros	167	4	336	101	122	730
Congo	–	–	–	–	4	4
Côte d'Ivoire	–	–	–	1	8	8
Democratic Republic of the Congo	–	–	0	1	10	12
Djibouti	–	–	–	–	3	3
Egypt	514	55	188	184	196	1 136
Equatorial Guinea	–	–	10	21	27	59
Eritrea	–	–	10	2	1	13
Ethiopia	–	–	112	–	0	112
Gabon	–	–	5	0	10	15
Gambia	–	–	–	–	2	2
Ghana	–	–	15	1	101	117
Guinea	–	–	1	–	26	27
Guinea-Bissau	–	–	1	–	5	6
Kenya	–	–	–	1	9	10
Libya	–	–	5	788	49	842
Madagascar	–	–	6	0	10	16
Mauritania	–	–	1	1	44	46
Mauritius	–	–	14	44	62	120
Morocco	–	64	11	14	328	416
Mozambique	–	–	7	–	34	41
Namibia	–	–	3	–	122	125
Nigeria	–	–	6	432	219	658
Saint Helena	–	–	–	–	2	2
Sao Tome and Principe	–	–	6	–	4	10
Senegal	–	–	2	0	51	53
Seychelles	–	–	43	122	37	202
Sierra Leone	178	24	483	173	115	973
Somalia	–	–	2	–	3	5
South Africa	–	–	0	13	154	168
Sudan	–	–	20	–	4	24
Togo	45	30	160	147	16	398
Tunisia	17	–	50	59	107	233
United Republic of Tanzania	39	–	369	50	39	497
DEVELOPING ECONOMIES OF AFRICA Total	**1 081**	**176**	**1 954**	**2 188**	**2 606**	**8 005**

Annex II (a). Merchant fleets of the world by flags of registration, groups of economies and types of ship, as at 1 January 2012 (Thousands of GT) *(continued)*						
	Bulk carriers	Container ships	General cargo ships [c]	Oil tankers	Other types	Grand total
DEVELOPING ECONOMIES OF AMERICA						
Anguilla	–	–	0	–	0	0
Argentina	14	13	33	319	222	601
Aruba	–	–	–	–	0	0
Barbados	536	157	260	308	139	1 399
Belize	303	–	800	81	297	1 482
Bolivia (Plurinational State of)	18	–	69	2	4	93
Brazil	359	366	210	938	471	2 344
British Virgin Islands	–	–	0	0	5	6
Cayman Islands	690	–	1 220	1 243	185	3 338
Chile	254	23	42	215	258	792
Colombia	–	–	28	15	49	91
Costa Rica	–	–	–	–	6	6
Cuba	0	–	4	0	34	39
Curaçao	40	–	852	99	166	1 157
Dominica	532	–	72	382	45	1 031
Dominican Republic	–	–	0	–	5	5
Ecuador	–	–	8	204	135	347
El Salvador	–	–	–	–	11	11
Falkland Islands (Malvinas)[d]	–	–	–	–	46	46
Grenada	–	–	1	–	1	2
Guatemala	–	–	–	0	4	4
Guyana	–	–	23	6	14	42
Haiti	–	–	1	–	0	1
Honduras	25	–	179	89	188	481
Jamaica	81	28	45	–	3	157
Mexico	144	–	39	757	633	1 573
Nicaragua	–	–	1	1	4	6
Paraguay	–	8	46	2	8	63
Peru	–	12	12	275	140	439
Saint Kitts and Nevis	227	39	390	176	171	1 003
Suriname	–	–	1	2	2	5
Trinidad and Tobago	–	–	1	3	47	50
Turks and Caicos Islands	–	–	0	–	2	2
Uruguay	2	–	6	13	78	98
Venezuela (Bolivarian Republic of)	110	–	32	419	445	1 007
DEVELOPING ECONOMIES OF AMERICA Total	**3 336**	**646**	**4 372**	**5 550**	**3 819**	**17 723**

Annex II (a). Merchant fleets of the world by flags of registration, groups of economies and types of ship, as at 1 January 2012 (Thousands of GT) *(continued)*						
	Bulk carriers	Container ships	General cargo ships [c]	Oil tankers	Other types	Grand total
DEVELOPING ECONOMIES OF ASIA						
Bahrain	33	247	0	107	156	544
Bangladesh	739	28	349	118	36	1 271
Brunei Darussalam	–	–	3	5	532	540
Cambodia	164	10	1 127	18	111	1 429
China	18 435	5 268	3 941	7 389	2 890	37 924
China, Hong Kong SAR	38 712	12 827	3 370	14 061	1 236	70 206
China, Macao SAR	–	–	–	–	0	0
China, Taiwan Province of	1 383	693	113	434	367	2 990
Democratic People's Republic of Korea	98	16	521	39	35	709
India	2 952	224	342	5 016	1 228	9 762
Indonesia	1 635	823	2 585	3 026	2 361	10 430
Iran, Islamic Republic of	137	31	242	244	215	870
Iraq	–	–	–	17	2	19
Jordan	–	–	39	137	24	201
Kuwait	46	269	96	1 766	231	2 408
Lao People's Democratic Republic	15	–	0	–	–	15
Lebanon	23	–	110	0	3	136
Malaysia	212	650	431	3 465	3 439	8 197
Maldives	1	–	70	6	11	88
Mongolia	320	8	163	21	25	538
Myanmar, Republic of the Union of	–	1	152	4	29	186
Oman	–	–	2	1	28	32
Pakistan	149	–	25	179	26	379
Philippines	2 099	318	1 420	500	674	5 012
Qatar	70	300	1	223	295	888
Republic of Korea	7 337	779	1 487	846	1 635	12 084
Saudi Arabia	–	172	266	955	310	1 704
Singapore	12 866	10 887	4 859	20 815	4 403	53 830
Sri Lanka	60	16	75	7	24	181
Syrian Arab Republic	40	–	47	–	3	89
Thailand	583	217	483	1 125	307	2 715
Timor-Leste	–	–	–	–	1	1
Turkey	2 822	564	1 482	1 065	485	6 419
United Arab Emirates	51	280	70	371	233	1 005
Viet Nam	1 163	124	1 385	922	202	3 796
Yemen	–	–	5	17	13	35
DEVELOPING ECONOMIES OF ASIA Total	**92 144**	**34 755**	**25 263**	**62 900**	**21 571**	**236 633**

Annex II (a). Merchant fleets of the world by flags of registration, groups of economies and types of ship, as at 1 January 2012 (Thousands of GT) *(continued)*						
	Bulk carriers	Container ships	General cargo ships [c]	Oil tankers	Other types	Grand total
DEVELOPING ECONOMIES OF OCEANIA						
Fiji	–	–	8	–	36	45
Kiribati	71	–	187	34	76	368
Micronesia, Federal States of	0	–	6	–	9	16
Papua New Guinea	18	–	74	4	23	119
Samoa	–	–	8	–	4	12
Solomon Islands	–	–	2	–	8	10
Tonga	–	–	26	1	9	36
Tuvalu	83	34	79	797	143	1 136
Vanuatu	1 145	25	245	–	1 099	2 515
DEVELOPING ECONOMIES OF OCEANIA Total	**1 317**	**60**	**635**	**837**	**1 408**	**4 257**
OPEN REGISTRY ECONOMIES						
Antigua and Barbuda	902	5 875	4 216	11	158	11 163
Bahamas	8 417	1 693	6 846	18 770	16 663	52 390
Bermuda	1 805	595	101	1 489	7 333	11 323
Cyprus	9 096	3 954	1 300	5 241	1 402	20 993
Isle of Man	3 980	91	471	6 913	1 886	13 341
Liberia	33 897	37 681	4 310	39 910	5 721	121 519
Malta	18 682	4 661	3 134	15 417	3 223	45 117
Marshall Islands	24 941	7 175	1 749	31 527	10 662	76 054
Panama	106 605	33 779	24 151	36 082	14 143	214 760
Saint Vincent and the Grenadines	1 260	81	1 959	181	540	4 020
OPEN REGISTRY ECONOMIES Total	**209 586**	**95 586**	**48 236**	**155 541**	**61 731**	**570 680**
DEVELOPED ECONOMIES						
Australia	298	–	153	37	1 117	1 604
Belgium	1 654	75	227	846	1 626	4 429
Bulgaria	183	–	112	6	16	318
Canada	1 240	16	140	552	1 107	3 056
Denmark	215	6 614	355	3 305	1 412	11 901
Estonia	–	–	11	8	300	319
Finland	52	29	556	363	581	1 581
France	181	1 962	153	2 905	1 851	7 052
Germany	377	13 486	372	345	740	15 320
Greece	12 687	2 280	256	23 953	2 100	41 276
Iceland	0	–	1	0	167	169
Ireland	–	5	144	13	67	229
Israel	–	243	2	3	9	256
Italy	4 666	863	2 736	5 196	5 032	18 492
Japan	6 206	115	2 917	3 532	4 653	17 423
Latvia	–	–	14	9	165	187

Annex II (a). Merchant fleets of the world by flags of registration, groups of economies and types of ship, as at 1 January 2012 (Thousands of GT) *(continued)*

	Bulk carriers	Container ships	General cargo ships [c]	Oil tankers	Other types	Grand total
Lithuania	–	10	192	–	205	407
Luxembourg	51	85	287	181	495	1 098
Netherlands	466	1 072	3 344	438	2 250	7 570
New Zealand	79	7	131	57	160	434
Norway	2 421	–	3 976	4 977	5 139	16 512
Poland	–	–	15	5	90	110
Portugal	56	50	322	365	448	1 241
Romania	–	–	8	4	72	84
Slovakia	–	–	19	–	0	19
Slovenia	–	–	–	–	3	3
Spain	32	35	336	559	2 066	3 028
Sweden	20	–	1 924	174	1 252	3 369
Switzerland	514	85	82	55	6	742
United Kingdom of Great Britain and Northern Ireland	1 874	9 820	3 559	1 878	2 676	19 807
United States of America	1 079	3 412	1 773	2 051	3 286	11 601
DEVELOPED ECONOMIES Total	**34 350**	**40 264**	**24 117**	**51 816**	**39 090**	**189 638**
ECONOMIES IN TRANSITION						
Albania	–	–	43	–	2	45
Azerbaijan	–	–	128	249	363	740
Croatia	696	–	27	701	138	1 562
Georgia	46	8	163	20	26	264
Kazakhstan	–	–	3	61	63	127
Montenegro	22	–	2	–	2	27
Republic of Moldova	67	–	339	17	60	484
Russian Federation	405	143	2 836	1 468	2 740	7 591
Turkmenistan	–	–	17	24	39	80
Ukraine	36	–	322	26	327	710
ECONOMIES IN TRANSITION Total	**1 272**	**151**	**3 880**	**2 566**	**3 760**	**11 629**
Unknown flag	**437**	**103**	**1 228**	**551**	**2 147**	**4 468**
World total [e]	**343 524**	**171 741**	**109 685**	**281 950**	**136 132**	**1043 033**

Annex II (b). Merchant fleets of the world by flags of registration,[a] groups of economies and types of ship,[b] as at January 2012 (Thousands of dwt)

	Bulk carriers	Container ships	General cargo ships [c]	Oil tankers	Other types	Grand total
DEVELOPING ECONOMIES OF AFRICA						
Algeria	204	-	66	27	512	809
Angola	-	-	13	10	34	58
Benin	-	-	-	-	0	0
Cameroon	-	-	3	-	6	9
Cape Verde	-	-	12	10	5	26
Comoros	269	5	410	177	85	946
Congo	-	-	-	-	1	1
Côte d'Ivoire	-	-	-	1	3	4
Democratic Republic of the Congo	-	-	1	2	12	14
Djibouti	-	-	-	-	1	1
Egypt	900	63	190	319	158	1 630
Equatorial Guinea	-	-	11	33	20	63
Eritrea	-	-	10	3	1	14
Ethiopia	-	-	146	-	-	146
Gabon	-	-	5	0	4	10
Gambia	-	-	-	-	2	2
Ghana	-	-	20	2	65	87
Guinea	-	-	0	-	12	12
Guinea-Bissau	-	-	0	-	2	2
Kenya	-	-	-	2	6	8
Libya	-	-	5	1 461	25	1 492
Madagascar	-	-	8	0	4	13
Mauritania	-	-	1	2	18	22
Mauritius	-	-	12	77	53	142
Morocco	-	78	8	20	132	239
Mozambique	-	-	12	-	25	37
Namibia	-	-	2	-	69	70
Nigeria	-	-	9	730	200	939
Saint Helena	-	-	-	-	1	1
Sao Tome and Principe	-	-	8	-	2	11
Senegal	-	-	3	0	19	22
Seychelles	-	-	56	201	31	287
Sierra Leone	265	30	587	276	111	1 268
Somalia	-	-	3	-	2	5
South Africa	-	-	0	18	82	101
Sudan	-	-	25	-	2	27
Togo	73	39	222	241	10	585
Tunisia	26	-	35	107	27	195
United Republic of Tanzania	63	-	510	81	25	679
DEVELOPING ECONOMIES OF AFRICA Total	**1 801**	**216**	**2 393**	**3 801**	**1 766**	**9 977**

Annex II (b). Merchant fleets of the world by flags of registration,[a] groups of economies and types of ship,[b] as at January 2012 (Thousands of dwt) *(continued)*

	Bulk carriers	Container ships	General cargo ships [c]	Oil tankers	Other types	Grand total
DEVELOPING ECONOMIES OF AMERICA						
Anguilla	-	-	0	-	-	0
Argentina	24	18	50	541	185	818
Aruba	-	-	-	-	0	0
Barbados	914	211	343	473	99	2 040
Belize	477	-	971	128	239	1 815
Bolivia (Plurinational State of)	29	-	91	3	2	124
Brazil	614	478	258	1 521	489	3 360
British Virgin Islands	-	-	1	1	0	1
Cayman Islands	1 084	-	458	2 056	205	3 804
Chile	418	30	47	362	209	1 066
Colombia	-	-	40	24	48	113
Costa Rica	-	-	-	-	2	2
Cuba	1	-	5	1	24	30
Curaçao	74	-	1 087	172	228	1 561
Dominica	1 003	-	101	701	38	1 843
Dominican Republic	-	-	-	-	1	1
Ecuador	-	-	8	344	68	421
El Salvador	-	-	-	-	2	2
Falkland Islands (Malvinas)[d]	-	-	-	-	34	34
Grenada	-	-	1	-	0	1
Guatemala	-	-	-	1	2	3
Guyana	-	-	29	9	7	45
Haiti	-	-	1	-	0	1
Honduras	45	-	235	160	75	514
Jamaica	128	35	54	-	0	217
Mexico	252	-	27	1 242	550	2 071
Nicaragua	-	-	1	1	1	3
Paraguay	-	10	53	4	1	67
Peru	-	15	14	433	85	546
Saint Kitts and Nevis	374	44	516	280	114	1 329
Suriname	-	-	2	3	1	6
Trinidad and Tobago	-	-	-	4	17	21
Turks and Caicos Islands	-	-	-	-	0	0
Uruguay	3	-	8	19	30	60
Venezuela (Bolivarian Republic of)	187	-	42	732	494	1 455
DEVELOPING ECONOMIES OF AMERICA Total	**5 627**	**841**	**4 441**	**9 216**	**3 248**	**23 374**

Annex II (b). Merchant fleets of the world by flags of registration,[a] groups of economies and types of ship,[b] as at January 2012 (Thousands of dwt) *(continued)*					
	Bulk carriers	Container ships	General cargo ships [c]	Oil tankers	Other types	Grand total
DEVELOPING ECONOMIES OF ASIA						
Bahrain	44	271	1	192	122	630
Bangladesh	1 263	39	493	219	27	2 041
Brunei Darussalam	-	-	3	7	411	421
Cambodia	231	14	1 418	24	53	1 740
China	32 041	6 323	4 962	12 787	2 083	58 195
China, Hong Kong SAR	70 993	14 646	4 444	25 544	1 177	116 806
China, Macao SAR	-	-	-	-	-	-
China, Taiwan Province of	2 549	784	154	725	117	4 328
Democratic People's Republic of Korea	165	22	735	68	32	1 023
India	5 225	294	353	9 052	1 217	16 141
Indonesia	2 753	1 090	3 258	4 916	1 494	13 512
Iran, Islamic Republic of	233	43	310	416	177	1 179
Iraq	-	-	-	27	2	29
Jordan	-	-	45	290	9	344
Kuwait	78	292	74	3 294	239	3 976
Lao People's Democratic Republic	20	-	2	-	-	22
Lebanon	36	-	103	1	3	143
Malaysia	364	794	471	6 079	3 187	10 895
Maldives	2	-	96	12	7	116
Mongolia	538	11	227	31	23	830
Myanmar, Republic of the Union of	-	-	178	7	14	198
Oman	-	-	3	2	12	17
Pakistan	271	-	36	329	26	663
Philippines	3 442	383	1 716	797	357	6 694
Qatar	116	331	0	393	307	1 147
Republic of Korea	13 608	987	1 843	1 430	1 290	19 157
Saudi Arabia	-	185	269	1 645	234	2 333
Singapore	23 612	12 785	3 633	37 293	4 760	82 084
Sri Lanka	99	17	99	13	16	245
Syrian Arab Republic	64	-	65	-	0	129
Thailand	966	297	698	2 009	280	4 249
Timor-Leste	-	-	-	-	0	0
Turkey	4 873	711	1 813	1 843	296	9 535
United Arab Emirates	72	307	75	622	198	1 273
Viet Nam	1 969	165	2 266	1 527	146	6 072
Yemen	-	-	2	28	6	36
DEVELOPING ECONOMIES OF ASIA Total	**165 624**	**40 792**	**29 844**	**111 619**	**18 324**	**366 203**

Annex II (b). Merchant fleets of the world by flags of registration,[a] groups of economies and types of ship,[b] as at January 2012
(Thousands of dwt) *(continued)*

	Bulk carriers	Container ships	General cargo ships [c]	Oil tankers	Other types	Grand total
DEVELOPING ECONOMIES OF OCEANIA						
Fiji	-	-	5	-	11	16
Kiribati	121	-	243	57	48	469
Micronesia, Federal States of	0	-	6	-	5	11
Papua New Guinea	24	-	93	6	18	141
Samoa	-	-	9	-	1	10
Solomon Islands	-	-	2	-	5	7
Tonga	-	-	30	1	4	35
Tuvalu	125	38	111	1 444	149	1 868
Vanuatu	1 881	29	232	-	917	3 058
DEVELOPING ECONOMIES OF OCEANIA Total	**2 151**	**67**	**732**	**1 509**	**1 157**	**5 616**
OPEN REGISTRY ECONOMIES						
Antigua and Barbuda	1 499	7 404	5 308	16	175	14 402
Bahamas	14 830	1 907	5 880	34 612	11 875	69 105
Bermuda	3 489	629	113	2 769	4 598	11 598
Cyprus	16 283	4 703	1 611	9 466	923	32 986
Isle of Man	194 843	37 686	18 112	65 623	11 946	328 210
Liberia	7 521	119	552	12 461	1 888	22 542
Malta	61 767	44 449	4 447	72 597	6 651	189 911
Marshall Islands	45 403	8 442	1 777	57 791	9 443	122 857
Panama	33 579	5 303	3 255	27 772	1 377	71 287
Saint Vincent and the Grenadines	2 181	109	2 601	322	424	5 636
OPEN REGISTRY ECONOMIES Total	**381 397**	**110 752**	**43 656**	**283 430**	**49 299**	**868 534**
DEVELOPED ECONOMIES						
Australia	481	-	144	52	1 137	1 815
Belgium	3 188	93	150	1 634	1 597	6 663
Bulgaria	297	-	123	10	11	440
Canada	1 914	17	136	922	544	3 532
Denmark	420	7 419	265	5 290	793	14 187
Estonia	-	-	15	13	58	86
Finland	81	37	408	609	123	1 258
France	348	2 148	86	5 367	941	8 890
Germany	752	15 432	392	522	385	17 482
Greece	23 832	2 491	270	44 882	1 083	72 558
Iceland	1	-	1	0	74	76
Ireland	-	7	212	18	25	263
Israel	-	297	3	5	5	309
Italy	8 630	948	1 696	8 895	1 594	21 763
Japan	11 440	125	2 513	6 560	2 934	23 572

Annex II (b). Merchant fleets of the world by flags of registration,[a] groups of economies and types of ship,[b] as at January 2012 (Thousands of dwt) *(continued)*						
	Bulk carriers	Container ships	General cargo ships [c]	Oil tankers	Other types	Grand total
Latvia	-	-	19	12	47	79
Lithuania	-	14	238	-	73	325
Luxembourg	85	98	157	278	613	1 231
Netherlands	804	1 256	4 307	669	1 242	8 279
New Zealand	124	8	170	89	63	454
Norway	4 205	-	2 853	8 634	4 081	19 774
Poland	-	-	20	7	47	73
Portugal	88	63	292	640	152	1 236
Romania	-	-	10	6	43	59
Slovakia	-	-	22	-	0	22
Slovenia	-	-	-	-	1	1
Spain	47	48	221	1 024	1 308	2 647
Sweden	26	-	1 059	255	279	1 619
Switzerland	872	118	106	87	7	1 189
United Kingdom of Great Britain and Northern Ireland	3 458	10 752	2 379	2 997	1 642	21 228
United States of America	2 075	3 678	904	3 480	1 861	11 997
DEVELOPED ECONOMIES Total	**63 168**	**45 048**	**19 168**	**92 959**	**22 765**	**243 108**
TRANSITION ECONOMIES						
Albania	-	-	62	-	0	63
Azerbaijan	-	-	133	357	180	670
Croatia	1 213		35	1 291	32	2 571
Georgia	70	12	196	34	19	331
Kazakhstan	-	-	2	103	39	145
Montenegro	35	-	2	-	1	37
Republic of Moldova	112	-	409	31	33	584
Russian Federation	565	149	3 261	2 117	1 322	7 413
Turkmenistan	-	-	15	34	31	81
Ukraine	56	-	388	45	189	679
TRANSION ECONOMIES Total	**2 051**	**161**	**4 503**	**4 012**	**1 848**	**12 574**
Unknown flag	**718**	**124**	**1 648**	**908**	**1 235**	**4 633**
World total	**622 536**	**198 002**	**106 385**	**507 454**	**99 642**	**1534 019**

Annex II (c).   Merchant fleets of the world by flags of registration,[a] groups of economies and types of ship,[b] as at 1 January 2012 (Number of ships)

	Bulk carriers	Container ships	General cargo ships [c]	Oil tankers	Other types	Grand total
DEVELOPING ECONOMIES OF AFRICA						
Algeria	6	-	12	11	108	137
Angola	-	-	15	6	156	177
Benin	-	-	-	-	8	8
Cameroon	-	-	4	-	57	61
Cape Verde	-	-	11	5	27	43
Comoros	17	1	117	22	120	277
Congo	-	-	-	-	22	22
Côte d 'Ivoire	-	-	-	2	31	33
Democratic People's Republic of the Congo	-	-	1	1	16	18
Djibouti	-	-	-	-	13	13
Egypt	14	3	31	37	269	354
Equatorial Guinea	-	-	6	6	33	45
Eritrea	-	-	4	1	8	13
Ethiopia	-	-	8	-	1	9
Gabon	-	-	11	1	39	51
Gambia	-	-	-	-	8	8
Ghana	-	-	15	1	216	232
Guinea	-	-	2	-	43	45
Guinea-Bissau	-	-	7	-	17	24
Kenya	-	-	-	2	26	28
Libya	-	-	3	19	141	163
Madagascar	-	-	16	1	53	70
Mauritania	-	-	3	1	133	137
Mauritius	-	-	5	4	47	56
Morocco	-	7	5	3	494	509
Mozambique	-	-	10	-	114	124
Namibia	-	-	1	-	166	167
Nigeria	-	-	11	86	467	564
Saint Helena	-	-	-	-	2	2
Sao Tome and Principe	-	-	9	-	12	21
Senegal	-	-	5	1	203	209
Seychelles	-	-	7	6	40	53
Sierra Leone	24	5	231	71	119	450
Somalia	-	-	2	-	10	12
South Africa	-	-	2	7	249	258
Sudan	-	-	2	-	17	19
Togo	4	3	69	24	30	130
Tunisia	1	-	5	1	69	76
United Republic of Tanzania	5	-	139	16	73	233
DEVELOPING ECONOMIES OF AFRICA Total	**71**	**19**	**769**	**335**	**3 657**	**4 851**

Annex II (c). Merchant fleets of the world by flags of registration,[a] groups of economies and types of ship,[b] as at 1 January 2012 (Number of ships) (continued)						
	Bulk carriers	Container ships	General cargo ships [c]	Oil tankers	Other types	Grand total
DEVELOPING ECONOMIES OF AMERICA						
Anguilla	-	-	1	-	1	2
Argentina	1	1	7	27	394	430
Aruba	-	-	-	-	1	1
Barbados	26	6	64	18	30	144
Belize	37	-	210	21	178	446
Bolivia	2	-	23	1	9	35
Brazil	15	16	23	45	385	484
British Virgin Islands	-	-	2	1	15	18
Cayman Islands	21	-	30	68	44	163
Chile	12	2	18	13	344	389
Colombia	-	-	22	9	120	151
Costa Rica	-	-	-	-	17	17
Cuba	1	-	5	1	42	49
Curaçao	1	-	88	4	44	137
Dominica	13	-	30	8	51	102
Dominican Republic	-	-	1	-	20	21
Ecuador	-	-	8	39	236	283
El Salvador	-	-	-	-	16	16
Falkland Islands (Malvinas)[d]	-	-	-	-	26	26
Grenada	-	-	3	-	4	7
Guatemala	-	-	-	1	11	12
Guyana	-	-	35	5	77	117
Haiti	-	-	2	-	1	3
Honduras	16	-	230	83	555	884
Jamaica	4	4	8	-	18	34
Mexico	5	-	9	40	803	857
Nicaragua	-	-	2	1	26	29
Paraguay	-	5	24	2	18	49
Peru	-	1	1	19	395	416
Saint Kitts and Nevis	15	3	101	63	104	286
Suriname	-	-	3	3	10	16
Trinidad and Tobago	-	-	1	1	128	130
Turks and Caicos Islands	-	-	1	-	6	7
Uruguay	1	-	4	7	106	118
Venezuela (Bolivarian Republic of)	4	-	21	22	284	331
DEVELOPING ECONOMIES OF AMERICA Total	**174**	**38**	**977**	**502**	**4 519**	**6 210**

Annex II (c). Merchant fleets of the world by flags of registration,[a] groups of economies and types of ship,[b] as at 1 January 2012 (Number of ships) *(continued)*

	Bulk carriers	Container ships	General cargo ships [c]	Oil tankers	Other types	Grand total
DEVELOPING ECONOMIES OF ASIA						
Bahrain	2	4	2	6	209	223
Bangladesh	30	4	86	72	120	312
Brunei Darussalem	-	-	8	3	69	80
Cambodia	38	3	451	10	89	591
China	681	220	1 048	512	1 687	4 148
China, Hong Kong SAR	868	295	240	336	196	1 935
China, Taiwan Province of	43	31	70	30	732	906
Democratic People's Republic of Korea	11	3	157	16	36	223
India	104	13	171	128	1 027	1 443
Indonesia	158	127	1 789	447	3 811	6 332
Iran, Islamic Republic of	13	4	260	14	356	647
Iraq	-	-	-	2	1	3
Jordan	-	-	6	1	16	23
Kuwait	2	6	15	22	161	206
Lao People's Democratic Republic	1	-	1	-	-	2
Lebanon	4	-	31	1	8	44
Malaysia	11	40	191	176	1 031	1 449
Maldives	1	-	38	13	27	79
Mongolia	19	2	51	14	52	138
Myanmar, Republic of the Union of	-	1	50	6	70	127
Oman	-	-	9	1	39	49
Pakistan	5	-	2	6	46	59
Philippines	86	16	663	193	1 037	1 995
Qatar	3	13	2	5	99	122
Republic of Korea	213	73	419	291	1 920	2 916
Saudi Arabia	-	3	17	50	259	329
Singapore	286	346	205	779	1 261	2 877
Sri Lanka	5	1	12	8	61	87
Syrian Arab Republic	3	-	11	-	14	28
Thailand	32	31	166	236	385	850
Timor-Leste	-	-	-	-	1	1
Turkey	109	43	471	188	549	1 360
United Arab Emirates	4	5	78	38	408	533
Viet Nam	156	20	975	109	265	1 525
Yemen	-	-	3	4	42	49
DEVELOPING ECONOMIES OF ASIA Total	**2 888**	**1 304**	**7 698**	**3 717**	**16 084**	**31 691**

Annex II (c). Merchant fleets of the world by flags of registration,[a] groups of economies and types of ship,[b] as at 1 January 2012 (Number of ships) *(continued)*						
	Bulk carriers	Container ships	General cargo ships [c]	Oil tankers	Other types	Grand total
DEVELOPING ECONOMIES OF OCEANIA						
Fiji	-	-	15	-	101	116
Kiribati	6	-	58	17	30	111
Micronesia, Federal States of	2	-	10	-	21	33
Papua New Guinea	7	-	65	4	74	150
Samoa	-	-	4	-	7	11
Solomon Islands	-	-	11	-	23	34
Tonga	-	-	15	2	19	36
Tuvalu	6	2	29	36	87	160
Vanuatu	39	1	35	-	426	501
DEVELOPING ECONOMIES OF OCEANIA Total	**60**	**3**	**242**	**59**	**788**	**1 152**
OPEN REGISTRY COUNTRIES						
Antigua and Barbuda	42	409	799	5	67	1 322
Bahamas	258	60	348	304	439	1 409
Bermuda	23	16	9	25	91	164
Cyprus	277	195	183	128	239	1 022
Isle of Man	67	6	68	144	125	410
Liberia	736	978	288	771	257	3 030
Malta	567	120	394	489	245	1 815
Marshall Islands	616	229	102	656	273	1 876
Panama	2 624	737	1 928	1 074	1 764	8 127
Saint Vincent and the Grenadines	62	12	319	16	448	857
OPEN REGISTRY ECONOMIES Total	**5 272**	**2 762**	**4 438**	**3 612**	**3 948**	**20 032**
DEVELOPED ECONOMIES						
Australia	12	-	67	11	648	738
Belgium	22	3	26	13	171	235
Bulgaria	9	-	20	9	46	84
Canada	63	2	40	31	794	930
Denmark	6	95	105	166	609	981
Estonia	-	-	5	5	97	107
Finland	3	3	84	12	178	280
France	5	26	57	55	676	819
Germany	5	278	84	37	464	868
Greece	257	35	92	417	585	1 386
Iceland	1	-	4	1	216	222
Ireland	-	1	39	2	205	247
Israel	-	5	1	6	24	36
Italy	112	19	133	240	1 163	1 667
Japan	401	15	1 465	623	3 115	5 619

Annex II (c). Merchant fleets of the world by flags of registration,[a] groups of economies and types of ship,[b] as at 1 January 2012 (Number of ships) *(continued)*

	Bulk carriers	Container ships	General cargo ships [c]	Oil tankers	Other types	Grand total
Latvia	-	-	8	6	119	133
Lithuania	-	1	34	-	61	96
Luxembourg	2	7	15	18	109	151
Netherlands	10	67	586	53	666	1 382
New Zealand	8	1	45	4	206	264
Norway	71	-	351	175	1 407	2 004
Poland	-	-	12	6	164	182
Portugal	6	6	56	20	371	459
Romania	-	-	5	6	69	80
Slovakia	-	-	6	-	1	7
Slovenia	-	-	-	-	8	8
Spain	8	5	52	33	1 157	1 255
Sweden	7	-	81	37	327	452
Switzerland	21	3	9	5	1	39
United Kingdom of Great Britain and Northern Ireland	47	202	339	174	1 203	1 965
United States of America	55	85	89	55	6 177	6 461
DEVELOPED ECONOMIES Total	**1 131**	**859**	**3 910**	**2 220**	**21 037**	**29 157**
Economies In Transition						
Albania	-	-	51	-	9	60
Azerbaijan	-	-	36	51	195	282
Croatia	29	-	33	20	218	300
Georgia	8	1	69	10	66	154
Kazakhstan	-	-	8	12	109	129
Montenegro	1	-	1	-	9	11
Republic of Moldova	4	-	133	4	18	159
Russian Federation	60	13	942	367	1 980	3 362
Turkmenistan	-	-	8	6	54	68
Ukraine	2	-	135	18	368	523
TRANSITION ECONOMIES Total	**104**	**14**	**1 416**	**488**	**3 026**	**5 048**
Unknown flag	**116**	**13**	**1 080**	**281**	**4 674**	**6 164**
World total[e]	**9 816**	**5 012**	**20 530**	**11 214**	**57 733**	**104 305**

Source: IHS Fairplay.

[a] The designations employed and the presentation of material in this table refer to flags of registration and do not imply the expression of any opinion by the Secretariat of the United Nations concerning the legal status of any country or territory, or of its authorities, or concerning the delimitation of its frontiers.

[b] Seagoing propelled merchant ships of 100 GT and above, excluding the Great Lakes fleets of the United States of America and Canada and the United States of America Reserve Fleet.

[c] Including passenger/cargo.

[d] A dispute exists between the Governments of Argentina and the United Kingdom of Great Britain and Northern Ireland concerning sovereignty over the Falkland Islands (Malvinas).

[e] Excluding estimates of the United States Reserve Fleet and the United States and Canadian Great Lakes fleets.

Annex III. True nationality of the 20 largest fleets by flag of registration, as at 1 January 2012

Country or territory of ownership		Total owned fleet	Unknown registry	All other registries	Total, top 20 registries	United Kingdom of Great Britain and Northern Ireland	Singapore	Republic of Korea	Panama	Norway (NIS)	Marshall Islands	Malta	Liberia	Japan	Italy	Isle of Man	India	Greece	Germany	Denmark (DIS)	Cyprus	China, Hong Kong SAR	China	Bahamas	Antigua & Barbuda
Belgium	Number of vessels	277	1	200	76	1	-	-	1	1	10	1	-	-	-	-	-	19	-	-	3	33	1	6	-
	1 000 dwt	14 521	2	9 336	5 184	6	-	-	11	35	444	7	-	-	-	-	-	2 951	-	-	18	1 569	59	84	-
Bermuda	Number of vessels	268	-	66	202	6	26	-	33	20	40	15	4	-	-	9	-	3	-	-	7	25	-	14	-
	1 000 dwt	29 996	-	4 646	25 350	157	1 986	-	5 078	944	6 804	468	915	-	-	2 643	-	138	-	-	322	4 021	-	1 874	-
Brazil	Number of vessels	172	-	119	53	12	-	-	10	-	4	-	22	-	-	-	-	-	-	-	-	-	-	5	-
	1 000 dwt	13 762	-	2 345	11 417	2 981	-	-	1 609	-	465	-	5 574	-	-	-	-	-	-	-	-	-	-	788	-
Canada	Number of vessels	456	-	237	219	4	-	-	11	-	10	10	3	-	-	1	-	-	-	2	2	74	-	102	-
	1 000 dwt	21 650	-	3 706	18 144	44	-	-	509	-	475	415	159	-	-	21	-	-	-	152	64	5 349	-	10 955	-
China	Number of vessels	3 629	57	334	3 238	11	31	6	535	-	16	6	13	-	-	-	1	-	-	-	7	550	2 060	2	-
	1 000 dwt	124 002	332	2 381	121 289	505	1 906	54	23 610	-	1 577	106	839	-	-	-	27	-	-	-	192	40 673	51 716	84	-
China, Hong Kong SAR	Number of vessels	853	12	44	797	12	48	-	157	-	9	4	58	-	-	-	2	-	-	-	2	470	31	4	-
	1 000 dwt	45 486	69	1 235	44 181	123	1 810	-	6 931	-	289	123	5 652	-	-	-	37	-	-	-	55	28 884	174	104	-
China, Taiwan Province of	Number of vessels	703	3	122	578	11	85	-	327	-	10	-	107	-	8	-	-	-	-	-	-	30	-	-	-
	1 000 dwt	39 045	26	4 146	34 874	733	4 110	-	14 061	-	1 869	-	11 443	-	426	-	-	-	-	-	-	2 232	-	-	-
Cyprus	Number of vessels	214	-	30	184	6	-	-	7	1	44	31	6	-	-	-	-	2	-	-	62	3	1	21	-
	1 000 dwt	7 137	-	211	6 926	136	-	-	853	4	1 349	891	465	-	-	-	-	11	-	-	2 044	240	54	880	-
Denmark	Number of vessels	1 043	1	155	887	45	163	-	41	7	8	34	9	-	2	56	-	-	1	371	8	51	-	74	17
	1 000 dwt	39 991	36	3 647	36 308	2 378	12 070	-	1 327	281	341	1 198	272	-	23	832	-	-	3	13 440	76	2 750	-	1 230	89
France	Number of vessels	485	1	354	130	39	10	2	12	2	9	7	2	-	4	-	-	-	-	-	17	4	-	22	-
	1 000 dwt	11 171	1	4 460	6 710	3 026	364	19	282	70	506	556	218	-	21	-	-	-	-	-	638	241	-	768	-

Annex III. True nationality of the 20 largest fleets by flag of registration, as at 1 January 2012 (continued)

Country or territory of ownership	Germany		Greece		India		Indonesia		Iran, Islamic Republic of		Isle of Man		Italy		Japan		Kuwait		Malaysia		Netherlands	
	Number of vessels	1 000 dwt	Number of vessels	1 000 dwt	Number of vessels	1 000 dwt	Number of vessels	1 000 dwt	Number of vessels	1 000 dwt	Number of vessels	1 000 dwt	Number of vessels	1 000 dwt	Number of vessels	1 000 dwt	Number of vessels	1 000 dwt	Number of vessels	1 000 dwt	Number of vessels	1 000 dwt
Total owned fleet	3 989	125 627	3 321	224 062	560	21 363	1 042	11 593	138	11 464	44	6 358	834	24 989	3 960	217 663	86	6 692	539	14 445	962	11 701
Unknown registry	7	7	4	177	–	–	6	168	–	–	–	–	2	39	3	4	–	–	2	4	2	4
All other registries	334	3 889	134	4 172	12	24	953	9 308	74	869	–	–	72	1 327	203	5 877	66	5 307	447	9 793	714	6 595
Total, top 20 registries	3 648	121 730	3 183	219 703	548	21 339	83	2 117	64	10 596	44	6 358	760	23 623	3 754	211 782	20	1 385	90	4 648	246	5 103
United Kingdom of Great Britain and Northern Ireland	58	1 628	5	397	–	–	1	14	–	–	1	10	12	65	5	91	–	–	–	–	28	35
Singapore	36	1 224	24	2 368	31	2 368	58	1 341	–	–	–	–	5	136	170	11 278	–	–	29	2 820	21	36
Republic of Korea	–	–	–	–	–	–	–	–	–	–	–	–	–	–	15	634	–	–	–	–	–	–
Panama	23	3 647	334	18 348	32	1 853	10	376	6	32	1	251	21	870	2 413	150 646	14	917	18	338	20	53
Norway (NIS)	–	–	–	–	–	–	–	–	–	–	–	–	–	–	–	–	–	–	1	68	1	5
Marshall Islands	247	12 070	450	32 384	4	10	1	48	–	–	14	1 358	1	27	70	5 820	2	135	16	574	28	864
Malta	106	2 351	486	31 943	4	269	–	–	48	7 385	–	–	47	1 003	5	159	3	292	1	3	4	132
Liberia	1 270	59 969	542	37 186	6	507	2	101	–	–	22	4 512	45	2 844	113	7 956	–	–	2	3	30	484
Japan	–	–	–	–	–	–	–	–	–	–	–	–	–	–	717	20 453	–	–	–	–	–	–
Italy	52	983	7	361	–	–	–	–	–	–	–	–	608	18 114	–	–	–	–	–	–	9	23
Isle of Man	–	–	64	6 511	–	–	–	–	–	–	6	227	6	685	23	2 738	–	–	–	–	–	–
India	–	–	–	–	455	15 277	–	–	–	–	–	–	–	–	–	–	–	–	2	32	2	10
Greece	9	28	738	64 921	–	–	–	–	–	–	–	–	5	30	–	–	–	–	–	–	–	–
Germany	422	17 296	–	–	2	9	2	82	–	–	–	–	–	–	2	25	–	–	5	32	5	32
Denmark (DIS)	–	–	–	–	–	–	–	–	–	–	–	–	–	–	–	–	–	–	–	–	–	–
Cyprus	265	6 197	199	12 247	5	358	–	–	10	3 179	–	–	6	27	20	526	–	–	–	–	41	464
China, Hong Kong SAR	14	1 018	35	1 724	–	–	9	155	–	–	–	–	–	–	80	3 985	–	–	–	–	–	–
China	–	–	–	–	–	–	–	–	–	–	–	–	–	–	2	2	–	–	–	–	–	–
Bahamas	27	2 325	247	13 659	–	–	–	–	–	–	–	–	–	–	105	7 127	1	41	15	125	41	2 888
Antigua & Barbuda	1 119	12 992	2	4	–	–	–	–	–	–	–	–	–	–	14	143	–	–	–	–	16	67

Annex III. True nationality of the 20 largest fleets by flag of registration, as at 1 January 2012 (continued)

Values are given as "Number of vessels / 1 000 dwt" for each country or territory of ownership.

Country or territory of registration	Norway	Qatar	Republic of Korea	Russian Federation	Saudi Arabia	Singapore	Sweden	Switzerland	Thailand	Turkey
Total owned fleet	1 992 / 43 100	85 / 4 627	1 236 / 56 186	1 787 / 20 368	192 / 12 740	1 110 / 38 563	307 / 6 396	181 / 4 890	344 / 5 154	1 174 / 23 481
Unknown registry	– / –	– / –	6 / 34	22 / 40	– / –	4 / 135	– / –	– / –	1 / –	2 / 6
All other registries	658 / 4 030	50 / 890	27 / 158	1 496 / 6 370	137 / 2 201	204 / 4 324	184 / 3 101	72 / 1 790	286 / 3 625	755 / 9 726
Total, top 20 registries	1 334 / 39 070	35 / 3 737	1 203 / 55 994	269 / 13 958	55 / 10 539	902 / 34 104	123 / 3 295	109 / 3 101	57 / 1 529	417 / 13 749
United Kingdom of Great Britain and Northern Ireland	42 / 753	– / –	3 / 95	3 / 216	1 / 2	– / –	31 / 589	2 / 34	38 / 1 005	1 / 57
Singapore	157 / 4 711	– / –	1 / 6	– / –	– / –	712 / 22 083	13 / 300	– / –	– / –	– / –
Republic of Korea	1 / 26	– / –	740 / 17 102	– / –	– / –	– / –	4 / 156	– / –	– / –	– / –
Panama	83 / 2 798	1 / 77	398 / 33 160	50 / 269	13 / 426	98 / 4 553	– / –	21 / 426	11 / 56	75 / 919
Norway (NIS)	437 / 14 647	– / –	– / –	– / –	3 / 112	1 / 5	27 / 851	– / –	– / –	– / –
Marshall Islands	83 / 3 502	29 / 3 609	55 / 5 330	7 / 252	– / –	35 / 3 437	1 / 75	11 / 361	– / –	77 / 4 176
Malta	109 / 1 179	– / –	3 / 51	45 / 424	– / –	3 / 240	4 / 49	21 / 272	– / –	234 / 7 584
Liberia	38 / 792	5 / 51	3 / 250	114 / 10 645	20 / 5 055	22 / 2 410	13 / 688	25 / 1 220	– / –	18 / 581
Japan	– / –	– / –	– / –	– / –	– / –	– / –	– / –	– / –	– / –	– / –
Italy	6 / 54	– / –	– / –	– / –	– / –	1 / 40	1 / 7	13 / 86	– / –	– / –
Isle of Man	62 / 2 126	– / –	– / –	– / –	– / –	– / –	– / –	– / –	– / –	– / –
India	– / –	– / –	– / –	– / –	– / –	2 / 6	– / –	– / –	1 / 291	– / –
Greece	– / –	– / –	– / –	– / –	– / –	1 / 302	– / –	– / –	1 / 30	– / –
Germany	– / –	– / –	– / –	– / –	– / –	– / –	– / –	– / –	– / –	– / –
Denmark (DIS)	3 / 6	– / –	– / –	– / –	– / –	– / –	17 / 161	– / –	– / –	– / –
Cyprus	34 / 182	– / –	– / –	45 / 2 135	– / –	– / –	3 / 11	– / –	– / –	1 / 35
China, Hong Kong SAR	42 / 2 975	– / –	– / –	1 / 8	– / –	17 / 956	– / –	5 / 199	– / –	1 / 178
China	– / –	– / –	– / –	1 / 3	– / –	– / –	– / –	– / –	1 / 4	1 / 30
Bahamas	228 / 5 274	– / –	– / –	2 / 5	18 / 4 944	8 / 53	9 / 408	– / –	5 / 143	3 / 155
Antigua & Barbuda	9 / 45	– / –	– / –	1 / 1	– / –	– / –	– / –	– / –	– / –	6 / 35

Annex III. True nationality of the 20 largest fleets by flag of registration, as at 1 January 2012 (continued)

Country or territory of ownership	Total owned fleet		Unknown registry		All other registries		Total, top 20 registries		United Kingdom of Great Britain and Northern Ireland		Singapore		Republic of Korea		Panama		Norway (NIS)		Marshall Islands		Malta		Liberia		Japan		Italy		Isle of Man		India		Greece		Germany		Denmark (DIS)		Cyprus		China, Hong Kong SAR		China		Bahamas		Antigua & Barbuda	
	Number of vessels	1 000 dwt	Number of vessels	1 000 dwt	Number of vessels	1 000 dwt	Number of vessels	1 000 dwt	Number of vessels	1 000 dwt	Number of vessels	1 000 dwt	Number of vessels	1 000 dwt	Number of vessels	1 000 dwt	Number of vessels	1 000 dwt	Number of vessels	1 000 dwt	Number of vessels	1 000 dwt	Number of vessels	1 000 dwt	Number of vessels	1 000 dwt	Number of vessels	1 000 dwt	Number of vessels	1 000 dwt	Number of vessels	1 000 dwt	Number of vessels	1 000 dwt	Number of vessels	1 000 dwt	Number of vessels	1 000 dwt	Number of vessels	1 000 dwt	Number of vessels	1 000 dwt	Number of vessels	1 000 dwt	Number of vessels	1 000 dwt
United Arab Emirates	430	8 796	5	20	199	1 394	226	7 382	8	56	27	200	–	–	90	2 172	–	–	17	901	–	–	40	2 458	–	–	–	–	–	–	4	56	–	–	–	–	–	–	11	85	1	299	28	1 156	–	–	–	–
United Kingdom of Great Britain and Northern Ireland	710	18 430	4	24	112	3 402	594	15 004	230	2 035	76	709	–	–	41	731	–	–	1	17	31	538	39	1 949	–	–	2	8	95	5 338	–	–	5	875	–	–	–	–	7	518	31	1 147	34	1 132	–	–	3	7
United States of America	2 055	54 623	11	67	1 202	11 312	842	43 243	46	147	42	2 134	8	135	136	3 938	11	811	267	20 552	36	766	61	4 968	–	–	23	174	2	21	–	–	8	394	–	–	–	–	13	94	48	4 863	115	4 223	–	–	25	23
Viet Nam	556	6 695	1	7	512	5 459	43	1 229	–	–	–	–	–	–	43	1 229	–	–	–	–	–	–	–	–	–	–	–	–	–	–	–	–	–	–	–	–	–	–	–	–	–	–	–	–	–	–	–	–
Total top 35 owners	35 734	1 326 957	157	1 202	10 564	141 054	25 013	1 184 701	592	12 355	1 834	76 558	772	17 970	5 140	282 733	511	17 797	1 573	109 842	1 307	58 843	2 675	170 171	717	20 453	684	19 337	377	22 173	469	15 475	783	69 942	430	17 356	402	13 786	770	29 488	1 524	103 466	2 100	52 023	1 151	61 121	1 202	13 812
All other owners	3 988	64 835	41	147	2 931	28 977	1 016	35 711	15	60	48	869	–	–	281	6 619	3	8	107	7 445	202	5 995	118	6 309	–	–	15	1 236	14	122	3	116	–	–	6	38	1	5	57	959	2	172	1	3	104	5 581	39	174
Unknown country or territory of ownership	7 179	126 317	477	1 950	3 361	21 642	3 341	102 725	107	6 118	140	4 321	91	543	1 318	37 950	17	89	153	5 553	213	6 338	203	13 289	55	351	49	1 039	6	238	47	344	76	2 486	10	25	9	20	86	2 510	235	13 109	401	5 616	77	2 382	48	404
World total	46 901	1 518 110	675	3 299	16 856	191 674	29 370	1 323 136	714	18 533	2 022	81 748	863	18 513	6 739	327 301	531	17 894	1 833	122 840	1 722	71 176	2 996	189 768	772	20 804	748	21 613	397	22 534	519	15 936	859	72 428	446	17 418	412	13 811	913	32 956	1 761	116 747	2 502	57 642	1 332	69 085	1 289	14 391

Source: Compiled by the UNCTAD secretariat on the basis of data provided by IHS Fairplay.

a Cargo-carrying vessels of 1000 GT and above.

Annex IV.	Containerized port traffic		

Country/territory	2009	2010	Rank 2010 (2009)
Albania	68 780	86 875	113 (114)
Algeria	250 095	279 784	89 (88)
Antigua and Barbuda	29 150	24 615	123 (123)
Argentina	1 626 835	2 021 675	42 (42)
Aruba	125 000	130 000	107 (107)
Australia	6 200 325	6 668 075	20 (20)
Austria	330 995	350 461	78 (82)
Bahamas	1 297 000	1 125 000	53 (43)
Bahrain	279 799	289 956	87 (91)
Bangladesh	1182121	1 356 099	48 (50)
Barbados	75 015	80 424	114 (113)
Belgium	9 701 494	10 984 824	13 (13)
Belize	31 344	31 919	122 (122)
Benin	272 820	316 744	84 (85)
Brazil	6 590 363	8 138 608	18 (18)
Brunei Darussalam	85 577	99 354	109 (111)
Bulgaria	136 444	142 611	104 (101)
Cambodia	207 577	224 206	95 (93)
Cameroon	245 538	285 069	88 (90)
Canada	4 191 568	4 829 806	28 (28)
Cayman Islands	44 215	40 281	121 (120)
Chile	2 795 990	3 171 958	34 (33)
China	108 799 933	130 290 443	1 (1)
China, Hong Kong SAR	21 040 096	23 699 242	4 (4)
China, Taiwan Province of	11 352 097	12 501 107	11 (11)
Colombia	2 056 789	2 443 786	38 (39)
Congo	291 917	338 916	82 (83)
Costa Rica	875 687	1 013 483	55 (56)
Côte d'Ivoire	677 029	607 730	69 (60)
Croatia	130 740	137 048	106 (105)
Cuba	290 098	228 346	93 (84)
Cyprus	353 913	349 357	79 (78)
Denmark	621 546	709 147	60 (63)
Djibouti	519 500	600 000	70 (69)
Dominican Republic	1 263 467	1 382 679	47 (44)
Ecuador	1 000 895	1 221 849	51 (52)
Egypt	6 250 443	6 709 053	19 (19)
El Salvador	126 369	145 774	103 (106)
Estonia	130 939	151 969	102 (103)
Finland	1 125 532	1 247 520	49 (51)
France	4 490 583	5 346 799	25 (25)

Annex IV. Containerized port traffic *(continued)*

Country/territory	2009	2010	Rank 2010 (2009)
French Guiana	40 923	47 511	120 (121)
French Polynesia	63 807	68 889	115 (115)
Gabon	132348	153 656	101 (104)
Georgia	181 613	226 115	94 (96)
Germany	13 296 300	14 821 766	9 (9)
Ghana	557 323	647 052	66 (71)
Greece	935 076	1 165 185	52 (54)
Guadeloupe	142 692	165 665	100 (100)
Guam	157 096	183 214	99 (98)
Guatemala	906 326	1 012 360	56 (55)
Honduras	571 720	619 867	67 (67)
Iceland	193 816	192 778	96 (94)
India	8 014 487	9 752 908	15 (15)
Indonesia	7 255 004	8 482 635	17 (16)
Iran, Islamic Republic of	2 206 476	2 592 522	35 (37)
Ireland	832 021	790 067	59 (58)
Israel	2 033 000	2 281 552	39 (40)
Italy	9 532 462	9 787 403	14 (14)
Jamaica	1 689 670	1 891 770	43 (41)
Japan	16 285 918	18 098 345	7 (5)
Jordan	674 525	619 000	68 (61)
Kenya	618 816	696 000	61 (64)
Kuwait	854 044	991 545	57 (57)
Latvia	184 399	256 713	90 (95)
Lebanon	994 601	949 155	58 (53)
Libya	158 987	184 584	98 (99)
Lithuania	247 982	294 954	86 (89)
Madagascar	132 278	141 093	105 (102)
Malaysia	15 922 799	18 267 475	6 (7)
Maldives	56 000	65 016	118 (118)
Malta	2 323 941	2 450 665	37 (35)
Mauritania	62 269	65 705	117 (116)
Mauritius	406 862	4 447 78	75 (75)
Mexico	2 874 312	3 693 956	32 (32)
Morocco	1 222 000	2 058 430	41 (49)
Mozambique	219 380	254 701	92 (92)
Myanmar, Republic of the Union of	163 692	190 046	97 (97)
Namibia	265 663	256 319	91 (86)
Netherlands	10 066 374	11 345 167	12 (12)
Netherlands Antilles	97 913	93 603	111 (109)
New Caledonia	119 147	90 574	112 (108)

Annex IV. Containerized port traffic *(continued)*			
Country/territory	2009	2010	Rank 2010 (2009)
New Zealand	2 324 969	2 463 278	36 (36)
Nicaragua	59 471	68 545	116 (117)
Nigeria	87 000	101 007	108 (110)
Norway	318 924	330 873	83 (81)
Oman	3 768 045	3 893 198	30 (29)
Pakistan	2 058 056	2 149 000	40 (38)
Panama	4 597 112	6 003 297	22 (23)
Papua New Guinea	262 209	295 286	85 (87)
Paraguay	7 045	8 179	125 (125)
Peru	1 232 849	1 534 055	45 (48)
Philippines	4 306 964	4 947 039	27 (27)
Poland	671 552	1 045 232	54 (62)
Portugal	1 233 482	1 622 246	44 (47)
Qatar	410 000	346 000	81 (74)
Republic of Korea	15 699 663	18 542 803	5 (6)
Romania	594 299	556 694	72 (65)
Russian Federation	2 427 743	3 199 980	33 (34)
Saint Helena	623	650	126 (126)
Saint Lucia	51 942	52 479	119 (119)
Saint Vincent and the Grenadines	16 238	18 852	124 (124)
Saudi Arabia	4 430 676	5 313 141	26 (26)
Senegal	331 076	349 231	80 (80)
Singapore	26 592 800	29 178 500	3 (3)
Slovenia	343 165	476 731	73 (79)
South Africa	3 726 313	3 806 427	31 (30)
Spain	11 803 192	12 613 015	10 (10)
Sri Lanka	3 464 297	4 000 000	29 (31)
Sudan	431 232	439 100	76 (72)
Sweden	1 251 424	1 390 504	46 (45)
Switzerland	78 285	99 048	110 (112)
Syrian Arab Republic	685 299	649 005	65 (59)
Thailand	5 897 935	6 648 532	21 (21)
Trinidad and Tobago	567 183	573 217	71 (68)
Tunisia	418 883	466 397	74 (73)
Turkey	4 521 713	5 574 017	24 (24)
Ukraine	516 698	659 541	64 (70)
United Arab Emirates	14 425 039	15 176 524	8 (8)
United Kingdom of Great Britain and Northern Ireland	7 671 299	8 590 282	16 (17)
United Republic of Tanzania	370 764	429 284	77 (77)
United States of America	37 353 574	42 337 513	2 (2)

Annex IV. Containerized port traffic *(continued)*			
Country/territory	**2009**	**2010**	**Rank 2010 (2009)**
Uruguay	588 410	671 952	62 (66)
Venezuela, Bolivarian Republic of	1 240 251	1 226 507	50 (46)
Viet Nam	4 936 598	5 983 583	23 (22)
Yemen	639 670	669 020	63 (76)
TOTAL	**472 273 661**	**540 693 119**	

Source: UNCTAD secretariat, derived from information contained in Containerisation International Online (May 2012), from various Dynamar B.V. publications and from information obtained by UNCTAD secretariat directly from terminal and port authorities.

Annex V.   UNCTAD Liner Shipping Connectivity Index (ordered by rank at 2012)

Country or territory	ISO3 2012	Index points			Average annual change 2004–2012	Change 2012/2011	Rank 2004	Rank 2012
		2004	2011	2012				
China	CHN	100.00	152.06	156.19	7.02	4.12	1	1
Hong Kong, China	HKG	94.42	115.27	117.18	2.84	1.91	2	2
Singapore	SGP	81.87	105.02	113.16	3.91	8.15	4	3
Republic of Korea	KOR	68.68	92.02	101.73	4.13	9.70	10	4
Malaysia	MYS	62.83	90.96	99.69	4.61	8.73	12	5
United States	USA	83.30	81.63	91.70	1.05	10.07	3	6
Germany	DEU	76.59	93.32	90.63	1.75	-2.68	7	7
Netherlands	NLD	78.81	92.10	88.93	1.26	-3.17	6	8
United Kingdom of Great Britain and Northern Ireland	GBR	81.69	87.46	84.00	0.29	-3.47	5	9
Belgium	BEL	73.16	88.47	78.85	0.71	-9.62	8	10
Spain	ESP	54.44	76.58	74.44	2.50	-2.14	15	11
France	FRA	67.34	71.84	70.09	0.34	-1.74	11	12
Taiwan Province of China	TWN	59.56	66.69	66.62	0.88	-0.07	13	13
Italy	ITA	58.13	70.18	66.33	1.03	-3.85	14	14
Japan	JPN	69.15	67.81	63.09	-0.76	-4.72	9	15
United Arab Emirates	ARE	38.06	62.50	61.09	2.88	-1.42	18	16
Saudi Arabia	SAU	35.83	59.97	60.40	3.07	0.43	19	17
Egypt	EGY	42.86	51.15	57.39	1.82	6.24	16	18
Morocco	MAR	9.39	55.13	55.09	5.71	-0.04	78	19
Turkey	TUR	25.60	39.40	53.15	3.44	13.75	29	20
Sweden	SWE	14.76	30.02	49.45	4.34	19.43	48	21
Viet Nam	VNM	12.86	49.71	48.71	4.48	-1.01	55	22
Oman	OMN	23.33	49.33	47.25	2.99	-2.09	31	23
Portugal	PRT	17.54	21.08	46.23	3.59	25.15	41	24
Greece	GRC	30.22	32.15	45.50	1.91	13.35	24	25
Malta	MLT	27.53	40.95	45.02	2.19	4.08	25	26
Denmark	DNK	11.56	26.41	44.71	4.14	18.30	64	27
Poland	POL	7.28	26.54	44.62	4.67	18.08	92	28
Sri Lanka	LKA	34.68	41.13	43.43	1.09	2.30	20	29
Lebanon	LBN	10.57	35.09	43.21	4.08	8.11	67	30
Panama	PAN	32.05	37.51	42.38	1.29	4.88	22	31
India	IND	34.14	41.52	41.29	0.89	-0.22	21	32
Mexico	MEX	25.29	36.09	38.81	1.69	2.71	30	33
Brazil	BRA	25.83	34.62	38.53	1.59	3.92	28	34
Canada	CAN	39.67	38.41	38.29	-0.17	-0.13	17	35
Thailand	THA	31.01	36.70	37.66	0.83	0.97	23	36
Colombia	COL	18.61	27.25	37.25	2.33	10.00	39	37
Russian Federation	RUS	11.90	20.64	37.01	3.14	16.37	62	38
South Africa	ZAF	23.13	35.67	36.83	1.71	1.16	32	39

Annex V.   UNCTAD Liner Shipping Connectivity Index (ordered by rank at 2012) *(continued)*

Country or territory	ISO3 2012	Index points					Rank 2004	Rank 2012
		2004	2011	2012	Average annual change 2004–2012	Change 2012/2011		
Argentina	ARG	20.09	30.62	34.21	1.76	3.59	37	40
Chile	CHL	15.48	22.76	32.98	2.19	10.22	44	41
Peru	PER	14.79	21.18	32.80	2.25	11.62	47	42
Uruguay	URY	16.44	24.38	32.00	1.95	7.62	43	43
Israel	ISR	20.37	28.49	31.24	1.36	2.75	35	44
Australia	AUS	26.58	28.34	28.81	0.28	0.48	26	45
Pakistan	PAK	20.18	30.54	28.12	0.99	-2.42	36	46
Bahamas	BHS	17.49	25.18	27.06	1.20	1.88	42	47
Indonesia	IDN	25.88	25.91	26.28	0.05	0.37	27	48
Ukraine	UKR	11.18	21.35	24.47	1.66	3.12	65	49
Mauritius	MUS	13.13	15.37	23.86	1.34	8.49	54	50
Dominican Republic	DOM	12.45	22.87	23.72	1.41	0.84	59	51
Romania	ROU	12.02	21.37	23.28	1.41	1.91	61	52
Ecuador	ECU	11.84	22.48	23.05	1.40	0.58	63	53
Jordan	JOR	11.00	16.65	22.75	1.47	6.10	66	54
Islamic Republic of Iran	IRN	13.69	30.27	22.62	1.12	-7.65	52	55
Slovenia	SVN	13.91	21.93	21.94	1.00	0.01	51	56
Nigeria	NGA	12.83	19.85	21.81	1.12	1.96	56	57
Jamaica	JAM	21.32	28.16	21.57	0.03	-6.59	33	58
Croatia	HRV	8.58	21.75	21.38	1.60	-0.38	85	59
Guatemala	GTM	12.28	20.88	20.07	0.97	-0.81	60	60
New Zealand	NZL	20.88	18.50	19.35	-0.19	0.85	34	61
Bolivarian Republic of Venezuela	VEN	18.22	19.97	18.93	0.09	-1.04	40	62
Trinidad and Tobago	TTO	13.18	17.89	18.90	0.71	1.02	53	63
Ghana	GHA	12.48	18.01	17.89	0.68	-0.12	58	64
Bahrain	BHR	5.39	9.77	17.86	1.56	8.09	111	65
Philippines	PHL	15.45	18.56	17.15	0.21	-1.41	45	66
Djibouti	DJI	6.76	21.02	16.56	1.23	-4.46	98	67
Côte d'Ivoire	CIV	14.39	17.38	16.45	0.26	-0.93	50	68
Cyprus	CYP	14.39	17.12	16.02	0.20	-1.10	49	69
Syrian Arab Republic	SYR	8.54	16.77	15.64	0.89	-1.13	86	70
Finland	FIN	9.45	11.27	15.51	0.76	4.24	77	71
Namibia	NAM	6.28	12.02	15.18	1.11	3.16	102	72
Benin	BEN	10.13	12.69	15.04	0.61	2.35	73	73
Costa Rica	CRI	12.59	10.69	14.13	0.19	3.44	57	74
Togo	TGO	10.19	14.08	14.07	0.48	-0.02	71	75
Angola	AGO	9.67	11.27	13.95	0.54	2.68	76	76
Puerto Rico	PRI	14.82	10.70	13.67	-0.14	2.97	46	77
Senegal	SEN	10.15	12.27	13.59	0.43	1.32	72	78
Cameroon	CMR	10.46	11.40	13.44	0.37	2.04	69	79
Yemen	YEM	19.21	11.89	13.19	-0.75	1.30	38	80
Ireland	IRL	8.78	5.94	12.99	0.53	7.05	82	81
Sudan	SDN	6.95	9.33	12.75	0.72	3.41	95	82
Congo	COG	8.29	10.78	12.57	0.54	1.79	87	83
Fiji	FJI	8.26	9.23	12.39	0.52	3.17	88	84
Madagascar	MDG	6.90	7.72	11.80	0.61	4.08	96	85

Country or territory	ISO3 2012	Index points			Average annual change 2004–2012	Change 2012/2011	Rank 2004	Rank 2012
		2004	2011	2012				
Kenya	KEN	8.59	12.00	11.75	0.39	-0.25	84	86
United Republic of Tanzania	TZA	8.10	11.49	11.07	0.37	-0.43	90	87
French Polynesia	PYF	10.46	8.59	10.86	0.05	2.27	70	88
Honduras	HND	9.11	9.42	10.03	0.11	0.61	80	89
Belize	BLZ	2.19	3.85	9.99	0.97	6.14	149	90
Mozambique	MOZ	6.64	10.12	9.82	0.40	-0.30	99	91
Lithuania	LTU	5.22	9.77	9.55	0.54	-0.22	115	92
New Caledonia	NCL	9.83	9.17	9.41	-0.05	0.24	75	93
Gabon	GAB	8.78	7.97	9.23	0.06	1.26	81	94
El Salvador	SLV	6.30	12.02	8.75	0.31	-3.27	101	95
Guam	GUM	10.50	8.76	8.41	-0.26	-0.35	68	96
Nicaragua	NIC	4.75	8.41	8.23	0.43	-0.19	122	97
Mauritania	MRT	5.36	5.62	8.20	0.35	2.58	112	98
Liberia	LBR	5.29	6.17	8.11	0.35	1.94	113	99
Bangladesh	BGD	5.20	8.15	8.02	0.35	-0.13	116	100
Gambia	GMB	4.91	5.24	7.81	0.36	2.57	119	101
Algeria	DZA	10.00	31.06	7.80	-0.28	-23.26	74	102
Libya	LBY	5.25	6.59	7.51	0.28	0.92	114	103
Guinea	GIN	6.13	6.21	7.42	0.16	1.21	104	104
Sierra Leone	SLE	5.84	5.41	7.40	0.20	1.99	107	105
Iraq	IRQ	1.40	4.19	7.10	0.71	2.92	156	106
Papua New Guinea	PNG	6.97	8.83	6.86	-0.01	-1.96	94	107
Kuwait	KWT	5.87	5.60	6.60	0.09	1.00	106	108
Curaçao [a]	CUW	8.16	8.14	6.59	-0.20	-1.56	89	109
Qatar	QAT	2.64	3.60	6.53	0.49	2.93	144	110
Seychelles	SYC	4.88	6.45	6.50	0.20	0.06	120	111
Bulgaria	BGR	6.17	5.37	6.36	0.02	0.99	103	112
Tunisia	TUN	8.76	6.33	6.35	-0.30	0.02	83	113
Solomon Islands	SLB	3.62	5.87	6.07	0.31	0.20	133	114
Aruba	ABW	7.37	6.21	6.03	-0.17	-0.17	91	115
Cuba	CUB	6.78	6.55	5.96	-0.10	-0.59	97	116
Latvia	LVA	6.37	5.51	5.45	-0.12	-0.06	100	117
Estonia	EST	7.05	5.84	5.43	-0.20	-0.41	93	118
Norway	NOR	9.23	7.32	5.31	-0.49	-2.00	79	119
Comoros	COM	6.07	7.14	5.17	-0.11	-1.97	105	120
Haiti	HTI	4.91	4.75	5.08	0.02	0.33	118	121
Georgia	GEO	3.46	3.79	4.99	0.19	1.19	136	122
Barbados	BRB	5.47	5.85	4.82	-0.08	-1.03	109	123
Iceland	ISL	4.72	4.68	4.68	0.00	0.00	123	124
Saint Lucia	LCA	3.70	4.08	4.55	0.11	0.47	132	125
Equatorial Guinea	GNQ	4.04	3.68	4.54	0.06	0.85	127	126
Cape Verde	CPV	1.90	4.24	4.48	0.32	0.24	152	127
Suriname	SUR	4.77	4.16	4.48	-0.04	0.31	121	128
Brunei Darussalam	BRN	3.91	4.68	4.44	0.07	-0.25	129	129
American Samoa	ASM	5.17	4.56	4.39	-0.10	-0.17	117	130
Samoa	WSM	5.44	4.56	4.39	-0.13	-0.17	110	131

Annex V.   UNCTAD Liner Shipping Connectivity Index (ordered by rank at 2012) *(continued)*

Country or territory	ISO3 2012	2004	2011	2012	Average annual change 2004–2012	Change 2012/2011	Rank 2004	Rank 2012
Somalia	SOM	3.09	4.20	4.34	0.16	0.14	139	132
Guinea-Bissau	GNB	2.12	4.07	4.31	0.27	0.24	151	133
Faeroe Islands	FRO	4.22	4.20	4.21	0.00	0.00	125	134
Republic of the Union of Myanmar	MMR	3.12	3.22	4.20	0.13	0.99	138	135
Eritrea	ERI	3.36	4.02	4.17	0.10	0.14	137	136
Cayman Islands	CYM	1.90	4.03	4.07	0.27	0.04	153	137
Guyana	GUY	4.54	3.96	4.06	-0.06	0.10	124	138
Democratic Republic of the Congo	COD	3.05	3.73	4.05	0.13	0.33	141	139
Grenada	GRD	2.30	3.93	4.04	0.22	0.10	148	140
Saint Vincent and the Grenadines	VCT	3.56	3.95	4.02	0.06	0.07	134	141
Vanuatu	VUT	3.92	3.70	3.88	-0.01	0.18	128	142
Federated States of Micronesia	FSM	2.80	3.62	3.58	0.10	-0.05	143	143
Palau	PLW	1.04	3.62	3.58	0.32	-0.05	157	144
Cambodia	KHM	3.89	5.36	3.45	-0.06	-1.91	130	145
Northern Mariana Islands	MNP	2.17	3.65	3.44	0.16	-0.21	150	146
Tonga	TON	3.81	3.72	3.37	-0.06	-0.35	131	147
United States Virgin Islands	VIR	1.77	3.39	3.34	0.20	-0.04	154	148
Kiribati	KIR	3.06	3.11	2.91	-0.02	-0.19	140	149
Marshall Islands	MHL	3.49	3.08	2.91	-0.07	-0.17	135	150
Saint Kitts and Nevis	KNA	5.49	2.66	2.67	-0.35	0.01	108	151
Antigua and Barbuda	ATG	2.33	2.40	2.41	0.01	0.01	145	152
Greenland	GRL	2.32	2.30	2.30	0.00	0.00	147	153
Sao Tome and Principe	STP	0.91	2.13	2.28	0.17	0.15	158	154
Dominica	DMA	2.33	2.08	2.08	-0.03	0.00	146	155
Maldives	MDV	4.15	1.62	1.60	-0.32	-0.02	126	156
Bermuda	BMU	1.54	1.57	1.57	0.00	0.00	155	157
Montenegro	MNE	2.92	4.04	1.35	-0.20	-2.68	142	158
Albania	ALB	0.40	4.54	0.53	0.02	-4.01	159	159

Source: UNCTAD, based on data provided by Lloyd's List Intelligence.

Note: The Liner Shipping Connectivity Index is generated from five components: (a) the number of ships, (b) the total container-carrying capacity of those ships, (c) the maximum vessel size, (d) the number of services and (e) the number of companies that deploy container ships on services to and from a country's ports. The index is generated as follows: for each of the five components, a country's value is divided by the maximum value of that component in 2004, and for each country, the average of the five components is calculated. This average is then divided by the maximum average for 2004 and multiplied by 100. In this way, the index generates the value 100 for the country with the highest average index of the five components in 2004.

a   2004 figure for Curaçao is based on Netherlands Antilles' data.

QUESTIONNAIRE

Review of Maritime Transport, 2012

In order to improve the quality and relevance of the Review of Maritime Transport, the UNCTAD secretariat would greatly appreciate your views on this publication. Please complete the following questionnaire and return it to:

Readership Survey
Division on Technology and Logistics
UNCTAD
Palais des Nations, Room E.704
CH-1211 Geneva 10, Switzerland
Fax: +41 22 917 0050
E-mail: transport.section@unctad.org

Thank you very much for your kind cooperation.

1. What is your assessment of this publication?

	Excellent	Good	Adequate	Poor
Presentation and readability	☐	☐	☐	☐
Comprehensiveness of coverage	☐	☐	☐	☐
Quality of analysis	☐	☐	☐	☐
Overall quality	☐	☐	☐	☐

2. What do you consider the strong points of this publication?

   _____

   _____

3. What do you consider the weak points of this publication?

   _____

   _____

4. For what main purposes do you use this publication?

Analysis and research	☐	Education and training	☐
Policy formulation and management	☐	Other(specify)	☐

   _____

   _____

5. How many people do you share/disseminate the Review of Maritime Transport with?

   Less than 10 ☐   Between 10 and 20 ☐   More than 20 ☐

6. Which of the following best describes your area of work?

Government	☐	Public enterprise	☐
Non-governmental organization	☐	Academic or research	☐
International organization	☐	Media	☐
Private enterprise institution	☐	Other (specify)	☐

_____

_____

7. Personal information

Name (optional): _____

E-mail: (optional): _____

Country of residence:_____

8. Do you have any further comments?

_____

_____

_____

_____

***

HOW TO OBTAIN THIS PUBLICATION

Sales publications may be purchased from distributors of United Nations publications throughout the world.
They may also be obtained by writing to:

UN Publications Sales and Marketing Office
300 E 42nd Street, 9th Floor, IN-919J
New York, NY, 10017 USA

Tel: +1-212-963-8302
Fax: +1-212-963-3489
Email:publications@un.org

https://unp.un.org/